# SAILING AND SEAMANSHIP

## FIFTH EDITION
## FIRST PRINTING

0288-51

## U.S. COAST GUARD AUXILIARY

Library of Congress Catalog Card Number: 76-29794
ISBN 0-930029-04-X

PRINTED IN THE UNITED STATES OF AMERICA

Contents approved by the
National Association of
State Boating Law Administrators
and recognized by the
United States Coast Guard

**THE COMMANDANT OF THE UNITED STATES COAST GUARD**
WASHINGTON, D.C. 20593-0001

FOREWORD

Experience has taught us that education is a key factor in the prevention of boating accidents. All too often, investigations into boating accidents reveal that the skippers and crew have not attended safe boating classes of any kind. This text will introduce you to such topics as basic piloting, navigation rules, seamanship and other skills to help you enjoy your sailing activities.

This text was prepared by the U.S. Coast Guard Auxiliary for use in the Sailing and Seamanship Public Education Course, 5th Edition. Presenting this training is one of the ways the Auxiliary helps boaters get more pleasure from their sailing experiences. Completing this program will give you the basic knowledge to help you make your sailing safer and more enjoyable.

As Commandant of the United States Coast Guard, I salute our Auxiliary for their concern and dedicated efforts in promoting safe boating, and for the development of this course. I heartily endorse it for all who use our country's waterways for recreational sailing.

P. A. YOST
Admiral, U. S. Coast Guard

# UNITED STATES COAST GUARD
## AUXILIARY

PREFACE

This 5th Edition of SAILING AND SEAMANSHIP has been produced by the Department of Education of the United States Coast Guard Auxiliary. The text has been completely updated to provide you with a comprehensive combination of sailing theory, seamanship techniques, legal responsibilities, the latest Federal regulations, and other subjects which will assist you to become a more proficient and SAFETY CONSCIOUS sailor.

The text and course reflect the resources of the entire Coast Guard Auxiliary, a volunteer, civilian organization dedicated to assisting the United States Coast Guard in its mission of BOATING SAFETY.

The course is presented by qualified and certified Auxiliary public education instructors, fellow sailors who voluntarily give their time to share with you their knowledge and experience in sailing and seamanship skills.

The material in this SAILING AND SEAMANSHIP course has been reviewed and approved by the U. S. Coast Guard and the National Association of State Boating Law Administrators. Many insurance companies discount premiums for their boat insurance to those graduating and holding certificates for this course.

Upon successful completion of this course you are invited to continue to enhance your seamanship skills by enrolling in the Auxiliary's ADVANCED COASTAL NAVIGATION public education course.

May your sailing be smooth and SAFE!

Sincerely,

William C. Harr
National Commodore
United States Coast Guard Auxiliary

# CONTENTS

Page

INSIDE BACK COVER

IALA Maritime Buoyage System

# Introduction

**Welcome Aboard!**

Boating is one of the most popular recreational activities today, and it is growing. In 1986, the latest year for which complete statistics are available, Americans went "down to the sea" for pleasure in 16 1/2 million recreational boats. This is up 10 million from just 20 years ago.

Obviously, boating today bears little resemblance to the "yachting" of yesterday, although that still exists. But for most recreational boaters, "boating" means a fun way for the family and a few friends to pass a weekend or a summer afternoon.

**Fig. I-1    The Basic Principles of Good Seamanship Apply...**

Unfortunately, for thousands of Americans every year, what boating involves is injury, financial loss, and even death. In 1984 over one thousand people were reported killed in recreational boating accidents, and thousands more received serious injuries. The death and injury rates for that year are lower than they have been since these records have been kept. Yet, when you consider the number of casualties in light of the very small amount of time that each boater actually spends boating, the rate of death and injury exceeds that in many traditionally hazardous occupations!

The victim of these boating accidents is typically a man between the ages of 24 and 34, fishing in a quiet lake on a late Saturday afternoon. He doesn't think of himself as a "boater"; the boat is just another part of his "fishing outfit."

Maybe he makes a sudden move with a fish on the line, or maybe he stands up to relieve himself of some of the beer he has drunk that afternoon. For whatever reason, the small boat capsizes, and the man falls into the water.

Of course, the life jackets he kept carefully in the boat drift away from him as he estimates the distance to shore and starts to swim away from the capsized boat. The one thing that could have saved his life he didn't have on, either because it was "uncomfortable," or because he was a "good swimmer," or because it isn't "manly." For whatever reason, the extra effort he expends swimming without a life jacket soon exhausts him, and he slips beneath the surface.

Of course, not all boating accidents happen this way. Many involve collisions, either with other boats or with fixed objects (piers, breakwaters, etc.). A very high percentage of these accidents, in turn, were due at least in part to the fact that the judgment of some of those involved was impaired by alcohol, drugs, or excess fatigue.

The Coast Guard and the Coast Guard Auxiliary believe that many of these losses could be prevented, or the consequences reduced, if more boaters knew more about seamanship, navigation, and related topics. Experience is a hard teacher, and lessons may be very hard, indeed. Formal instruction and training can help, but few people have formal training. Education cannot make you accident-proof. But experience has shown that a good fundamental course in seamanship (such as this one) is the single most cost-effective means of reducing losses.

Had our fisherman described above taken this course, for instance, he would have known to buy and wear a well-fitted PFD (life jacket) whenever he was underway. He would also have known that, by far, it is best to stay with the boat if he fell in.

He would also have known how to load his boat for best trim and balance, and how not to exceed load limits.

He would also have learned the importance of keeping a lookout at all times, to avoid collisions.

And, finally, he would have known what alcohol and fatigue can do to impair balance and judgment.

## Family Activity

By and large, recreational boating is a family activity. Something about boating will appeal to every member of the family. If you are a member of a boating family and the other members of your family are not also enrolled in this

Fig. I-2    ...Regardless of the Size of the Boat...

course, you should talk with your instructor about enrolling them as soon as possible.

## This Course

The purpose of this course, then, is to help you become a better recreational boater by gaining knowledge and skills. This knowledge can help you avoid difficulties and enjoy your on-the-water activities more. In addition, we would like to raise your awareness of things that might happen, and thereby help you avoid them. Finally, we hope to help you to help yourself in case you have problems on the water, or to help you help others should the need arise.

Fig. I-3    ...or the Amount of Money It Cost.

## Your Instructors

This course is being taught by members of the United States Coast Guard Auxiliary. Your instructors are all volunteers, and most of them are recreational boaters who started out in just such a class as this one. They are here to share with you some of their experience and some of the benefits of the special training they have received from the United States Coast Guard, the "parent" of the Auxiliary.

The members of the Coast Guard Auxiliary are civilians. They have no military or law enforcement duties or powers. They are concerned individuals who give freely of their time and energies by being involved in public education activities such as this one, or in other Auxiliary programs supporting the Coast Guard. If you would like to know more about the Coast Guard, the Coast Guard Auxiliary, or any of its programs, one of your instructors will be happy to talk to you about it. In the meantime, be sure to read the "Invitation" on the inside front cover of this book for more information.

**Fig. I-4    The Members of the Coast Guard Auxiliary are Concerned Civilian Volunteers.**

**Course Format**

Depending on local needs and the resources of the Auxiliary unit offering the course, a variety of formats may be followed, ranging from as few as seven to as many as fourteen lessons. Your instructor will tell you what format this course will take.

Whatever the format, the course will contain a core of specific lessons. Each

lesson is outlined briefly here to give you a preview.

Chapter 1, What Makes a Sailboat, decribes the basic components of a sailboat and its rigging, the functional requirements of hulls, their shapes, and the varieties of different sailboat rigs in use today.

This lesson also introduces you to the language of boats. We do not intend to make you sound like an "old salt," or to overwhelm you with a strange vocabulary. Nevertheless, it is useful to be able to recognize (and use) some of the terms that you find in common use among boaters.

In Chapter 2, How a Boat Sails, the nature of wind, its relation to the different points of sailing, and the basic principles of sail shaping techniques are covered.

Chapter 3, Basic Sailing Maneuvering, introduces you to tacking and jibing maneuvers, how to determine a safe and efficient course to sail to your destination, and various means of controlling the boat's motion and tipping tendencies.

**Fig. I-5    Boaters Must Be Able To Rely On Their Equipment.**

Chapter 4, Legal Requirements and Aids to Navigation, explains what you must carry aboard your boat, what your obligations are under the law, and introduces you to the principles of the U.S. Aids to Navigation system which control and mark the sea lanes and channels.

Rigging and Boat Handling is covered in Chapter 5. The procedures for stepping the mast, adjusting the boat's standing rigging, hoisting sails, and mooring, docking, and anchoring are discussed.

In Chapter 6, Tuning and Heavy Weather, the finer points of sail shape and means of controlling the helm's balance are discussed. The varieties of headsails, heavy weather procedures, capsizing, and man-overboard situations are also introduced.

Chapter 7 on Navigation Rules is a vitally important one, since its sole purpose is to help you prevent the most common injury-producing accident, a collision. This chapter describes the internationally-enforced "rules of the road" that guide your movements in the presence of other boats.

Several additional lessons may be offered, based upon the course format your instructors have elected to use. These include the following:

Chapter 8, Marlinspike Seamanship, covers the art and science of doing useful things with ropes and lines. You will learn the difference between a line and a rope, between a knot and a hitch. Afterwards, you will be able to tie the three knots (and one hitch) which you will need most often. You will learn to tie up your boat, and to care for your lines so they will give you better, longer service.

Chapter 9, Engines for Sailboats, describes the elements of a sailboat's auxiliary power plant, inboard or outboard, including basic maintenance and emergency repairs. Safe operating and fueling procedures are also discussed.

Trailering, Chapter 10, introduces some of the techniques of trailering your boat, techniques that can expand your boating horizons. This lesson discusses the selection of a trailerable boat, the choice of a trailer, and the things that you have to consider in selecting an appropriate tow vehicle. Techniques for launching and

Fig. I-6    An Understanding of the Elements of Weather Forecasting is Important to Good Seamanship.

retrieving your boat are also discussed, as well as highway driving tips to make your boating trips more enjoyable.

After the Weather lesson, Chapter 11, you will be able to recognize most common weather patterns and form your own short-term weather forecasts based on local conditions, trends, and official weather information. You will learn about better and more reliable sources of weather information that are available, and you will be able to make more sense of broadcast weather forecaster's charts and symbols.

Chapter 12, The Radiotelephone, introduces the marine radiotelephone. You will learn about licensing, how to use the radiotelephone to make necessary calls to marinas, locks, and bridges, to keep track of developing conditions that may affect your safety, and to summon help (or extend help to others) in times of distress.

Chapter 13, Inland Waterways, Locks and Dams, describes the thousands of miles of inland waterways (rivers, canals, and the Intracoastal Waterway). The lesson describes the particular cautions necessary in these waterways, and gives you many hints of things that can enhance your enjoyment of the unique pleasures these waterways afford.

**Fig. I-7    The Inland Waterways Make Recreational Boating Available to Millions.**

Chapter 14, Piloting, introduces you to basic techniques of using charts and aids to find your position. It gives you the basic techniques you need to read a chart, keep track of your position by dead reckoning, and keep a deck log.

You may have noticed that the most frequently-used word in the past few paragraphs was "introduce." In a course as brief as this one it is not possible to do more than introduce you to the material. There is much, much more to learn. We hope that your experience in this course will stimulate your interest in further study. Your instructor will be glad to discuss further learning opportunities available in your area.

### Additional Information

Even if certain lessons are not covered in the schedule of the course, you should feel free to read those chapters. If you have any questions, one of your instructors will be glad to discuss it with you and help you find answers.

In addition, there is supplemental material in appendices in the back of the book. This supplemental material is not part of the course, but is included for you to read and use, since it is material a responsible boater should know about. It includes useful information about hypothermia, drugs and alcohol.

### The Responsible Skipper

"The skipper of a vessel is responsible for everything that happens on her or to her." This is certainly true in merchant vessels on the high seas, and in naval vessels. It is true of the officer in charge of a lifeboat, no matter what his rank. And it is true of the skipper of a small recreational boat. The skipper is responsible, no matter what. It's the law!

But responsibility is not just the right to get blamed if things go wrong. The responsible skipper has the authority (right) to expect that things be done properly on his boat. Along with that goes the assumption that he knows what the "proper" way is.

### Crew Training

One of the first things that a responsible skipper does is to make sure that his crew (family as well as guests) understand what is expected of them and how they are to behave in an emergency. This begins even before anybody arrives at the boat. Common courtesy and common sense dictate that guests (especially inexperienced ones) should be given explicit guidance about such things as what clothing to bring, and what accommodations they can expect. You can imagine how you would feel if you showed up at a formal dinner in casual clothes! So shall your guests feel if they are invited for a day on your "yacht," and show up dressed for a 65-footer, only to learn that your "yacht" is a 17' open boat!

More is involved here than just embarrassment at wearing the wrong clothes. The wrong shoes can be deadly on a slippery deck, and a guest who appears for a weekend visit on a larger boat carrying hard-sided luggage can unknowingly create a dangerous condition below decks if the boat starts to pitch and such objects fly about the cabin.

## Safety

The responsible skipper takes the time to show his guests where the emergency equipment is and how it works. This need not be handled like the preflight briefing on a commercial airliner (although that is not too bad an idea), but can be worked into the guided tour you will inevitably want to give your guests.

Make sure each crew member and guest has a personal flotation device ("life jacket") and knows how to wear it. Make sure everybody knows where the fire extinguishers are. (Also make sure there are enough of them, that they are located in appropriate places, and that they are all charged and in good condition.)

These items, and many more that are covered in Chapter 4, are part of your being a responsible skipper.

## Health

Another aspect of the skipper's responsibility is monitoring, and if necessary controlling, behavior. You are the knowledgeable one on board; your guests may not appreciate as you do the effects of too much sun too soon, or of the effects of alcohol taken with a lot of fresh air, noise and sunshine. Do not permit your guests to "overdo." Keep an eye on their behavior, be alert for signs that they may

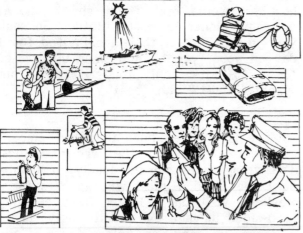

Fig. I-8  **Special Care May Be Needed for Very Young or Very Old to Protect Their Health.**

not be functioning as they should. If they do not cooperate, or if they appear to be suffering ill effects, halt your boating activities and return to shore at once.

Above all, do not tolerate "substance abuse." Alcohol, drugs and boating are a deadly mixture, no less than in an automobile. You are the leader; be firm, be fair, and set a good example.

Be sensitive, too, to the needs of the very young and of the elderly. Either may be adversely affected by environmental effects that may not bother others at all. Hypothermia, heat exhaustion, sun stroke and dehydration are extremely dangerous life-threatening emergencies. Differences in clothing, diet, and general health can be critical in determining who is stricken. Be sensitive to the possibilities, and prevent or correct potentially dangerous situations, even if it may mean cutting your boating activities.

## Special Considerations for Smaller Pleasure Craft

The smaller pleasure craft are very sensitive to speed, loading, balance, and rough water. For this reason special care should be taken when operating these types of boats.

When loading your boat, weight should be evenly distributed from bow (front) to stern (back) and athwartships (from side to side). The more weight you put into a boat, the deeper it sinks into the water, thus reducing the amount of freeboard. Freeboard is the vertical distance from the gunwale (pronounced gun'l), or top ends of the hull, to the water. The more you reduce the freeboard, the greater the tendency to swamp (fill with water) or capsize (turn over). An overloaded or improperly loaded boat is unstable and dangerous.

Whether you should carry the maximum weight recommended by the manufacturer (see pages 4-8 and 4-9 for discussion on capacity plates) depends on several factors.

First, consider the anticipated sea state, or water conditions. It is important to realize that if rough water is expected, less weight should be carried. A heavily laden boat will ship water more easily than one which is riding higher in the water. Watch your freeboard. Many small boats have swamped or capsized when they were loaded to the point where they had insufficient freeboard.

Second, consider the activity in which you expect to engage while underway. For instance, if you want to do some fishing, it's possible that persons will stand up occasionally in the boat. Standing up in a small boat is extremely dangerous, especially if it is done in choppy water conditions or if the boat is too heavily laden. By standing up you will change the center of gravity of the boat, and if the hull is being buffeted about appreciably, it could cause the boat to capsize, or for you to fall overboard.

Other factors to consider would be weight of the equipment, fuel, tools, food and other gear which will be carried. The more gear loaded aboard, the less passenger-carrying capacity you will have left.

Be wary of sea and wind conditions when you operate your boat. If you run too fast you can buffet your boat excessively and damage it. You also lose control if you buffet too much. You could flip if you caught a wave at too fast a speed, or even capsize if you took a curve too hard.

One other thing. Stay out of restricted areas, especially swimming areas and areas near (above or below) dams. Swimmers and boats don't mix! Dam gates can open without warning, with the resulting water flow either pulling your boat over the dam (or through the gate) if you are behind the dam, or flooding you out should you be caught below it.

**Boat Theft Prevention**

Pleasure boats of all sizes, small outboard motors (less than 25 HP), radios,

compasses, binoculars, and other boating gear are stolen every year. With a few simple measures and some forethought, most of this theft could have been avoided. Some of these simple precautions include:

1. Permanently mark your Hull Identification Number (HIN)--for boats built after 1972--at some hidden location on your boat. Although the HIN is permanently stamped or engraved on the outboard, starboard side of the transom, or on the starboard, outboard side of the hull, aft, or on the aft crossbeam of catamarans and pontoon boats (see page 4-8), this number can be defaced or altered. A hidden HIN would provide positive identification when the boat is recovered, if the visible HIN is altered.

2. Mark all of your valuable equipment with an identification number. Operation Identification, supported by police and sheriff departments, provides identification numbers for this purpose. Your local police can provide you with an engraving tool with which you can scribe your ID number on the hard surfaces of your equipment. Soft materials, such as cloth covers, sleeping bags, blankets, tents, etc., can be marked with paint, indelible "magic markers," or invisible ink which shows up under special ultra-violet light. Visible identification numbers, boat name, and owner's name have been deterrents, discouraging thieves, and providing assistance to law enforcement authority in return to the owner after recovery.

3. Keep valuables out of sight! When you park your car, put your gear in the trunk, and lock the car. Leave your car in a well lighted area for personal safety as well as theft prevention if you expect to be gone after dark.

4. Remove valuable, portable equipment from your boat, such as binoculars, radios, compasses, depth finders, personal flotation devices (PFDs), signaling equipment, etc., and lock them in a safe place. Also take your keys and boat registration card when away from your boat.

5. If you trailer your boat, whether you keep it at home or in a storage area, you may prevent theft of the trailer and boat by securing the trailer to some immovable object, such as a fence post. A case-hardened steel bolt or eye-bolt can be set in concrete, and serve as a theft-deterrent anchor for a chain wrapped around the trailer axle or frame and locked tight to the anchor bolt. You can also jack up the trailer and remove a wheel, locking it in your trunk. If the trailer is not to be used for some time, such as during the winter, remove all of the wheels from your trailer, and store them in a safe place. This will not only prevent their theft, but save them from the elements.

6. Use a trailer hitch lock to keep the trailer from being removed from your car, or hitched to another if the trailer is left unattended.

7. If you have a small outboard motor, usually less than 25 HP, remove it from your boat when not in use, or fasten it with a motor lock or locked chain (across the clamps). On larger, less portable, permanently-mounted outboard motors, you can use special transom retainer bolts, which may only be removed with special sockets.

8. If you keep your boat at the dock or on a mooring buoy, secure it with a case-hardened lock and chain. You may also wish to remove portable fuel tanks and some vital engine component (such as a distributor rotor, ignition wire(s) or other difficult to replace part). A hidden cutoff switch, installed between the engine and ignition power, can also be a useful deterrent.

9. Work with your neighbors and fellow boaters in keeping watch for strangers or suspicious activity. Call your local law enforcement officials if you have any doubts whether someone is authorized to work on a boat or trailer. Write down a description of any suspicious individuals, and the license number of their vehicle or registration number and description of their boat.

To assist law enforcement officials in the recovery of any stolen property, and to document any losses for your insurance company, keep an up-to-date inventory of your boating and fishing equipment. Make sure you record the name of the equipment, its description, any serial numbers, and other means of identification. Color photographs or slides provide an excellent means of identifying and documenting the condition of your boat and its equipment.

Make sure that your insurance covers theft of your boat or equipment. Homeowner's policies may not provide adequate coverage of marine equipment. Marine coverage including your boat, trailer, outboard motor(s), and associated equipment, is usually worth the generally low premium.

Stolen vessels can be used for a number of illegal purposes, from simple--but dangerous--joy riding, to use in the illicit drug trade, or for resale to another unsuspecting victim. It's up to the boat owner to make sure that his or her property doesn't end up being used for a purpose they did not intend. Although not foolproof, the precautions discussed above can go a long way toward theft prevention.

# Chapter 1

# What Makes A Sailboat?

Sailboats and powerboats together make up the world of recreational boating. Sailboats and powerboats differ considerably, not only in their appearance and locomotive power; but also in the way people use them. Sailboats don't make very good fishing platforms, and you can't waterski behind one. But they bring you closer to nature, to the wind and the waves. They challenge the skipper's skill and judgment. They require greater effort than most powerboats, but the rewards are often proportional to the effort expended.

To many people, the thrill of getting there, the ability to master the elements, is more important than the destination itself. These are the folks we see sailing in local waters week after week while their powerboating friends head off to new and exotic destinations. However when we look at the other extreme, we find that most around-the-world cruises are carried out in sailboats that are not dependent on refueling facilities, are more seakindly and less noisy. There is room for all kinds of recreational boating on our increasingly crowded waterways, but only if all boaters respect both the interests and the rights of others.

Although there are literally hundreds of types of sailboats afloat today, all sailboats are basically similar. In this book, we will concentrate on more common kinds of boats, but the principles that apply to them will generally hold true for the exotic, unusual craft as well.

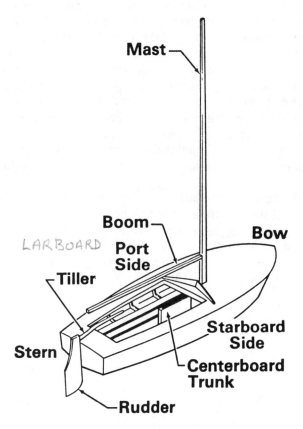

Fig. 1-1   Basic Sailboat Nomenclature

It is important for a beginner to pick up a basic sailing vocabulary. As one of man's more ancient activities, sailing has developed a language of its own over the centuries. Although many of the words may seem strange at first, there's a reason for nearly all of them. Sailors' jargon exists because the terms have no equivalent in ordinary speech. Once you become accustomed to using sailors' terminology, it will come naturally. And it's a lot easier in the long run to have at your command a word like <u>halyard</u>, for instance, than to grope for the approximate equal in everyday English - <u>rope or wire that raises and lowers a sail.</u>

## Components of a Sailboat

There are two basic parts of any sailboat - the <u>hull</u> (or hulls) and the <u>rig.</u> A sailboat <u>hull is simply the load-carrying part of the vessel.</u> Besides supporting the crew, their equipment, the engine (if any) and the mast and sails, the hull has other functional requirements. It must move efficiently through the water in the direction the boat is steered while at the same time resisting forces that attempt to push it in other directions. Meanwhile it must stay reasonably upright, opposing the pressure on the sails. <u>The rig is the collective term for the various elements that form a sailboat's power system.</u> There are basically three interacting parts--the spars, the rigging, and the sails.

### Parts of the Hull

Many sailboat terms are so much part of the language that you'll find you know them already. Some other terms are less well known. Let's run through the ones that pertain to the hull.

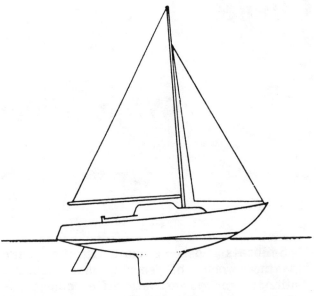

Boat is out of trim by having weight too far aft - she is down by the stern. Note that waterline of boat is visible at bow while stern is squatted down.

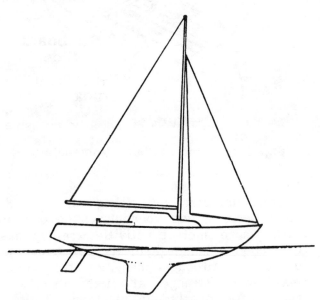

Boat is out of trim by having weight too far forward - she is down by the bow. Note that waterline of boat is visible at the stern, as opposed to vessel in illustration above.

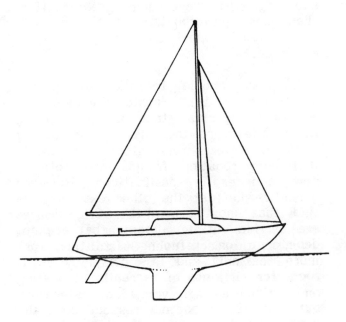

Boat shown above is properly trimmed, fore and aft. She is well balanced as evidenced by waterline's attitude relative to surface of water.

Fig. 1-2  Hull Trim-Correct vs Out-of-Trim

As in all boats, the front or <u>forward</u> end of a sailboat is the <u>bow</u>, pronounced as in the exclamation, "ow!" The other, or <u>after</u>, end is the <u>stern</u>. Facing forward, <u>port</u> is to your left and <u>starboard</u> to your right. If you measured the length of the boat along the deck from bow to stern, the dimension would be labeled as <u>length over all</u>. When the dimensions of sailboats appear in magazines or sales literature, this term is frequently abbreviated <u>LOA</u>. Length at the waterline is called <u>LWL</u> for short. The width of the hull at the widest point is her <u>beam</u>, and the depth of water required to float her is known as the boat's <u>draft</u>. Many sailboats have retractable appendages called <u>centerboards</u> or <u>daggerboards</u>, so in this case two figures may appear for draft - <u>board up</u> and <u>board down</u>.

The <u>waterline</u> is the line of intersection of the surface of the water and the boat's hull. A line painted along and above the waterline when the boat is floating upright is called the <u>boot top</u> or <u>boot stripe</u>. It serves as a useful reference point to determine if the boat has been properly loaded. When the waterline shows clear around the hull and parallel to the surface of the water, the boat is said to be correctly <u>trimmed</u>. If the hull is down by the bow or stern, or tipped to one side or the other, or too high or low in the water, she's <u>out of trim</u>. (See **Fig. 1,2**)

Very small sailboats may be completely open, with only a seat or two for the crew. Most boats, however, have a covering, the <u>deck</u>, over the forward part of the hull at least. And in many craft there are side decks as well. The deck keeps rain and spray out of the hull, provides a place to attach hardware, and helps keep the mast in place. The cut-out area in the center of the deck, from which the crew operates the boat, is the <u>cockpit</u>. There's frequently a raised lip around the edge of the cockpit - the <u>coaming</u> - that serves to deflect water.

Inside the cockpit are <u>floorboards</u> which form the surface on which the crew stands. In older boats this surface is

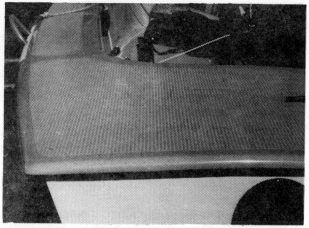

Fig. 1-3  Non-skid Deck Surface

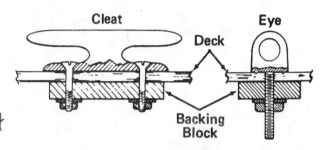

Fig. 1-4  Typical Thru-Bolted Cleat

composed of boards in a grid shape, but in many newer boats, floorboards are represented by a molded fiberglass cockpit <u>sole</u>, or deck. Like other walk-on surfaces aboard, it should be <u>non-skid</u>. The effect may come from paint with sand in it, or (more commonly) from a molded-in pattern. If your boat doesn't have non-skid where it's needed, you can buy, at most boating supply stores, waterproof tape with a slightly abrasive surface. It's a good investment in safety.

Most hardware on a sailboat is connected with handling the sails, but some pertains to the hull itself. Even the smallest boat should have a <u>cleat or eye</u> bolt at bow and stern for the attachment of mooring or towing lines. Cleats may be wood, metal or plastic, but they should be bolted through the deck and preferably through a <u>backing plate</u> under the deck as well. More and more fiberglass sailboats have built-in <u>flotation</u> between the outer skin of the hull and the inner skin, called the <u>liner</u>. This

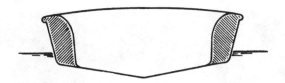

**Fig. 1-5  Cross Section of Hull Flotation**

flotation is usually in the form of rigid plastic foam, inserted in quantity sufficient to keep the water-filled boat plus her crew afloat.

Some boats have <u>self-bailers</u> built into the bottom. These are valves which operate to draw bilge water from the hull - but they only work when the boat is moving at a good clip. Don't count on them to empty the boat when she's at rest. For that you'll need a pump or bailer. Some self-bailers actually take in water if the boat isn't moving, and must be shut off once the boat slows down. If you have such a device built into your boat, make sure you know how it works before setting out.

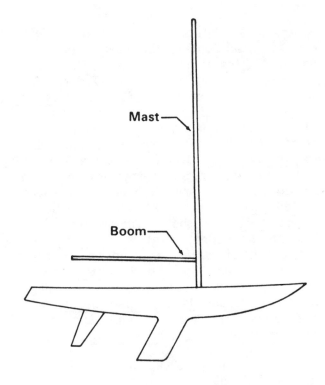

**Fig. 1-7  Mast and Boom**

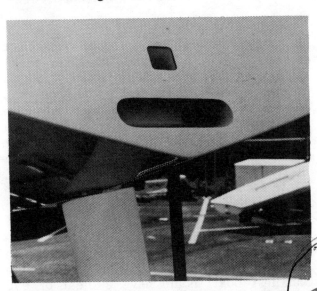

**Fig. 1-6  Typical Self-Bailer in Hull**

### Spars

Spar is the general term for the rigid members that support and extend sails and other parts of the rigging. The primary spar is the <u>mast,</u> a vertical member that holds the sails up. Most boats also have a <u>boom,</u> which holds out

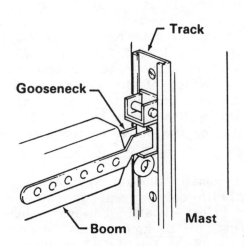

**Fig. 1-8  Gooseneck Installation**

the foot or bottom of the sail at right angles to the mast. The mast and boom are joined by a kind of <u>universal joint</u> called a <u>gooseneck,</u> which allows the boom to pivot up, down or sideways.

There are other types of spars - gaffs, yards, spinnaker poles, to name the most common - but they are restricted to specialized boat types or advanced forms of sailing, and will be dealt with later.

Spars may be made of several kinds of materials. Because of its strength, relative light weight, and good durability, aluminum is the most popular spar material. On some smaller boats where bending spars are useful, fiberglass spars, rather like oversize fishing poles, are occasionally seen. Older boats and ones of traditional appearance may retain wood spars, either hollow sections glued together or solid pieces of timber.

Whatever the construction material, spars have much the same kinds of fittings attached to them. As we shall see in a later chapter, it's important to be able not only to extend a sail, but also to vary the amount of tension along any one of the sail's edges. The sail control fittings on the spars perform this function. Once we've had a chance to consider how the sails are shaped and made fast to the spars, we can consider the various types of fittings and how they work.

A basic (in several senses) fitting is the step. This is a socket in the bottom of the boat, often set directly into the keel (the backbone) of the vessel. The mast fits into or onto the step, which is so shaped that the spar's heel, or base, cannot slide off. In most boats, the mast is held in place by being passed through a tight-fitting hole in the deck or a forward seat. Often, in larger boats, the

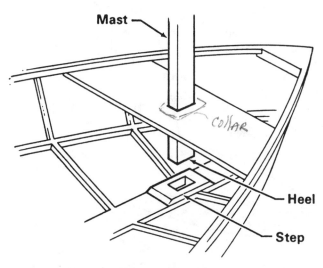

**Fig. 1-9  Typical Small Boat Mast Step**

mast passes through the cabin roof, where a reinforcing collar is placed to help take the strain of the spar. On some small boats, this arrangement is enough support for the mast, but on most a certain amount of rigging, varying with the size of boat, is necessary to keep the mast up and straight. Sailboats that are trailered, and have to keep putting the mast up and down, have the mast stepped on the deck or cabin top in a pivot fitting called a tabernacle.

## Standing and Running Rigging

There are two types of rigging - standing and running. Standing rigging stays put; it supports the mast under tension. Running rigging moves: it runs through blocks (the nautical term for pulleys) to raise and lower or extend and pull back the sails.

## Standing Rigging

The standing rigging of the average sailboat is not complicated. Its purpose is to keep the mast upright and straight. (There are exceptions, but this statement remains true for most boats, large and small.) Remember also that any pull on the mast from one direction must be matched from the opposite side, if the spar is to remain in position and untwisted.

Standing rigging which keeps the mast from falling forward over the bow or backward over the stern consists of one or more forestays and backstays. As you might easily guess, a forestay is in the forward part of the boat. It runs from a metal plate on deck - the tack fitting - to a position at or near the top of the mast, and it keeps that spar from toppling backward. In opposition to it is the backstay, which runs from the stern up to the masthead. In some cases where the rudder and tiller are in the way, or the boat has a long boom, two backstays are fitted, running to corners-the quarters-of the stern. And sometimes a backstay is shaped like an inverted Y, for the same reason.

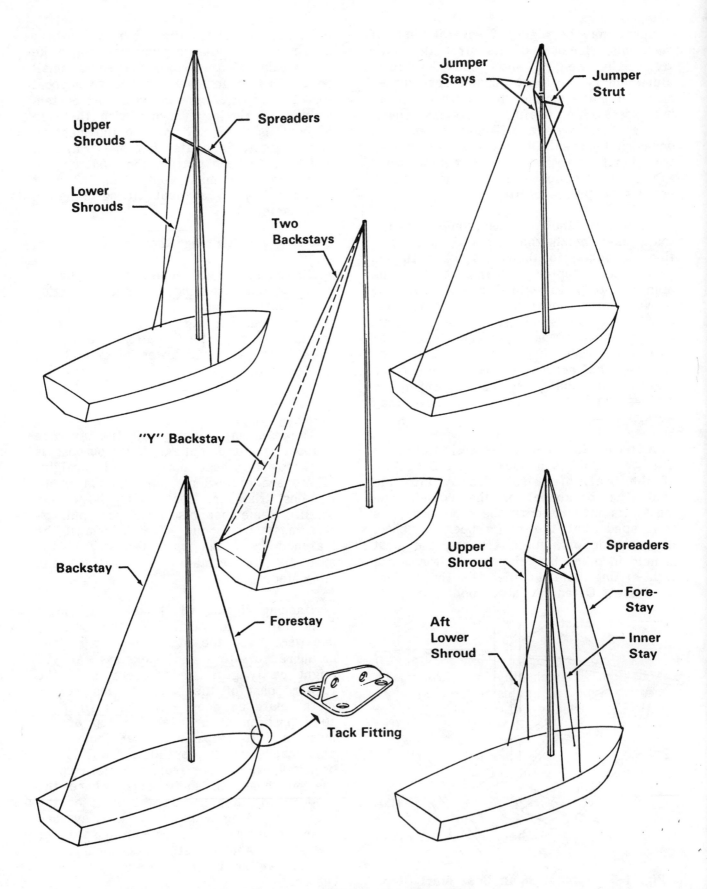

Fig. 1-10   Rigging Nomenclature

When, for reasons of design, the forestay doesn't end near the masthead, tension to balance the backstay is provided by short, horizontal spars called jumper struts, over which run jumper stays. On small boats, where the mast is thick and strong enough to take such strains, jumper struts and stays aren't necessary.

A mast is kept from falling to the side by standing rigging called shrouds. On small boats there is usually only one set, running from the side of the hull up to the masthead. Sometimes, to make a more mechanically effective lead of the shrouds to the masthead, a pair of horizontal spars called spreaders are fitted about two-thirds the way up the mast. The spreader, as its name suggest, simply widens the angle at which the wire reaches the masthead, giving a more effective sideways angle of pull.

The shrouds which run over spreaders to the masthead are called upper shrouds, or just uppers. Other shrouds run from the sides of the hull to the mast just beneath the intersection of the spreaders; these are lower shrouds or lowers. There may be one or two pairs of them. On some boats, an inner forestay does the same job as the pair of forward lowers.

Both shrouds and stays are normally made of stiff wire rope, generally stainless steel. Since it's necessary to balance off the stresses of the various pieces of standing rigging against their opposite numbers, adjuster fittings are provided at the bottom of each stay and shroud. The standard type of adjuster is called a turnbuckle, usually cast in bronze or stainless steel. It allows for a limited amount of adjustment of wire tension, a process called tuning, dealt with in more detail in a later chapter.

The turnbuckles are in turn fitted to toggles, small castings that allow the turnbuckle to lie in the same straight line as the stay or shroud to which it is fitted. And many toggles, in turn, are secured to chainplates - heavy metal

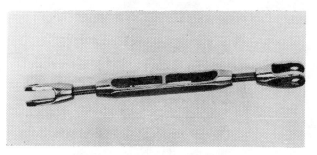

Fig. 1-11  Turnbuckle

straps bolted and/or fiberglassed to the hull or its principal bulkheads (partitions).

## Running Rigging

While standing rigging is almost invariably wire, running rigging may be wire or rope or both. The two most common types of running rigging are halyards, which raise and lower the sails, and sheets, which control the set of a sail. There are other kinds of running rigging, but they are specialized in nature, to be discussed later.

Each sail has at least one halyard, which normally takes its name from the sail it raises. Because rope stretches, halyards are frequently half rope and half wire, so that when the sail is fully raised, all the tension is taken by non-stretching wire. Sheets, which are also named by the sail they control, are normally Dacron line. The type of wire used for halyards is quite flexible, and different in construction, if not in material, from the wire used for stays and shrouds. Rigging materials are discussed further in Chapter 5.

Each sail has a halyard, but in some cases the same halyard is used by more than one headsail, one at a time. Halyards run either through rollers - called sheaves - set into the top of the mast, or through blocks attached to the mast, depending on how high the sail is to be raised. Most halyards terminate at cleats on the mast itself, and in many cases (especially aboard larger craft) the halyard is led around a winch to increase the tension on it and, by extension, on the sail it is hoisting.

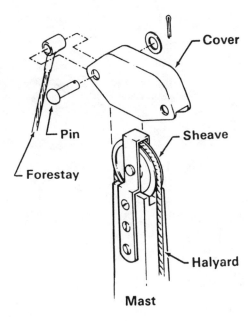

Fig. 1-12   Masthead Fittings

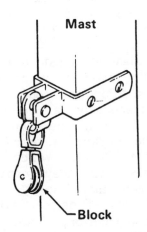

Fig. 1-13   Halyard Block

Once raised, a sail must be adjusted so it sets at a particular angle to the wind. The lines controlling this adjustment are the sheets. They normally run from the after corner of the sail, known as the clew, or from the mainsail boom down to the cockpit. Mechanical advantage of the sheets may be increased by the use of winches or block-and-tackle systems as required. The end of a sheet is made fast to a cleat. While the traditional, anvil-shaped cleats are often seen, more and more skippers are turning to one or another style of quick-release cam or jam

cleats. In these devices, the rope is simply led through a gripping pair of jaws which hold it fast until it's forcibly released by a crew member. The attachment is as secure as cleating the line, and a great deal quicker both to make fast and to let free - and in smaller boats quick release of a sheet may be the difference between capsizing and staying upright.

A third type of running rigging is the topping lift, which is used to support the boom when its sail is not raised. The topping lift is usually run from the masthead to the aft end of the boom.

**Sails**

All this structure - spars, standing and running rigging - exists to make the sails function efficiently. Today's sailboats use triangular sails which are set fore-and-aft on rigs known as jib-headed, Marconi or Bermudan. When sailboats functioned as fishing craft or ferries, the sails employed in everyday business were known as the working sails. Now, we use our boats for cruising and racing, and we often call our smaller, stronger cruising sails "working sails" to distinguish them from larger, more expensive racing sails.

The most common American sailboat type is the sloop - a vessel with a single mast and two sails, one set ahead of the mast and one behind. The sail behind the mast is the mainsail, usually shortened to main, and the sail in front is the jib. The sails have a number of terms associated with them.

A triangular sail has three corners - the head, at the top; the tack, at the forward lower corner; and the clew, at the after lower corner. The sail's leading edge is the luff, sometimes referred to by old-timers as the hoist; its lower edge is its foot, and its after edge is the leech. Each sail is formed from a number of cloths sewn together in one of several patterns. A sail, unlike a flag, is a three-dimensional airfoil (think of an airplane's wing). The cloths are sewn to

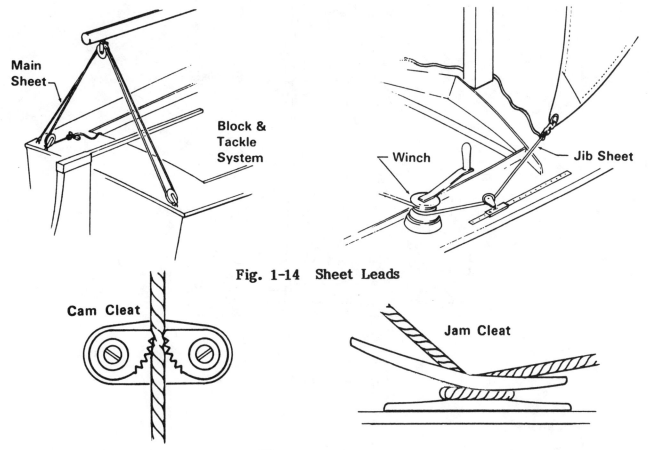

Fig. 1-14   Sheet Leads

Fig. 1-15   Cleats

create this airfoil, either flat or full. The sail's edges are reinforced with rope or extra thicknesses of cloth, or with wire sewn to the luff of the sail. Figs 1-16, 1-17

A mainsail is attached to the mast along its luff and to the boom along its foot. It is fitted with slides, which ride along a surface track on the top of the spar, slugs, which fit a groove recessed into the mast or boom, or bolt rope which fits inside the track groove. The sail's leech is the free side, and it is normally reinforced and to a great extent supported by wood or plastic battens, strips set into pockets at right angles to the leech. The reason for these supports is that the mainsail's leech, unlike its luff or foot, is cut into a convex curve called the roach, for greater sail area. Fig. 1-17

At each corner of the sail is a cringle, a circular metal reinforcement for attaching hardware: the halyard is made

fast to the head cringle; the gooseneck is fitted to the tack cringle; and the outhaul, a carriage riding on the boom to extend the foot of the sail, is fitted to the clew cringle.

The jib is a somewhat simpler sail to describe: it has the same names as the main for its three sides, three corners and its three cringles. The jib usually has no boom; its luff is hanked or snapped along the forestay; and the leech and the foot fly free. The jib tack fastens with a shackle to the tack fitting that holds the forestay, and the jib's head takes the halyard shackle. The jib clew cringle accepts the jib sheets - usually a pair of lines that lead aft to winches or cleats on either side of the cockpit.

Today's sails are nearly all made from synthetic fabric, usually Dacron but sometimes nylon. Dacron stretches less than nylon, and is used for mainsails and

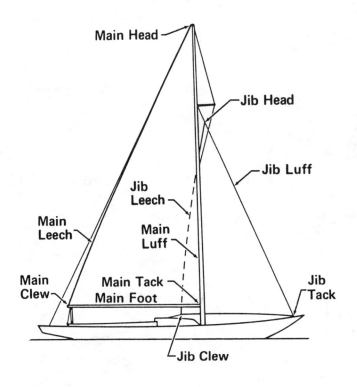

Fig 1-16  Sail Parts

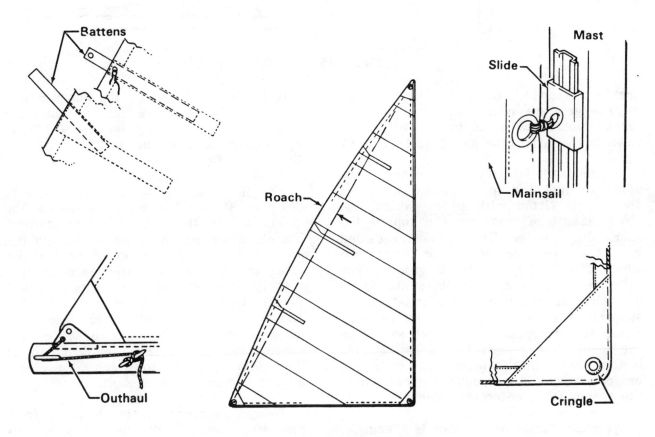

Fig. 1-17  Sail Construction

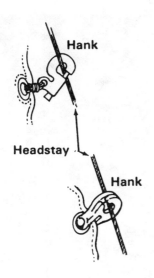

**Fig. 1-18    Typical Jib to Forestay Attachment**

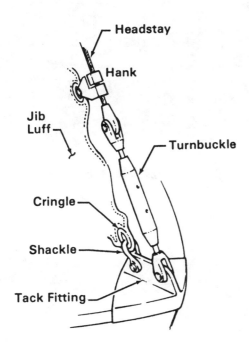

**Fig. 1-19    Tack Fitting**

mildew (which will not affect Dacron except to make unsightly stains on its surface). Sails should be stowed neatly after each excursion, either furled (on the boom) with a sail cover, or folded in a sailbag. Like all artificial fibers, Dacron is sensitive to prolonged sunlight, and it will weaken if left uncovered. Increasingly, sails used for racing are now constructed of Mylar and Kevlar fabrics. These materials are considerably more expensive and harder to care for than Dacron.

Brown

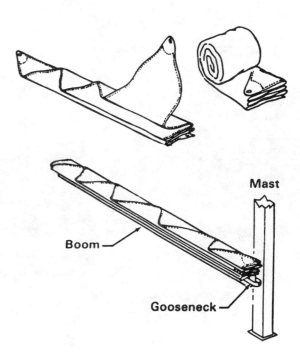

**Fig. 1-20    Folding Sail for Storage**

**Hull Types**

jibs, while nylon is used for sails where slight shape deformation is no problem. Dacron sails require little or no care compared to their cotton predecessors: if you sail on salt water wash the salt out of them from time to time. If possible, dry the sails before stowing them in their bags for prolonged periods to avoid

As sailboat designers are painfully aware, the hull characteristics that keep a boat moving efficiently, resist handling difficulties and keep a sailboat upright, are sometimes in mutual opposition. It can be a tricky job to reconcile them. All boats, sail or power, are compromises, but sailing craft embody more trade-offs in their design than do other types. Most modern sailboats give nearly equal attention to stability, load-carrying ability and a speedy hull, with perhaps a slight tilt toward one factor or another, depending on the designer's special aims. As one gets into the nearly "pure" racing sailboats speed-producing elements are emphasized to the detriment of other factors. Cruising sailboats tend to be designed for comfort and cabin amenities instead of speed.

Fig. 1-21  International Class Type Hull

Fig. 1-22  Motor Sailer

A few years ago, when nearly all boats were built of wood, the most obvious basic distinction between hull types was that of shape: <u>hard chine</u> or <u>round bottom</u>. Round or at least curved bottoms have been the traditional hull shape for centuries. They are easy to move through the water, but are also easy to tip or heel. Their construction in wood planking requires both time and skill, and as the cost of workmanship has become a larger and larger factor in boatbuilding expense, round-bottom boats have become increasingly costly.

By contrast, flat-bottom boats are easy to build, even for amateurs. With the advent of sheet plywood, flat-bottom

Fig. 1-23  Hard Chine Hull

craft became outstandingly inexpensive, but their tendency to pound in even a slightly choppy sea caused designers to draw in a mildly V-shaped bottom. The chine - or intersection between side and bottom - remained hard, or abrupt, giving the hull type its name. Hard-chine craft sail well as long as they remain upright, and they have considerable initial stability: they resist tipping easily. To illustrate for yourself the relative tipping tendencies of hard-chine and round-bottom hulls, lay a round bottle and a rectangular

**Fig. 1-24   Round Bottom Hull**

**Fig. 1-25   Hull—Plywood Construction**

cardboard milk container in water. The bottle will spin easily around its axis, while the carton--with its hard chines--will not.

With the advent of fiberglass-molded hulls, it was as easy to produce a curved hull as a flat one. More important, fiberglass engineering makes use of some curvature in strengthening the hull. Because of this fact, and the great predominance of fiberglass hulls today, most boats' shapes are more or less curved and the hard chine has been considerably modified.

**Displacement vs. Planing Hulls**

Sailboats can have displacement hulls or planing hulls. The displacement hull pushes through the water; the planing hull rides on top of it.

Any floating object at rest displaces an amount of water equal to its own weight. If you could freeze the water around and below a floating vessel, then remove the boat without cracking the ice, the hole left behind could contain an amount of water equal to the boat's weight.

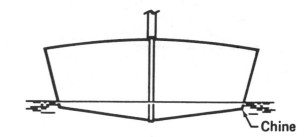

**Fig. 1-26   Hard Chine**

**Fig. 1-27   Tipping Tendency**

As a boat begins to move, it still displaces its own weight of water: it must push aside the water ahead, while the water behind rushes in to fill the space vacated by the hull. This sounds like a process that requires a lot of effort, and it is. What's more, a boat

Fig. 1-28  Displacement Hull at Rest

Fig. 1-29  Displacement Hull Underway

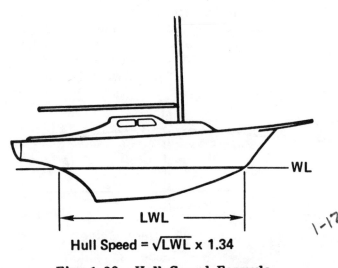

Hull Speed = $\sqrt{LWL}$ x 1.34

Fig. 1-30  Hull Speed Formula

which can only move by displacing its own weight in water is restricted to a relatively low top speed.

Displacement boats generally cannot go faster than a certain speed which is closely related to the boat's waterline length. You can figure your boat's maximum displacement speed - called its hull speed - quite easily: take the square root of the boat's length at the waterline (often known as its LWL) in feet, and multiply it by 1.34, to find the boat's

approximate maximum speed in nautical miles per hour. (A nautical mile is approximately 6,080 feet, as opposed to 5,280 for a land mile. A speed of one nautical mile per hour is called one knot.)

It doesn't matter if the boat in question is propelled by oars, sails or engine, nor does it matter how much power is applied; unless the boat can escape from displacement-type movement through the water, it cannot increase its speed much above 1.34 x the square root of the water-line length. A displacement boat which is 16 feet long at the waterline cannot go much faster than 5.36 knots. A considerably larger boat, 25 feet on the waterline, will only go about 6.7 knots.

A displacement sailboat won't even go this fast most of the time. A boat that can average a speed in knots equal to the square root of its waterline length in feet - 4 knots for a 16-foot boat - is doing very well. What's holding the boat back is both friction from the water and the wave formation caused by the boat's motion through the water. The speed-reducing waves are not the familiar, V-shaped swells that form the boat's wake. In addition to these waves, the displace-

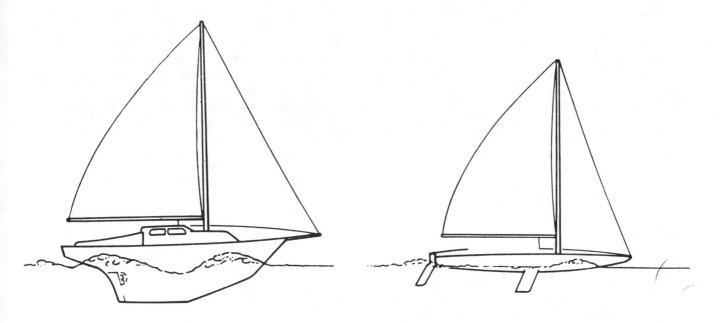

Fig. 1-31   Wave Formation—Displacement vs Planing Hull

ment hull forms two transverse - at right angles to the hull - waves, one near the bow and another at a variable distance back toward the stern. As the boat gathers speed, the stern wave drops further aft, until at hull speed the boat is virtually suspended between the two. The only way to escape is for the boat to receive enough additional propulsive force to ride up and over the bow wave, and then move over, instead of through, the water, rather like a ski moving on snow. This kind of motion, very familiar to powerboat people, is called planing. While there are practical limits to planing speed in a boat, there is no theoretical maximum speed - iceboats, which have virtually no surface friction to contend with, have been clocked at well over 100 miles per hour.

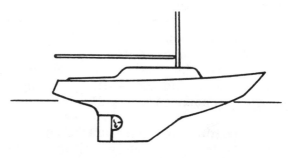

Fig. 1-32   Hull—Planing—505 Design        Fig. 1-33   Full Keel

While there are many factors that go into sailing hulls, the main requirements of planing are fairly obvious. The hull must be fairly shallow in shape, able to move easily over the water rather than through it; it cannot carry great loads; it requires sufficient power - whether in engine or sail area - to get it up and over the watery "hump" between displacement and planing and keep it in the latter type of movement.

Boats that aren't designed to plane have deeper, fuller shapes. They can carry greater loads relative to the size of the boat, and the power required is less - because more power will not move them faster than design hull speed. To counterbalance the weight of masts and sails, displacement hulls frequently have a weighted appendage called a keel, which we'll discuss next. When deep keeled displacement boats are overpowered either by wind or by surfing ahead of large waves, steering becomes erratic or difficult, larger bow and secondary waves are formed and the hull actually tends to ride relatively lower in the water. Planing boats seldom have deep keels and achieve stability either through hull shape or through the use of the crew as counterweights: anyone who's seen sailing photos has undoubtedly encountered at least one shot of a planing boat with the crew hiked out over the side to keep the craft from heeling over too much.

## Keel and Centerboard

Sailboat hulls are designed to pursue a straight-ahead course with as little disturbance of the water as possible. At the same time the boat is moving forward, wind pressure on the sails is frequently attempting to push it to one side. This lateral or sideways movement caused by the wind is called leeway and is partially counteracted by the hull shape. When the boat is moving in the direction the wind blows it is moving to leeward (pronounced "loo'ard").

The portion of the hull shape that minimizes leeway is called either a keel or centerboard depending upon which is used in the design of the boat. This fin-shaped feature in the bottom of the hull allows forward movement, but increases the side profile of the hull thereby increasing lateral resistance. The obvious difference, of course, is that the keel is normally fixed in place - bolted or molded to the hull - while the centerboard is raised and lowered through a slot in the bottom. Within the hull, the board is housed in a structure called the trunk.

## Fixed Keel

A keel has no moving parts, hence nothing to break or jam. A lead keel bolted to the bottom of a boat's hull is also soft enough to absorb the sudden jolt of a grounding on rock or coral without damaging the hull. But keels have their disadvantages, too. Lead is an expensive metal, and the depth of a keel may add so much to a boat's draft that she is excluded from many shallow-water sailing areas. In addition, a boat with a fixed keel is difficult to launch from a highway trailer and it will probably never have the potential for planing.

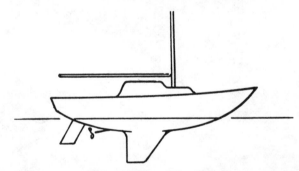

Fig. 1-34   Fin Keel

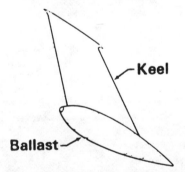

Fig. 1-35   Externally Ballasted Keel—
Bulb Type

The keel is usually weighted and the centerboard normally is not. While many boards are metal and quite heavy, their weight relative to the boat's displacement is small. A keel, however, may contain an amount of weight-usually in the form of lead ballast-equal to half the boat's total displacement. This much weight is there for a reason. While the shape of the keel performs the function of preventing or minimizing leeway, its weight helps add to the boat's stability by counterbalancing the heeling or overturning forces of wind on the sails and the weight of the mast, rigging and sails. Since "Australia II" won the America's Cup in 1983, the wing keel has become featured on a number of production sailboats. It's popularity is due to the fact that it provides a deeper draft when heeling, therefore improving the upwind performance of the boat.

**Swing Keel**

Some designers have produced swing-keel boats: in these, the weighted keel can be partially retracted into the hull or locked in the fully-lowered position. For many people, swing-keel vessels are a good compromise, for while their sailing with the keel raised is sometimes limited, they can be launched from a standard trailer and they can be motored to and from deep water.

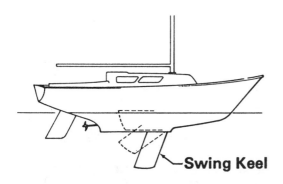

**Fig. 1-36   Typical Swing Type Keel**

**Centerboard**

When shallow draft is important the centerboard craft is the first choice. A centerboard can be fully raised, and since it pivots at the forward corner of the board, the fin can be moved forward and backward by lowering or raising the board. As we shall see, this has an important effect on the boat's sailing ability under certain conditions. To counterbalance its advantages, a centerboard has several drawbacks: to begin with, it is easily damaged if the boat should hit an underwater obstruction. Although the centerboard will sometimes pivot up into its trunk when it hits something, it's more likely to splinter or crack (if wood), bend and jam in the trunk (if metal) or exert a sudden strain on the trunk and the hull, often leading to a serious leak.

Centerboard trunk leaks are not as common in fiberglass boats as they were in wood craft, but they still happen, and they are still among the most stubborn defects to repair.

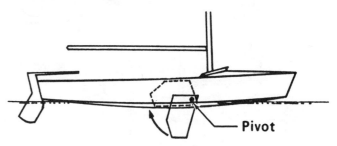

**Fig. 1-37   Centerboard**

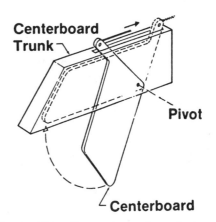

**Fig. 1-38   Centerboard and Trunk**

Finally, a centerboard has the disadvantage of taking up space in the boat. Although some centerboard trunks don't protrude very much above the floorboards, they are still visible, and it's difficult to use that area of the cockpit or cabin for anything else. Some high trunks require bracing to the sides of the hull. It's sometimes possible to make these braces into seats, but for the most part a centerboard trunk is merely a problem in an already crowded area.

Besides a centerboard, there are three other types of fin used in boats. Each is designed to have some advantage over a centerboard in a specialized application.

The Leeboard - invented centuries ago by the Dutch, and now seen mostly on small dinghies. Leeboards are mounted on the sides of the hull, instead of in a trunk inside. They pivot in the same manner as a centerboard, but there may be two of them. The name derives from the fact that only the board on the leeward side of the boat - the side away from the wind - is lowered at any one

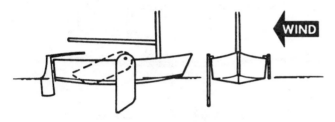

**Fig. 1-39   Leeboard**

time. Leeboards are not as efficient as centerboards, but they don't take up space in the boat, and are cheaper - even in pairs. They are vulnerable to damage when coming alongside piers or other boats.

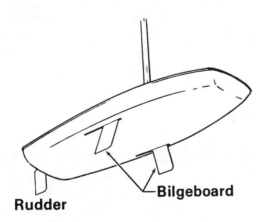

**Fig. 1-40   Bilgeboard**

The Bilgeboard - sometimes seen on flat-bottomed sail racers, bilgeboards are paired like leeboards, but are placed on either side of the cockpit. They are said to aid in sailing efficiency, and they also make construction more complicated.

The Daggerboard - by far the most popular alternative to the centerboard, the daggerboard slides up and down in its trunk, instead of pivoting. It has the advantage of simplicity over the center-board, requiring no pennant, or line, to raise and lower it. Its cheapness and simplicity have made it a standard installation on smaller boats. In small boats, the daggerboard usually has a handle fixed to the top to make lifting easier. The problem with a daggerboard is that, since it's not pivoted, it must when raised extend above the top of its trunk. This has two implications: first, the trunk cannot be capped at the top, which allows water to splash into the cockpit. Second, when fully raised the dagger greatly interferes with operations in the cockpit and may get in the way of maneuvering. Although a centerboard may pivot upward out of harm's way if a submerged object is struck, a daggerboard almost certainly cannot slide upward, and it is thus considerably more vulnerable.

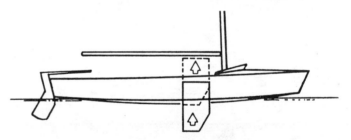

**Fig. 1-41   Daggerboard**

**Using the Centerboard or Daggerboard**
One advantage of both the centerboard and the daggerboard over the fixed keel is that they can be raised or lowered in varying heights to counter the effects of leeway and minimize underwater hull resistance. The racing skipper knows that when running downwind with the board raised the boat will move faster than another boat which has its board down. This same skipper will have to drop the

board when reaching or beating if leeway is to be minimized.

As you will learn later, the underwater shape and hull profile can be varied by adjusting the board height (either centerboard or daggerboard) and that the ultimate trim and steering of the boat are affected by the position of the board. The amount that a skipper varies the board will depend upon experience and confidence as well as individual preference. Many successful skippers drop the centerboard or daggerboard completely and never raise it except when sailing into shallow water or onto a beach.

### Care of the Centerboard or Daggerboard

As either the centerboard or daggerboard is adjustable, care should be taken to make sure that it can be raised or lowered with ease. Occasionally on wooden boats a tight fitting board or the trunk itself will swell or expand when the boat is left in the water for a period of time. This swelling usually results in damage to the trunk itself as well as extreme difficulty in raising or lowering the board when required.

Centerboard boats which must be left in the water require attention to prevent the centerboard from being jammed in the trunk in the "up" position by marine growth. In addition to regular haulouts and bottom painting, proper prevention could be underwater hull cleaning or brushing and movement of the centerboard through constant or routine use.

### Centerboards and Daggerboards on Multihulls

Most trailerable catamarans (two hulled boats) do not have a centerboard in either hull. Large catamarans which must be kept in the water will often have either a keel or centerboard in each hull. The design and depth of the hulls will often provide enough area that a centerboard or keel is not required. Ballast for either centerboards or keels is not usually required because the design of the two hulls, side by side, provides great initial stability (resistance to overturning forces).

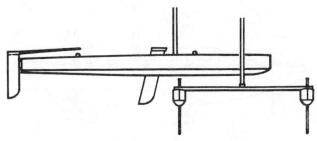

**Fig. 1-42   Catamaran**

Trimarans (three hulled boats) will have either a centerboard or a keel in the center hull which might be either ballasted or unballasted, depending upon the size of the hull and the speeds for which the craft is designed. Trailerable trimarans will usually have an unballasted centerboard.

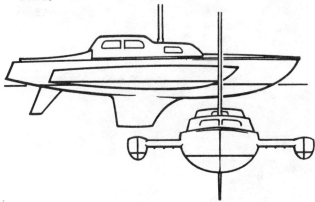

**Fig. 1-43   Trimaran**

### Twin keels

The twin keel or bilge keel is a popular keel design in some shallow water areas or areas subject to extreme ranges in tide. Twin keels provide an opportunity for a boat so designed to rest on its bottom upright at low tide if necessary. This design is similar to that of the bilgeboards except that the keels are permanently fixed and are not lowered or raised through the hull. The depth of the twin keels is less than that of one single keel.

### Steering Systems

Most people, even if they've never seen a boat, are aware that it is steered by means of a rudder. A rudder is a fin located toward the stern of the boat. On small craft, it's usually hinged to the

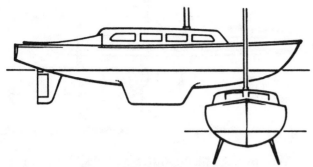

Fig. 1-44 Twin Keel

Fig. 1-45 Rudder

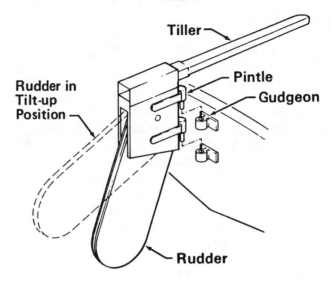

Fig. 1-46 Typical Transom Mounted Rudder

transom, at the very stern. As it pivots from side to side, the rudder has one face or the other to the pressure of water streaming past the moving boat. The pressure of water on the rudder blade pushes the stern to one side or the other.

On most smaller sailboats, the rudder is worked by a simple lever called a tiller, which makes it possible to turn even a fairly large rudder on a fast-moving boat without too much effort. On larger craft steering wheels are quite common and provide even more mechanical advantage than do tillers. A steering wheel on a boat works in the same manner as the one on your car: turn the wheel to the right, the boat turns to starboard, and vice versa.

A tiller, on the other hand, operates in reverse: push the tiller to port, and the boat swings to starboard. What happens is that the boat's stern is thrust sideways by water pressure against the rudder blade. As the stern swings to port (let us say), the boat pivots around its keel or center-board, and the bow must swing away to the other side - to starboard, in this case. It takes beginning sailors a little while to get used to this fact of tiller steering, but once one has become accustomed to pushing the tiller in one direction to have the boat turn in the other, it's quite natural.

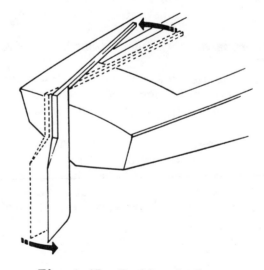

Fig. 1-47 Rudder Action

1-20

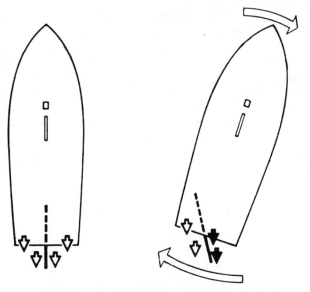

**Fig. 1-48   Rudder Turning Boat**

In steering a boat with a tiller, a few things are important to remember. First, don't forget that the boat pivots like a weathervane around a point somewhere near <u>amidships</u> - the center of the boat. In this, a boat is quite unlike a car, which follows its front wheels through a turn. A boat turning is more like a car skidding - the bow describes a small circle, while the stern swings in a wider circle outside it. This means that careless skippers frequently hit docks and other boats with their own boats' sterns when turning sharply.

**Fig. 1-49   Braking Action of Rudder**

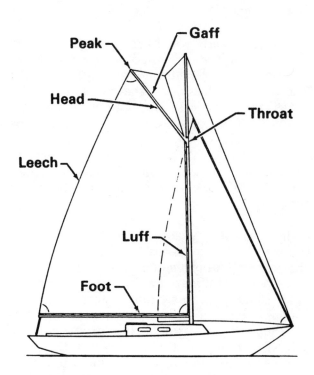

**Fig. 1-50   Parts of Gaff Rig**

Second, bear in mind that a rudder cannot function unless water is moving past it. For this reason a boat must gain speed before it can be steered - unless, of course, it's anchored in a place where water is running swiftly past the hull while the boat is standing still, as in a river.

Third, a rudder pushed too hard to one side or the other acts more like a brake than a turning force. With the face of the rudder at right angles (or nearly) to the moving water, the boat's tendency is simply to slow down and even become unmanageable. One of the first things to learn about any boat is how far the tiller must be put over to one side in order to make the boat turn. Chances are it's less than you think.

This, then, is the basic boat: a hull to carry crew and equipment, a keel or centerboard to keep the boat from sliding sideways, and a rudder (with tiller or wheel) for steering.

## Other Rigs

The sailboat we have been describing in this chapter is called a sloop and has a triangular Bermudan mainsail and jib. There are other sail shapes and rigging types that you will see and very possibly choose. The conventional sloop is the most efficient, cheapest to make (if one includes the cost of the rig) and easiest to handle. Modern sloops generally perform better upwind than any of the other rigs.

In the early years of the 20th century, before aluminum spars and stainless steel shrouds and stays made tall masts practical, most sailboats were gaff-rigged. A gaff mainsail has four sides, and is supported by a gaff spar across the top of the sail. It provides a great deal of sail area close to the water, but the rigging also is more complicated and requires an extra spar and two halyards, one at each upper corner.

The gaff-rigged sail is demonstrably less efficient than a Bermudan sail most of the time, but many people have an affection for gaff sails because of their traditional appearance. Gaffs are still popular among working sailboats such as the **Newfoundland fishing schooner**, a tribute to the usefulness of the rig. A sloop with a gaff mainsail has, of course, a jib of normal shape.

On some small sailboats, the tall mast required for an effective Bermudan rig may be a danger at anchor, when the weight of the spar can cause the boat to tip over or capsize. Shorter masts also are more convenient to carry on a cartop and to rig before each sail. Such short masts, are usually combined with a gunter rig or carry a lateen, lug or sprit sail. The upper spar, called a gaff on the gunter rigged boats and a yard on the other rigs, allows the head of the mainsail to be raised above the top of the mast without having an overwhelming spar weight to make the boat top heavy and unstable at anchor. The most common of these rigs, the lateen, is found on sail-

boards such as the Sunfish, which are easy to sail, fast, portable, and fairly inexpensive.

Another sail variation common, but not exclusive to, smaller sailboats is the loose-footed mainsail. The lug sail has no boom, but more common loose-footed mainsails are attached to a boom only at the clew to permit the sail to assume its proper shape over more of its total area. A windsurfer, which is neither a surfboard nor a sailboat, has a loose-footed main controlled by a wishbone boom.

## Single Masted Boats

There are three different single mast sailboat rigs. The mast on a catboat is set quite near the forward end of its waterline. Small catboats are the simplest of all boats to sail because they have only one sail to worry about. Consequently, a large number of small boats are cat rigged, they are popular beginners' sailboats which provide all the thrills of sailing with a minimum of sail setting problems.

The catboat rig is less attractive for larger boats because the boat's balance, which is discussed in a later chapter, can not be maintained when the mainsail is reefed (its size reduced) in heavy weather. Large catboat mainsails become very difficult to handle; since sail areas over 400 square feet are considered unwieldy, the maximum catboat size is limited. On the other hand, small sails yield less drive per unit area than large sails. So all other things being equal, catboats, with their single sails, are more efficent than rigs having the same sail area divided among two or three sails. Catboats such as the fourteen foot Laser, a planing hull sailboat that weighs only 130 pounds, are extremely popular for both daysailing and racing and are capable of speeds as high as 15 knots in strong winds.

The sloop rig divides its sail area between two sails, gaining much in both versatility and handling characteristics. If the jib is hoisted from the top of the

A cutter has several advantages over a sloop. It provides a greater choice of sail configurations for the cruising sailor. In stormy weather, the jib can be dropped or roller-furled and the boat sailed with main and staysail. To tack this abbreviated rig, one simply puts the tiller over – each of the two boomed sails is self-tending. In light weather, the cutter can drop its staysail and set from the jibstay a truly immense drifter or reaching jib. Disadvantages of the cutter are extra cost and more things to break or go awry.

**Fig. 1-51  Classic Catboat**

mast, it is called a <u>masthead</u> rig; if it is hoisted from anywhere below the mast top, the rig is termed <u>fractional.</u> Navy daysailers and cruising sailboats have fractional rigs. The jibs on fractional rigs usually are smaller than the mainsail even if they overlap the mast. On most masthead rigs, the <u>genoa jibs</u> contain more square footage than the mainsail, overlap the mast considerably, and are trimmed far aft.

59   The third single masted rig is the <u>cutter</u> with its mast stepped anywhere from 40% to 50% of the deck length back from the bow. A cutter normally sets three sails – the main, which is smaller than on a sloop of comparable size; the <u>forestaysail</u> (<u>staysail</u> for short), which is often self-tending and set on a staysail boom; and outside and forward of it, the jib, which is often a high-cut sail set on a <u>tack pendant,</u> a length of wire running from the jib tack to the deck.

**Fig. 1-52   Cutter**

## Multi-Masted Rigs

As sailboats get larger, the sail area necessary to drive them at hull speed increases. Because of handling limitations on the size of individual sails, the rigs have to be divided to carry the necessary sail area. Today, ease in sail handling has introduced divided rigs to sailboats somewhat smaller than the divided rigs found on older working boats. Most pleasure boats are limited to two masts although working schooners in the last century carried up to seven masts.

Fig. 1-53  Ketch

The most common two-masted yachts are ketches and yawls. The classic definition of each is:

Ketch: A two-masted sailing vessel in which the forward mast, called the mainmast, is the larger, and the after mast, the mizzen, is stepped forward of the rudder post. Ketches are often cutter rigged.

Yawl: A two-masted sailing boat with a large mainmast and a small mizzen aft of it. The mizzen mast of a yawl is stepped aft of the rudder post.

While these definitions are accurate as far as they go, they are not terribly helpful in identifying a ketch from a yawl at a distance, or in suggesting why these are really two quite different types of boats.

### Ketch

A ketch is a two-masted boat in which the sail area of the jib and the mizzen combined are approximately equal to the area of the mainsail; in modern ketches, the jib is usually somewhat larger than the mizzen. The rig came about because, beyond a certain point, a sail becomes too big for one person to handle, even with mechanical aids like winches. Dividing the sail area makes for less aerodynamic efficiency but easier handling, which is why a ketch is usually a cruising boat, and is seldom seen in lengths under about 30 feet. When running, a ketch's mizzen will often blanket the mainsail, unless it can be set on the opposite side of the boat.

### Yawl

A yawl, on the other hand, is really a sloop with a small balancing sail well aft. Many yawls race - and the yawl is essentially a racing rig - with or without the mizzen. Off the wind, both ketch and yawl can set a mizzen staysail, a large, light-air sail that is set flying from the mizzen masthead and sheeted to the end of the mizzen boom. The staysail's tack is on deck, more or less amidships at the foot of the mainmast - thus it's a sail that's often as large as the mainsail, and far easier to control than a spinnaker, as it is entirely within the boat.

The mizzen sail itself is often dropped when the staysail is up.

## Schooner

The schooner is a rig associated with America, although it did not originate on this side of the Atlantic. Most schooners today - the few remaining - are two-masted vessels of some size with the mainmast aft and the smaller foremast forward. A three-masted schooner's masts are the fore, main and mizzen. The schooner is a complex and inefficient rig except off the wind, and having its

**Fig. 1-55  Schooner**

largest sail aft, the mainmast usually winds up blocking the cabin. Its proponents argue that a schooner is the fastest of the rigs on a reach, which may or may not be true, and is easy to handle short-handed.

Most schooners are gaff-rigged on the main and foremasts, though some have marconi mainsails and gaff foresails, and there are other arrangements possible. Off the wind, a schooner may set a big fisherman staysail in the space between fore and main. No matter how inefficient she may be compared to a modern sloop, a schooner driving along on a reach is a splendid sight.

**Fig. 1-54   Yawl**

# Chapter 2

# How A Boat Sails

A sailboat's rig is its engine, and the fuel is the wind. As with any useful engine, the power the rig transmits to the boat can be controlled. We do this by altering the position of the sail or sails in relation to the wind's direction.

The sheets control the set of the sails; as we trim or ease a sheet, we move the after edge of the sail closer or further away from the boat's center line. Providing the boat's direction remains the same, we alter the sail's position with the wind at the same time we change its angle with the boat's center line. We can produce the same effect without trimming our sails - by changing the direction or heading of our boat. Therefore we have two throttles with which we can control the transmission of wind power through the rig to our hull - the sheets and the rudder.

**True Wind**

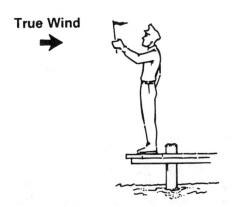

Fig. 2-1 True Wind

As we look further at the reasons why and how wind is transformed into boat motion, try to remember these two throttles. If you feel overwhelmed at any time, you can slow your boat and reduce its heel by either easing the sheets or heading closer to the wind. In a real emergency you can do both.

### The Nature of Wind

Wind is air in motion. When you stand on a pier and feel the breeze on your face, what you're sensing is the true, or geographic wind - moving air. With a little experience, you'll learn to tell how strongly the wind is blowing and what direction it's coming from. (Wind directions are always given in relation to where the wind is blowing from: thus, a north wind is blowing from north to south. Weather forecasts always report the wind's true direction, not its magnetic compass direction.)

A moving vehicle, on land or sea, creates a "wind" of its own as it moves through the air. This is called "wind of motion." Suppose, for example, that you're in a powerboat on a day when no true wind is blowing at all. You're cruising north at 10 knots. If you raise your head above the windshield, you'll feel a "north wind" of that same strength - 10 nautical miles per hour - blowing straight at you. This is the boat's wind of motion.

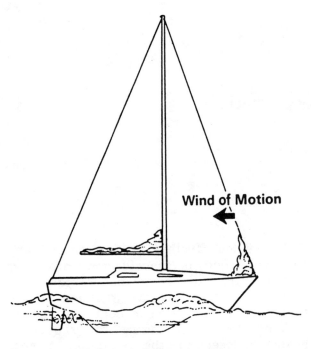

**Fig. 2-2 Wind of Motion**

This result is called <u>apparent wind</u>: the wind perceived from a moving vehicle. This wind is the combined force and direction of true wind and wind of motion.

Sometimes the apparent wind is less than either of its two components: imagine that we're still in our powerboat, moving at 5 knots to the north into a north wind that's blowing at seven knots. The apparent wind is 12 knots. We turn the boat in the opposite direction and go south at 5 knots, with the same 7 knot wind now blowing from directly astern. Our apparent wind is now 7 knots <u>minus</u> 5 knots, or a mere 2 knots.

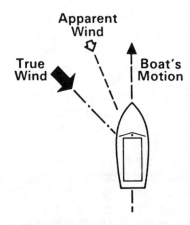

**Fig. 2-4 Apparent Wind**

Now take the example one step further: you're again in a powerboat, again moving north at 10 knots. But this time, there is a wind blowing <u>from</u> the north at five knots. What do you feel, riding in the boat? <u>A 15-knot wind</u> - your boat's wind of motion, added to the true wind.

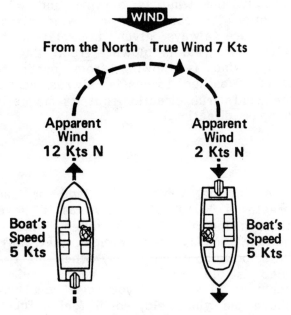

**Fig. 2-3 Relation Between True Wind and Boat Speed**

Apparent wind is easy to calculate when the wind is directly ahead or astern. It's more complicated when the wind is blowing from somewhere on either side of the boat. In a situation like this, if we know the true wind's speed and direction (which we can observe before we set out) and the boat's speed and direction, we can figure out the apparent wind by use of a diagram called a <u>wind vector</u>.

On small boats, few people bother to calculate apparent wind in detail, except very intense racing skippers. All you have to know is the general idea of apparent wind and what makes it up, because it's apparent wind you sail by, determining the directions in which your boat can sail and how much or little sail you should raise. Sailors who don't consider apparent

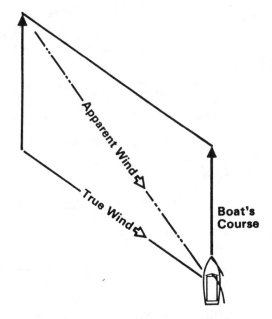

**Fig. 2-5 Wind Vector Diagram**

**Fig. 2-6 Telltales on Shrouds**

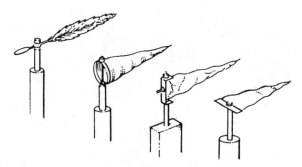

**Fig. 2-7 Types of Masthead Wind Vanes**

appeared a gentle zephyr when heading downwind is quite blustery when going the other way.

To be aware of wind direction, most skippers use a form of wind vane or <u>tell-tale</u>. It may be a rigid, pivoting vane at the masthead, a cloth pennant, or a strip of fabric tied to one of the shrouds. The vane is located in a place where it can easily be seen and where the wind hitting it will not have been deflected by the sails or rigging. On small boats, a practical location for a vane is at the masthead. In larger boats the wind at the top of the mast may be blowing in a slightly different direction than the breeze at deck level, so larger sailboats usually have extra telltales tied or taped to the upper shrouds about four or five feet from the deck, and another, for measuring the wind astern, made fast to the backstay.

On cruising sailboats, where the mast may be 30, 40 or even 50 feet high, an electronic device at the masthead may measure both wind direction and speed, for readout on a pair of instrument dials in the cockpit. This instrumentation is available for quite small craft. It is convenient, but it's really not necessary.

### Points of Sailing — Running

It's easy to visualize a sailboat moving with the wind behind it - being pushed downwind. When the wind is more or less directly astern of a boat, she is said to be <u>running</u>. For most efficient sailing, the main and jib should, if possible, be at right angles to the apparent wind (which

wind can get an unpleasant surprise when, after sailing with the wind for some time, they suddenly head their boat into the breeze - only to find that what

**Fig. 2-8 Mast Head Wind Devices**

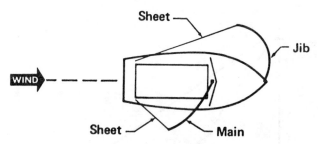

**Fig. 2-9 Running Wing and Wing**

**Sailing Wing-and-Wing**

A good way to keep the boom in its place, especially on very windy days, is to sail with the wind coming from either <u>quarter</u> - over the corners of the transom. On this heading, the mainsail will be reasonably efficient and you should be able to set the jib on the opposite side. You may require a portable spar called a <u>whisker pole</u> to keep the jib standing and filled. A whisker pole is a light aluminum tube with a snap hook at one end and a narrow prong at the other. The snap hook fits to an eye on the forward side of the mast, while the prong goes through the jib clew cringle. When the jib sheet is pulled back, the pole acts like a boom.

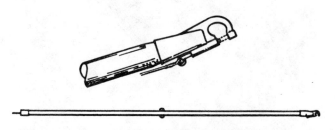

**Fig. 2-10 Whisker Pole and Fittings**

It takes a good deal of practice to be able to sail a boat wing-and-wing, and for a long time it will seem that it's more trouble than it's worth. If your boat has a very small jib, it may indeed be too much effort to bother winging it out - concentrate at least for the time being on sailing with the main alone.

Try to keep the sail at right angles to the apparent wind, watching either the telltale on the backstay or the masthead vane. To adjust the angle at which the wind strikes the sail, you can either turn

will be from the same direction as the true wind).

Because the mainsail is likely to <u>blanket</u> , or keep the wind from, the jib if both sails are extended to the same side of the boat, when running the sails are set <u>wing-and-wing</u> - the main fully out on one side, and the jib out on the other side of the vessel. A boat sailing directly before the wind can be difficult to steer, responding sluggishly to her rudder. In addition, stern seas throw the stern sideways and the wind direction is constantly changing in small degrees. It's possible for the wind to get behind the fully extended mainsail and blow it - boom and all - across the boat to fully extended on the other side. This is called an <u>accidental jibe</u>, and can cause injury or put serious strains on the rigging and should be avoided. A "preventer" can help prevent accidental jibes, but must be watched carefully. (See Chapter 6.)

the whole boat or play the mainsheet in and out. Many experienced sailors never cleat the mainsheet at all, and certainly the sheet should always be ready to let run, to spill the wind from the sail in a hurry. At the same time, it's tiring and dull to have to hold a piece of line all day. A quick-release cleat works very well and is quite safe.

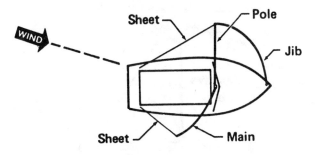

**Fig. 2-11    Wind Over the Quarter – Using Whisker Pole**

## Points of Sailing — Close Hauled

We can see how a boat can sail before the wind, but it's harder to understand how a boat moved by the wind can sail into the direction from which the wind is blowing - yet modern, well-designed sailboats can sail to within 40° of the <u>true</u> wind. Even old-fashioned, nonperformance craft can sail to within about 50° of the direction from which the wind is blowing. We usually say that the average boat can sail to within approximately 45° of the <u>wind's eye</u> - the direction from which the true wind is coming.

That means, of course, that a sailboat skipper in a reasonably good boat has a choice of headings covering 270° of the conventional 360° circle. This is a major improvement over the old square-rigged sailing vessels of the age of sail. They could only sail about 200 of the 360°.

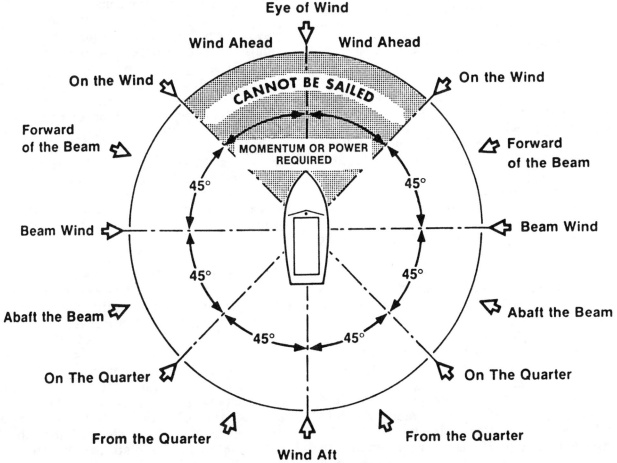

**Fig. 2-12 Eye of the Wind**

A sailboat heading at approximately 45° to the true wind is said to be sailing <u>close hauled</u>. She may also be referred to as <u>beating to windward</u>, being <u>on the wind</u> or simply <u>beating</u>. All these terms mean the same thing - the boat referred to is sailing as close to the direction from which the wind is blowing as she efficiently can.

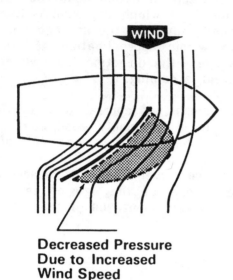

**Decreased Pressure Due to Increased Wind Speed**

**Fig. 2-13 Airfoil Section of Sail**

How is it done? Essentially, a sail on a boat going to windward is performing like an airplane wing. It is an <u>airfoil</u>. In Chapter One we mentioned a sail as having a three-dimensional shape built into it. That shape - a curve - is such that the flow of wind over the <u>leeward</u> side of the sail (the side away from the wind) acts the same way as does the flow of air over the upper side of an aircraft wing.

To simplify what's happening, the air is split by the sail or wing. Part of the air passes closely over each side of the airfoil; the air passing the leeward side of the sail or the upper side of the wing creates a negative pressure, or <u>lift</u>, which tends to move sail or wing upward and forward. This lift is generated in the forward quarter of the sail, along the luff and a relatively small distance back; the direction of the lift is at right angles to the sail, which is why a fairly pronounced

curve is cut into the luff of a mainsail or jib.

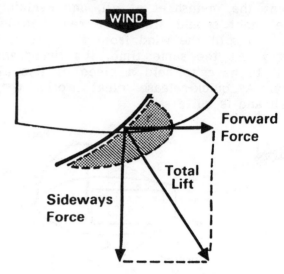

**Fig. 2-14 Forces on Sail**

When going to windward, the force developed by the wind on the sails can be divided into two components - a <u>forward force</u> that propels the boat, and a <u>sideways force</u> which both pushes the boat sideways and causes the boat to tip or <u>heel</u>. Heeling can be counteracted by a ballast keel, by crew weight (on a small boat), or by sail trim. Hull shape, whether the boat has a keel or centerboard, is so designed that <u>leeway</u>, or sidewise motion, is strongly resisted while minimum resistance to forward motion is encountered. Sail shape and trim can maximize the forward component of the sail's lift, but it remains less than sideways force on even the best-designed rig.

**Function of Jib Close Hauled**

Thanks to great refinements in hull and sail design, today's sailboats move to windward very efficiently, all things considered. Both sails function in this process, but the jib - if it is a large one, as many are today - contributes more lift than does the main. Lift over the mainsail surface is at least partially canceled out by the effects of turbulence caused by the mast, while air striking the jib luff is only mildly disturbed by the forestay, jib snaps and sail luff.

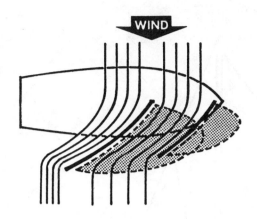

**Fig. 2-15 Sail Slot Effect**

Not only does the jib provide its own lift to windward, it also helps funnel wind across the leeward surface of the main-sail. This creates a "slot effect" which accelerates the wind over the main and thus makes its lift more effective.

If lift is to be created, the wind flow must pass smoothly over the surfaces of the sail, with as little turbulence as possible. In order for smooth flow to occur, the sail must be at the proper angle to the wind. If the angle between sail and wind is much too small, the sail will luff, or shiver, along its windward edge; a luffing sail is an obvious warning that the sail is set too close to the wind. It is possible, however, to sail with enough wind in the sails to fill them, yet at an incorrect angle, so that lift isn't nearly as great as it should be. Until fairly recently, it was hard to sail to windward efficiently, and most people took many hours of practice to develop a "feel" for when the boat was moving most efficiently to windward.

Now such a feel, while useful in getting the last ounce of drive from a boat, isn't really necessary. A person at the helm can now "see" how the wind is moving over the sails of his or her boat. Simply thread two or three pieces of knitting yarn, in a color that contrasts with the sail, through the jib luff at evenly spaced intervals. These tell tales, sometimes called woolies, streamers, or

wind tallies, should be four to six inches back from the jib luff and eight inches to a foot in from the mainsail luff. They should be long enough - six inches or so on either side of the sail - to hang freely, yet not so long that they catch in seams or get snagged when the sail is bagged or set. (Fig. 2-16)

When sailing to windward, pull the jib sheet as tightly as possible and hold it, while edging the boat up into the wind. As the jib approaches its optimum angle with the wind, both windward and leeward tell tales will stream straight back across the sail. If the boat is too close to the wind, windward streamers, on the concave side of the sail, will begin to lift and twirl, graphically indicating the air turbu-lence around them. When the boat heads too far off the wind for the set of the jib, the leeward streamer will begin to twirl.

For most vessels, there is an area of two to five degrees of heading where the sail trim is good enough so the windward tell tales stream evenly and the leeward tell tales just barely lift off the sail surface. As a general rule, the leeward tell tale can be seen through the sail fabric, at least in sunlight, but many people have a sailmaker put a small, clear plastic window in the sail where the key jib tell tale - about one-third the length of the luff up from the deck - is located.

Having trimmed the jib for maximum efficiency, one can then proceed to do the same with the mainsail. The main can be trimmed with tell tales on the edge of the leech. On most boats, it should be possible to trim each sail till both are drawing properly, but on some modern boats with very large jibs, when the foresail is properly trimmed, the air will flow off its leeward side with such velocity that it will interfere with the mainsail, causing mild luffing. There is usually no good solution to this problem, but in many cases, the jib is so much more effective in moving the boat upwind that it really doesn't seem to matter.

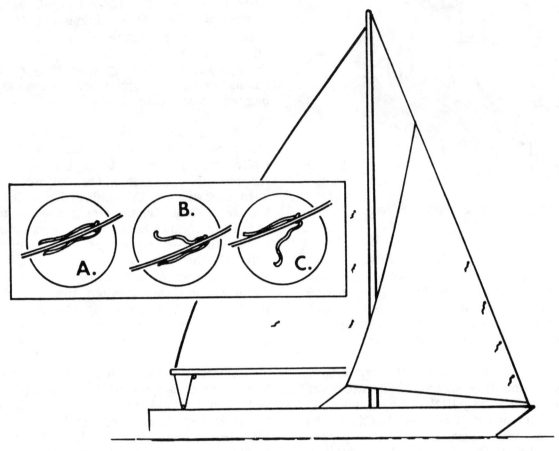

**Fig. 2-16 Luff Woolies**

When sailing to windward, the fact of ever-changing wind direction becomes quite apparent. Although in many parts of our country the prevailing summer breeze seems to blow from the same direction for days at a time, in fact its actual direction will shift constantly a few degrees to either side of its general direction. These shifts aren't noticeable to most people, but to sailors trying to urge their craft to windward, they can be crucial. Called playing the puffs, the helmsman's technique of responding with the tiller to each slight wind shift can make a dramatic difference to a boat's progress over a reasonable distance.

### Points of Sailing — Reaching

A boat may be said to be sailing close-hauled within perhaps five degrees of its optimum windward course. Likewise, a boat is running when the wind is anywhere within a 10- or 15-degree arc dead astern. That's a total of perhaps 25° in the total 270° a boat may head at a given moment. The remaining 245° consists of various types of reaching, from almost-beating all the way around to almost-running.

Almost-beating is known as close reaching. The wind's action on the sails is much as it is when sailing close-hauled—most of the force moving the boat is lift, with perhaps a little more push than when beating. Close reaching is slightly faster than beating—because of the extra push—and there's a slight degree of extra flexibility, too. Because the boat is not already sailing as close to the wind as it can, the person steering may head into the wind a trifle (called heading up, as opposed to turning away from the wind, which is falling off), trimming the sheets in as the boat turns.

2-8

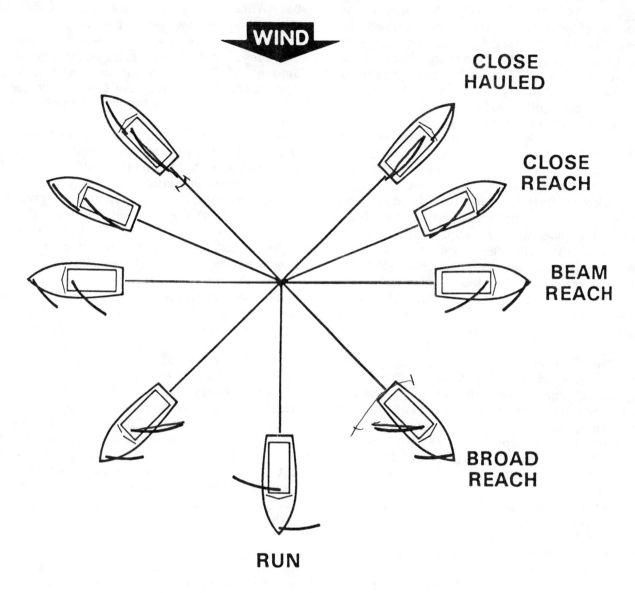

**WIND**

CLOSE
HAULED

CLOSE
REACH

BEAM
REACH

BROAD
REACH

RUN

**Fig. 2-17 Points of Sailing**

Use of the tell tales is just about the same as in beating, and they should be just as helpful. As the boat's bow is turned farther away from the wind, she approaches a beam reach, which occurs when the apparent wind is blowing over the boat at more or less right angles. A beam reach combines excellent lift over the leeward side of the sail with good thrust on the windward side. For this reason, beam reaching is usually a boat's fastest point of sailing. It also offers maximum maneuverability and is probably the safest point of sailing for the beginner.

When beam reaching, the tell tales should still be reasonably effective, at least the ones on the leeward side of the sail. If in doubt, try the old trick of letting the sails out till they begin to luff just a little, then trimming them back in till the luffing stops, then trimming them a hair more. This rule-of-thumb system should leave you with the sails drawing effectively.

As the wind moves aft from a beam reach, one is said to be on a <u>broad reach</u>. Probably the tell tales will cease to be effective, as the force moving the boat is mostly thrust from astern, with just a little lift remaining over the leeward side of the sail. Broad reaching is safe, reasonably fast in any kind of wind, and quite exhilarating. The only common mistake new sailors make is to fail to let the sails out far enough. Trimmed in, the sails seem to be catching more wind; the boat heels and appears to be roaring along. In fact, however, easing (letting out) the sheets a bit may bring the boat back up on her feet, and while she may not appear to be going as fast, she will really be moving more swiftly. The proper way to trim sails for broad reaching is the luff-and-let-out system described above. A log or knot-meter will help you determine if your boat is moving at her best.

The differences between beating, close reaching, and broad reaching, the three types of reach, are not instantly apparent, nor do they matter a great deal in practice. The important thing to learn is proper sail trim for each heading, and for this the concepts of beating, reaching and running are useful.

Perhaps the best way to test sail trim is to get another boat identical to yours and sail the same courses, with each skipper varying sail trim, one at a time. The most effective trim for every major heading will soon become apparent, and it will soon become second nature. Another good way to learn sail trim is to sail with someone who knows your kind of boat. Don't be afraid to ask him or her questions about what's the best practice. Most sailors are only too eager to impart what they know, and your only problem may be absorbing more information than you really need.

## Sail Shape

The curvature which gives your sail its aerodynamic shape is built into the sail by the sailmaker. While all the seams between the sail's panels look parallel when your sail is set, each panel is cut with curved sides where the seams will be. When the panels are sewn together the sail is somewhat concave.

Today, sailmakers can determine the amount of "belly" to put in a sail with a computer. The sail's built in curvature, called its draft, can be determined mathematically for high efficiency at a specific wind speed. The relationship between the depth of the curvature and a straight line distance between the luff and leech of the sail is called the sail's camber ratio, or simply "camber." The greater the camber, the more belly in the sail.

Sails cut for light wind use have a large camber ratio. Increasing the bow shape in the sail increases the velocity difference between the air flowing over the front and back of the sail - that velocity difference determines the sail's lift.

In the days of cotton sails, serious sailboat skippers often bought a new set of sails every spring. Those sails were usually heavy weather sails, that is they had a small camber. The more these sails were used in strong winds, the more the cloth stretched. By the next spring those cotton sails had stretched enough to become light air sails and the skipper bought another set of heavy weather sails.

Today, sail material is much more durable and many more sail cloth weights are available. Serious sailors buy different weight sails for different wind conditions, each with an appropriate camber that, with care, lasts for several seasons.

But what about the not so serious sailor who tries to get by with one set of sails? Sailmakers try to meet the casual sailor's needs by designing a set of sails that meet the average wind conditions in the sailor's home waters. These sails are at peak efficiency only when the wind blows at average conditions; but at wind speeds near the average, the average skipper can't tell the difference. When the wind speed drops considerably, the skipper's boat won't be as fast as if it were rigged with light air sails. In heavier than average winds, the sails will overpower the boat more often. In very heavy winds, the sails may be permanently stretched or ripped.

## Sail Adjustments

You can control the draft of your sails within limits to increase their aerodynamic efficiency. Serious sailing text books cover the art of draft control in great detail. We will just touch on a few major principles here so you will know what to look for.

For windward work, the point of maximum draft (the deepest part of the curve in the sail) should be located 33 to 40 percent aft of a jib's luff and about half way back on the mainsail. If you have "slot effect" problems, you may have to move the draft back as much as 55 percent from the main's luff. The maximum draft location on a catboat's mainsail should be located the same as a jib, 40 percent aft of the luff.

You can control the draft by changing the luff tension. More tension pulls more cloth out of the central area of the sail, reducing the "belly" and moving the deepest draft location forward. Consequently, if the wind increases enough to move the draft aft (because of sail stretch), you can reduce excessive heeling and increase the sail's forward drive by tightening the halyard or downhaul.

The tension along the boom controls the draft in the lower part of the main; reducing the foot tension by easing the outhaul will increase the draft in that area.

The sheet tension controls the shape of the main's leech. If the sheet is too tight, the leech will curve to windward, increasing the draft in the after part of the sail and moving the deepest draft location aft. Slacking the sheet tension causes the end of the boom to rise and the leech to fall off to leeward, reducing the total draft and moving the deepest

part of the draft forward. Further loosening the sheet will allow the main to twist, causing the top of the sail to luff before the bottom does. This can be considered a safety measure when the wind is a little too strong for comfort, but under normal conditions the leech should not twist in either direction.

Since the jib sheet controls both foot and leech tension on your jib, you can't change one without affecting the other. Consequently, the best you can do is to move your jib sheet block until the whole jib luffs at once. If the block is too far forward, the lower part of the jib will luff first; if it is too far aft, the upper part of the jib will luff first. Don't forget that if you then change the jib's luff tension you will move the jib clew in relation to the jib block. You should reposition the jib sheet blocks and retrim the jib sheet. Generally, if the leech is touching the spreader while the foot is touching the shroud at the turnbuckle, the lead is set correctly.

After you sail your boat for a while, you will most likely adjust your jib first when you are sailing to windward because the jib's trim has so much effect on set of your mainsail. When you sail off the wind, on a broad reach or run, you will find the sail's aerodynamics are not as important. In fact, on a run, you can reduce all the edge tensions so that you don't reduce the sail area due to tension curl. Your mainsail's leech may still give you a little problem if it spills air. A properly rigged boom vang (see Chapter 6) will keep your leech firm.

## When the Wind Picks Up

All these sail adjustments can be pretty confusing to a beginner. The time you will most want to remember them is when you go for an afternoon's sail and the wind picks up unexpectedly. While a sail in a good breeze can be quite exhilarating, if you are constantly being overpowered it can be irritating or even frightening. So let's review what you can do when its not breezy enough to shorten sail and you want to move faster upwind rather than just heel over more. When the wind increases:

- Tension the jib halyard to move the jib's draft forward,

- Move the jib block aft to get the jib drawing properly again,

- Tighten the downhaul or main halyard to move the mainsail's draft forward,

- Tighten the outhaul to reduce the draft in the lower mainsail area,

- Check to see if your main is being back winded, if so, move your traveler in or slack off your jib, and

- If your main still luffs near the top of your mast, trim your main sheet to counter sheet or sail stretch.

# Chapter 3

# Basic Sailboat Maneuvering

We've considered the three major points of sailing - close hauled, reaching and running - and the subdivisions of reaching. In a modern fore-and-aft rigged boat, in which the sails at rest lie along the boat's centerline, the wind can blow on either side of most sails. When the breeze is coming over the boat's starboard side and the main boom is extended out to port, we say the boat is sailing on <u>starboard tack</u>. When the opposite is true, and the wind is coming over the boat's port side, she is said to be on <u>port tack</u>.

## Identification of Tack

A boat is always on one tack or the other, even when running directly before the wind: in that case, we use the position of the main boom to determine tack; if the boom is extended to <u>port</u>, the boat is on <u>starboard</u> tack and vice versa. We assume that the wind strikes the boat on the side opposite to that on which the boom is extended.

Any description of how a boat is sailing includes both point of sailing and tack: "We were close hauled on starboard tack," for instance, or "reaching on port tack." It's important to know which tack your boat or any other in sight may be on. Which sailboat is "stand-on" or "give-way" is often determined by who is on what tack. (See chapter 7)

In Chapter Two, we showed how most sailboats could at any moment sail a heading on any of 270° of a 360° circle. The two 45° segments on either side of

the wind's eye are not sailable by the average boat. A boat can sail headings equal to only 135° without taking the wind on the opposite side of the boat.

If a boat is running on starboard tack, with the main boom fully extended to port, and she changes course only slightly to bring the wind to the port quarter, the main boom will swing across the boat to the starboard side, and the vessel is now on port tack. If a boat is sailing fast and well while close hauled on port tack, and the skipper steers her through the wind's eye, she will soon be heading at about 90° to her previous course, and the sails will fill from the other side. She will be close hauled on starboard tack.

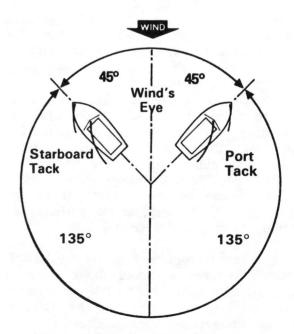

Fig. 3-1 Starboard vs Port Tack

3-1

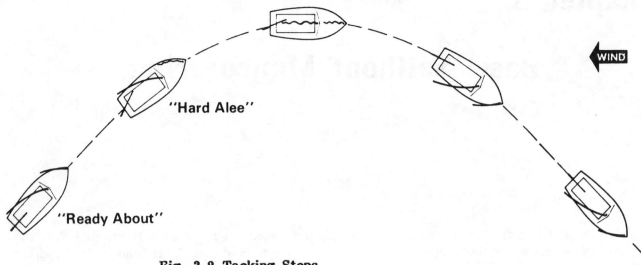

"Hard Alee"

"Ready About"

WIND

## Fig. 3-2 Tacking Steps

These are the two basic sailing maneuvers, _jibing_ and _tacking_ (also called _coming about_), both of which result from the need to change tacks from time to time. Because _tacking_ is the more important of the two maneuvers, let's examine it in detail first.

### Tacking (Coming About)

Tacking can be defined as moving the boat's bow through the wind's eye from close hauled on one tack to close hauled on the other. Coming about means exactly the same thing as tacking.

During the tacking maneuver, the sails will not be drawing or helping the boat to move. They will be causing drag as the boat continues to move forward while turning. It's important, therefore, to make the tacking maneuver as quick as possible, to retain the boat's momentum. At the same time, if the tiller is pushed too far over, the rudder acts as a brake, which also cuts down on the boat's forward speed. Thus, a well-executed tack is a compromise between a turn that's too slow, causing air drag, and one that's too abrupt, causing water drag.

Let's run through a tack to see how it works. Assume a small boat with a mainsail and a jib, handled by a crew of two. One of the two is the skipper, usually whoever's steering. The important thing, is to make sure that there's only one skipper. You can discuss a sailboat maneuver before you do it or afterward, but never during the action itself. To do so is just asking for trouble.

The skipper decides when to tack. The reason may be a wind shift (that is, a change in wind direction), another boat in your way, or simply the desire to change course. Having decided to come about, the skipper says, "Stand by to come about." This is a warning to prepare to change tack. Each crewmember has a job to do in getting ready. The skipper must be sure the boat is moving at a good, steady speed while close hauled, and be ready to release the main sheet if necessary (it shouldn't be, but the skipper should be prepared); the crew normally handles the jib sheet. The crew must uncleat but not release the cleated end of the sheet so it's ready to let go.

When the skipper sees everything's in hand, the immediate preparatory command "Ready about," short for "Get ready to come about," is given. The actual maneuver follows the command "Hard alee!" or "Helm alee!" These words signify that the tiller has been pushed to leeward. At this time, the tiller is put over to leeward away from the direction the wind is coming from, called windward. In wheel steering, the wheel is turned in the desired direction. The stern moves leeward and the bow swings into the wind.

The jib sheet is usually double, with the ends running to cleats at each side of the cockpit. To make the jib set on the opposite side of the boat, the other half of the jib sheet has to be taken in and cleated. (Some jibs, by the way, have a boom - the <u>club</u> or <u>jib-boom</u> - and sheet like the mainsail; these jibs are known as <u>self-tending</u> sails because they sheet themselves properly on the opposite tack.)

The maneuver should be swift enough so the boat is still moving easily ahead as she turns. As the bow comes up more and more into the wind, the sails will begin to flutter, or <u>luff</u> - first the jib, then the main. As soon as the jib luffs, <u>but not before</u>, the crew should let go the held sheet and grasp the other one, taking in the slack without forcing the sail to set on the other side of the boat.

Fig. 3-3 Jib Boom

As the bow swings into the eye of the wind, the sails will luff straight down the boat's centerline. Then, as the bow continues its turn, the sails will begin to fill out on the other side. As the jib luffs

over the deck, the crew takes in the sheet on that side, until the sail begins to stop luffing and draw. It's not necessary to tend the mainsheet - the mainsail will usually fill and adjust itself.

When the boat has made a complete turn of 90° from its original heading, the sails should both be filled in approximately the same position on the new tack that they were on the old. The boat now settles down and begins to gain speed. As the boat gains speed, trim the jib, then the main.

### Skillful Tacking
The skipper should put the tiller only as far over as is necessary to turn smoothly and fast, without unnecessary braking. This amount of helm will depend on the boat, and you can only discover it by practice. Generally speaking, a heavy, narrow keel boat has more momentum and requires less tiller action than does a light, wide centerboard-type hull, which loses speed dramatically as it comes into the wind.

In the course of tacking, the crew should avoid pulling the jib across onto the other side of the boat prematurely. Doing so only causes the sail to <u>backwind</u> - to take the breeze on its forward side, braking the boat's forward motion and turning the bow back to the old tack. The crew should, when possible, simply allow the jib to come across the boat, easing out the old part of the sheet and taking in the slack of the other part, so there's no great amount of loose line flapping on the foredeck to get tangled.

While most boats tack through 85-95 degrees, remember the effect of apparent wind, noted in Chapter Two: just before tacking, with the boat moving well close hauled, the <u>apparent</u> wind will probably be about 25° off the bow. When the tack is completed, and the boat has begun to move off on the new heading, the <u>apparent</u> wind will probably be more like <u>40°</u> off the other side of the bow. As the boat gains speed, the apparent wind direction will move forward.

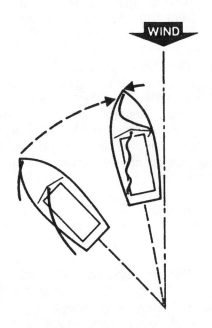

**Fig. 3-4 Premature Backwinding**

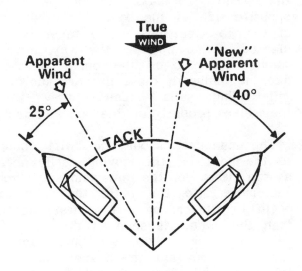

**Fig. 3-5 Tacking—Apparent Wind Effect**

This means that the crew will normally not trim the jib in as far on the new tack as it was trimmed in on the old. Then as the boat regains its speed, the jib will have to come in a little, to account for the changing apparent wind.

### Caught In Irons

It sometimes happens, especially in small, light boats, that a vessel will get halfway through a tack and stall with the bow facing directly into the wind. This is called being in irons, and it happens to everyone from time to time. It usually happens because the boat wasn't moving fast enough when the tack was begun, or because the skipper tried to tack from a reaching point of sailing, without edging up to close hauled first. Sometimes you can get into irons on a very windy day if a wave slaps your bow as you're turning the boat, and stops you cold. Sometimes when there's very little wind, the boat will simply not tack at all.

To avoid getting into irons, make sure - especially while you're still not familiar with the boat - that you're moving fast and smoothly before trying to tack. Many skippers will fall off - delib-

erately head the bow away from the wind five degrees or so - and pick up a bit of extra speed before coming about.

On very windy days, when there are steep, short waves, put the helm over more abruptly than usual, and a bit farther. The idea is to get the bow through the wind's eye, wind blowing directly against bow, even at a sacrifice of forward speed, before the boat's forward momentum is stopped by wind or wave.

On very calm days, put the helm over gently, not quite so much as usual, and let the boat ease through the turn. In this case, you're trying to maintain all the momentum you can, at some cost in turning speed.

Most boats will come about from a close reach, but many cannot do it from a beam reach, even if the sails are trimmed in during the turn. Better to trim the sails in slowly, while heading up to a proper close hauled heading, then make your tack from there.

Every boat tacks slightly differently from every other boat, and learning how to handle a new craft is just a matter of time and practice. A top skipper will spend hours tacking and tacking again in a new boat, till the maneuver is down pat and the skipper knows just what to expect.

But even top skippers can make a mistake. Sooner or later you'll be in the embarrassing position of finding yourself stalled - dead in the water, with the sails luffing helplessly down the boat's center-line. In irons.

### Getting Out of Irons

Getting out of irons isn't particularly difficult. How you do it depends on what kind of boat you have. Here are several methods you can try to see which works best for you. (See Figures 3-7 & 3-8)

First, if yours is a light boat, just release the sheets, pull up the center-board (if there is one), and wait. In a short time, the boat should swing around broadside to the wind, with the sails luffing out to leeward. Drop the board, sheet in the sails and sail off.

Next, you can <u>back the jib</u>. Have the crew hold the jib clew out to one side of the boat, while you (the skipper) put the

tiller over to the opposite side. Your boat will slip backward, and her stern will swing in the same direction the jib is extended, while the bow turns the other way. Once you're beam to the wind, you can straighten the tiller, sheet in both sails normally, and sail off.

On a boat with no jib, such as a boardboat or small dinghy, you can back the mainsail in the same manner. This may cause the boat to move straight backward, until you put the tiller over. Small catamarans will often begin to sail in reverse almost immediately after getting into irons. Just wait for the boat to pick up a knot or so of speed, then put the tiller over, while letting the sheet run.

There are only a couple of things to keep in mind when getting out of irons. First, before taking action, consider which direction you'll want to be heading after you get out of irons. If you back the jib, the bow will wind up headed in the opposite direction, but the stern will slide toward the side the jib is backed. Plan ahead.

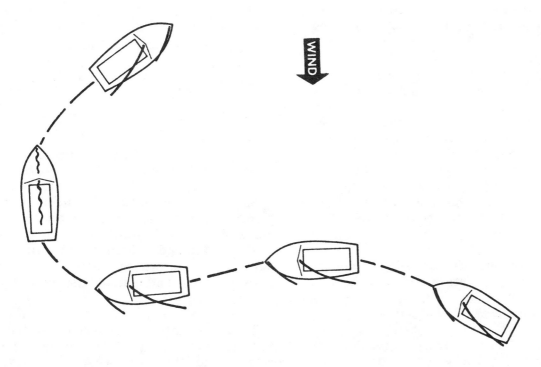

**Fig. 3-6  Avoiding Irons by Falling Off**

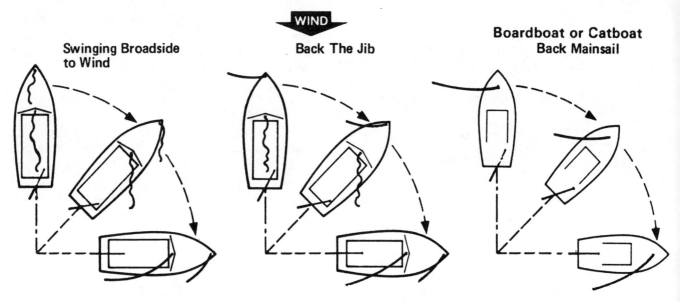

Swinging Broadside
to Wind

**WIND**

Back The Jib

Boardboat or Catboat
Back Mainsail

Fig. 3-7  Getting Out of Irons

In heavy winds, be cautious about sheeting in as the boat comes beam-on to the breeze. If you take the sheet in too quickly, the sudden wind pressure may spill the boat before it can get going. Better to sheet in just enough to let the boat gain headway, then complete the sheeting operation when you're moving well.

Generally speaking, the heavier the boat, the more positive action will be required to get out of irons. As keel boats are normally heavier than centerboard boats of the same length, they'll need the jib backed and rudder hard over to get out of irons, while a centerboard boat may respond to rudder action alone. This is another of the things you'll have to learn about how your boat reacts.

### Jibing

Jibing, pronounced Jybe-ing, occurs when you move the <u>stern</u> through the eye of the wind, in order to bring the breeze onto the other side of the sail.

The jibe is the downwind equivalent of tacking. Sometimes a wind change may be such that continuing along the tack you're on will mean you'll have to steer a course that's less direct than you'd like.

Fig. 3-8  Getting Out of Irons by Backwinding the Jib

Many smaller boats sail much faster on a broad reach than on a run, so they "tack downwind," using a series of jibes, first to one side, then to the other, and actually arrive where they're going faster than if they had sailed the straight-line course.

The essential difference between tacking and jibing is the wind direction relative to the sail. When you <u>tack</u>, the wind blows across the luff, the controlled edge of the sail; when you <u>jibe</u>, the wind hits the leech, the free side of the sail.

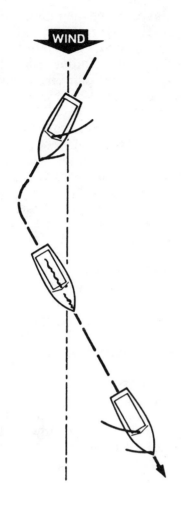

**Fig. 3-9   Jibing**

Thus, when you're tacking, the sail flutters across the boat with no wind filling it until you sheet in. When you jibe, on the other hand, the sail always has wind filling it, except for the split second when it's halfway across.

This means that jibing is, potentially hazardous, a less controlled, more violent maneuver than tacking. This does not mean you should be afraid to jibe your boat - a good sailor uses tack or jibe with equal confidence, according to what the maneuvering situation calls for. Until you can do the same, you're not handling your boat well.

Jibing may require a bit more maneuvering room than tacking, especially when jibing a small boat in a stiff breeze.

This, too, is a question of control, and while a tack is a very predictable evolution, a fast jibe may result in a sudden burst of speed or a moment's out-of-control stagger. Allow enough room to cope.

The actual operation is very simple; let's assume the same kind of small sloop we had when discussing tacking, with a crew of two. To jibe you'll need to put the boat on a run. If you're running wing-and-wing, jib set on opposite side to main, with a whisker pole extending the jib, remove the pole and stow it out of the way. The jib may or may not fill. Forget it. The mainsail gets your principal consideration.

The boat is now running, main boom fully extended. The skipper calls out, "Stand by to jibe," or words to that effect. The crew may handle the mainsheet or the skipper may hold it; that's something each crew must decide for themselves. The skipper then calls, "Ready to jibe," as a final warning to the crew. The sheet handler takes in the mainsheet as the boat begins to turn until the boom is nearly amidships. On the command, "Jibe-oh," the skipper puts the tiller over, as always in the direction away from that in which he wants to go. When jibing, the tiller is put over away from the boom.

As the tiller is put over, the boat's stern begins to swing into the wind, and a moment later the main boom will move across, its speed depending largely on the strength of the wind and the control of the sheet handler. The desired effect is to push the boat's stern through the wind's eye.

When the boom crosses the centerline, the crew lets the mainsheet run, but keeps some tension on it. This can be accomplished by running the line under the horn of a cleat, for friction, or simply employing hand pressure. Let the sheet out in a controlled run, as the boat is still turning, then gradually increase resistance until the sheet is stopped with the boom short of hitting the lee shrouds. Settle down on the new course. It's as simple as that.

In light winds, it won't be necessary to harden in very much before jibing, and in very light zephyrs, the crew may have to push the boom across by hand.

## Uncontrolled Jibe

The important aspect of jibing is control: never allow the boom to swing across without controlling the sheet. In a brisk wind, aboard a small boat, the jar of boom's hitting shrouds can snap a wire, bend the boom or capsize the boat. If your boat has a single backstay, the boom can swing up as it moves across out of control and snag on the backstay.

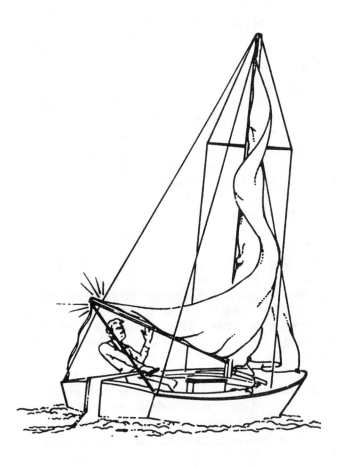

**Fig. 3-10   Uncontrolled Jibe**

Wear gloves when handling sheets. Some sailors prefer fingerless mitts (it's the palms that need protection) made of chamois or some similar material. Others buy cheap cotton painters' gloves in the hardware store.

One of the dangers of running is that you are not aware of true wind strength. When heading downwind, your boat's speed is subtracted from the true wind speed, and the apparent wind you feel may be very much less than the true wind, which may slam the boom across with quite a crash if you're not ready for it.

And watch your heads! The boom doesn't shout a warning as it comes across the cockpit, and more than one sailor has incurred a painful or even serious whack on the head from an accidental or uncontrolled jibe.

## Sailing a Course

Any boat moving from point to point over the water can be said to be sailing a course. Some of the time nothing more is involved than heading directly toward your objective, but frequently things are somewhat more complicated.

If, for instance, the objective is directly upwind, it is impossible to sail directly to it. The straight line from you to your objective is called the "rhumb line." The way to work a sailboat to windward involves a series of tacks, so that the boat zigzags its way to its ultimate destination. When it's necessary to sail a set of tacks to a windward mark, it's usually a good idea to choose a mark that is within sight. If the destination itself is out of range, then intermediate marks may be chosen, preferably ones that appear on nautical charts of the area.

In sailing an upwind course you have to decide whether to sail long or short tacks to either side of the straight-line course to the objective. There is no right way to do it. Time spent tacking is time lost and the same distance covered in many short tacks should take longer than a few long

3-8

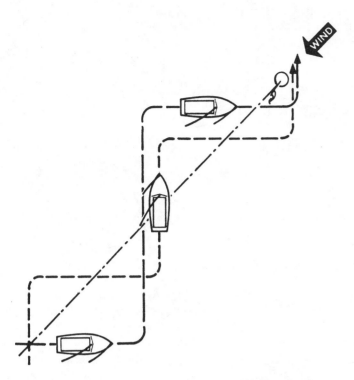

**Fig. 3-11   Sailing a Course Upwind**

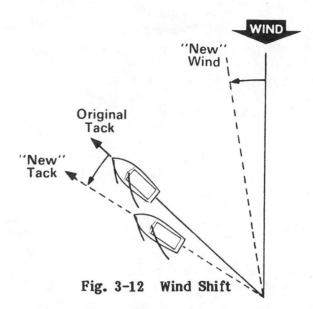

**Fig. 3-12   Wind Shift**

tacks. It is easier to keep track of one's direction and position when short-tacking than when long tacks may take the boat well away from the base course. Finally, long tacks take you away from the intended course, and, if the wind shifts, you can be a long time getting back. Staying close to the intended course protects you from adverse wind shifts.

For example, you are tacking toward a mark directly upwind on starboard tack and the wind shifts 10° to port. This means that, to hold the same course relative to the wind while remaining on starboard tack, the boat will have to head 10° away from your objective. This wind shift is called a <u>header</u>. But if you tack over to port, it will be possible to sail 10° closer than the former best course. A wind change in one's favor is known as a <u>lift</u>, and enables you to sail closer to the wind than anticipated. Generally, tack on a <u>header</u>, and you convert it into a <u>lift</u>. If you are <u>lifted</u>, you can sail closer to the intended course.

When running downwind it may pay to head off the direct course to benefit from a considerable gain in speed when reaching. The boat type and the wind strength will have a great deal to do with deciding whether this tactic is a good one. Racing sailors frequently carry inexpensive plastic slide rules that read out the advantages and disadvantages of tacking downwind, revealing how much faster one must sail to make up the extra distance of an indirect course.

Normally, the way to change direction when running is to jibe, but sometimes, especially in rough weather, a controlled jibe may be rather tricky, and the skipper may elect to sail a series of broad reaching headings, coming about each time the course is changed. This tactic keeps the wind relatively safely on the quarter, where a sudden wind shift is not likely to cause an unexpected jibe.

When tacking from a broad reach, it's usually necessary to come up toward the wind slowly until the boat is sailing a very close reach, with the sails properly trimmed, then come about. Instead of settling down on the opposite close reach, simply keep the boat coming around until the new downwind course is reached. It's a safe and only moderately inefficient way to handle a boat in heavy winds and seas.

3-9

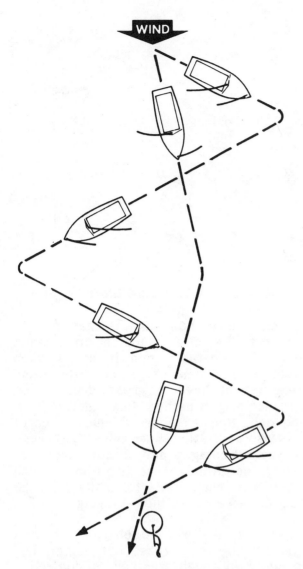

**Fig. 3-13** Running Downwind in Heavy Weather

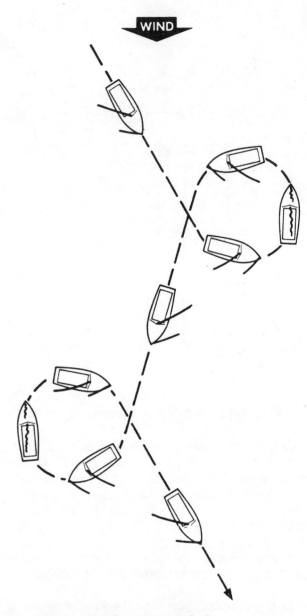

**Fig. 3-14 Tacking Downwind**

A boat beating to windward or sailing a close reach makes a certain amount of leeway - the sideways slippage caused by wind pressure, which hull design cannot cancel out. The maximum amount of leeway under sail would be made by a centerboard boat close hauled, with the board fully raised. Try this with your own boat or a friend's. Put her on a close hauled heading with the board down, sailing right at some mark. Even better, try to line up a <u>range</u> - two marks in line. Sail toward it and see how your boat slides gently off to leeward. Now line up the marks again and try the same thing with the board all the way up. The difference will be dramatic.

**Important Note** Not all sailboats are designed to sail close hauled with the board up without capsizing!

Every skipper should have a pretty accurate idea of the amount of leeway his or her boat will make close hauled, close reaching and beam reaching, with the board all the way down, halfway down and fully raised. After a while, this becomes instinctive, but it takes practice.

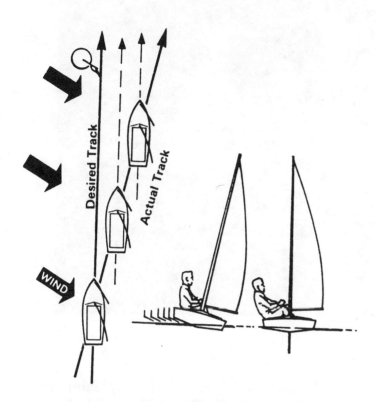

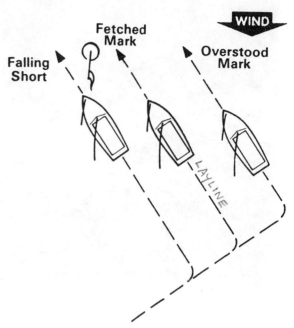

Fig. 3-16   Fetching The Mark

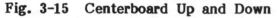

Fig. 3-15   Centerboard Up and Down

When sailing toward a windward mark, the final tack is the crucial one. If you find yourself, following this tack, heading straight for your goal (allowing for leeway), then you have fetched the mark you are sailing down the layline, which is the course line you need to reach.. If, after you've come about, you find you don't have to sail a close hauled course to make your target, you've overstood and should have tacked sooner. Far more common, however, is the problem of falling short, when one tacks too soon for the final leg, and then finds that another tack will be required.

The temptation is to come about as soon as the mark is at 90° to your present heading. Theoretically, that should put you on a course directly toward it. But your leeway will make you fall short. In addition, knowing exactly when the mark is at 90°, or directly abeam, is very tricky. More often than not, wishful thinking will cause you to tack too soon. Be sure you have reached the layline before you tack. It is better to hold on another 30 seconds and overstand a bit.

## Stability and Angle of Heel

A sailboat normally heels in response to wind pressure, and we have seen (Chapter One) how the degree of heeling is partly controlled by hull shape and partly by ballast. Another important factor is the disposition of crew weight. Even in a stiff wind, a small boat that's dramatically heeled can be brought level by the crew hiking out to windward. In older boats, hiking meant sprawling along the windward gunwale, but in most up-to-date small sailboats, hiking straps are built in. The crew puts his or her feet under the straps; with one's seat on the gunwale, this allows the entire upper body to project out to windward as a living counterbalance. On some high-performance boats, the crew stands on the windward gunwale, seat supported by a trapeze hung from the masthead, and arches back to windward. This is the most exciting use of human ballast possible, but it's not for beginners. [See Figs 3-17, 3-18]

There are times when a boat should heel and times it shouldn't, and the degree of heel is also a variable. Within limits, heeling is a safety factor. When a sudden gust of wind strikes a boat's sails,

**Fig. 3-17   Hiking Out**

**Fig. 3-18   Use of The Trapeze**

and the boat heels, not only does the heeling action absorb some of the wind's force (which would otherwise damage the rig), but the sails of a heeled boat present considerably less wind resistance than those of an upright craft. An excessively heeled boat offers a distorted underwater shape and becomes less efficient.

On days of very light breeze, there may not be enough wind to make the sails assume a proper airfoil shape. The cloth just hangs there. But by heeling the boat five degrees or so to leeward, the sails may be induced to sag into the proper curve. In this case, heeling is induced by the crew sitting on the leeward, not the windward, side of the boat.

On some boats with long overhangs at bow and stern, heeling can effectively extend the length of the waterline. This means that the boat's potential speed, which is related to waterline length (Chapter One) is somewhat increased.

Some sailboats can be slightly heeled to leeward in faint breezes to reduce the

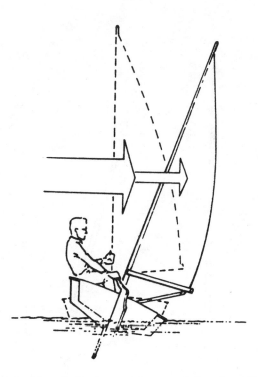

**Fig. 3-19  Sail Area Exposed During Heel**

amount of hull surface in contact with the water, and thus lessen the friction impeding the boat's movement. (See Figures 3-20 & 3-21)

Some boats have a more effective underwater shape when slightly heeled, but this is generally true of older craft. Today's high-performance daysailers are almost always at their best when sailed flat or very nearly so. In almost no case is a boat's performance going to improve beyond 20° of heel, and in most boats performance will deteriorate badly from 25° or so on.

Boats have two kinds of stability: initial and ultimate. Initial stability is a boat's tendency to resist heeling at all. Ultimate stability is the boat's ability to resist capsize. Round bottom keel boats have relatively little initial stability. They heel easily - but only to a point. Once the counterbalancing effect of the ballast keel is felt, a round bottom boat will be very hard to heel any further. It has good ultimate stability.

**Fig. 3-20  Crew's Weight Shifted to Lee Side in Faint Breeze (Induced Sag)**

Almost the opposite is true of hard chine, centerboard boats. Their hull shape resists easy heeling, and they are very steady at first. But once there's enough heeling force to heel the boat more than a few degrees, the initial stability sud-

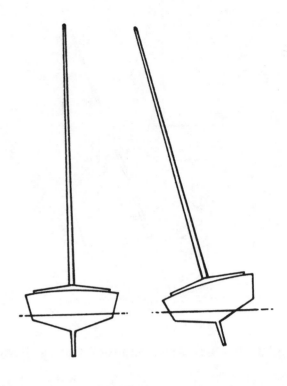

Fig. 3-22   Surface Area of Hard Chine Hull

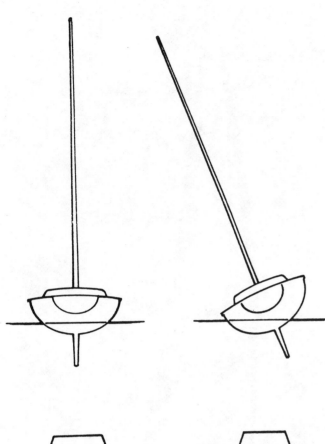

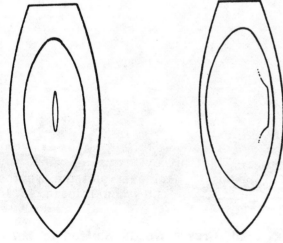

Fig. 3-21 Waterline Changes by Heeling

denly begins to lessen, until at some point it's easier for the hull to keep going over than to right itself. This is a matter of good initial stability and poor ultimate stability.

The most extreme case is that of the multihull - a catamaran with two hulls or a trimaran with three. Because of hull shape, these boats have tremendous initial stability, and a catamaran will seldom heel more than five degrees or a trimaran more than 10. But once the windward hull of a catamaran leaves the water, stability is on the point of evaporating and a "cat," once capsized, will tend to turn completely upside-down. A trimaran is more initially stable, but again, if sufficient force is applied to flip her, she will settle in a completely upside-down position. Both cats and tris are normally without ballast and have daggerboards, so there is no counterbalancing weight to bring them back up.

Each type of hull has its advantages and drawbacks. There is no "perfect" hull for all conditions, and in choosing a boat you must aim for that compromise between stability and other attributes (such as speed or maneuverability) that your sailing area demands.

**Fig. 3-23 Catamaran**

**Fig. 3-24 Trimaran**

**Knowing Your Boat**

Practice is the key to good boat handling. New sailors tend to sail erratically until they develop a feel for their tiller and their boat's motion. We have already seen that the relationship of the sails to the wind's direction is the secret of making a boat move well, as opposed to just making a boat move. You must concentrate on maintaining that relationship, keeping your boat in the "groove," in spite of other distractions. It's easy to lose your orientation to the wind when you take your eyes off your sails to look

at another boat or to chat with your crew. You can easily head up or bear off unknowingly until you develop enough awareness to know when a change in course has changed your boat's angle of heel.

Small changes in wind direction or wind speed while sailing close hauled or reaching also give novices problems. Unless you are careful, you will tend to oversteer to account for these variations. Such changes can usually be felt through your tiller unless you have a strong weather helm. When you get hit by a gust of wind, your boat begins to heel over and the weather helm increases. You should learn to let the tiller pull your hand slightly to leeward to head up a little in a puff; if you push your tiller, you will head up too far too fast and slow your boat. A drop in tiller pressure usually means that the apparent wind direction has shifted forward, either because of a true wind direction change or a lower true wind speed. Of course if you hang onto your tiller as if it were going to run away, you won't feel any subtle changes in tiller pressure.

The tendency to oversteer while sailing before the wind is even greater. The tiller has less sensitivity, the apparent wind is less and seems to shift around more, and the seas tend to push your boat's stern off course. When you find yourself using your tiller like a saw to keep a steady course on a run, try holding your tiller amidships to see what your boat will do. It takes a certain amount of determination to reduce your steering efforts, and you can never eliminate them entirely, but you may be surprised at how well your boat will stay on course when you stop fighting it.

Oversteering slows your boat; your rudder acts like a brake any time it is turned from your boat's centerline. Try steering your boat through a series of abrupt turns on a broad reach in light air to see just how much braking effect your rudder has.

There are several games you can play to get to know your boat better. They all require practice and plenty of sea room the first few times you try them. For instance, you can bring your boat slowly into the wind, let your jib sheets fly, and see what your boat does after it loses headway. It may fall off the wind and, because the mainsheet is still secured, the mainsail will fill and the boat will sail off. Or your boat may fall astern (move backward). If this happens, try to put your boat on a tack of your choice. Remember, since your boat is moving backward, you turn your rudder in the direction you want your stern to go. If you want the bow to fall off to starboard, you push your tiller to starboard to move the rear edge of your rudder to port. Keep trying this until you are sure that you can make your boat fall off on whichever tack you choose.

There are a couple of variations to this game. You can try to back your boat straight backward. This may be quite difficult. If so, try backing your jib and steering straight back; then try backing your main and steering straight back.

Eventually, you will know all about backing your boat if it can be done. You will know how much rudder you need to apply to control your boat, the right time to put your rudder over after your boat starts backing, and when to straighten your rudder as your mainsail fills and your boat starts forward. You will, in effect, know if you can get out of irons without backing a sail, and how efficiently you can get out of irons backing either your main or your jib.

Another game you can try starts in the same way as the one described above. This one is best tried in no more than a moderate breeze. As your boat slows with its bow into the wind's eye, trim your jib tightly on the side opposite the direction you want the bow to swing. In other words, back your jib and secure it. Once you have lost all way, let your mainsheet go and put your rudder over to speed up your turn. For example, if you want to fall off to starboard, trim your jib to port and push your tiller to starboard. Your boat should fall off very quickly to starboard. As the wind comes abeam, turn the rudder in the opposite direction; in our example, pull your tiller to port. Your mainsail should begin to fill by this time, make sure you control your mainsheet so your boom doesn't hit a shroud. Continue to turn, jibe as your stern comes through the wind's eye, and sail off close hauled on the opposite tack.

Once you have sufficient way on, try to put your bow through the eye of the wind again. This time keep both your jib and main sheets trimmed. Since you are sailing in a moderate breeze, your boat, unless it is small and light, should be able to carry enough way on to complete this maneuver. If you can complete your turn go through the exercise again, this time with both your jib and main fully trimmed. Your mainsail will change sides when either your bow or stern go through the wind, but otherwise you will not have changed your sail trim at all during the second loop.

What does this game teach you? First of all, it should make you more comfortable when jibing your boat. If you were able to complete your second loop, you are able to compare the room needed to turn a loop with and without your main sheeted in. If you couldn't start your second loop, you'll know that it is impossible to come about in your boat without letting go your jib sheets in moderate breezes. As you practice, you and your crew will become more nimble and proficient and much more at home in your boat. You will, at the same time, have learned a possible technique for leaving a mooring in a crowded harbor.

The next game is most suited to test the balance of small cruising sailboats. When sailing on a close reach, tack your boat without trimming or letting go either your jib or main sheets. Once you have put your rudder over, hold it there so that your boat continues to circle. Like the previous game, this should be played in moderate air. You can start this maneuver further and further off the wind until you can no longer put your

**Fig. 3-25  Sailing Loops**

bow through the eye of the wind. Once many boats make it through the first tack, they will continue to jibe and tack as long as you hold the rudder over in the same position. The loops in this game will not be as small as they were in the previous one because you haven't moved your rudder this time.

You can also use this last game to decide how to best heave-to or stop your boat without mooring it. The conventional method of heaving-to is to bring your boat close to the wind, trim your jib tight to the windward side, trim your mainsail in, and secure your tiller to leeward. Your rudder is supposed to head your boat into the wind while your jib forces your boat off the wind, resulting in a scalloped course through the water at a slow speed with the mainsail alternately luffing and filling. As we can deduct from the previous game, many modern boats do not lie as calmly as we might like. Some boats begin to swoop vigorously, moving considerable distances; and many boats begin to sail around in a circle.

If your boat doesn't want to heave-to in the conventional manner, you can try the following: trim your jib to weather until its clew is at your mast, ease your mainsheet until it lies at a 45° angle to your boat's centerline, and then lash the tiller or wheel so the rudder is all the way over (heading your boat into the wind).

Very few modern sloops will heave-to successfully. Storybooks tell of adventurers riding out a storm hove-to but that is not your average recreational sailor's cup of tea. However the ability to stop your boat at sea does have its advantages if you need to recover a man overboard, sort out your navigational problems, get in out of the rain, or just eat a peaceful meal.

Lying-to is a variant of heaving-to. If you free all your sheets and lash your tiller to leeward, you will lay abeam the wind with all sails luffing to leeward.

This results in considerable strain on your nerves, sails and rigging in any but the lightest breeze. However lying-to does reduce leeway and is a handy maneuver if you need to stop along side something in the water such as your hat.

Many sailboats will lie-to under bare poles, that is they will lie beam-on to the wind with no sails up if their tillers are lashed to leeward. Their rate of drift is reduced considerably from that of an uncontrolled sailboat hull which normally drifts with its bow downwind and at about 45° to the wind direction. This has at least two implications: if your motor stops, you can cut your rate of drift by lashing your tiller hard over while you work on your problem (you can also put your sail up and have complete control over your boat while your crew works on the motor); or you can direct your downwind drift. In effect, you may be able to "sail" downwind with bare poles, sometimes at angles of up to 30 to 45° from the downwind direction.

As you gain confidence you will think of other games that will increase your ability to handle your boat. The more you experiment, the more confidence you will have in both your boat and yourself. Wear your personal flotation device while you practice these maneuvers. Not because there is any more danger to maneuvering than to straight sailing under normal conditions, but because it's a good idea to see if your PFD will hamper your actions when conditions might not be so good. And remember to let your crew try these maneuvers too; after all sailing is supposed to be fun for everyone on the boat - and some day your life may depend on your crew's seamanship - and their wearing of PFD's.

If your PFD does inhibit your movements, try one of the newer Type III flotation aid vests. They are softer, more comfortable, and made to fit well. It is possible to find a PFD that will not be a problem for the sailor.

# Chapter 4

# Legal Requirements
# and
# Aids To Navigation

## Introduction

The Congress of the United States has recognized the need for safety in boating, and in August of 1971 major federal legislation, PL 92-75 or the Federal Boat Safety Act of 1971 was signed into law. Through this law Congress gave the U. S. Coast Guard a mandate to improve recreational boating safety. In addition, there are numerous state and local regulations which go beyond federal requirements. As in all other areas of our society, ignorance of the law does not exempt you from prosecution if you violate it. You as skipper, owner or crew must be aware of your responsibilities on the water and equip your craft according to federal and state requirements.

Some of the items covered by law are vital to safe operation; others are purely administrative in nature.

The first part of this chapter describes the federal laws and regulations applicable to boats and boatmen. State and local requirements vary so much across the country that it is impossible to cover them here. You can obtain information concerning these from the nearest state or local boating law enforcement agency responsible for your boating area.

## Numbering of Vessels

Power boats operated on (federally-controlled) navigable waters of the United States must be numbered, regardless of length. In general, the term "navigable waters of the United States" refers to waters which provide a "road" for transportation between two or more states or to the sea.

This numbering requirement excludes boats used exclusively for racing in organized and sanctioned regattas and vessels documented as yachts. Other exceptions include public vessels, state and municipal vessels and ships lifeboats. Vessels that have a valid temporary certificate may operate without displaying the registration number on the bow while awaiting issuance of a permanent certificate.

Under the Federal Boating Act of 1958, most states have assumed this numbering function. Their systems are compatible with the Federal system. If you intend to operate principally on waters in a state which has received federal approval of its numbering system you must determine that particular state's requirements. For information regarding individual states with approved systems, consult your marine dealer, the Coast Guard, the Coast Guard Auxiliary, or the State Boating Law Administration.

If your boat must be numbered, the place of application depends upon the waters of principal use. Where these waters are within a state that has a Federally approved numbering system, application is made in accordance with that state's instructions. If you live in one state but operate your boat principally in another state, your boat should be

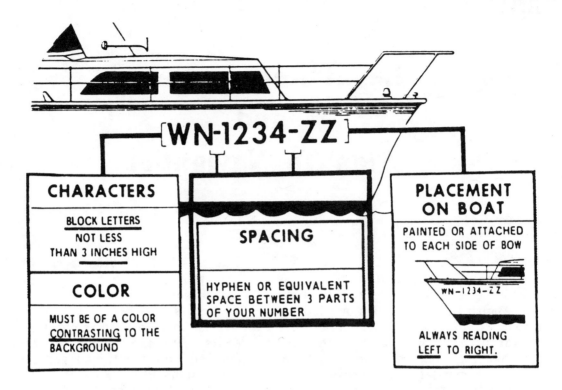

**Fig. 4-1  Proper Number Placement**

registered in the state where it is operated.

When a boat is used principally on the ocean or waters of the Gulf of Mexico or on similar bodies of water, the place where it is normally moored becomes the determining factor in where the application is made. If the state where the boat is moored has a federally approved system, application is made to that state. When the state system has not been federally approved, application is made to the appropriate District Commander (see Appendix C). However, most states have enacted numbering laws approved by the Federal government.

The number assigned by the certificate is to be painted on or attached to each side of the forward half of the vessel (the bow), and no other numbers there. Numbers are to read from left to right, are to be vertical plain block numbers that must be of contrasting color to the background and not less than three inches high. Between the prefix, the numerals, and the suffix, there must be a hyphen or

space equal to the width of any letter or number except "I" or "l" (about 3").

The number shall not be placed on the obscured underside of a flared bow where the angle is such that the number cannot be easily read. When the vessel configuration is such that the number cannot be so placed on the bow, it will be placed on the forward half of the hull or on the permanent superstructure located on the forward half of the hull, as nearly vertical as possible, and where easily seen. If all of these methods are impossible or do not result in clear, readable numbers, the number may be mounted on a bracket or fixture firmly attached to the forward half of the vessel.

**Sales and Transfers**

Boat numbers and Certificates of Numbers are not transferable from person to person, nor from boat to boat. This number stays with the boat unless the state of principal use is changed, in which case it must be renumbered in the new state. When numbered by the Coast Guard, a new application with a fee must be filed by each owner for every boat (except dealers) with the appropriate District Commander (see Appendix C).

## Sales to Aliens

Federal law restricts the sale or lease of certain types of boats to aliens. If the sale or lease involves a vessel powered by more than 600 hp, it must be specifically approved by the Maritime Administration.

The same stipulation applies to the sale, transfer, mortgage, or lease (to an alien) of any vessel presently documented or last documented or numbered in the United States, regardless of its length or specified horsepower.

Specific advance approval of the Maritime Administration is also necessary for the sale of any vessel to a citizen or resident of certain Communist-controlled countries.

For approvals or further information, communicate with the Division of Ship Disposals and Foreign Transfers, Department of Transportation, Washington, D.C. 20593.

## Documenting of Vessels

Under navigation laws administered by the U. S. Coast Guard, a vessel of 5 net tons or over owned by a citizen of the United States and used exclusively for pleasure may be documented as a yacht. If your yacht is documented, you may have the privilege of recording and retaining copies of mortgages, bills of sale, and other instruments of title with the U. S. Coast Guard. Mortgages which are so recorded may, upon compliance with the applicable requirements, become preferred mortgages, thus giving additional security to the mortgagee. You may also properly fly the yacht ensign, and you may find some advantages in clearing customs on returning to the U. S. from cruises in foreign waters.

## Length of Boats

The law specifies minimum equipment for various classes of boat, categorized by length. (See Figures 4-3 thru 4-6.) Manufacturers may specify length in any of a variety of ways, but the official length of a boat is the end-to-end length of the boat over the deck, parallel to the keel line, excluding bow sprits, boomkins, rudders, brackets, outboard motors or outdrives, or other such attachments. (See Fig. 4-2.)

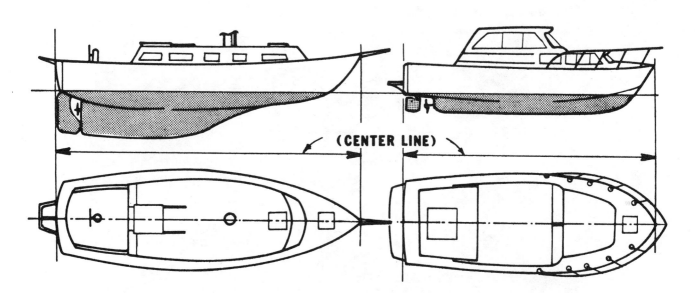

**Fig. 4-2 Measuring the Boat**

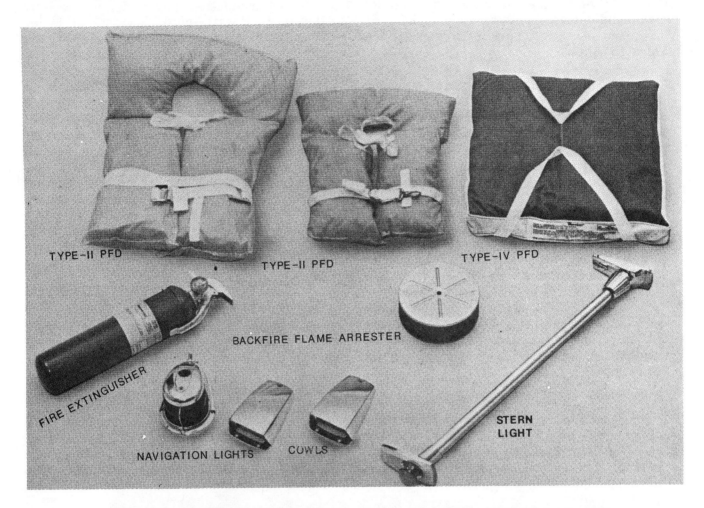

**Fig. 4-3  Types of Equipment For Boats Less Than 16 feet in Length.**

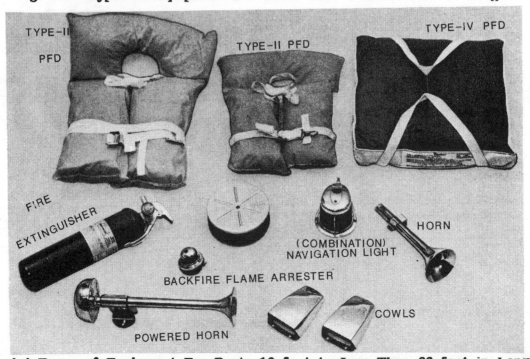

**Fig. 4-4 Types of Equipment For Boats 16 feet to Less Than 26 feet in Length.**

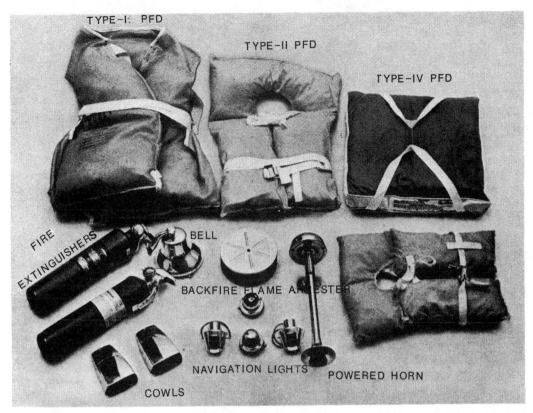

TYPE-I: PFD

TYPE-II PFD

TYPE-IV PFD

FIRE EXTINGUISHERS

BELL

BACKFIRE FLAME ARRESTER

NAVIGATION LIGHTS

COWLS

POWERED HORN

Fig. 4-5 Types of equipment for boats 26 feet to less than 40 feet in length.

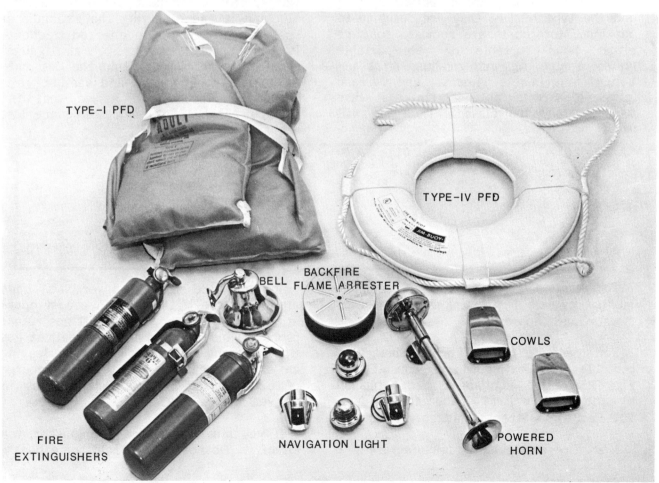

TYPE-I PFD

TYPE-IV PFD

BELL

BACKFIRE FLAME ARRESTER

COWLS

FIRE EXTINGUISHERS

NAVIGATION LIGHT

POWERED HORN

Fig. 4-6 Types of equipment for boats 40 feet to not more than 65 feet in length.

All motorboats (including sailboats either temporarily or permanently equipped with a motor) may be required to carry up to eight different items of equipment: navigation lights, fire extinguishers, personal flotation devices, flame arresters, ventilation devices, bells, whistles, and visual distress signals. Additional equipment may be required by state or local law or ordinance, or by good judgment and the requirements of good seamanship. (See Figs. 4-3, 4-4, 4-5, & 4-6.)

## Lights

By day, a vessel's movements are fairly obvious. By night, practically nothing can be determined about another vessel unless the vessel is lighted according to the Navigation Rules. As with the rules for maneuvering, the provisions for lights vary according to the place, the size of the vessel and her use. Lights for vessels will be discussed in Chapter 7.

## Fire Extinguishers

Fire extinguishers are classified by size and the type of fire they are designed to put out. Motorboats are required to have either hand portable or semi-portable units capable of extinguishing fires involving flammable liquids and grease (class "B" fires). Table 4-I makes it easy to understand the classifications you will use:

prior to 1 January 1965, do not have the Coast Guard approval number of the nameplate. When a fire extinguisher does not show the Coast Guard approval number, the nameplate should be checked against the listing in COMDTINST M16714.3, Equipment Lists at Coast Guard Marine Inspection Offices, or Underwriters' Laboratories, Inc., Fire Protection Equipment List. To be acceptable by the Coast Guard for use, they must be in good and serviceable condition.

If there is a doubt about the approval status of any fire extinguisher, you should contact the nearest Coast Guard Marine Safety Office, Marine Inspection Office or Marine Safety Detachment.

You should make frequent checks to be sure your extinguishers are in their proper stowage brackets and undamaged. Cracked or broken hose should be replaced and nozzles should be kept free of obstructions. (In some areas, insects such as wasps, etc., often nest inside the nozzle, blocking it and rendering the extinguisher useless. They should be checked frequently.) Extinguishers having pressure gauges should show pressure within the designated limits. Locking pins and sealing wires should be checked to assure that the extinguisher has not been used since last recharge.

| Class B Fire Extinguishers | | | | |
|---|---|---|---|---|
| Classification (type-size) | Foam | Carbon Dioxide | Dry Chemical | "Freon" "(Halon)" |
| B-I | 1-1/4 gals. | 4 lbs. | 2 lbs. | 2-1/2 lbs. |
| B-II | 2-1/2 gals. | 15 lbs. | 10 lbs. | -- |
| B-III | 12 gals. | 35 lbs. | 20 lbs. | -- |

**TABLE 4-I**

To meet Federal equipment requirements, portable fire extinguishers must be Coast Guard approved.

For current listings of marine type portable fire extinguishers, consult the Fire Protection Equipment List published by the Underwriters' Laboratories, Inc., 207 East Ohio Street, Chicago, Illinois.

Most fire extinguishers manufactured

Extinguishers should never be tried merely to see if they are in proper operating condition. The valves will not reseat properly and the remaining propellent gas will leak out within a short time, leaving an extinguisher with nearly a full charge of extinguishing material and no way to deliver it to a fire.

If you must use a fire extinguisher, use all of it. Do not try to "hold some back" for later. The fire may flare up again if you do not smother it completely and any that you might save by "holding back" will be useless in a few minutes when the propellant pressure has leaked away.

A discharged extinguisher should be recharged at the first opportunity.

FOAM  CARBON DIOXIDE  FREON (HALON)  DRY CHEMICAL

## Fig. 4-7 Typical Fire Extinguishers

The following tests and inspections should be made by qualified persons:

### Foam

Once a year discharge the extinguisher. Clean the hose and inside of the extinguisher thoroughly. Recharge and attach a tag indicating the date of servicing.

### Carbon Dioxide or Freon (Halon)

Twice a year weigh the cylinder and recharge if the weight loss exceeds 10% of the weight of the charge. Inspect hose and nozzle to be sure they are clear. Inspect the lead seals on the operating levers to insure they are not broken. Attach a tag to indicate when the extinguisher was serviced or inspected.

### Dry Chemical

With visual pressure indicator:
Regularly check the pressure indicator to insure the extinguisher has the proper amount of pressure. Check the nozzle to insure that there is no powder in it; if there is, weigh the extinguisher to insure that it has a full charge. Check the seals to insure that they are intact. Occasionally invert the extinguisher and hit the base with the palm of your hand to insure that the powder has not packed and caked due to vibration. Opinion among experts is divided as to whether or not this does any good. It is a known fact, however, that caking of dry extinguisher agent is a major cause of failure of dry chemical fire extinguishers. This would argue for spares over the minimum requirement. Also—one large is better than two small.

Without indicator:
Once every six months the extinguisher must be taken ashore to be checked and weighed. If the weight is 1/4 ounce less than that stamped on the container it must be serviced. The seals indicating that it has not been tampered with must be intact. If there is any indication of tampering or leakage such as powder in the nozzle, the extinguisher must be serviced. All servicing must be indicated by the servicing station on an attached tag.

### Fire Extinguisher Requirements

Outboard motorboats less than 26 feet in length which are so constructed that entrapment of flammable vapors cannot occur are not required to carry fire

| MINIMUM NUMBER OF HAND PORTABLE FIRE EXTINGUISHERS REQUIRED | | |
|---|---|---|
| Length of Vessel | No fixed system in machinery space | Fixed fire extinguishing system in machinery space |
| Less than 16' | 1 B-I | None |
| 16' to less than 26' | 1 B-I | None |
| 26' to less than 40' | 2 B-I or 1 B-II | 1 B-I |
| 40' through 65' | 3 B-I or 1 B-II and 1 B-I | 2 B-I or 1 B-II |

TABLE 4-II

(FINAL-1)

extinguishers but they are recommended. All other motorboats must be equipped with fire extinguishers according to Table 4-II.

The construction arrangements listed below are considered to permit entrapment of flammable vapors and no boat having one or more of them may be exempted from the requirement to carry fire extinguishers.
1.  Closed compartments under the thwarts and seats wherein portable tanks may be stored.
2.  Double bottoms not sealed to the hull or which are not completely filled with flotation material.
3.  Closed living spaces.
4.  Closed stowage compartments in which combustible or flammable materials are stowed.
5.  Permanently installed fuel tanks.

Conditions which, by themselves, would not require fire extinguishers to be carried on outboard motorboats less than 26 feet in length include:
1.  Bait wells.
2.  Glove compartments.
3.  Buoyant flotation material.
4.  Open slatted flooring.
5.  Ice chests.

## Hull Identification Number
Boats manufactured between 1 November 1972, and 31 July 1984, were required to use a hull identification number such as those shown in Fig. 4-8. The letter "M" in Fig. 4-8(b) indicates the optional method for displaying the date of certification. The last three characters of Fig. 4-8(b) indicate the Month and Model Year. Note that under this method the model year begins in August.

Effective 1 August 1984, all boats must use a new Hull Identification format, such as shown in Fig. 4-8(c). The 9th character indicates the month of certification or manufacture. Character #10 indicates the last digit of the year of manufacture. Characters #11 and #12 indicate the Model year.

Two identical hull identification numbers are required to be displayed on each boat hull.

The primary number must be affixed:

1.  On boats with transoms to the starboard side of the transom within two inches of the top of the transom, gunwale, or hull/deck joint, whichever is lowest.

2.  On boats without transoms or on boats on which it would be impractical to use the transom, to the starboard outboard side of the hull, aft, within one foot of the stern and within two inches of the top of the hull side, gunwale or hull/deck joint, whichever is lowest.

3.  On catamarans and pontoon boats which have readily replaceable hulls, to the aft crossbeam within one foot of the starboard hull attachment.

The duplicate hull identification number must be affixed in an unexposed location on the interior of the boat or beneath a fitting or item of hardware.

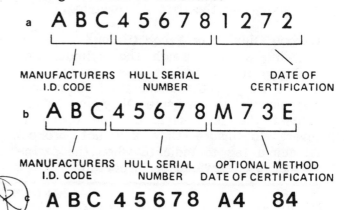

Fig. 4-8  Hull Identification Number

## Display of Capacity Information
All monohull recreational boats less than 20 feet in length the construction of which began after October 31, 1972, except sailboats, canoes, kayaks, and

inflatable boats, must have a legible capacity marking permanently displayed where it is clearly visible to the operator when he is getting the boat underway. The information required to be marked must be displayed as illustrated in Figures 4-9 and 4-10.

## Manufacturer's Certification of Compliance

A certification of compliance must be affixed to any vessel for which a Coast Guard Standard applies. Each label must contain (1) the name and address of the manufacturer who certifies the boat or associated equipment and (2) the words: "This ('Boat' or 'Equipment') complies with U. S. Coast Guard Safety Standards in effect on the Date of Certification. Letters and numbers must be no less than one-eighth of an inch in height. The certificate of compliance label may be affixed at any easily accessible location on the boat or associated equipment. This label may, at the manufacturer's option, be combined with the capacity plate. Examples of the Manufacturer's Certificate of Compliance are illustrated in Figures 4-11 and 4-12.

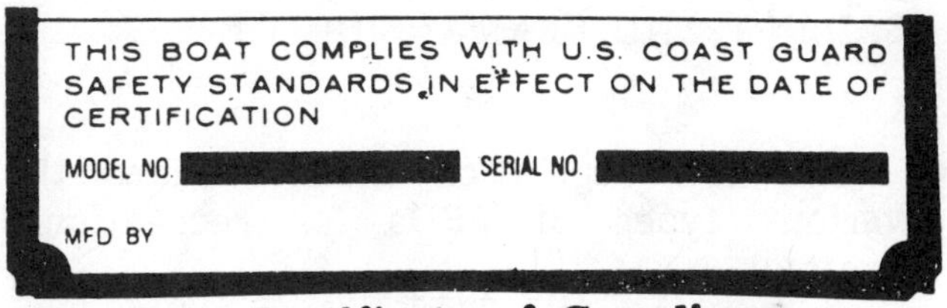

THIS BOAT COMPLIES WITH U.S. COAST GUARD SAFETY STANDARDS IN EFFECT ON THE DATE OF CERTIFICATION

MODEL NO.                    SERIAL NO.

MFD BY

**Fig. 4-11 Certificate of Compliance**

**U.S. COAST GUARD CAPACITY INFORMATION**

MAXIMUM HORSE POWER
MAXIMUM PERSONS CAPACITY (POUNDS)
MAXIMUM WEIGHT CAPACITY
    PERSONS MOTOR & GEAR (POUNDS)

THIS BOAT COMPLIES WITH U.S. COAST GUARD SAFETY STANDARDS IN EFFECT ON THE DATE OF CERTIFICATION

MODEL NO.                    SERIAL NO.

MFD BY

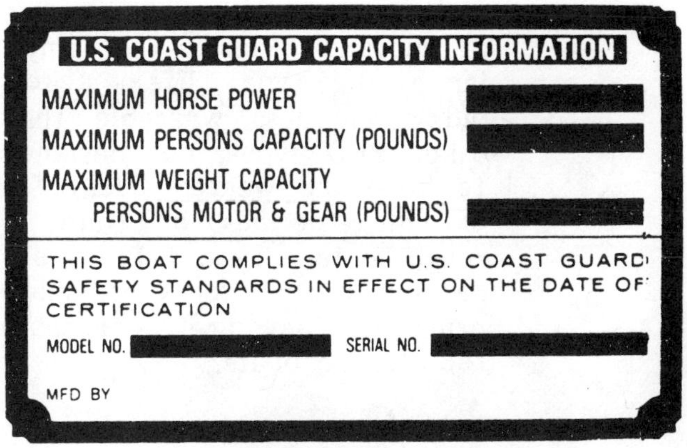

**Fig. 4-12 Combination Capacity Plate and Certificate of Compliance**

**U.S. COAST GUARD CAPACITY INFORMATION**

MAXIMUM HORSE POWER
MAXIMUM PERSONS CAPACITY (POUNDS)
MAXIMUM WEIGHT CAPACITY
    PERSONS MOTOR & GEAR (POUNDS)

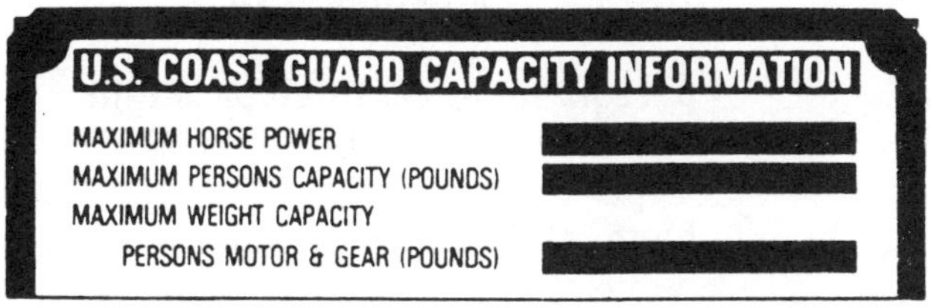

**Fig. 4-9 Capacity Plate for Outboards**

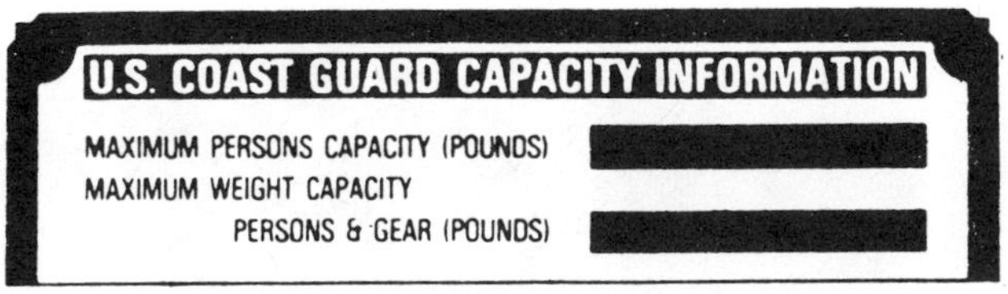

**U.S. COAST GUARD CAPACITY INFORMATION**

MAXIMUM PERSONS CAPACITY (POUNDS)
MAXIMUM WEIGHT CAPACITY
    PERSONS & GEAR (POUNDS)

**Fig. 4-10 Capacity Plate for Inboards, etc.**

## Personal Flotation Devices

The law requires that (1) all recreational boats less than sixteen (16) feet in length, including sailboats and rowboats, and all kayaks and canoes, carry at least one Type I, II, III or IV PFD for each person on board, and (2) all recreational boats sixteen (16) feet or over in length, including sailboats and rowboats, carry at least one Type I, II, or III (wearable) PFD for each person on board and one Type IV (throwable) PFD in each boat.

The new regulation below defines the various types of PFDs for recreational boats: - A Type I PFD (Off-Shore Life Jacket) is a Coast Guard approved device designed to turn an unconscious person in the water from a face downward position to a vertical or slightly backward position, and to have more than 20 pounds of buoyancy. This is the familiar collar-type life jacket, bulky and less wearable than other PFD types, but designed to keep the wearer afloat for extended periods of time in rough water. Type I PFDs are recommended for off-shore cruising. They are acceptable for all size boats.

**Type I**

*#10*

Fig. 4-13    Type I Personal Flotation Device(Off-Shore Life Jacket)

**Type II**    A Type II PFD (Near-Shore Life Vest) is a Coast Guard approved device designed to turn an unconscious person in the water from a face downward position to a vertical or slightly backward position, and to have at least 15.5 pounds of buoyancy. This is a more wearable device than the Type I and is recommended for closer, inshore cruising. Type II PFDs are also acceptable for all size boats.

**Type III**    Type III PFD (Flotation Aid) is a Coast Guard approved device designed to keep a conscious

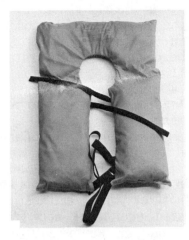

Fig. 4-14    Type II Personal Flotation Device (Near-Shore Life Vest)

Fig. 4-15    Type III Personal Flotation Device (Flotation Aid)

person in a vertical or slightly backward position. Like the Type II PFD, Type III must have at least 15.5 pounds of buoyancy. However, it has a lesser turning ability than either Type I or Type II. Type III PFDs are recommended for in-water sports, or on lakes, impoundments, and close inshore operation. They are acceptable for all size boats.

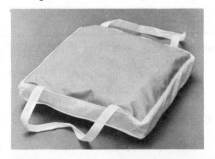

Fig. 4-16    Type IV PFD (Buoyant Cushion)

**Type IV** A Type IV PFD (Throwable Device) is a Coast Guard approved device designed to be thrown to a person in the water and not worn. It must have at least 16.5 pounds of buoyancy. Type IV PFDs are acceptable for boats less than 16 feet in length and canoes and kayaks, and at least one Type IV PFD is required for boats 16 feet and over in length.

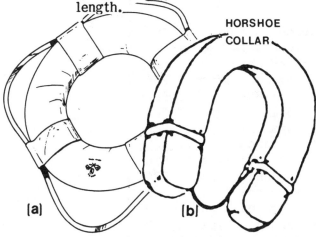

HORSHOE COLLAR

(a)        (b)

All Coast Guard approved personal flotation devices bear markings indicating the manufacturer, the type, and an approval number. However, since the above type designations were adopted in 1973, there are many kinds of Coast Guard approved PFDs in existence which are not marked as "Type I, II, III, IV, or V." Table 4-III gives equivalent "type" information for previously existing devices.

Personal flotation devices can have excellent flotation materials, be expertly manufactured and be in serviceable condition without being a good personal flotation device. The proper use of any personal flotation device requires the wearer to know how it will perform. The only way to gain this knowledge is through personal experience. Every person going out on the water in a boat should first understand how to properly fit and wear the personal flotation device intended for his use. He should then understand how the device will react when the wearer and device are in the water. Only then can he be sure he and the device are ready for an emergency which would cause him to leave the boat. Children, especially, require this practice. Any wearable PFD shall be of an appropriate size for the person who intends to wear it. Child size devices are acceptable only for persons weighing less than 90 pounds.

It is recommended that all PFDs be marked indelibly with the vessel's name and number and hailing port. This can be important in a search and rescue effort, and could help concentrate effort where it can do the most good.

**Life Preservers (Type I PFDs)**
Life preservers will last for many years if they are given reasonable care. They should be dried thoroughly before being put away and should be stowed in a dry, well-ventilated place. Do not stow in the bottom of lockers or deck storage boxes where moisture might accumulate. Frequent airing and drying in the sun is also recommended. Life preservers should not be tossed about haphazardly, used as fenders or cushions, or otherwise roughly treated.

Life preservers are most often of the kapok type, although buoyant fibrous glass, cork, balsa wood, and unicellular plastic foam are used. They are either jacket or bib design.

The jacket type is constructed with pads of buoyant materials inserted in a cloth covering. This covering is fitted with the necessary straps and ties.

Bib type life preservers are constructed of unicellular plastic foam with a vinyl-dip surface or cloth cover. They are fitted with an adjustable strap. Adult and child sizes are available. All Coast Guard approved life preservers (Type I) are required to be Indian Orange colored.

The jacket type life preserver should be put on the same as a coat with all ties and fasteners secured to obtain a snug fit. When the bib type is worn the body strap should be drawn snugly.

```
         APPROVED PERSONAL FLOTATION DEVICES

Number on      Devices Marked       are Equivalent to
  Label


160.002    Life preserver.....Performance Type    I PFD
160.003    Life preserver.....Performance Type    I PFD
160.004    Life preserver.....Performance Type    I PFD
160.005    Life preserver.....Performance Type    I PFD
160.009    Ring life buoy.....Performance Type   IV PFD
160.047    Buoyant vest.......Performance Type   II PFD
160.048    Buoyant cushion....Performance Type   IV PFD
160.049    Buoyant cushion....Performance Type   IV PFD
160.050    Ring life buoy.....Performance Type   IV PFD
160.052    Buoyant vest.......Performance Type   II PFD
160.053    Work Vest.........Performance Type     V PFD
160.055    Life preserver.....Performance Type    I PFD
1.60.060   Buoyant vest.......Performance Type   II PFD
160.064    Special purpose....A device intended to be
           water safety       worn may be equivalent
           buoyant devices     to Type II or Type III.
                               A device that is equiva-
160.077    Hybrid             lent to Type III is
                               marked "Type III Device-
                               may not turn unconscious
                               wearer." A device in-
                               tended to be grasped is
                               equivalent to Type IV.
                               Performance Type  V PFD
                               Must be worn to be ac-
                               ceptable.
```

**TABLE 4-III**

All life preservers are required to be ready for use and readily accessible. This means they should be ready to be worn without adjustments as well as being within reach. The straps should be adjusted for the person for whom it is intended and the fasteners unhooked to eliminate that step when time is most critical.

When underway in a small open boat, life preservers should be worn by children and non-swimmers. When rough weather is encountered on any type of boat, or when in hazardous waters, life preservers should be worn by everyone. As a matter of good seamanship and common sense, all unsatisfactory lifesaving equipment should be left ashore. Its replacement should be Coast Guard approved equipment. An emergency is no time to conduct an inspection to determine whether or not the equipment is serviceable.

## Buoyant Vests (Type II PFDs)

Coast Guard approved buoyant vests are manufactured in several designs. They can be constructed of pads of kapok, fibrous glass or unicellular plastic with cloth covering, with straps and ties attached. The kapok and fibrous glass pads are enclosed in plastic bags. Other models of buoyant vests are made of unicellular plastic foam which has a vinyl-dip coating. They are made in three sizes: adult, child (medium) and child (small), and may be any color.

Buoyant vests are identified by a Coast Guard approval number and the model number which are contained on a label attached to the vest. Vests must be in good and serviceable condition.

As with life preservers, buoyant vests have a variety of adjustable straps which should be adjusted to fit before leaving the mooring. Be sure to make children's adjustments for proper fit, too. Vests should be worn snugly with all ties and fasteners pulled tight and worn by children and non-swimmers when underway in small boats or open construction type craft. They should be dried thoroughly before being put away, and when stowed

on board should be in a readily accessible location which is dry, cool, and well ventilated. Buoyant vests should not be tossed about haphazardly, used as fenders or cushions, or otherwise roughly treated.

## Buoyant Cushions (Type IV PFDs)

Buoyant cushions approved by the Coast Guard contain kapok, fibrous glass or unicellular plastic foam, come in a variety of sizes and shapes, may be any color, and are fitted with grab straps. Some unicellular plastic foam buoyant cushions are vinyl-dip coated.

Buoyant cushions are generally more readily accessible since they are sometimes used as seat cushions. However, the kapok or fibrous glass cushions used as seats become unserviceable rather rapidly because the inner plastic envelope may be punctured.

Cushions are usually available in time of emergency. However, they are difficult to hang on to in the water and do not afford as great a degree of protection as a life preserver or buoyant vest. For this reason, buoyant cushions are not recommended for use by children or non-swimmers. The straps on buoyant cushions are put there primarily for holding-on purposes. However, they may also be used in throwing the cushion. Cushions should never be worn on a person's back since this tends to force the wearer's face down in the water.

Approved buoyant cushions are marked on the side (gusset), showing the Coast Guard approval number and other information concerning the cushion and its use.

## Ring Life Buoys (Type IV PFDs)

These personal flotation devices can be made of cork, balsa wood or unicellular plastic foam, and are available in 30, 24, 20, and 18-inch sizes. Their covering is either canvas or specially-surfaced plastic foam. All buoys are fitted with a grab line and may be colored either white or orange.

It is desirable to attach approximately 60 feet of line to the grab rope on the ring buoy. When throwing a ring buoy, care should be taken not to hit the person in the water. Ring buoys should be stowed in brackets topside, readily accessible for emergencies.

Cork and balsa wood ring buoys must bear two markings, the manufacturer's stamp and the Coast Guard inspector's stamp. Plastic foam ring buoys bear only one marking, a nameplate attached to the buoy.

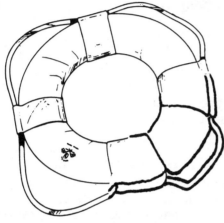

**Fig. 4-17  Type IV PFD (Ring Buoy)**

### Special Purpose Water Safety Buoyant Devices

### Type III PFDs
Approved special purpose water safety buoyant devices are manufactured in many designs depending on the intended special purpose. These include water ski jump vests, hunters' vests, motorboat racing vests, flotation jackets, and others. Additional strength is added where needed for the intended purpose of the device.

Devices are made for either wearing or grasping and devices intended to be worn are available in adult and child sizes. Their markings include the Coast Guard approval number, indication of the purpose for which the device is intended, instructions for use and maintenance, and other necessary information, such as the wording: "Warning--Do not wear on Back" for device intended to be grasped and not worn.

### Type V PFDs [SPECIAL USE DEVICE]
There are two groups of Type V PFDs. The first group consists of "special purposes" PFDs, such as light-weight jackets for kayak racers, exposure suits, and some types of "float coat." The second group within Type V consists of so-called "hybrid PFDs."

Special purpose PFDs are, as their name implies, designed and intended for particular application. In general, they are not suitable (or approved) for general use aboard a recreational boat.

Hybrid PFDs, on the other hand, are designed to meet a need for a comfortable, easy-to-wear PFD for recreational boaters. They are called "hybrid" because they have some inherent buoyancy (closed-cell plastic foam, etc.), but depend on inflatable chambers for additional support in the water.

Hybrid PFDs are designed to keep you afloat should you fall into the water, but they do not provide as much buoyancy as other types. The inflatable chambers or bladders may be inflated by a built-in compressed gas cylinder or by mouth to provide additional buoyancy.

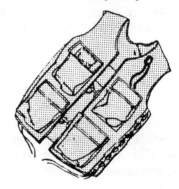

**Fig. 4-18    Type V Personal Flotation Device**

Some manufacturers provide a mechanism that will inflate the flotation bladders automatically when the jacket and wearer enter the water. Such mechanisms, while they are convenient and may provide an extra margin of safety should the wearer be injured or unconscious and unable to inflate the chambers when he/she falls into the water, they do require careful maintenance to keep them workable.

Type V PFDs meet the legal requirements for wearable PFDs on board a vessel only if they are actually being worn at the time. On the other hand, they are designed to be comfortable enough that wearing them at all times when you are on the water should be no problem. The Type V PFD may be substituted on a pleasure craft for a Type I, II or III device — if worn.

## Ventilation Systems

While ventilation is required on most power boats, there is no such thing as a ventilation system "approved" by the Coast Guard. A variety of systems exist, depending which designs and conformity of individual boats, for the purpose of conveying fresh air into each engine and fuel tank compartment and dangerous vapors out of the vessel. To create a flow through the ducting system, at least when underway or when there is a wind, cowls (scoops) or other fittings of equivalent effectiveness are needed on all ducts. A wind-actuated rotary exhauster or mechanical blower is considered equivalent and preferred to a cowl on the exhaust duct.

To scavenge gases from ventilated spaces and avoid undesirable turbulence within the spaces, at least one inlet duct must be installed to extend to a point at least midway to the bilge, or at least below the level of the carburetor air intake.

At least one exhaust duct must extend from the open atmosphere to the lower portion of the bilge. Ducts should not be installed so low in the bilge that they may become obstructed by normal accumulation of bilge water.

The minimum size of the duct must be 2 inches in diameter or have a cross-sectional area of at least 3 square inches.

## Open Boats

The use of gasoline in boats will always present a safety hazard because the vapors are heavier than air and may find their way into the bilges from which there is no escape except through the ventilation systems. In an open boat these vapors may be dissipated through the scouring effect of exposure to the open atmosphere. Open boats are, therefore, exempted from the above ventilation requirements.

All three of the following conditions should be met in order to consider a boat "open":

1. Engine and fuel tank compartments have a minimum 15 square inches of open area directly exposed to the atmosphere for each cubic foot of net compartment volume.
2. There are no long or narrow unventilated spaces accessible from such compartments in which a flame could propagate.
3. Long, narrow compartments (such as side panels), if joining engine or fuel compartments and not serving as ducts thereto, have at least 15 square inches of open area per cubic foot provided by frequent openings along the full length of the compartment formed.

## Technical Details

### Intake (Air Supply)
There must be one or more intake ducts in each fuel and engine compartment, fitted with a cowl (scoop), extending from the open atmosphere to a level midway to the bilge (fuel compartment) or at least below the level of the carburetor (engine compartment).

### Exhaust
There must be one or more exhaust ducts from the lower portion of the bilge of each fuel and engine compartment to the free atmosphere, fitted with a cowl or an equivalent such as a wind actuated rotary exhauster or a power exhaust blower.

### Ducting Materials

Depending on the design, vent cowls could be a major source of bilge water from rain, washdown, breaking seas. Also, periodic inspection is desirable - plastic ducting may break, fall down, etc.

### Positioning of Cowls

Normally, the intake cowl will face forward in an area of free underway airflow, and the exhaust cowl will face aft. They should be located with respect to each other so as to prevent the return of displaced vapors to any enclosed space, or to avoid the pick up of vapors from fuel filling stations.

### Carburetion Air

Openings in engine compartment for entry of air to the carburetor are additional to the ventilation system requirements.

### General Precautions

Ventilation systems are not designed to remove vapors caused by breaks in fuel lines or leaking tanks. If gas odors are detected repairs are generally indicated. Prior to each starting of the engine, the engine compartment should be opened to dissipate vapors which may be present. The smaller the compartment the quicker an explosive mixture of gasoline vapors can be expected to develop.

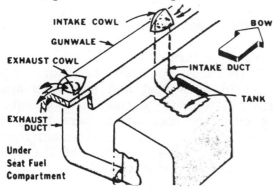

**Fig. 4-19 Ventilation (Boats Built Before July 31, 1980)**

### Play it Safe—Keep Your Boat Free of Explosive Vapors!

Note: Vessels which are intended for carrying more than six passengers for hire

are subject to special regulations. Owners should contact the nearest Coast Guard Marine Safety Office, Marine Inspection Office or Marine Safety Detachment for inspection requirements.

### Ventilation Systems — Boats Built Before July 31, 1980

Both (1) powered and (2) natural ventilation requirements are in effect after July 31, 1980, for boats built after that date. Some boat builders have been in compliance since July 31, 1978. If you are building a boat, check with the Coast Guard for details.

1. Any compartment on a boat containing a permanently installed gasoline engine with a "cranking motor" (e.g., starter) must have a power ventilation system and a label close to the ignition switch and in plain view of the operator: WARNING - GASOLINE VAPORS CAN EXPLODE. BEFORE STARTING ENGINE OPERATE BLOWER FOR 4 MINUTES AND CHECK ENGINE COMPARTMENT BILGE FOR GASOLINE VAPORS.

2. Other engine and/or fuel compartments may require natural ventilation.

All ventilation regulations, as in the past, require the operator to maintain them.

**Fig. 4-20 Backfire Flame Arrester**

### Backfire Flame Arresters

Gasoline engines (other than outboard engines) that have been installed since April 25, 1940, must have an acceptable means of backfire flame control. The usual method is by installation of a Coast

Guard approved flame arrester. Alternate methods are a special Coast Guard approved reed valve system or a closed metallic duct system which would carry all backfire flames outside the vessel in a manner to permit dispersion without endangering the vessel, persons on board, or nearby vessels or structures.

## Whistle or Horn

Whistle signals are required to be given by all boats under certain circumstances. Equipment requirements vary according to the length of the boat.

For compliance with (Navigation Rules) and for distress signaling purposes, all boats must carry some type of sound-producing device capable of a 4 second blast audible for 1/2 mile. Athletic whistles are not acceptable on boats over 12 meters.

Athletic whistles

Note that even though a boat less than 16 feet in length is not required to have a whistle on board, it still must give the proper whistle signals when needed.

Fig. 4-21  Sound Producing Devices

## Bell

Bell signals are required when a vessel is at anchor under conditions of restricted visibility. Under both the International and Inland Navigation Rules (see Chapter

Fig. 4-22  Bell

All vessels 39.4 feet or longer must also carry a bell in operating condition with a minimum diameter at the mouth of at least 7-7/8 inches (200 mm).

## Visual Distress Signals

All recreational boats 16 feet or more are required to be equipped with visual distress signaling devices at all times when operating on coastal waters as of 1 January 1981. Also, boats less than 16 feet are required to carry visual distress signals when operating on coastal waters at night. Coastal waters are defined as (1) The ocean (territorial sea) (2) The Great Lakes (3) Bays or sounds that empty into those waters, and (4) Rivers over two miles across at the mouth, upstream to a point where they narrow to two miles. Completely open sailboats, less than 26 feet, without engines are excepted in the daytime, as are boats propelled manually. Also excepted are boats in organized races, regattas, parades, etc. Visual Distress Signals must be Coast Guard approved, readily accessible, serviceable, and, for those applicable, bearing a legible, unexpired date.

All vessels that operate in U. S. coastal waters or the Great Lakes are required to carry Coast Guard-approved visual distress signals (VDS's). In addition, vessels operating in inland lakes and rivers are strongly urged to carry them.

VDS's have been found to be extremely effective in attracting attention and in guiding rescuers in a search and rescue situation. The wrong type of signal, or one that is not used to best advantage, can be of no help at all, and can even be dangerous to you or to your vessel.

Vessels that are required to carry VDS's must carry types appropriate for day use and night use.

## Types of VDS

VDS's may be of several possible types. The simplest is a bright orange flag bearing a black square and a black circle. This signal is, of course, usable only during the day, but it has the advantage of being constantly on display.

Another signal that is usable only in daylight is orange smoke. A smoke flare is particularly effective in attracting attention from aircraft. They have the disadvantage, however, of not lasting very long, and they are much less effective in conditions of poor visibility or in high wind.

A signal that can be used at night is an electric flashing light. This device, in order to meet Coast Guard approval standards, must be able to blink SOS (... --- ...) automatically.

Some VDS's are usable in either day or night conditions. These include a variety of aerial flares and handheld flares.

One serious disadvantage of flares of either sort is that they last for only a short time, possibly only seconds, after they are ignited. An aerial VDS, depending on the type it is and the conditions under which it is used, may not go very

high. These facts should suggest that VDS's are best saved for use ONLY when other vessels ARE IN SIGHT. If you cannot see another vessel, the chances are that they will not see your signal.

Coast Guard approved flares have an expiration date stamped on them. Be careful when you buy flares. It is possible that some VDS flares sold in stores or by mail order may be very near the end of their shelf life. Devices that have expired do not meet the legal requirement. They may still work, but they should not be counted on to save your life in an emergency. If you carry flares to meet the VDS requirement, you must have at least three on board in good condition and bearing current dates. Of course, it is recommended that you carry more than the minimum number.

Even flares that are within their legal "lifespan" may fail to work if they have been damaged or abused. They are designed to withstand most "normal" on-board conditions, but they can be damaged, especially if they are allowed to get wet.

It is recommended that you keep outdated flares after you have replaced them with new, current-dated ones. They do not meet the legal requirement, but there is no penalty for carrying outdated spares. In an emergency, use the oldest devices first. There is no way to test either handheld or aerial flares, and it may be dangerous or illegal to discharge them unless a genuine emergency exists.

If you do use a VDS in an emergency, do so carefully. They are designed to be as safe as possible, but there are some hazards that cannot be avoided. (Hazardous as they are, approved flares are significantly LESS hazardous to handle in a marine environment than non-approved types. Road hazard flares, for instance, can easily start fires on boats, while approved marine types are carefully designed and manufactured to minimize this risk, even if it cannot be eliminated altogether.) Aerial flares should be given the same respect as firearms, which, of course, they are. (Note that some states regulate aerial flare launchers as firearms. Check with local law enforcement officials in your area for information about local enforcement policies regarding such devices.)

NEVER point a flare pistol at another person. Never allow children to play with or around them. If you discharge a flare pistol, check for overhead obstructions (sails, rigging, etc.) that may be damaged by the flare or deflect it to where it can cause damage.

Of course, in an emergency you can use any means at your disposal to attract attention. Probably the most effective means of summoning help, if you have it available, is the marine VHF radiotelephone. Your crew and guests should all be checked out on emergency procedures with the radiotelephone, since there is seldom time to learn effective operating during an emergency. See Chapter 12 for more information about the radiotelephone.

There are a large number of other means of signaling distress that have been developed and more or less recognized over the years, some more effective or widely recognized than others. On large vessels, for instance, it may be possible to build a large smoky fire on board in such a way that it will not endanger the ship. Smoke and flames will obviously attract attention, but it is equally obvious that it is difficult to build a "safe" fire on most small boats! In general, this is NOT a recommended distress signal for recreational boaters.

A mirror can be used to good advantage on sunny days to attract attention from great distances. It cannot reach searchers over the horizon, but the horizon for an observer in an aircraft can be many miles away. Not only is this an effective signaling device, but it needs no batteries, it always works as long as the sun is shining, and any shiny object can be used.

In most recreational boating situations the best distress signal to use when another boat is in sight may be waving the arms up and down slowly. This gesture is simple, seldom misunderstood, and requires no equipment.

Other "traditional" distress signals, such as flying the American flag upside down, probably have little impact. In an emergency, your efforts would probably better be put into more effective signaling methods.

## Marine Sanitation Devices (MSDs)

Each vessel with an installed toilet must have attached to it either: (1) a marine sanitation device (MSD) certified by the Coast Guard; or (2) a holding tank. Operating a boat with a non-approved MSD is illegal in the navigable waters of the U.S., including the "territorial sea" ("three mile limit"). In addition, certain bodies of fresh-water have been declared no-discharge areas. To comply, all installed toilets must be certified by the Coast Guard or designed to retain waste onboard for pumpout at a land site. All non-approved overboard discharge toilets must be removed or permanently disabled, but there is no requirement to install toilet facilities on vessels not currently having them. These regulations do not affect portable toilets on vessels.

## Your Responsibility as a Boatman

You are responsible for any damage your boat may cause other craft or for any injuries suffered by your passengers or others. For instance, if you pass close to a cruiser at high speed and your wake rocks this vessel so that the dishes in the galley are broken, you may be held responsible. If this should happen when hot foods are being prepared or served on board the cruiser and someone suffers serious burns as a result of the violent rocking caused by your wake, you may be held liable. You could be summoned into court and equitable civil damages assessed against you. In addition, you might also be cited for negligent or grossly negligent operation.

## Water Pollution and Discharge of Oil

The recreational boatman has an important stake in the effort to keep the nation's waters free from pollution and to maintain the purity of water supplies and the environment of wildlife. You must help to provide and protect clean water not only for your own recreation but also for the enjoyment of sport fishermen, divers, swimmers, and all who appreciate a beautiful and bountiful natural resource. An important part of the responsibility to protect the marine environment is observing the Federal water pollution laws.

The law prohibits the throwing, discharging, or depositing of any refuse matter of any kind (including trash, garbage, oil, and other liquid pollutants) into the waters of the United States to a distance of three miles from the coastline. The Federal Water Pollution Control Act prohibits the discharge of oil or hazardous substances into the waters of the United States to twelve miles offshore. You must immediately notify the U. S. Coast Guard if your vessel or facility discharges oil or hazardous substances into the water.

Federal water pollution controls are rigidly enforced and provide penalties for individuals who violate them, even accidentally.

Federal regulations issued under the Federal Water Pollution Control Act require:

1. All vessels under 100 gross tons must have a fixed or portable means to discharge oily bilge slops to a reception facility. A bucket or bailer is considered a portable means.

2. Vessels 26 feet in length and over must have posted a placard at least 5 by 8 inches, made of durable material, fixed in a conspicuous place in the machinery spaces, or at the bilge and ballast pump control station, stating the following:

### DISCHARGE OF OIL PROHIBITED

The Federal Water Pollution Control Act prohibits the discharge of oil or oily waste into or upon the navigable waters and contiguous zone of the United States if such discharge causes a film or sheen upon, or discoloration of, the surface of the water, or causes a sludge or emulsion beneath the surface of the water. Violators are subject to a penalty of $5,000.

3. No person may drain the sumps of oil lubricated machinery or the contents of oil filters, strainers, or purifiers into the bilge of any U.S. vessel.

You must also help to ensure that others obey the law. You are encouraged to report polluting discharges which you observe to the nearest U.S. Coast Guard office. Report the following information:

a. location,
b. source,
c. size,
d. color,
e. substance,
f. time observed.

Do not attempt to take samples of any chemical discharge. If you are uncertain as to the identity of any discharge, avoid flame, physical contact, or inhalation of vapors.

## Boating Accident Reports

The operator of any vessel involved in an on-the-water accident must stop, render assistance to those in danger and offer identification. If a person disappears from a vessel or a death occurs as a result of a boating accident, local authorities must be notified immediately. A written boating accident report is required within 48 hours if, as a result of the accident a person dies, disappears from a vessel, or is injured and requires treatment beyond first aid. In addition, a written boating accident report must be submitted within 10 days if a vessel is lost or damage to the vessel or other property exceeds $200.

Boating accident report forms can be obtained from, and should be returned to the state authorities having jurisdiction over the waters on which the accident occurred. If an accident occurs on the waters of the state of New Hampshire which does not have an approved numbering system, the Accident Report Form (CG-3865) can be obtained from the nearest Coast Guard Marine Safety Office, Marine Inspection Office or Marine Safety Detachment. Accident reports are used to compile accident prevention data and the information contained in the individual reports are not made public.

## Law Enforcement - Penalties

Coast Guard boarding vessels will be identified by the Coast Guard ensign and personnel will be in uniform. A vessel underway, upon being hailed by a Coast Guard vessel or patrol boat, is required to stop immediately and lay to or maneuver in such a way as to permit the boarding officer to come aboard. Failure to stop to permit boarding may subject the operator to a penalty.

The owner or operator of a vessel which is not numbered as required or who fails to file notice of transfer, destruction or abandonment of a vessel or fails to report a change of address, is liable to penalty which could be as much as $500.

A civil penalty may be imposed by the Coast Guard for negligent or grossly negligent operation, for failure to obey the Navigation Rules or failure to comply with regulations.

The law also provides for a fine of up to $1,000 and imprisonment of not more than 1 year for the criminal offense of reckless or negligent operation of a vessel which endangers the life or property of any person.

The law also authorizes a Coast Guard Boarding Officer, when in his judgment continued unsafe use of a boat creates an especially hazardous condition, to direct the operator to correct the hazardous condition immediately or return to a mooring and to remain there until the situation creating the hazard is corrected or ended. Reasons for using the authority could be insufficient personal flotation devices or firefighting equipment aboard, or overloading. Failure to comply with the orders of the Boarding Officer subject the offender to penalties provided for under the law.

Additionally the law authorizes any Coast Guard District Commander to issue regulations for a specific boat designating that boat unsafe for a specific voyage on a specific body of water when he has determined that such a voyage would be manifestly unsafe.

## Courtesy Marine Examination

As a courtesy to pleasure boat owners and operators, members of the Coast Guard Auxiliary check thousands of boats each year for safety requirements. These members are qualified as Courtesy Examiners under strict requirements set by the Coast Guard and are very knowledgeable in their field. The examinations are performed as a courtesy, and only with the consent of the pleasure boat owner. To pass the examination, a vessel must satisfy not only federal equipment requirements but also certain additional safety requirements recommended by the Auxiliary. If the boat passes the examination it is awarded a safety decal which is placed conspicuously on the vessel.

## SEAL OF SAFETY CHECK LIST
### (To Be Completed by Your
### Auxiliary Courtesy Examiner)

UNITED STATES COAST GUARD AUXILIARY

# COURTESY

U.S. COAST GUARD
AUXILIARY

# EXAMINATION

No. _____
CG-2902 (Rev.    )

| | YES | NO | NOT APPL |
|---|---|---|---|
| 1. NUMBERING | | | |
| 2. REGISTRATION/ DOCUMENTATION | | | ▒ |
| 3. NAVIGATION LIGHTS | | | ▒ |
| 4. SOUND PRODUCING DEVICES ○ BELL - BOATS 12M (39.4 ft) OR LONGER | | | ▒ |
| 5. PERSONAL FLOTATION DEVICES | | | ▒ |
| 6. FIRE EXTINGUISHERS | | | ▒ |
| 7. VISUAL DISTRESS SIGNALS ○ INLAND  ○ INTERNATIONAL | | | ▒ |
| 8. VENTILATION | | | |
| 9. BACKFIRE FLAME ARRESTER | | | |
| 10. FUEL SYSTEMS | | | |
| 11. ANCHOR AND ANCHOR LINE | | | ▒ |
| 12. ALTERNATE PROPULSION | | | |
| 13. DEWATERING DEVICE | | | ▒ |
| 14. GENERAL CONDITIONS ○ SEAWORTHINESS ○ ELECTRICAL  ○ GALLEY | | | ▒ |
| 15. STATE REQUIREMENTS | | | ▒ |

The following items are not a requirement for the CME decal. These additional items are required by Federal and State laws. The Courtesy Examiner has checked these items to assist the boater in determining if the vessel is within the requirements of these laws.

| | | | |
|---|---|---|---|
| 1. CG CAPACITY PLATE | | | |
| 2. CERTIFICATE OF COMPLIANCE LABEL | | | |
| 3. HULL IDENTIFICATION NUMBER | | | |
| 4. MARINE SANITATION DEVICE ○ BOATER INFORMED | | | |
| 5. POLLUTION PLACARD | | | |
| 6. NAVIGATION RULES | | | |

ADDITIONAL COMMENTS:

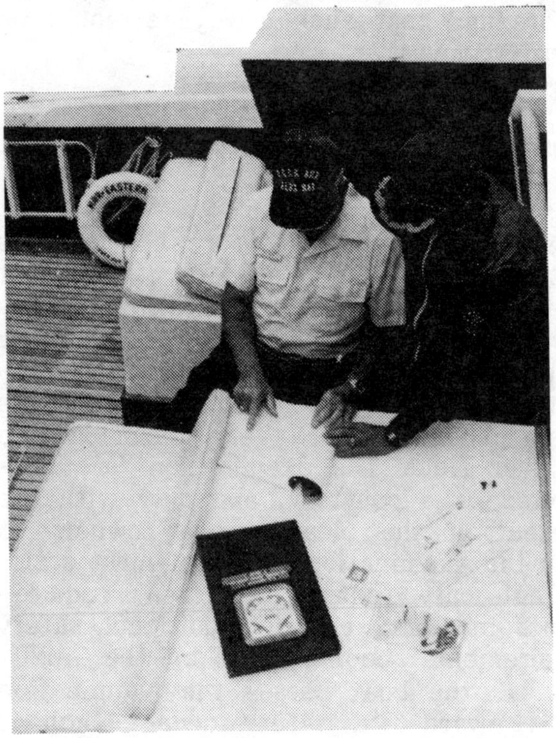

**Fig. 4-23 Legal Requirements and Requirements For the Seal of Safety Decal**

## Aids To Navigation

When man first went to sea he rarely left sight of land, and his only navigational aids were familiar landmarks. Today, our dependence on visible reference points is still great; however there are many more sophisticated means of determining our position.

An aid to navigation is any device external to a vessel intended to assist a navigator to determine his position or safe course, or to warn him of dangers or obstructions to safe navigation. Short range aids to navigation are buoys, daybeacons, lighthouses, and fog signals. Electronic aids to navigation include radiobeacons and LORAN-C to assist us in finding our position on the water. As all aids to navigation serve the same general purpose, structural differences, markings, and other aid characteristics are solely for the purpose of meeting the conditions and requirements of the particular location at which the aid is established.

Although not Aids to Navigation, prominent landmarks, both natural, such as mountain peaks and promontories, and man-made objects, such as church spires, water tanks and radio towers can be useful to the navigator, but they must be visible from the water, and be shown on the applicable chart for the area. The chart symbols for these objects are covered in the chapter on charts.

## Buoy System

The principal system of buoyage in the United States has been the Lateral System; however, in April of 1982, the United States agreed to conform to the International Association of Lighthouse Authorities (IALA) system B, or IALA-B.

The IALA maritime buoyage System B applies to buoys and beacons that indicate the lateral limits of navigable channels, obstructions, dangers such as wrecks, and other areas or features of importance to the mariner. This system provides five types of marks: lateral marks, safe water marks, special marks, isolated danger marks, and cardinal marks. Cardinal marks are not used in the United States. Each type of mark is differentiated from other types by distinctive colors, shapes, and light rhythms.

The change to IALA-B is in process, and involves an interim stage, known as the Modified U. S. Aid System. This involves changing all black painted, odd-numbered marks (aids) to green; changing all existing white lights on lateral aids (with one exception) to either red or green, to match the mark color. The exception is the "safe water" mark, marking a fairway or mid-channel. This mark will always have a white light. The specific light characteristics for all marks will be covered in a later section of this chapter.

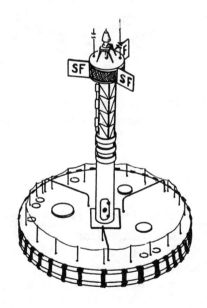

**Fig. 4-24  A Large Navigational Buoy.**

This book covers both the old system and the new system.

In the lateral buoyage system, marks indicate sides of a navigable channel, and also mark channel junctions, and indicate the safe side of a hazard for the navigator to use. In addition, some marks indicate the centerline of a particular channel. Buoyage systems differ among nations, and boaters navigating abroad should become familiar with other systems.

The navigator must be able to identify all aids to navigation accurately, quickly and easily in order to make the best use of them for safe navigation. Therefore, all marks are identified in various ways, and this identification is displayed on charts, along with the appropriate chart symbol for that mark. Knowing the color and number of an ATON (Aid to Navigation) will be of little use without the appropriate chart to tell the navigator the mark's position in that water area.

Aids to navigation will all have one or more of the following identifying marks: color significance (including specific combinations of more than one color in either horizontal bands or vertical stripes); number and/or letter significance; daymark significance; light significance; and sound significance.

Both our present Lateral System and the IALA-B System use odd numbers with all black or green marks and use even numbers with all red marks. On all navigable waterways returning from the sea, the black or green odd-numbered marks are on the port (left) side of the channel, and the red even-numbered marks are on the starboard (right) side of the channel.

An easy memory phrase is "RED RIGHT RETURNING!" (Note this is not always true, which will be covered later in this chapter.)

For the sea buoys that delineate channels off the coast of the United States, and for the Intracoastal Waterway (ICW) red is on the right when proceeding in a clockwise direction (looking at a map of the U.S.). Therefore, red is on the right when proceeding south along the East Coast, either at sea or in the ICW, proceeding north along the West Coast of Florida, proceeding west and southwest along the Gulf Coast, and proceeding north along the West Coast in the Pacific Ocean.

For the Great Lakes, the outlet ends are defined as the seaward ends.

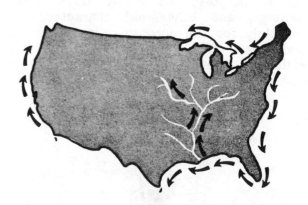

Fig. 4-25 Conventions About Directions of Travel in Coastal Waters.

Marks with horizontal red and green bands indicate bifurcations or junctions in a channel, or wrecks or obstructions that can be passed on either side. If the upper band is green, the preferred channel when proceeding from the sea is followed by keeping the mark on the port side of the vessel; if the upper band is red, keep the mark on the starboard side.

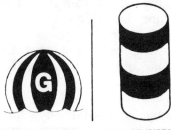

PASS EITHER SIDE    STAY FAIR DISTANCE AWAY

**Fig. 4-26   Vertically–striped and
Horizontally–banded Buoys.**

Marks with vertical red and white
stripes are "safe water marks" indicating
the mid-channel or fairway. Such marks
may also be used at the beginning of a
vessel Traffic Separation Scheme.

Both the junction or obstruction marks
and the safe water marks will not be
numbered, but may have letters for iden-
tification if necessary.

**Characteristics of Aids to Navigation**

Depending upon the location and needs
of identification, aids have many shapes
and characteristics. Generally they fall
into six categories; 1) buoys, 2) daybea-
cons, 3) lights, 4) sound (fog signals), 5)
ranges, and 6) radio and radar beacons.

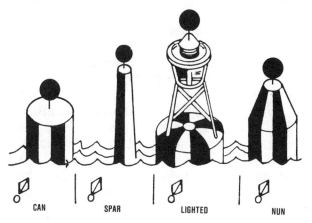

CAN        SPAR        LIGHTED        NUN

**Fig. 4-27   Vertically–striped Buoys Mark
the Fairway or Mid–channel.**

**Buoys**
Buoys are floating aids that warn the
mariner of some danger, some obstruc-
tion, or change in the contours of the sea

bottom, or to delineate channels so that
he may avoid dangers and continue his
course safely. Such features as size,
shape, color, numbering (or other mark-
ings), and signaling equipment of buoys
are for the purpose of identification and
also telling the navigator what the aid
stands for. For example, under System B,
a spherical buoy with vertical red and
white stripes indicates "safe water" or
"mid-channel."

However, a word of caution should be
included concerning buoys. They are at
anchor! Just like a vessel, they will drift
around the anchor position with wind or
current or may even drag anchor such
that they may be out of their charted
position. The chart symbol for a buoy is
a diamond shape with a small circle at
the bottom indicating an approximate
position.

Navigators should not rely completely
upon the position of floating aids, but
should use bearings toward fixed aids or
objects onshore where possible. The lights
on lighted buoys may be extinguished, or
sound-producing devices on sound buoys
may not function. Buoys fitted with bells,
gongs, or whistles are normally activated
by wave action and do not produce sounds
at regular intervals, making positive
identification near impossible without
visual observation.

**Buoy Types**
The spar buoy is similar in shape to a
section of telephone pole and can be red,
even numbered, or green, odd numbered.
They can also be used with horizontal
bands for junction buoys.

The nun buoy has the topmost section
conical in shape, is painted red and even
numbered, and normally marks the star-
board hand side of the preferred channel
entering from seaward.

Fig. 4-29  A Can Buoy.

Fig. 4-28  A Nun Buoy.

The can buoy is cylindrical in shape, black or green, odd numbered, and normally marks the port hand side of the preferred channel. It also can be used to signify junctions or mid-channels with appropriate bands or stripes.

The spherical buoy (ball-shaped) is used for a mid-channel marker in the IALA-B System, with vertical red and white stripes. If the buoy is not spherical, it will have a red spherical top mark, instead.

A lighted buoy consists of a float on which is mounted a short structural or skeleton tower with a battery powered light mounted at the top. The batteries, or other power source, are placed in the body of the buoy. Under the older system, the light would be either white or green for black aids, and white or red for red aids. Under the new system, the light is either green or red, depending upon the basic color of the mark. Also, the light color will match the top band color on horizontally banded lighted marks.

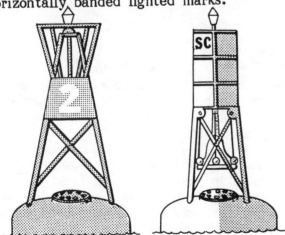

Fig. 4-30  A Lighted Buoy.

A bell buoy is a similar float and tower structure in which is hung a bell with usually four clappers suspended externally to the bell such that the clappers strike the bell as wave action rocks the buoy.

A gong buoy is similar to a bell buoy, but with usually four gongs mounted in the tower, in a vertical stack, each of a different tone. Each gong has its own clapper, of a different length, such that the wave action will cause four different tones to be sounded.

Fig. 4-31  A Lighted Bell Buoy With Radar Reflectors.

A whistle buoy is constructed similarly to the bell or gong buoy, but with a low-pitched whistle, actuated by trapped air as the buoy moves up and down in the wave action. A horn buoy is similar, but the horn is powered from electric batteries.

Combination buoys are those with a light combined with a sound source; a lighted bell or gong buoy, etc.

The navigator should be aware fog and very calm water often go together. In a flat calm, there may not be enough motion to activate sound buoys.

As stated previously, most marks will be numbered, lettered, or a combination, depending upon their use. All solid color marks will be numbered, odd numbers for green marks, and even numbers for red marks. They will be numbered sequentially from seaward, the outermost mark being 1 or 2, depending upon its color.

Some numbers may be omitted along a channel when only one side is buoyed for some distance. For example, green marks numbered 1 through 5 might be installed on the port hand side, whereas only two red marks might be required on the starboard hand side, numbered 2 and 6, accordingly. Marks may also be added to a channel at a later date, in which case letters will be added. This could mean mark 7A added between numbers 7 and 8. Some numbered channel marks may also have letter abbreviations added to further identify their purpose, as 8 "CS." The number is in the usual sequence, but the "CS" would stand for Capri Shoal.

### Daybeacons

Daybeacons are marks which are normally restricted to shore or shallow water use as they are fixed rather than floating, and less expensive to maintain. They are generally constructed of plywood signboards, called daymarks, painted, and affixed with a reflective border of the proper color and shape and an identifying number or letter (also of reflective material). They are mounted on single piles or multiple pile structures (dolphins).

**Fig. 4-32  Daymark On a Piling.**

Daymark shape and color identifies the purpose for the mark. To be specific:

1. Triangular shape, red, and even numbered indicate a mark that should be kept on the starboard hand when returning from sea.

2. Square shape, green (or black), and odd numbered daymarks should be left on the port hand under the same conditions.

### Ranges

Ranges are pairs of ATON's placed a suitable distance apart, with the far daymark mounted higher than the near daymark. When the two are aligned, one above the other, they will also be aligned with the center of a straight channel. The daymarks usually have lights attached at the top for guiding the mariner along a mid-channel route at night. The mariner must keep the pair of daymarks or lights in line for safe passage.

**Fig. 4-33  Open Range - Not in Center of Channel.**

**Fig. 4-34  Closed Range - In Center of Channel.**

### Lighted Aids

Many of our buoys and daybeacons are fitted with lights to aid the mariner. A lighted daybeacon is one type of <u>minor light</u>. Minor lights are automatic unmanned lights on fixed structures such as a single pile, dolphins (multiple piles cabled together), or skeletal steel towers of varying heights. Minor lights are established in harbors, along channels, rivers and isolated locations. The skeletal tower is often found fixed to the end of a breakwater at a harbor entrance. It can also be fixed to a concrete foundation in shallower water, marking the side of a channel. Their lights are usually of low to moderate intensity. They are usually part of the Lateral System, with the same numbering, coloring, light and sound characteristics.

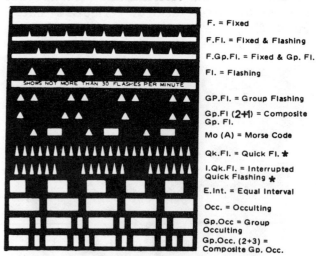

Fig. 4-35  A 'Texas Tower' Offshore Light Structure.

The characteristics of the lights (termed light rhythms) are designated on charts adjacent to the aid's symbol as well as in the applicable "Light List," published by the United States Coast Guard. Different rhythms use lights of various colors, fixed lights that shine continuously, flashing lights (off more time than on) and occulting lights (on more time than off). The standard colors are red, green, white, and yellow.

The lighted aid displaying a steady light, ("fixed"), marks a waterway which has no background lights to cause confusion. For coastal cruising mariners or anyone cruising in waters where background lights could cause confusion, flashing lights are used. The rhythm of the flashing light must be identified by the navigator and then referred to the local chart for determining position.

The flashing light blinks on at a rate of less than 50 flashes per minute with the duration of light shorter than that of darkness (it is off more than on). The flashing light draws attention, and nearby flashing aids have different flash rates or different colors for easy identification. The mariner must have a means of determining the flash period (the time difference between the beginning of one flash to the beginning of the next flash). An occulting light is one that is on more than it is off. It will also have a charted period.

The period of a flashing aid will be shown on the chart, adjacent to the aid symbol, as "10 sec" or "10s." This means the light will flash briefly, possibly 1 second, and then be off for 9 seconds, and continuously repeat. Obviously, this also means this example would only flash 6 times in one minute. Many lights will have a period of 2 or 3 seconds, or flash 20 to 30 times in one minute. A navigator must very carefully observe the characteristics of the navigation aid lights, because except for the specific light rhythms, many of such lights in a given area are very similar, and difficult to tell apart. By careful observation, during both day and night, the novice will gain valuable experience and learn to distinguish between the various lighted aids, regardless of their similarities.

F. = Fixed

F.Fl. = Fixed & Flashing

F.Gp.Fl. = Fixed & Gp. Fl.

Fl. = Flashing

SHOWS NOT MORE THAN 30 FLASHES PER MINUTE

GP.Fl. = Group Flashing

Gp.Fl (2+1) = Composite Gp. Fl.

Mo (A) = Morse Code

Qk.Fl. = Quick Fl. ★

I.Qk.Fl. = Interrupted Quick Flashing ★

E.Int. = Equal Interval

Occ. = Occulting

Gp.Occ = Group Occulting

Gp.Occ. (2+3) = Composite Gp. Occ.

*Will no longer be used after 1989.

Fig. 4-36  Light Rhythms.

Some flashing aids have group flashing, in which a group of flashes, specified in number, is regularly repeated. The period is measured from the beginning of a group of flashes to the beginning of the next group. Major waterways often utilize this characteristic for rapid identification.

Where there is a need to indicate that special caution is required such as at sharp turns, sudden constrictions, or for marking wrecks or obstructions to be passed on one side only, a quick flashing light will be displayed. It will blink on similar to the flashing light, but the rate will be more than 50 flashes per minute but less than 80 flashes per minute.

For channel junctions and obstructions, for the "old" system, the Interrupted Quick Flashing was used. It is a quick-flashing light in which the sequence of flashes is interrupted by regularly repeated eclipses of constant and long duration. A typical example would be 5 seconds of quick flashes followed by 5 seconds of darkness. After 1989, the Interrupted Quick Flashing characteristic will be discontinued.

Under the Modified Aid System, for junction and obstruction aids which can be passed on either side, composite group-flashing (2 + 1) lights are used. On these red and green horizontally banded aids, the light color matches the color of the top band on the structure.

Mid-channel markers (also known as safe water or fairway marks) display a white light. To distinguish them further, they emit a dot-dash (short-long) light characteristic indicating the International Morse Code (A). As the name implies, they should be passed on the appropriate side to help separate incoming from outgoing traffic and eliminate collisions.

### Directional Lights

The directional light is used when it is not practicable for some reason to install a pair of range lights. This light is installed at one end of the straight section of a channel, high enough to be seen the full length of the channel section. This single light projects a high-intensity, narrow width beam of white light. On either side, through separate lenses, will be a broader red sector and green sector.

The red and green sectors will be on the same respective sides of the channel as the red and green buoys. The arcs covered by each sector will be shown on the chart. A vessel in the center of the channel will only see the white light.

### Articulated Lights

The articulated light is a recent addition to available aids to navigation. It is a combination of a minor light and a lighted buoy. It consists of a sealed hollow cylinder, up to 50, or more, feet in length. The lower end is attached by a swivel to a normal buoy "sinker" or anchor, and the cylinder will float in a vertical position. Sometimes, an additional buoyancy chamber is attached to the upper end, somewhat below the water surface.

The length of the cylinder will be equal to the normal water depth, plus tidal range, plus some 10-15 feet above the surface. Mounted at the top is a typical light and corresponding daymarks. These are to be used when a more precise marking of a position is required, but the water is too deep to make a normal pile or dolphin structure practicable. Since no anchor chain scope is involved, the aid is always directly over the sinker, with only a relatively small swinging circle.

### Special Purpose Marks

A departure from our old system of yellow buoys indicating Quarantine areas is that special marks will be established which will be yellow in color; and, if lighted, will show amber (yellow) lights. These special marks will indicate the following areas:

Ocean Data Acquisition Systems (ODAS),
Traffic Separation Schemes where conventional channel marking would be confusing,
Fish Net Areas,
Spoil Grounds,
Military Exercise Zones,
Anchorage Areas.

## Light Structures

Lighted aids to navigation vary from the simple battery powered lantern on a wooden pile in a small creek to the tallest lighthouse on the coast with millions of candlepower. Their basic function is still the same as a buoy; however, they are established in positions where they perform more suitably than buoys. Also, with the exception of lighthouses, they have the same numbering, coloring, light, and sound characteristics of buoys.

There are Short Range Aids (SRA) which are not part of the buoyage system. Lighthouses are normally in this category, and are placed where they will be of most use; on prominent headlands, at channel entrances, on isolated dangers (although this will soon have a separate aid), or at other points where it is necessary that mariners be warned or guided. Their primary purpose is to support a light at a considerable height above the water displaying appropriate light characteristics. In many instances, automatic fog signals and/or radiobeacon equipment are installed, as well as quarters for personnel.

Fig. 4-37  A Lighthouse.

Lighthouse structures vary considerably, depending upon the desired height, and on the location and available foundation at that location. However, the Light List briefly describes their structure, such as "gray conical tower covered way to dwelling," or "white cylindrical granite tower connected to dwelling." Cylindrical or conical towers may have distinctive color combinations painted on them, such as the black and white spirals on the Cape Hatteras Light. The structure itself, together with any distinctive colors, make up a lighthouse "daymark" to help the navigator identify them during the day. During bright daylight, the light is normally turned off.

A major factor in both location and height above the water for the light are the differences in how far they need to be seen, for safety, from the sea. The higher the light is above the water and the more brilliant (greater candlepower) the light, the farther away it can be seen at night.

Lights are given classifications. These are primary seacoast light, secondary light, river or harbor light (also minor lights, normally part of a buoyage system) and these terms indicate, in a general way, lighted ATON's that are "fixed" rather than "floating." They are described in the Light List by:

a. Name and Light rhythm,
b. Location, including latitude and longitude,
c. Nominal Range,
d. Height above the water,
e. Structure, including height above ground and daymark,
f. Characteristics of sound devices present and year built.

Lighthouse light rhythms may encompass more than the light characteristics previously discussed. Sectors and alternating colors are also used.

A light sector is provided when sections of colored glass are placed in the lantern to warn the navigator of shoals or nearby land in that sector. Sectors are angular portions of the 360° circle around the light. When the light is cut off by a land mass or structure adjoining it, or by deliberately obscuring it toward its landward side, an obscured sector is also created. Both types of sectors are shown on the chart by broken lines that extend from the light on each side of the sector. These lines will be labeled with the true bearing in degrees, from the vessel to the light, and an arc between them will indicate the color. Any such sectors will also be described in the Light List.

When a navigator is heading toward a light, and finds he is in the red sector, he is definitely heading into danger. If a navigator sees a red sector light when crossing such a sector, he may or may not be heading into danger. For example, heading into South River from the Chesapeake Bay requires a navigator to cross a red sector from Thomas Point light, even though a safe passage is available if the navigator is paying attention to his chart and the South River channel buoyage.

The lightship has disappeared from the North American coast. At one time these vessels could be found at the entrances of many major seaports. All of them have been replaced by offshore light towers resembling oil drilling structures, or by large navigational buoys. These structures are equipped with lights, fog signals, and radiobeacons, and take the place of lighthouses which would be impractical to build in that location.

## Light Structure Sound Signals

A significant sound producing aid to navigation is the fog horn. Most lighthouses and major aids and some minor light structures are equipped with fog horns to aid the mariner during periods of low visibility. These signals are operated by either mechanical or electrical means and may be recognized by the timing of the signal, its silent period, and its tone. Where the number of blasts and the total time for a signal to complete a cycle is not sufficient for positive identification, reference may be made to details in the Light List regarding the exact length of each blast and silent interval.

In boating areas there might be several fog horns with different periods and tones being heard at the same time. The mariner needs to recognize them for safe passage.

An important electronic aid to navigation is the radiobeacon. The navigator must be equipped with, 1) a Radio Direction Finder (RDF) adjustable throughout the marine frequencies in use, 2) a chart showing the location, frequency, and International Morse Code characteristics of such aids, 3) some experience tuning in and recognizing these radio signals, and 4) a deviation curve for the receiver in the location for which it is to be operated. (Radio signals are affected similar to deviation of a compass, discussed in Chapter 14.)

These radiobeacons can be used in two ways. Using an RDF, a relative bearing from the vessel to the radiobeacon can be obtained, converted to a true bearing, plotted on the chart from the vessel to the radiobeacon (chart symbol "R Bn"). Two or more bearings will provide the navigator with an "RDF fix," although the precision of such bearings is nowhere near the quality of a visual one. A vessel can also home in on a radiobeacon. After the signal is found with the RDF, the vessel is steered directly toward the radiobeacon. This takes place when the vessel's heading is such that the RDF relative bearing is 000°.

Great caution must be observed when homing because the vessel is obviously heading toward the land where the antenna is mounted on a tower, or possibly toward a lighthouse mounted on a steel structure out in the water, surrounded by riprap. The navigator should be taking depth soundings, and attempting to determine his position more accurately by other means. In a fog or other reduced visibility, the prudent decision might be to anchor until other ATON's can be seen.

## Visibility of Lights

The nominal visibility of lights on light structures is **printed**, along with the height of the light, on the chart, i.e. 10M = 10 nautical miles.

## Bridges

Bridges across navigable waters are often encountered and have fixed light combinations. Of special importance is vertical clearance, which can be determined from the local chart. Additional aids are also provided for the mariner's safe passage.

Red lights mark piers and other parts of the bridge or to show that a drawbridge is in the closed position. Green lights are used to mark the centerline of navigable channels through fixed bridges or for indicating a drawbridge in the open position. For major bridges where there is more than one safe passage, the preferred channel will be marked by three white lights in a vertical line above the green light.

## Intracoastal Waterway Aids

The Intracoastal Waterway route runs parallel to the Atlantic and Gulf Coasts from Manasquan Inlet on the New Jersey shore to the Mexican border. Marks for this route are very similar to those of the old Lateral System and the new Modified U. S. System. There are some differences in aid markings between the Intracoastal Waterway and open ocean waterways.

Aids marking the Intracoastal Waterway have some portion of them marked with yellow. Otherwise, the coloring and numbering of buoys and beacons follow a lateral system similar to that used in other U. S. waterways, with red on the right side of the channel clockwise around the United States.

In order that vessels may readily follow the Intracoastal Waterway route where it coincides with another marked waterway, such as an important river, special markings are employed. These special markings are applied to the buoys or other aids that already mark the river or waterway for other traffic. These aids are then referred to as "dual purpose" aids.

The mark consists of a yellow square or a yellow triangle, placed on a conspicuous part of the dual purpose aid. The yellow square, in outline similar to a can buoy, indicates that the aid on which it is placed should be left on the left hand side when following the Intracoastal Waterway clockwise around the United States. The yellow triangle has the same meaning as a nun; it should be kept on the right hand side when proceeding clockwise around the United States. When such dual purpose aid marking is employed, the mariner following the Intracoastal Waterway should disregard the shape and color of the aid and be guided solely by the yellow mark.

## Uniform State Waterway Marking System

The Uniform State Waterway Marking System (USWMS) includes a system of marks to supplement the federal system in marking of state waters and a system of regulatory markers to warn a vessel operator of dangers or to provide general information and directions.

For the supplemental portion where standard federal aids are inappropriate, much smaller buoys of a cylindrical shape are generally utilized although the shape has no significance in itself. Channel marks are cylindrical, all black (or green) or all red, numbered odd or even, respectively, with red on the right when heading upstream.

Fig. 4-38 A dangerous area is indicated by an open diamond shape, as shown below.

**Fig. 4-39 A prohibited area is marked by a diamond with a cross inside, as shown below.**

**Fig. 4-40 A controlled area, such as one which excludes water skiing or fishing, is indicated by a circle, as shown below.**

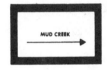

**Fig. 4-41 General information and directions are shown on a square or rectangular marker, as shown below.**

Other marks are normally white in color with a topmost color of green or red indicating safe passage areas similar to federal aids. Mooring buoys are also of the same shape and color except that a blue horizontal band located near mid-buoy marks their intended function.

The important difference between the USWMS and the standard federal system is that of regulatory marks. They are colored white with international orange horizontal bands completely around the buoy. One band is at the top of the mark, and the other is just above the waterline so that both orange bands are clearly visible to approaching vessels. With these marks, there are four different purposes and four different markings to indicate the purpose. Two of these markings indicate dangerous conditions, one indicates caution and one is for information.

Of the two types of danger markings, both have an international orange diamond located between the horizontal bands. The diamond with an internal cross means "boats keep out" whereas the standard danger marking without the cross may have additional information inside the diamond to indicate the nature of the danger (e.g. rocks, shoal, etc.).

The controlled area marker, as its name implies, provides instruction to the boater. The basic recognition factor is that there will be an international orange circle between the horizontal bands and within that circle may be such regulatory information as speed limits, no fishing, no anchoring, no wake, etc.

## Navigation Publications

The most important publication to be kept on the boat is a current chart of the boating area. Since the location, characteristics, and maintenance status of aids to navigation may change from time to time, an obsolete chart can be dangerous. While there are a number of sources of charts, the charts produced by NOAA are the most up-to-date and complete. They can be obtained at marinas, boat stores, and other designated chart dealers.

To keep your charts current, and to get news of all matters of interest in your boating area, the Coast Guard publishes Local Notice to Mariners, which may be obtained for free from your Coast Guard District.

A copy of the Light List will help you identify aids to navigation. Published by the Coast Guard, it is available in several volumes:

Volume I, Atlantic Coast, describes aids to navigation in United States waters from St. Croix River, Maine to Ocean City Inlet, Maryland.

Volume II, Atlantic Coast, describes aids to navigation in United States waters from Ocean City, Maryland to Little River, South Carolina.

Volume III, Atlantic and Gulf Coast, describes aids to navigation in United States waters from Little River, South Carolina to Econfina River, Florida and the Greater Antilles.

Volume IV, Gulf Coast, describing aids to navigation in United States waters from Econfina River, Florida to Rio Grande River, Texas.

Volume V, Mississippi River System, describes aids to navigation on the Mississippi and Ohio Rivers and navigable tributaries.

Volume VI, Pacific Coast and Pacific Islands, describes aids to navigation in United States waters on the Pacific Coast and Pacific Islands. For the convenience of mariners, there is also included some of the lighted aids on the coast of British Columbia, maintained by Canada.

Volume VII, Great Lakes, describes aids to navigation maintained under the authority of the U. S. Coast Guard, and some aids maintained by Canada, on the Great Lakes and on the St. Lawrence river above the St. Regis river.

Light Lists are sold to the public by the Superintendent of Documents, Government Printing Office, Washington, D. C. 20402, from Government Printing Office Branch Bookstores, located in many cities, and by sales agents located in most major ports. A list of sales agents is published yearly in the Notice to Mariners, and also in a pamphlet available free of charge from the National Ocean Survey (C-44), Washington, D. C. 20840.

# Chapter 5

# Rigging And Boat Handling

As anchorages become more crowded and marinas more costly, sailors have turned in increasing numbers to trailering their sailboats (see Chapter 10). Even if you keep your boat at a pier or mooring, it may be helpful for you to know how to set up the rigging from scratch - a task well within the capabilities of most skippers of boats under about 25 feet in length.

## Stepping the Mast

The difficulty of setting up the mast depends on two things: The size and weight of the spar itself, and the manner in which it's stepped in the boat. In our introductory chapter on parts of a boat we considered the simplest kind of step, in which the mast foot fits into or around a socket grounded on the boat's keel. Such a mast may first lead through a brace at gunwale level - either a hole in the deck or a seat.

Fig. 5-2 Mast Step on a Hinge

On larger boats, such as small, trailerable cruisers, the mast may step on deck in a hinged fitting which allows it to be raised and lowered quite easily. In principle, stepping the mast in either case is much the same and should offer no problems if a few, orderly steps are followed.

First, select the location for mast stepping. If yours is a small boat without floorboards, or one in which the hull is thin enough so it flexes under your weight, then the boat has to be launched first. Make sure she is tied securely to float or pier, so she won't shift under you as you step aboard with the spar on your shoulder. If you step the mast while the boat is still on its trailer, as many do, first check to be sure that there are no

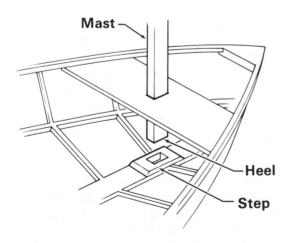

Fig. 5-1 Stepping the Mast

Mast

Heel

Step

overhead wires either near you or between you and the launch ramp. A significant number of sailors have been electrocuted in recent years when their metal spars or standing rigging came in contact with uninsulated wiring. Before raising the mast, check all parts of the rig, particularly those that will be inaccessible once the mast is up. Make sure the halyards are free to run and lead to the proper sides of the mast. Have your cotter and/or clevis pins ready to use, along with any necessary tools.

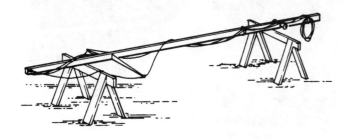

**Fig. 5-3 Mast on Horses**

If you haven't done so already, tie off the stays, shrouds and halyards against the mast. The easiest way to do this is first to set the spar on two or three sawhorses for support. No tie should be higher up the mast than you can reach while standing on the deck when the spar is stepped, for obvious reasons.

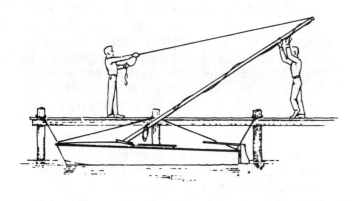

**Fig. 5-4 "Walking" the Mast Up**

For masts that are deck-stepped in a hinged fitting, you may now place the

mast foot in the hinge and secure it. If there's no way to secure the foot, or if the spar must first be guided through a deck hole, at least two people will be required to step even a rather small mast - one to locate the foot and the other to raise the spar.

Walk slowly and carefully forward, watching where you put your feet, and raise the mast to the vertical. At this point, one person will have to steady the mast (unless the deck-level support is enough to hold it upright) while another quickly makes fast (secures or fastens) the key pieces of standing rigging. These are the fore- and backstays and the upper shrouds, both port and starboard. Once these turnbuckles are attached to the proper chainplates and taken up enough to hold the mast reasonably steady, then it's no longer necessary for anyone to hold the spar erect. For heavier masts, the shrouds and backstay should be loosened, but attached to the chainplates prior to raising the mast. This makes it easier to keep the mast vertical while attaching the forestay.

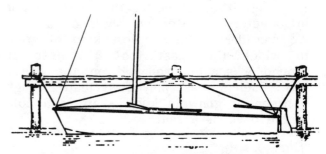

**Fig. 5-5 Mast Stepped**

Make fast the remaining shrouds to their chainplates and be sure the halyards are free to run without being tangled in the rigging or the mast hardware. Although actual tuning of the standing rigging is a matter of trial and error, initial tensioning is no great problem. The wire running to the masthead, whether it be shrouds or stays, should be quite taut - enough so that it vibrates when plucked - while wire that runs part way up the mast should be tight enough so it

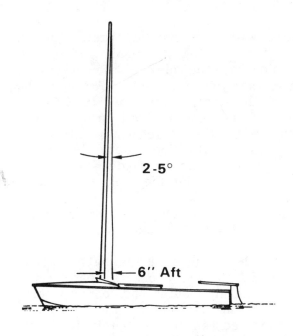

Fig. 5-6 Mast Rake

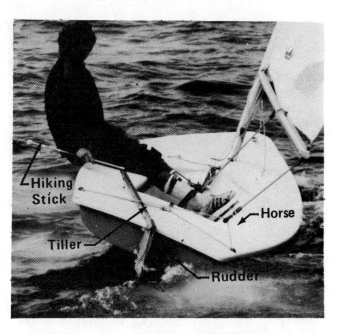

Fig. 5-7    Rudder and Tiller –
Note Hiking Stick

doesn't flap to and fro, but should not have serious tension on it. Once you're sailing, you'll know soon enough if your turnbuckles need adjusting, so for the moment don't overdo.

What's important is to have the mast standing straight in the boat. Sight over the bow to make sure the spar isn't tipped to one side or the other, and from the side to determine that the amount of fore-and-aft tilt, known as rake, is proper. On most boats, the mast is designed to rake aft slightly – two to five degrees at most. If yours is a class or production boat, other skippers or the manufacturer's literature will tell you the amount of rake that works best. Lacking this information, try a slight tilt aft – enough so that the halyard, allowed to swing free, will touch the deck about six inches aft of the mast step for a 20-foot spar. The mast rake affects the action of your boat when you let the tiller go. The further aft the mast is raked, the more the boat wants to head into the wind. This is called a weather helm and is highly desirable as a safety measure. However too much weather helm both tires the helmsman and slows the boat.

With the mast in place, you can attach the boom to the gooseneck track or fixed fitting, whichever your boat is equipped with. Attach the mainsheet to boom and deck fittings, making sure the line is free to run through its blocks. If your boat has a topping lift, a light line or wire running from the masthead to the outer end of the boom, make it fast to hold the boom off the deck.

Now set up the rudder and tiller, if they're not already attached. On small boardboats having a rope or wire traveler or horse, a bridle or bar under which the tiller fits, be certain that the tiller is in fact under the traveler or horse. If the fittings on the rudder and boat transom allow, the rudder should be locked in so it cannot float free. If you have a tilt-up rudder and the boat is not yet launched, be sure that the rudder is in the "up" position. Many boats with heavy centerboards are trailered with the board resting on a crossbeam of the trailer, so as to take the strain off the centerboard pennant. Before launching, check to make sure the board is fully retracted and the pennant tied off. Otherwise, the board will almost certainly jam in the trailer frame and make it impossible to launch the boat. Once afloat, however, the centerboard or daggerboard should be lowered.

**Fig. 5-8 Tilt-Up Rudders**

## Making Sail

Before attaching the sails to the spars and forestay, head the boat more or less into the wind so that the sails, once hoisted, will luff freely. Ideally, a boat should be swinging free at a mooring when making sail, but in many cases you'll be at a pier or float where you line up only generally into the wind.

Work with the mainsail first. Usually, you'll have to take the sail out of the bag and find the clew - the lower aft corner, as you remember. Arrange the sail so the foot, from clew to tack, is untwisted and feed the sail onto (or into, depending on the attachments) the boom track, pulling the foot along the boom until the clew can be made fast to the outhaul. Next, make the tack cringle fast to the gooseneck fitting, and pull the outhaul toward the outer end of the boom until the sail's foot is taut.

Insert the battens in the batten pockets. Old-fashioned pockets had small grommets at the outer end, corresponding to a hole in the end of the batten. A light line secured the batten in its pocket. Nowadays, however, most sailmakers use the type of pocket illustrated, which holds the batten in place without tying. Battens should fit snugly into the pockets

**Fig. 5-9  Bending On Main - Feeding Foot into Boom Track**

**Fig. 5-10 Inserting Batten in Sail**

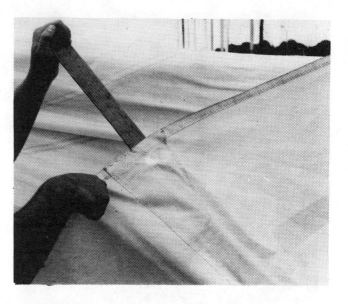

**Fig. 5-11 Detail of Batten & Sail Pocket**

that hold them, but not so tightly that they stretch the fabric. Remember that the thinned-down end of a wood batten goes into the pocket <u>first</u>. It might seem that just the opposite would be true, but consider that a batten's job is to support the roach of the sail and to impart an

even curve, hence the more easily bendable thin edge should be further forward in the sail, where the curvature is greater.

If your mainsail luff is fitted with <u>slides</u> (for an exterior track) or <u>slugs</u> (for

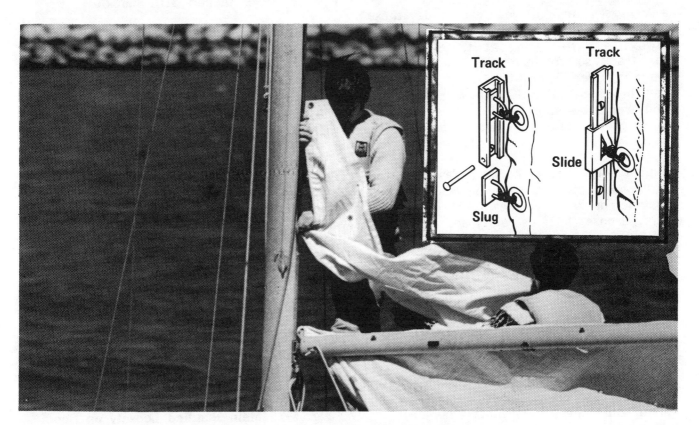

**Fig. 5-12    Bending on Main — Inserting Mainsail Slides**

**Fig. 5-13  Sail's Head Cringle –
Attached with Bowline**

**Fig. 5-14  Sail's Head Cringle –
Attached with Shackle**

a recessed track), you can slide these onto or into the track. There's nearly always a gate fitting at the bottom of the track so you can keep the slides or slugs in place, once attached. If, however, you have a mainsail with a roped luff, you won't be able to slide this into the mast groove until you are actually ready to make sail.

Last, make the halyard fast to the sail's head cringle. Most halyards have a shackle or other piece of hardware for this purpose, but it's really not necessary. A bowline (see Chapter 8, Marlinspike Seamanship) will serve just as well. Before making fast the halyard, sight up along it to make sure that it isn't twisted or snagged.

If your boat has only a mainsail, you're now ready to hoist it and go. But we're assuming that your boat has a sloop rig and you have yet to deal with the jib. (In practice, one crewmember will attach the main while the other handles the jib.)

**Fig. 5-15  Main Bundled Loosely on Boom**

Fig. 5-16  Making Jib - Attaching Tack
           to Stem

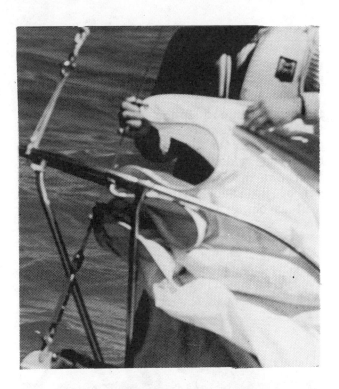

Fig. 5-17 Bending On Jib - Hanking On

Bundle the mainsail loosely atop the boom (see Fig. 5-15) and wrap it in place with a couple of sail stops - lengths of sail fabric or rubberized shock cord (the latter is recommended) that are carried for just this purpose.

Generally speaking, you can attach the jib to the forestay right from the sail bag, if you've taken the precaution to fold and bag the sail so that its tack cringle is right on top. Shackle or snap the tack in place, then work up the luff of the jib snap by snap to the head. As you do so, it may help to run the luff through your hands to keep the edge from being twisted in the process of attachment. When you're done, check that all the jib snap jaws are facing the same way. Virtually all American sailmakers sew on jib snaps so their openings face to port.

When you get to the sail's head, make fast the jib halyard, using the same procedure as with the main.

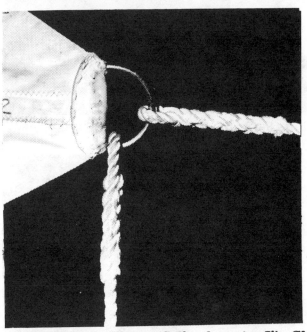

Fig. 5-18 Jib Sheets-Spliced on to Jib Clew

The jib sheets are another story. Remember that they're nearly always double, with half the sheet running to one side of the cockpit and the other half to the other side. How you attach the sheets is an open question, and here are some of the methods among which you can choose.

Splicing - a splice is a permanent way of making an eye at the end of a line or attaching two lines together. It will never, when properly done, work free, no matter how briskly the sail luffs or flutters. A good splice is not heavy, so two of them won't weigh down a corner of the sail. On the other hand, a splice can't be undone, so if you have more than one jib, you'll need more than one set of jib sheets, which is a nuisance as well as being expensive.

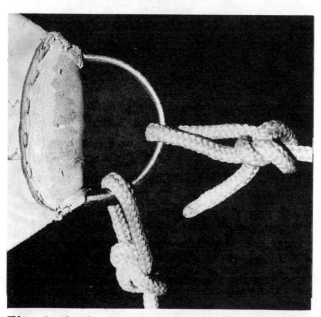

Fig. 5-19 Jib Sheets—Bent on with Bowline

Fig. 5-20 Jib Sheets - Bent on with Fisherman's Bend

Tying - there's no reason you can't tie each part of the jib sheet to the jib clew cringle, using a bowline. This good knot is easy to tie, once you get the hang of it, and is also easy to untie. Normally, it will not shake itself loose except if badly tied and repeatedly shaken. A bowline is, however, a fairly large and clumsy knot, and two of them will weigh down the jib clew in light breezes, as well as offering potential snags when tacking.

Fig. 5-21 Jib Sheets - Attached with Snap Shackle

Snapshackles - for those who prefer or require a quick release, the snap shackle, into whose ring both jib sheets are spliced, is often the answer. Stainless steel or bronze snapshackles are relatively light and streamlined, but they are also expensive. And although they have been carefully engineered so as not to pop open, still they do so from time to time, and it can be very difficult to capture the wildly flapping clew of a big jib on a windy day. In addition, the hardware can be dangerous or damaging even if it doesn't snap open. More than a few sailors have received bloody noses from being whacked across the face by an untamed shackle.

When hoisting sail, a double-check of three things is recommended. First, be sure the boat is facing as nearly into the wind as possible. Second, check again before putting tension on a halyard to see that it's free and untangled. And third, be sure that main or jib sheets are ready to run free, so the sail won't hold any puff of breeze it may catch, and start your boat sailing before you're ready.

Raise the mainsail first, hoisting it quickly and smoothly. Once the mainsail is raised, your boat will act like a weather vane if it is on a mooring and the main happens to catch any wind. If your boat has a sliding gooseneck, release the downhaul line, allowing the sail to be raised all the way to the top of the track. On some smaller boats, there may be a halyard lock which will engage, holding the sail fully raised. On most boats, you'll have to tie off the halyard on a cleat. Now put tension on the downhaul until the sail's luff is approximately as taut as the foot and secure the downhaul line.

For rigs without a downhaul, you will have to raise the sail and put tension along the luff by pulling on the halyard. In most cases where this type of rig is fitted, there's a mainsail halyard winch fitted to the starboard side of the mast, and by taking four or five turns of the halyard wire around the winch drum, then turning the winch, you can increase tension on the mainsail luff. When the sail shows vertical creases along the luff, it's properly taut.

The tail of the halyard - a length of line about equal to the height of the mast - now must be coiled and stowed where it cannot get free, but where it can be freed and released on a moment's notice. There are several ways of coiling and stowing a halyard.

With the mainsail raised, it's now time to raise the jib, having gone through the same three checks of boat direction, halyards and sheets. On nearly all boats, the jib luff should be as taut as you can

**Fig. 5-22 Main Halyard Coiled and Stowed on Cleat**

get it, but not tauter than the forestay itself. Boats over about 16 or 17 feet usually have a jib halyard winch mounted on the port side of the mast, but few craft have jib tack downhauls because of the difficulty of fitting such a piece of gear so close to the deck. Remember which side of the mast each halyard runs

**Fig. 5-23 Coiled Halyard Stowed Between Halyard and Mast**

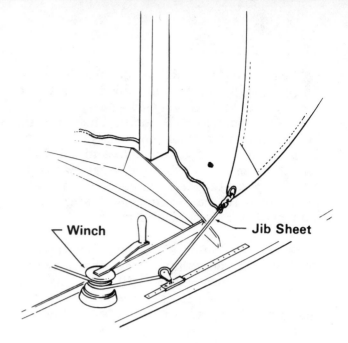

**Fig. 5-24 Jib Sheet Led Through Block**

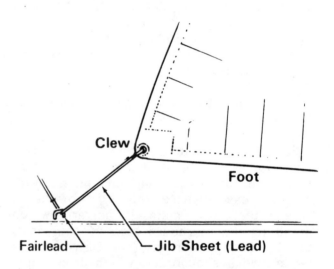

**Fig. 5-25 Jib Details at Clew**

down--starboard for the main and port for the jib. This is a universal tradition, so that if you go aboard a strange boat you can assume with confidence that the halyard on the port side of the mainmast raises the jib, and vice-versa.

If a boat flies more than one jib at a time, both headsail halyards lead down to port; and if she is gaff-rigged, the two mainsail halyards - peak and throat - both lead to starboard.

With the jib fully raised, check the sheet leads. In order for the sail to set properly when filled with wind, the jib sheet should lead to the block or non-turning <u>fairlead</u> on deck. Many boats have a length of jib sheet track on either side of the deck, so the position of the jib sheet lead can be varied.

Once you're away from mooring or pier (see page 5-21), put the boat on a close-hauled heading on either tack. Now sight up the mast from the side and from forward, to make sure it's straight. If there's a bend or hook in it, use the turnbuckles on the appropriate shrouds or stays to straighten it out, but work slowly.

If the head of the mast is hooked to windward, try tightening the windward

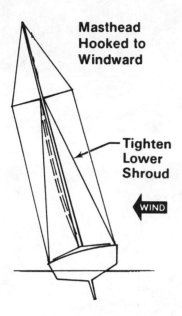

Masthead
Hooked to
Windward

Tighten
Lower
Shroud

WIND

Fig. 5-26 Mast Bowed to Leeward

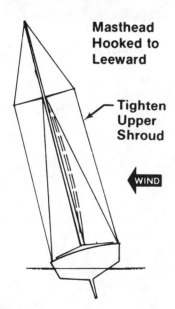

Masthead
Hooked to
Leeward

Tighten
Upper
Shroud

WIND

Fig. 5-27  Mast Bowed to Windward

lowers; if it's hooked to leeward, tighten the windward upper shroud. When the masthead hooks forward, chances are you'll want to tighten the backstay.

Having gotten the mast straight on one tack, come about and repeat the process on the other. You may have to run

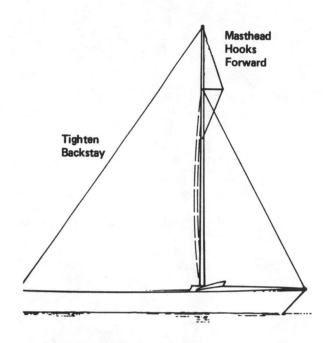

Masthead
Hooks
Forward

Tighten
Backstay

Fig. 5-28 Masthead Hooked Forward

Fig. 5-29  Turnbuckle with Cotter Pins Turned in to Prevent Sail Damage

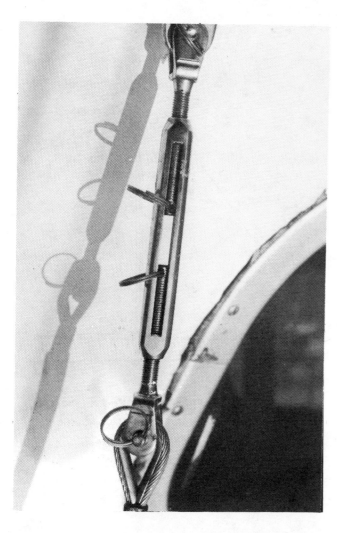

Fig. 5-30    Turnbuckle with Ring Clips in
Lieu of Cotter Pins

Fig. 5-31   Chafing Gear – Plastic Tubing
Over Turnbuckles

several tacks before you have the rig
properly adjusted, but once you've accom-
plished this, a dab of paint at the proper
spot on the turnbuckle will show how far
it should be turned next time. Remember
if you are trailer sailing, marking the
turnbuckles will only work if you just
loosen them to remove your mast. Once a
turnbuckle is completely unscrewed, it is
unlikely that you will fit it together
again in exactly the same position.

With the shrouds and stays at the
correct adjustment, insert the cotter pins
through the threaded stems and tape the
turnbuckles with waterproof tape (availa-
ble at any store handling sailing gear) so
that the bent-over pins can't snag or tear
the sails. Some skippers use inexpensive

Fig. 5-32 Stuffing Jib in Bag

**Fig. 5-33 Folding the Jib**

**Fig. 5-34 Rolling Jib for Bagging**

plastic tubing instead of tape. It can be employed over and over, but it's another thing to remember when hooking up the turnbuckles.

When returning from a sail, head into the wind before dropping sail, then do it in reverse order of raising the sails. Lower the jib first, then the main. To drop a sail, first capsize the halyard coil on deck - turn it upside-down so it's free to run when uncleated. One crewmember should tend the halyard to make sure the end doesn't snake up the mast out of reach, or to prevent a snag.

**Fig. 5-35 Dropping the Main**

The jib may be simply stuffed into its bag with the tack fitting accessible at the top. If you're in a hurry, it won't do the sail much harm. It's better practice, however, to take the sail ashore and lay it out flat. Now flake it from foot to head as shown and then loosely roll the flaked sail before bagging for overnight or longer. This will prevent wrinkles in the sail fabric and, more importantly, will keep the artificial fibers from cracking as they may if the sail is jammed forcibly into its bag.

The mainsail, too, should be folded and bagged (after the battens are removed, of course) in the same manner as the jib.

Fig. 5-36 Furling - Rolling on Boom

Fig. 5-37 Furling - Main Stowed on Boom

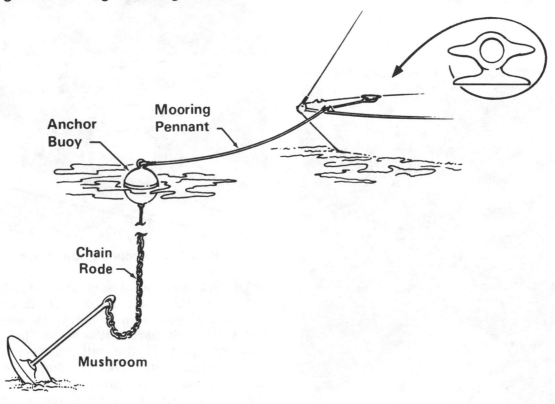

Anchor Buoy

Mooring Pennant

Chain Rode

Mushroom

Fig. 5-38 Permanent Mooring

On many larger boats, however, the main is furled on the boom and left there under a sail cover. This is quite acceptable and should do the sail no harm, provided that you first remove the battens, slack off the outhaul, and then furl the sail properly.

This is easy enough to do. As the sail is lowered, try to drop it slightly to one side of the boom. After detaching and securing the halyard, pull a large flake of sail out from the foot to form a semi-bag. Now flake out the rest of the main within this fold. Roll it tightly on top of the boom in a smooth, sausage-shaped form. Secure it in place with shock cord sail ties - three should be enough for the average length boom, but it's always a good idea to have one extra.

**Rigging Ground Tackle**

Before we consider actually getting into our boat and sailing away, we need to know something about what we are sailing away from, and what we will do with our boat after we have finished our sail. One option is to sail from a mooring. If we choose this option, we will need to prepare a mooring before we depart for our first trip either from or to that mooring. Even if we sail from a dock, prudent seamanship requires that we carry and know how to use an anchor. The time to learn about any safety equipment is before you need it. You should carry the right size ground tackle on your boat the first time you go out, but you should know how to use it before you ever depart.

A permanent mooring is a ground tackle system designed to remain in place for whole seasons at a time. Mooring anchors are generally cast iron mushrooms, so named because of their appearance. A mushroom (except in the smallest sizes) is an uncomfortable device to carry aboard, and its relative holding power is not great compared to modern lightweight anchors. It does have a couple of outstanding advantages for permanent installation. First, even a very heavy mushroom is extremely cheap (relatively speaking), and second, a dug-in mushroom will resist pulls from any side.

A variety of other anchors are used for permanent mooring, including drums filled with concrete, scrap engine blocks, and what have you. Some of these provide unreliable holding. Check carefully before you entrust your boat to a questionable mooring.

Normal mooring rigs today employ a heavy mushroom (see Table 5-1) shackled to a length of chain approximately equal in length to three times the high water depth in the anchorage. At the far end of the chain is a buoy, often made from polystyrene. To the buoy is attached the mooring pennant, a heavy, nylon rope with a large eye spliced in the extreme end. The only thing to be extra careful of, when setting up a mooring rig, is that the buoy has a metal rod running through it, to take the strain of the boat at one end and the mushroom at the other. Most mooring buoys are so reinforced, and one can tell at a glance. In some cases, a

**TABLE 5-1**

# Mooring Rig Sizes

| Boat length | Anchor | Chain | Shackle | Pennant |
|---|---|---|---|---|
| under 16' | 75 lbs. | 1/4" | 1/4" | 3/8" |
| 17'-20' | 100 lbs. | 1/4" | 5/16" | 7/16" |
| 21'-25' | 150 lbs. | 5/16" | 3/8" | 1/2" |
| 26'-30' | 200 lbs. | 3/8" | 1/2" | 5/8" |
| 30'-40' | 250-300 lbs. | 7/16" | 1/2" | 3/4" |

**TABLE 5-2**

# DESIGN LOADS AND RECOMMENDED GROUND TACKLE TABLE

| ITEM | | BOAT SIZE | | | | | |
|---|---|---|---|---|---|---|---|
| | | -15' | 16-20' | 21-25' | 26-30' | 31-35' | 36-40' |
| Design Loads in lbs.* | Lunch hook | 60 | 90 | 125 | 175 | 225 | 300 |
| | Working | 250 | 360 | 490 | 700 | 900 | 1200 |
| | Storm | 500 | 720 | 980 | 1400 | 1800 | 2400 |
| | Mooring | 750 | 1080 | 1470 | 2100 | 2700 | 3600 |
| DANFORTH Standard | Anchors Working | 4 S | 8 S | 8 S | 13 S | 22 S | 40 S |
| | Storm | 8 S | 13 S | 13 S | 22 S | 40 S | 65 S |
| Hi-tensile | Working | — | 5 H | 5 H | 12 H | 12 H | 20 H |
| | Storm | 5 H | 5 H | 12 H | 12 H | 20 H | 35 H |
| Plow (CQR) | Working | 5 lbs. | 10 lbs. | 15 lbs. | 15 lbs. | 20 lbs. | 30 lbs. |
| | Storm | 10 lbs. | 15 lbs. | 20 lbs. | 25 lbs. | 35 lbs. | 60 lbs. |
| Yachtsman | Storm | 25 lbs. | 40 lbs. | 50 lbs. | 60 lbs. | 75 lbs. | 100 lbs. |
| Shackel Galvanized | Working | 1/4" | 5/16" | 5/16" | 5/16" | 3/8" | 7/16" |
| | Storm | 5/16" | 5/16" | 5/16" | 3/8" | 7/16" | 1/2" |
| Chain Galvanized | Working** | 1/4" | 1/4" | 1/4" | 1/4" | 5/16" | 5/16" |
| | Storm | 1/4" | 1/4" | 5/16" | 5/16" | 3/8" | 7/16" |
| Nylon Rode 3-strand | Working*** | 5/16" | 3/8" | 7/16" | 1/2" | 1/2" | 5/8" |
| | Storm | 3/8" | 7/16" | 7/16" | 1/2" | 5/8" | 3/4" |

*The design loads are the forces which can be expected to be developed under ordinary use and moderate shelter from seas.

**The proof test load (elastic limit) for chain is $\frac{1}{2}$ times the load at the breaking point.

***The working load for 3-strand Nylon line is $\frac{1}{5}$ times the breaking strength and the loaded length is 1.5 times the rest length.

NOTE - In order for the ground tackle to dig in to the bottom, the proper length of rode must be let out. This is referred to as SCOPE. Anchors hold best when the pull of the rode on the shank of the anchor is as near to horizontal as possible. For this reason, the holding power of an anchor increases as the scope is increased. The following ratios of scope to water depth are considered adequate ( remember to take into account the rise and fall of the tide during the period of anchoring ):

| | |
|---|---|
| Lunch hook in calm conditions | 4 to 1 |
| Normal and overnight conditions | 7 to 1 |
| Storm anchors | 10 to 1 |

small pickup buoy, additional to the mooring buoy, is made fast to the loop in the pennant, so the crewmember on the bow can see and grab the pennant more easily.

## Anchors

Basically an anchor is a hook. Its point or points (flukes) dig into the sea bottom while a line connects it to the boat. The whole process seems so simple, but in fact several elements in the equipment and in the anchoring process are critical, and if they fail, the boat can drift to disaster.

There are several common types of anchors in use throughout the United States today. Probably the most popular is the Danforth and other makes derived from it. Known collectively as "light-weight burying anchors," all the Danforth-types have a pair of long, wide flukes that pivot at one end, where they are connected to a pipe-shaped stock. The amount of pivot of the flukes is very important, as it controls the angle between the flukes and the shank, to which the anchor line is attached; a proper angle between shank and flukes insures that the sharp-pointed flukes will dig in

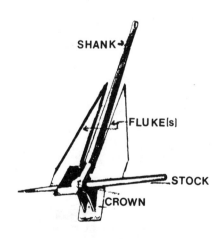

**Fig. 5-39 Danforth Anchor**

deeply and quickly, instead of skidding along the bottom.

Danforth-style anchors are lightweight for their size and holding power (see Table 5-2). They are most often employed where the sea bottom is sand, mud or just about anything except rocks, gravel, coral or kelp (a thick, ribbon-like "seaweed" that clogs the flukes of nearly any anchor).

**Fig. 5-40 Plow Anchor**

Popular among sailors with larger boats is the plow, an anchor developed in England. It has but one oversize fluke shaped like a plowshare, hence the anchor's name. The plow will work well in mud and will sometimes work in rocks or kelp. For the same size boat, a plow should be heavier than the corresponding Danforth.

The kedge, or yachtsman's, anchor is the traditional design, dating back to Roman times in its basic form. Actually, there are a number of subtle but important variations in fluke design among kedges designed for different types of bottom. In recent years the kedge almost died out of commercial production but now seems to be coming back, at least to some degree.

The standard kedge has two opposed, curving flukes, so that only one can dig in at a time. There is a relatively long shank at right angles to the flukes, and then a folding stock at the anchor's upper end. A kedge anchor can dig into types of bottom that defy other flukes, but considerably more weight in the anchor itself is required to make the design function - for normal use, one pound of anchor per foot of boat length. Since one fluke is exposed after the anchor is dug in, it's easy for the boat to swing around, foul the anchor line, and jerk the anchor free.

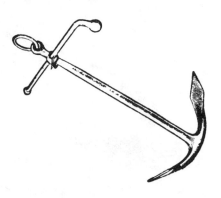

**Fig. 5-41  Yachtsman's Anchor**

Kedge anchors are popular with tradition-oriented sailors and with those whose anchorages include large patches of rocky or kelp ridden bottom. Since most sailing areas include anchorages with varying types of bottom, most cruising sailboat owners carry two different types of anchor, to be ready for anything. In all but the smallest daysailers it is also convenient to have an everyday, or working, anchor and one a size heavier, the storm anchor.

The anchor itself is only one part of the whole ground tackle system. The prudent skipper will shackle a length of chain - 12 to 20 feet or more - to the anchor ring. This not only precludes chafe at a point where it is most likely to occur, but also, by its weight, aids the anchor in digging in. To the chain is attached, with a shackle and an eye splice, the anchor rode, usually nylon line tied to the boat. Check the chart of your sailing area for anchorages, and try to carry a rode at least 10 times longer

than the high-tide depth of the deepest anchorage you expect to use. If this is impossible, a 100- or 150-foot rode should be adequate for most circumstances.

When a boat is at anchor, she normally has no motive power of her own. She will respond to the force of the current or the wind or both. Different kinds of boats react differently to these forces. Deep-draft keel boats, with a great deal of underbody, will often swing according to the current, while shallow centerboarders will respond primarily to wind pressure. When wind and current are in different directions, this can cause problems for dissimilar boats anchored close together, as they may swing into each other.

**Anchoring**
Generally speaking, when there is a choice it's best to anchor among boats of a size and type similar to your own. Try to calculate roughly the swinging circle of nearby craft - you can always ask other skippers, if they're aboard. If you know the depth of the anchorage (you can mark the depths in advance on your anchor line with plastic tags) and the amount of line a boat has out, it's easy to figure her swinging circle. Do bear in mind, too, that in anchorages the first boat has priority, and you must keep clear if you're a late arrival.

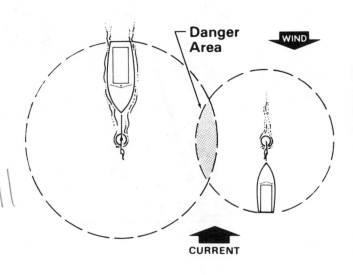

**Fig. 5-42  Anchoring Too Close**

4 parts Anchor, Rode, Shackle + Chain

5-18

**Fig. 5-43    Anchor Stowed on Foredeck Chocks**

Having selected your anchorage, you should set up the boat and her gear for the final approach. If your anchor is stowed in <u>chocks</u> or otherwise carried on deck ready for use, undo the lashings and make sure that the anchor line is clear to run out. It's a good idea to lower and furl the jib before your approach, to give you a clear foredeck.

Bring up as much anchor line as you expect to use and coil it loosely on deck so it will run out easily. The coil should be <u>capsized</u> - upside down - so that the end of the rode closest to the anchor is on top.

When you've reached the spot where you want to anchor, head up into the wind until all momentum is lost. When the boat stops moving forward, lower the anchor hand-over-hand from the bow. Don't throw it and don't drop the coil of rode over in one lump. You'll feel the anchor touch bottom, at which point make a mental note of how deep the water is. Now, as the boat drifts backward, have one crewmember lower and furl the mainsail while the other pays out the anchor line until approximately five to seven times the water depth has been used.

Take a quick turn around the deck cleat and let the boat's momentum snub the anchor line and dig in the hook. You can tell if the anchor is holding by grasping the rode forward of the bow. If the boat is dragging, you'll feel the anchor bouncing along the bottom. You can also sight on objects ashore, to see if their positions change relative to the boat.

**Fig. 5-44   Plow Anchor Stowed at Bow**

If your boat has an engine, it frequently helps in setting the anchor to give a burst of reverse, once the anchor is down and the rode is fully extended. If the anchor refuses to bite in, retrieve it. Chances are a rock or clump of seaweed has fouled the flukes. If, after several attempts, the anchor still won't set, try another place in the anchorage.

If you anchor among rocks, it's a good idea to buoy the anchor, by tying a light line to the lower end of the anchor and running the line to a lightweight buoy or float. If the anchor's flukes get stuck under a large rock, you can then draw it out backwards. When using this type of trip line, it will have to be paid out independently of the anchor rode, to avoid one line fouling the other.

## Sailing Away

Once you know about rigging your boat and ground tackle, it's time to think about boarding your sailboat and getting underway. The most important part of getting a sailboat underway is planning ahead. And conversely, the easiest way to get into trouble is to leap before you look. Let's assume that our boat is swinging at a mooring buoy in an anchorage. This is close to the ideal situation, as the boat can (at least in theory) sail off on any heading permitted by the wind direction. As a matter of practicality, of course, this is seldom true. One must take into account other boats, both anchored and moving, structures like piers and aids to navigation, water depth, and the shape of the harbor itself.

The wise skipper will also consider that what he or she is planning may not come off. If counting on sailing off in one direction and then tacking quickly to a new heading, bear in mind that this crucial first maneuver may be where your boat finds herself in irons. Or an unseen boat or swimmer may suddenly appear from behind another vessel, throwing off your calculations.

Here are some important things to remember in getting underway:

1. A sailboat cannot be steered until the sails are drawing and it's moving; therefore, only the lightest craft will be able to maneuver as soon as they cast off, or when the line holding them to mooring buoy or pier is released.

2. When casting off from a buoy, your boat will be effectively in irons - headed into the wind with the sails luffing. So your first tactics will be the same as those noted in the previous chapter for getting out of irons.

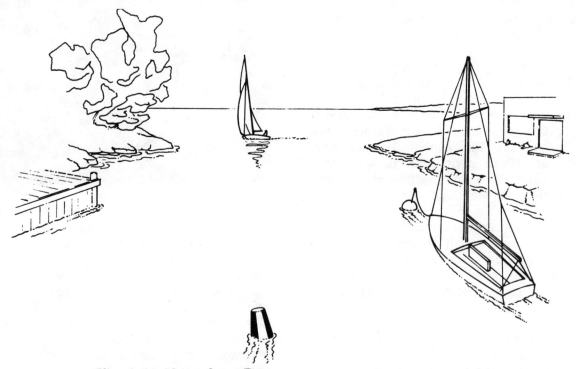

**Fig. 5-45 Moored on Buoy**

3. Remember to allow the boat to fall back from its mooring buoy a few feet before backing the jib, especially in a quick, lightweight boat. Otherwise you run the risk of taking off and overrunning the buoy or snagging the mooring line (which is usually permanently attached to the buoy).

4. Plan on sailing off on a beam or close reach if possible, as you'll then have the greatest maneuverability. If the harbor is very crowded, however, don't be ashamed to paddle out to open water before making sail. Every small sailboat should have a pair of paddles and larger craft should have a motor.

As a general rule, when at a mooring your boat will automatically point into the wind. At the same time, however, the current, which is the horizontal movement of the water, may be carrying your boat in a different direction. With small sailboats, the effect of wind overrides that of current; where the current is strong and the wind light, and when the boat in question is a deep-keel type, the current may have more effect than the wind, even to the point of forcing the boat to ride stern-first to the breeze.

In this case, there are two tactics you can choose between. First, you can lead the mooring line around to the stern, allowing the boat to swing end for end so her bow is again into the wind. Then make sail and head off in the normal way, except that you'll drift forward instead of backward after casting off. Second, you can hoist only the jib and let it stream out over the bow. Cast off, sheet in the jib, and sail downwind until you are clear of the anchorage area. Then head up into the wind and raise the mainsail. Most boats will sail reasonably well under either the jib or the mainsail, and many skippers use only one sail when the wind is strong.

Sailing away from a pier should not be too difficult as long as there's one edge of the structure that lines up more or less into the wind. If possible, lay your

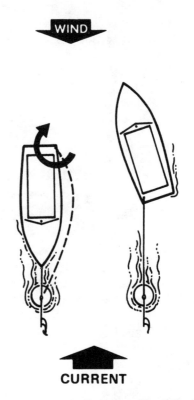

Fig. 5-46   Current Vs Wind

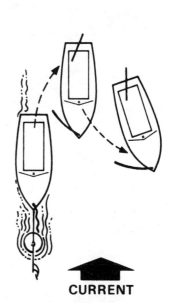

Fig. 5-47   Using Current to Cast Off

boat along an axis of pier or float so that the hull is in a closehauled position relative to the breeze before you cast off. Release the bow line first, let the

**Fig. 5-49   Sailing Off the Beach—
Carrying Boat to Water's Edge**

**Fig. 5-50   Sailing Off the Beach—
Shoving Off to Deeper Water**

**Fig 5-51   Sailing Off the Beach—
Sailing Through the Surf**

bow swing away, then cast off the stern line. Now <u>harden in</u> (pull in the sheets) and sail off.

If no side of the pier offers you a sailaway position, you'll just have to paddle or motor out to clear water before raising sail. It may be annoying, but it's a lot less embarrassing than being pinned helplessly against the float with your sails raised and no way to get off.

Sailing off a beach, one crewmember will usually have to stand about waist-deep in the water holding the boat in place until all is ready for sailing. Unless your boat is extremely maneuverable, don't try to stay a bit drier by sailing out of shallow water with the centerboard raised. When setting out from a standstill, the centerboard should be completely lowered.

**Returning to Port**
Heading back to beach, pier or mooring is just the reverse of sailing away, with a few necessary exceptions. As always, the first item of importance is to plan the approach.

Coming into an anchorage, the best tactics call for retaining as much maneuverability as you can, consistent with reduced speed in case something does go wrong. Until you are very familiar with your anchorage, it may help to sail up to your buoy a few times from different directions, without trying to pick it up. This will not only provide good information on the best paths among the other anchored boats, but it will also make you think in terms of what to do should you sail up to the mooring and miss picking it up - something that happens to the best sailors sooner or later.

If the spacing of other boats allows, try to approach the mooring buoy on a close reach. Thus, you have good speed

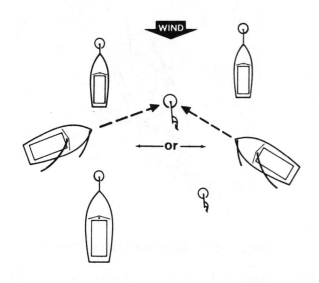

**Fig. 5-52 Approaching a Buoy**

and good maneuverability. Make your approach—other conditions permitting--on whichever tack will allow you to fall away from the wind safely if you miss the buoy. You probably won't have enough momentum left to come about, but you should, by the time you know whether you'll make the buoy or not, have speed enough to head the bow away from the wind.

If your boat will handle reasonably well under mainsail alone, it's often a good idea to drop, remove and bag the jib before making your final approach to the buoy. This procedure will give you far better visibility forward in critical moments, and it will provide an unobstructed foredeck for the crewmember who must grab the mooring line or buoy: not only is a Dacron or nylon sail very slippery underfoot, but it can also get muddied or torn if used for a carpet while mooring.

Your centerboard should be fully lowered for maximum maneuverability when making the final approach. At some point between one and three boat lengths from the mooring, head right into the wind and coast up to the buoy with the sail luffing and the sheet (or sheets) uncleated. Ideally, the boat should stop dead in the water with the mooring buoy in easy reach.

It sounds hard, but you may be surprised at how easy it becomes once you're used to your boat and familiar with her <u>carry</u>, the amount of distance she requires to lose momentum when headed into the wind from a close-hauled course. In addition, you can fudge a little just before the final approach, slacking the sheets and letting the sail luff if you're moving too fast, or heading off to gain a little speed.

What is tricky, however, is getting the mooring line aboard and made fast before the boat begins to move off in a new direction. Unlike an automobile, a boat won't stand still while you figure out a new approach to that parking spot. If you miss the mooring, you've got to be ready to do something else right away. Usually the safest tactic is simply to sail right clear, get your crew and gear sorted out, and start over from scratch. Trying to make a missed approach into a good one almost never works, and you're far better off to sail clear while you have the momentum and the room, then try again.

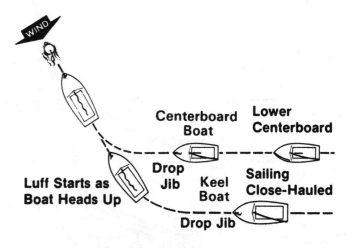

**Fig. 5-53 Mooring with Main Alone**

These remarks have been predicated on the usual mooring conditions, in which the wind direction is the dominant factor. As in leaving a mooring, it may sometimes be that the current is against the wind and stronger in its effects on the boat. When this happens, you may have to sail downwind to the mooring, in which case it may be easier to do so under jib alone, especially if that sail is smaller than the main.

Sailing to a pier involves much the same problem as coming up to a mooring, with the drawbacks being that only three sides of the pier, at most, will be accessible. Also, a pier or even a float is much more likely to damage a boat in case of collision than is a buoy. For relative beginners to sailing, it's probably not a good idea to sail into a slip or up to a pier unless the final shot can be made almost directly into the wind. When the pier is downwind, it's far safer to lower sail offshore and paddle in.

When sailing to a pier, someone aboard the boat must be ready to fend off. In small boats up to 16 feet or so, it's practical to sit on deck and fend off with your feet - which should have boat shoes on them. Don't try to stop the boat's momentum with an arm or a leg while standing up. And if the boat is a large

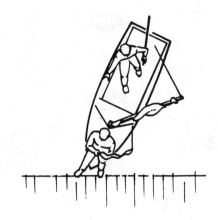

Fig. 5-54  Approaching a Pier

one, fend off with a fender - it will absorb much more shock than you can, and do it better, and in any case it's much more seamanlike to sacrifice a piece of gear than to risk injuring a crewmember.

Sailing in a crowded harbor, be ready for sudden wind shifts which may be caused by large buildings ashore, high piers or even anchored boats. As in the case of approaching an unfamiliar anchor-

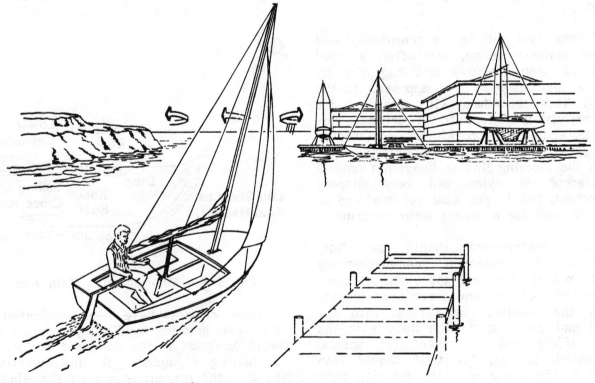

Fig. 5-55  Causes of Wind Shift in a Harbor

age, it often pays to sail close by your intended pier without committing yourself to the final approach, then return (if all is well) for the actual maneuver. Many small boats are advertised as being capable of being sailed "right up on the beach." With some of them, this may be true. But for most, a beaching at speed is an invitation to a wrenched rudder, a broken centerboard, or perhaps personal injury. Providing surf conditions will allow, it is far better to sail in close to the beach until the water is about waist-deep, then round up into the wind while one crew member goes overboard to hold a line attached to the bow. The person going over the side should be wearing a PFD (Personal Flotation Device) and sneakers and should know how to swim in case the water is deeper than waist-high.

If you must sail onto the beach, do so only when you have a very accurate idea of how steeply the shore shelves. Pull the centerboard or daggerboard all the way up (don't expect it to pop up by itself),
and be prepared to flip up the rudder the instant before the boat touches shore, or the second you feel the rudder blade touch bottom, whichever is first.

All maneuvers with a small boat require practice to perfect. A boat's behavior in a five-knot wind may change considerably when the same boat is facing 10- or 15-knot breezes. One of the best ways to practice approaches to moorings or piers is to use an inflated air mattress or a plastic detergent bottle anchored to the bottom and practice making landings alongside from every possible sailing direction. With a full afternoon's experience in hand, you'll be far more confident and rightly so. And don't forget to change places with your crew from time to time. Not only will you have a happier and more satisfied sailing companion if you share the tiller, but you'll also have a crewmember who knows much better what the skipper's problems are - just as you'll better appreciate what the crew can and cannot do.

# Chapter 6

# Tuning and Heavy Weather Sailing

In Chapter Five, we discussed basic rigging technique. In order to make your boat sail at peak efficiency, however, merely having the mast more or less upright isn't enough. Since most beginners' boats have rigid, or non-bendy, masts, let's look at the proper tuning of that type of rig.

The average small sloop has between four and six lengths of wire comprising its standing rigging system. There are the fore- and backstays, the masthead, or upper shrouds on each side, and perhaps lower shrouds. In larger craft, there are more elements to the rigging system, but the principle remains the same—every piece of standing rigging exerting tension on the mast must be balanced in some manner, usually by another piece of wire leading to the same spot on the mast. Tightening the various pieces of standing rigging to make a balanced system is called tuning the rig, and of course the devices most used in exerting tension on the stays and shrouds are turnbuckles.

## Setting Up Rigging

In remembering how to set up the rigging, it may be worthwhile bearing in mind the old adage, "the higher the wire, the tauter it is." Masthead shrouds are set up most taut, and stays and shrouds terminating below the masthead are correspondingly slacker. The important thing, when first tensioning the fore-and backstays and the upper shrouds, is to set them up evenly, so the mast is straight as you sight upward along the mainsail luff track or groove. If you can, get off the boat and look directly over the stern, checking that the spar is straight in the

boat, tilted neither to port nor starboard. Chances are the mast should angle aft a little—this is called rake, and the degree is usually specified in your owner's instruction. If no literature exists to tell you how many degrees aft to rake the mast, ask some skipper knowledgeable in your class to help you set the rig up the first time.

For those students who are technically inclined, the mast is usually raked aft between two and five degrees as indicated in Chapter 5 and shown in Figure 5-6. A rake of three degrees will displace the top of a mast approximately six inches for each ten feet of length. Consequently, if the distance from the center of halyard sheave (Figure 1-12) to the deck is 20 feet, a 3° mast rake will cause a freely swinging halyard to touch the deck twelve inches from the face of the mast. The rake of that same mast could also be determined by measuring down the mast 15 feet from the sheave and making a mark. When the free swinging halyard hangs 9 inches aft of that mark, you have a 3° rake in your mast. Check at the same time to see if the halyard hangs directly behind the center of the mast, if not your mast may not be upright. Remember, in a small sailboat your weight may affect the trim.

Normally, start adjusting your rigging with the lower shrouds being taut enough that there is no visible slackness. Bear in mind that the function of the lowers is to keep the bottom half of the spar from buckling when the load of a wind-filled sail pulls it to one side. When there is no side load on the mast, there should be no stress on the lowers.

## Adjusting Rigging

Now raise the sails, cast off and sail out to some area where there isn't any disturbing traffic. Both main and jib luffs should be taut enough so there is no sign of scalloping. Put the boat on a close-hauled course on either tack and check the mast (it may be necessary to do this from another boat the first time). Should the spar be straight as you sight upward, everything is fine. However, it's more likely that one of the following problems will exist.

1. Mast hooks forward. The forestay is too taut or--more likely--the backstay is not taut enough.

2. The mast hooks aft. The forestay is too slack or the backstay too taut.

3. The mast hooks to windward. The windward side upper shroud is too taut or the windward lower is too loose.

4. The mast hooks to leeward. The windward upper is too slack or the windward lower is too taut.

When adjusting turnbuckles, do so a little at a time. The forces created by the turnbuckle can be considerable. Remember to turn the center section of the turnbuckle, holding the upper part to keep it from turning as well. There should always be as much turnbuckle screw showing above the center section as below it.

Once the mast is straight on the original tack, come about to a close-hauled heading on the opposite tack, and repeat the adjustment. Do this until the spar is vertical on either close-hauled tack as well as at rest. You should begin each day's sail by checking the straightness of the mast. Although the stretch of stainless steel shrouds and stays is negligible, the wire has a certain amount of slack in its construction and will loosen a bit, especially early in the sailing season.

When the standing rigging is adjusted to your satisfaction, pin the turnbuckles with cotter pins or rings, to keep them from backing off. Be sure to bend the sharp ends into the turnbuckle to avoid protruding snags. After you've done so, tape over any remaining sharp edges or points on which sails, clothing or skin might snag. A roll of waterproof tape--sold in any marine supply store--should be a part of your ditty bag.

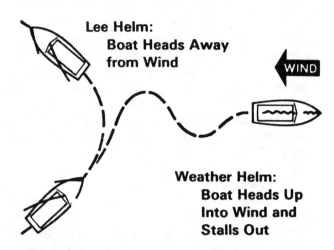

**Fig. 6-1  Lee Helm vs Weather Helm**

## Lee and Weather Helm

The average, modern small sailboat is remarkably well balanced, compared to boats of equivalent size from previous periods. Even so, certain adjustments may be required to create the optimum balance of which the boat is capable.

What we mean, when we talk about balance in reference to a sailboat, is the boat's ability--or lack of it--to sail a straight course without pressure on the tiller. A perfectly balanced boat would sail straight with no hand on the tiller when the sails were properly set for the direction and force of the apparent wind. Obviously, waves and weight distribution in the boat can upset the most neutral balance. Not so obviously, totally neutral balance is not normally considered an asset in a boat.

For most skippers, a perfectly balanced helm feels dead and unresponsive. Since most helmspeople sit on the up or wind-

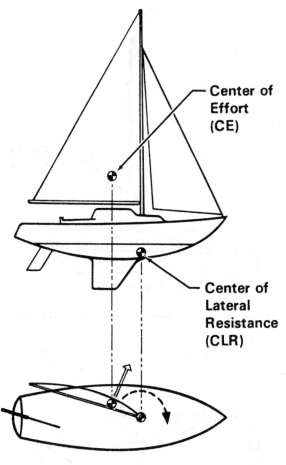

Center of
Effort
(CE)

A boat with weather helm has the Center of Effort (CE) (The combined effort of the headsail and main) acting aft of the Center of Lateral Resistance (CLR) of the hull underwater. The overall effect is a tendency for the boat to turn into the wind.

Center of
Lateral
Resistance
(CLR)

Note that the Center of Lateral Resistance acts as the pivot point about which the turning force of the sails must be balanced by the force exerted on the rudder.

Force must be exerted
on tiller to counter
turning force of Aft
Center of Effort

WIND

**Fig. 6-2  Effect of Weather Helm on Rudder**

ward side of the boat, a degree of imbalance that causes the tiller to pull against them is most comfortable. If you doubt this, try it yourself: sit first on the low side and try pushing against the average tiller; then switch. Unless you are quite unusual, you'll find the slight pull of a normal helm gives you a better feel of how the boat is progressing through the water.

If you let go of the tiller in an average boat, she will round up into the wind more or less quickly—a centerboard boat will often spin right up, while a long-keeled vessel may take 10 seconds or so. Turning to windward—or to weather, to use the old term--when the tiller is released is the mark of a boat with

weather helm. A slight amount of weather helm is not only advantageous for steering, it is also a safety factor, as the boat will head up into irons and stall out if an emergency causes the skipper to let go of the tiller.

Some boats have weather helm all the time, and some have it only under certain conditions, as we shall see later. Other boats have the opposite condition, the tendency to head away from the wind when the tiller is released, and this is called lee helm. Lee helm is generally considered a negative attribute in a boat, as it makes for tiring steering and is a potential danger. When the tiller is released, a boat with lee helm will head off the wind and into a jibe.

A boat with Lee Helm has the combined Center of Effort (CF) forward of the Center of Lateral Resistance (CLR) of the underwater hull. The overall effect is the tendency for the boat to turn away from the wind, and must be corrected by moving the tiller to the left, thus creating a force which turns the boat into the wind.

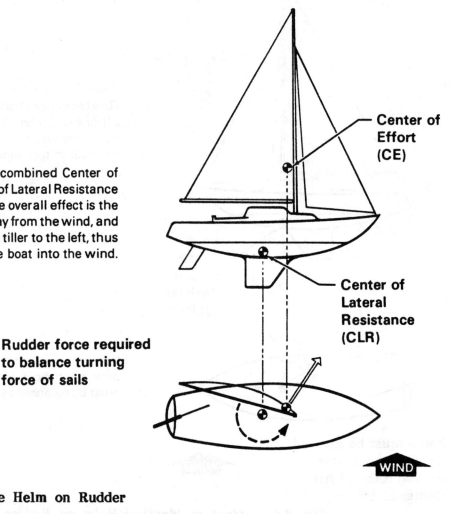

Center of Effort (CE)

Center of Lateral Resistance (CLR)

Rudder force required to balance turning force of sails

WIND

**Fig. 6-3   Effect of Lee Helm on Rudder**

The Center of Effort (CE) of the sails on your boat is a theoretical point calculated by the designer. It represents the single point where all the force of the wind on the sails is concentrated. Think for a moment of trying to balance a dish on a pool cue stick. If you can find the right point on the bottom of the dish, you can balance the dish as we have all seen on television. The weight of the dish can be thought of as the force of the wind on your sail, and the point where the cue stick balances the dish is the dish's Center of Gravity which is the same as the sail's Center of Effort.

The concept of Center of Lateral Resistance (CLR) of your boat's hull is similar. It too is a point representing a concentration of forces. In the case of your hull, it is a calculated single point representing the location of all the force

that the hull presents to lateral movement or overturning due to the wind. This point can also be thought of as the location where the dish is balanced on the cue stick.

Helm balance is affected by the relative location of these two points. The wind tries to rotate the hull around the hull's CLR unless the CE is almost directly above the CLR. The helmsman uses the boat's rudder to resist this rotation by applying pressure on the helm. The wind also causes the boat to heel over for the same reason: the CE is above the CLR when the boat is under sail.

Helm balance can therefore be changed in two ways, either by moving the Center of Effort or the Center of Lateral Resistance. We can adjust this relation-

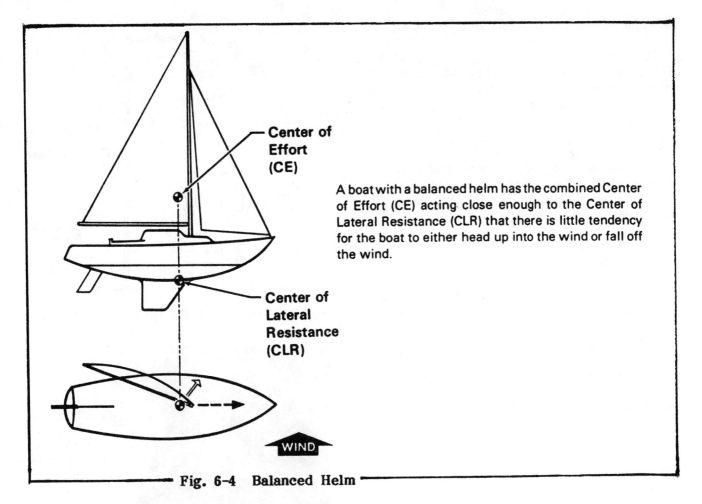

Center of
Effort
(CE)

A boat with a balanced helm has the combined Center of Effort (CE) acting close enough to the Center of Lateral Resistance (CLR) that there is little tendency for the boat to either head up into the wind or fall off the wind.

Center of
Lateral
Resistance
(CLR)

WIND

Fig. 6-4  Balanced Helm

ship by moving the mast forward or aft, an impractical solution in most cases; by changing the rake of the mast; by changing the headsail/mainsail area ratio; or by moving an underwater surface, such as the centerboard.

### Correction of Weather Helm

Causes of excess weather helm may be temporary or permanent. If your boat's tiller requires uncomfortable amounts of pull under way, or if your rudder is at an angle to the transom greater than about five degrees, your craft probably has too much weather helm.

Temporary causes of weather helm may be any one of the following:

1. Jib too small or mainsail too large for conditions.

2. Jib not trimmed enough or main trimmed in too much.

3. Mast raked too far aft.

4. Centerboard too far down and forward.

5. Too much weight forward in the boat.

6. Boat heeled too much.

The cures for the causes of temporary weather helm are, of course, implicit in the problems themselves. If none of the foregoing remedies works, then the weather helm may stem from something more basic to the boat. Causes of permanent weather helm include:

1. The foretriangle is too small. (The foretriangle is the area contained within the forestay, the mast and the deck.)

2. The mainsail is too large.

3. The mast is stepped too far aft.

4. The centerboard drops too far down.

It may or may not be worth trying to fix these problems. In most small boats, 2 and 4 can be remedied, while 1 or 3 might be a good reason to sell the boat.

## Correction For Lee Helm
Lee helm, too, is either permanent or temporary. Temporary causes tend, reasonably enough, to be the opposites of what creates weather helm:

1. Jib too large or main too small for conditions.

2. Jib overtrimmed or main not trimmed enough.

3. Mast raked too far forward.

4. Centerboard not dropped enough.

5. Too much weight aft.

Permanent lee helm problems are again the opposites of conditions causing permanent weather helm:

1. Mainsail too small or jib too large.

2. Mast stepped too far forward.

3. Centerboard too small.

## Mainsail Trim
Trim, or shape adjustment, of the mainsail under way is accomplished by tension on the three corners of the sail or by bending the mast. Let's look at how and why the main is trimmed in this way. The basic adjustment comes from the halyard, which regulates luff tension and—if the main boom is on a sliding gooseneck—sail height off the deck. When sailing on or near the wind—beating or on a close reach—the mainsail luff is normally quite taut, but as the air lightens, more <u>draft</u> (sail curvature) is required to keep the boat moving. Easing the halyard is one way of gaining fullness.

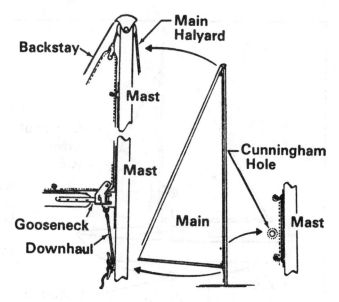

**Fig. 6-5  Points of Mainsail Adjustments**

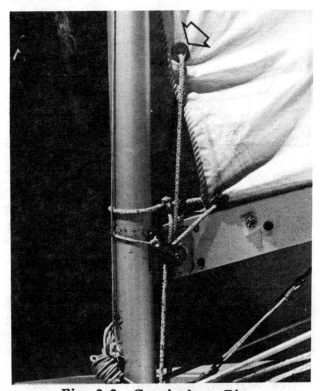

**Fig. 6-6  Cunningham Rig**

To prevent your sailboat from becoming overpowered in heavy winds, you must reduce the draft if you wish to sail on a close reach. One way to move the draft forward and reduce the fullness of your mainsail is to use the downhaul under the gooseneck. To get really hard tension along the luff, the main is frequently

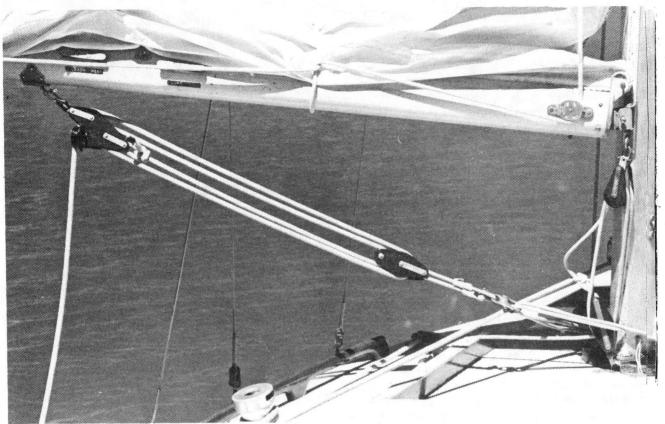

**Fig. 6-7   Boom Vang**

raised as high as it will go with the halyard, after which tension is applied to the gooseneck downhaul. On mains without a sliding gooseneck, the same effect can be obtained with a Cunningham--a grommeted hole in the mainsail luff slightly above the foot. A hook in the Cunningham is pulled downward to exert stress on the luff and flatten the sail.

The third adjustment point is the outhaul. Normally taut, the sail's foot is slackened when sailing off the wind by easing the outhaul. This and easing the halyard cause the main to bag somewhat, creating a more efficient downwind shape.

**Adjusting Backstay**

On some boats, the backstay tension can also be regulated underway, either by a sophisticated hydraulic tensioner or by something as simple as putting a wrench to the backstay turnbuckle. Tightening the backstay, especially on a boat whose forestay runs only partway up the mast, puts a bow in the spar, flattening the

mainsail for upwind sailing. Off the wind, the backstay is eased, the mast straightens, and the main becomes fuller. It's worth mentioning that a sail and spar must be properly designed for bending and flattening in this manner: trying to bow a rigid spar will just damage it.

**Boom Vang**

Off the wind, a boom vang-a tackle from the boom down to deck or gunwale-is used to hold the boom down to control leech tension, and rigged to prevent (hence the term preventer) an accidental jibe when running directly before the wind. Some boats have permanent vangs rigged from the underside of the boom to a point at the base of the mast. A four or five part tackle can exert tremendous force on a boom, so it's a good idea to go easy with the vang, using just enough pressure to bring the boom down parallel to the water.

One disadvantage of a vang set to the gunwale is that it must be cast off with each jibe and attached to the other gunwale. An accidental jibe using this type of vang would possibly result in a damaged or bent boom.

## Light-Weather Sails

In addition to the average sloop's working sails—her mainsail and jib—she may have any number of light-weather sails. The most common of these is perhaps the <u>Genoa jib</u>. By definition, a Genoa is simply a jib that overlaps the mast. Genoas come in all sizes and shapes and in many cloth weights. An offshore racer may have as many as half a dozen such sails, each intended for different weather conditions.

Genoas are often described by numbers that refer to their size and to the weight of the cloth—nearly always Dacron—from which they are made. A #1 Genoa is the largest, with a luff running the full length of the forestay and a foot that greatly overlaps the mast and extends just about back to the cockpit. A #2 Genoa is only slightly smaller, but is made from perceptibly heavier cloth. It's hoisted when the wind is strong enough possibly to stretch the #1 out of shape. A #3 is smaller and heavier still, and the numbers usually run as far as #5, which is rather short on the luff but which still has the considerable overlap characteristic of Genoas.

## Luff Perpendicular (LP)

A Genoa is also sometimes described by its <u>luff perpendicular</u>, a term derived from racing. Thus, we may hear a sail called "a 150% Genoa." This term simply refers to a sail with a luff perpendicular (LP) that is one-and-a-half times as long as the distance from the boat's jib tack fitting to the forward side of the mast. The <u>LP</u> measurement itself is the straight line from the Genoa clew to the sail's luff, making a right angle with the luff. The standard #1 Genoa, because of handicap rules, is a 150%, but there are sails that come as large as 180% (or even larger—the only limit is the length of the boat).

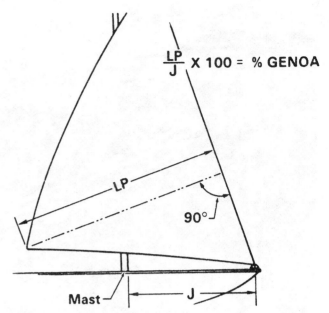

$$\frac{LP}{J} \times 100 = \% \text{ GENOA}$$

**Fig. 6-8  Genoa Formula**

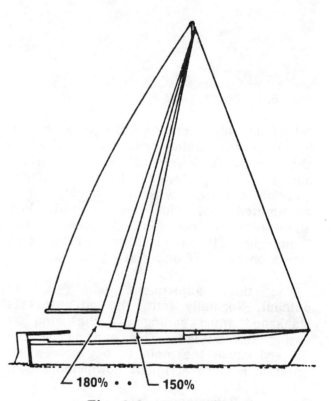

**Fig. 6-9  Genoa Sizes**

A Genoa's sheets usually lead to a block which is mounted on a sliding car. The car rides in a track running fore and aft on the deck or gunwale. This arrangement allows a proper lead for nearly any size of Genoa, simply by moving the car forward or back along the track. The same sheeting rules apply to a Genoa as to a working jib. When you hoist the sail, pull the clew aft and set the block at the corresponding position on the track. Now sail the boat close-hauled and observe the Genoa's foot and leech. If the foot appears loose while the leech is stressed, it means the sheeting point is too far forward. If the leech is loose and the foot taut, the Genoa sheet block should be moved forward. When the leech and foot appear equally tensioned, luff the boat slowly up into the wind. The Genoa should begin to ripple all along its luff, and if it does, your sheet lead is correct. If the ripple appears first at the head of the sail, then the leech is still a bit too loose, and vice versa if the sail luffs first toward its foot.

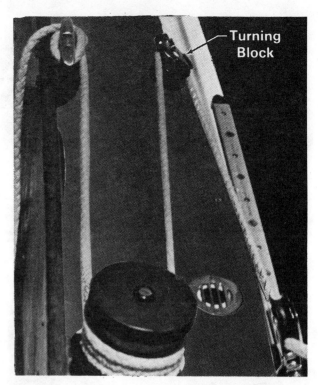

Fig. 6-11  Genoa Turning Block

Fig. 6-10  Jib Sheet Block

The sheet block on the opposite track should be set to match the first one. This will usually be the correct setting, but some slight adjustment may be required. This just means that your boat is imperceptibly out of shape, or the two tracks do not quite match, and is nothing to worry about. In many cases, the Genoa sheet is led from the sail's clew through the block to a winch mounted on the cockpit coaming. This mechanical aid is

required because of the amount of pull a Genoa can create. If your Genoa has a very long foot, or if the winch is mounted well forward in the cockpit, you may be faced with a sheet that leads rather abruptly upward from the sheet block to the winch. In this case, you will need a turning block at the aft end of the track, so the sheet comes to the winch at the flattest possible angle. The turning block must be extra strong, as it will be taking stresses nearly twice those on the sheet block. If you doubt this fact, ask any high school physics student.

For maximum efficiency, many Genoas are cut to be so-called deck sweepers. The sail's foot is in contact with the deck for nearly its whole length. When close-hauled, this kind of sail can cause a blind spot for the helmsman running from dead ahead to amidships on either side. Some skippers have their sailmaker put a transparent plastic window in the foot of the sail, and this is a help. But there's no substitute for a lookout, and one of the crew should be specifically assigned to sit down to leeward or up by the tack to keep an eye out forward.

Fig. 6-12 Genoa Window

Fig. 6-14 Lapper

Fig. 6-13 Window in Main

Tacking with a Genoa sometimes offers problems, as the sail drags and whips its way around the shrouds. After a few times out, you will know from exasperating experience which deck or rigging attachments are likely to catch the Genoa. These fittings should be taped smooth or relocated if possible. In some large boats, a crewmember is assigned to walk the Genoa clew around the shrouds when the boat tacks, but hopefully you won't require this.

There are three variants of the Genoa worth knowing about. These sails exist for special conditions which are fairly common in many parts of the United States, but which may or may not exist where you are.

Fig 6-15 Reacher

Lapper: The cross between a working jib and a Genoa. Its luff runs nearly the length of the forestay, but its foot only just overlaps the mast, hence the name. A 110% Genoa is often called a lapper.

Reacher: As big in area as a Genoa, but of lighter fabric, the reacher is usually a 180% LP sail with a very high foot. As the name suggests, it is used for reaching and is normally sheeted right aft to the transom or sometimes to a block at the end of the main boom.

Drifter: For very light airs, when most non-racers will turn on their auxiliary engines. The drifter is cut like a big Genoa, but is made of very light nylon. It often has no snap hooks along the luff, being made fast only at head, tack and clew.

## The Spinnaker

The light-air sail called the spinnaker is the queen of the racing sails. Shaped like a triangle with two convex sides, the spinnaker is often cut from brightly-colored nylon in individualistic patterns. It is a sail that's often maddening to set, fly or lower, but no serious racing boat would be without one, if the sail plan and class rules allow it.

Although there are a number of different ways to arrange the panels of a spinnaker, for the purposes of this book only two are mentioned. The sail with panels parallel and horizontal across the bottom half of the sail, and an arrangement of triangular panels at the top, is called a radial head. It's commonly used for broad reaching and running. The spinnaker that appears to have a three-pointed star superimposed on it is a starcut. Relatively flatter and smaller than a radial head, the starcut is used downwind in heavier weather or for beam and close reaching in normal conditions.

The spinnaker's nomenclature employs the same words that are used to describe any triangular sail, but the terms are defined differently. The lower edge of the sail is the foot, and the two sides are

Fig. 6-16   Drifter

Fig. 6-17   Radial Head Spinnaker

the leeches--until the sail is set, as we shall see. Likewise, the two lower corners are the clews and the upper corner is the head. Once a spinnaker is set, the side of the sail held by the <u>spinnaker pole</u> becomes the luff, its clew becomes the tack, and its sheet is called the <u>spinnaker guy</u>.

Unlike the sails described previously, the spinnaker is set <u>flying</u>--that is, it's connected to the boat by its halyard and the lines from its clews, not along any one of its edges. Once the sail is raised, it assumes a position in front of the mainsail. It rides outside all shrouds and stays--an important point to remember, With its five attendant lines--halyard, sheet, guy, lift, and downhaul--the spinnaker adds considerable complexity to any boat. Crews need to be well-rehearsed in sail handling, beginning in the dock before you get underway.

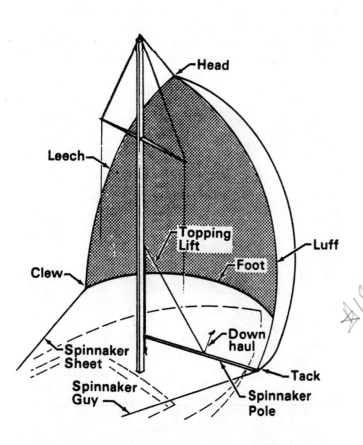

**Fig. 6-18   Spinnaker Nomenclature**

Up to this point we have been looking at methods and equipment used to make your boat sail at peak efficiency. This assumes that the weather is suitable for efficient sailing. When the weather worsens, efficiency must give way to prudent seamanship. The time to prepare your sailboat and to learn how to use your equipment in uncomfortable conditions is before you encounter those conditions. Remember, sailing a boat is not like driving an automobile--you cannot pull over to the side and stop when it is no longer pleasant to go on.

**Emergency Handling In Squalls**

Sooner or later you're going to find yourself and your boat caught out when the wind is stronger than you'd like it to be. In such a case remember that your boat was almost certainly built to take a great deal of punishment and she will come through, as long as you keep your head and use proper sailing technique. There are two kinds of bad weather to consider--the first is the sudden and unexpected squall, the second is heavy weather that you expect.

Squalls can be unnerving simply because they give you little time to prepare. Even the fastest-moving squall line will nevertheless allow you the few minutes you need to get your boat in shape to handle it. And always remember that a fast-moving squall has one great virtue--it's over in a hurry. Often a squall will last only a few minutes, seldom more than half an hour.

The <u>first step</u> when it becomes obvious that you're likely to be caught by a squall long before you can reduce sail is to have all hands put on their Personal Flotation Devices, the Coast Guard's technical term for what most people call lifejackets or lifevests. Not only should every crewmember have a personal lifesaving device of the proper size capable of supporting his or her weight, but everyone should wear it whenever there's any threat of bad weather. A good PFD will give the crewmember confidence, will conserve body heat, and will absorb the bumps that happen in rough weather. Racing sailors and those sailing offshore make it a habit always to wear a PFD in the cockpit or on deck, and many add a lifeline and harness.

Fig. 6-19  PFDs-Personal Flotation Devices

The second step is to luff up into the wind and drop the sails and furl. A serious squall can pack winds over 60 miles per hour and advance as fast as 50 miles per hour, so don't take chances. Until you know the strength of the advancing storm, drop the sails and furl them securely. Drop the centerboard or daggerboard, if it isn't already lowered.

Secure all loose equipment, have a bailer or pump ready to operate, and tell the crew to keep their weight low in the boat. With these precautions you and your boat will be ready to deal with whatever is likely to come. If you're upwind from a beach or shore, it would be well to put your anchor out and set it to avoid being blown ashore.

If a squall moderates to where you can set sail, but the winds are still too strong to sail under main and jib, you can do one of several things. First and probably best is to reef your sails--reduce the area of the mainsail and/or jib.

There are basically two ways of accomplishing this on most modern sailboats. First is roller reefing, in which the boom is so designed that it can be rolled around its axis, with the sail tightly wound around it like an old-fashioned window shade. To roller reef a mainsail, put the boat on a close reach. Now ease

Fig. 6-20  Luffing Up Into the Wind to Drop Sail

the mainsheet just a little, so there's wind in the sail but not the full force of the breeze. Now, while one person eases the main halyard, the other works the crank that turns the boom.

Most roller reefing gear has the crank located at the forward end of the main boom, which usually means that one person can ease the halyard and turn the boom. In this case, the person at the helm should if possible grasp the mainsail

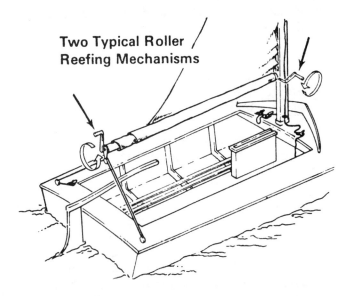

Two Typical Roller Reefing Mechanisms

Fig. 6-21  Mainsail—Roller Reefing

**Fig. 6-22    Mainsail Roller Reefing at the Gooseneck With the Hand Crank in Place**

leech and pull back, exerting a force parallel to the boom. This makes for a tighter, more even roll of sail.

If you roll a deep enough reef in the sail so that the lower batten becomes twisted, remove it—a wood batten can easily break under this kind of treatment, and even a flexible plastic batten does the sail no good when it's rolled up inside.

Some boats have a different form of reefing gear. Some sailors call it point reefing and other sailors call it jiffy reefing, but it is essentially the same operation. The boat is luffed up into the wind and the main dropped or partially lowered. The crew now run lines through grommets partway up the luff and leech (called the luff cringle and leech cringle) and then lash these lines tightly around the boom. In boats equipped with jiffy reefing, the luff cringle is secured to a hook welded to the gooseneck. The leech cringle reef line is also led through the outhaul, or a cheek block on the boom to pull the clew of the sail both down to the boom and out along it.

In point reefing, individual lines hang down both sides of the sail in a line from leech cringle to clew cringle. These reef points, as they are called, are used to lash the unused foot of the reefed sail in a neat roll along the boom. Unlike luff and leech cringle lines, the reef points do not lead under the boom, but only under the foot of the sail—thus, if the reef points are evenly tied (with reef knots), the pull along the sail's foot will be evenly transferred from slides to sail.

A jiffy-reefed main, however, does not require reef points, and the unused foot of the sail may be left to hang without any problem. Jiffy or point reefing may also be used on a jib equipped with a boom, but most jibs cannot be reefed, which is why modern racers carry a large assortment of them to match many possible wind conditions. Increasing numbers of racing boats are being

**Fig. 6-23    Sailing With Roller Reefed Mainsail**

equipped with jiffy reefing jibs, but their use is not yet general. Jibs may, however, be equipped with <u>roller furling</u>, which is quite different from roller reefing.

Fig. 6-24  Reef Grommets

A roller-furled jib is one in which the luff wire turns around its own axis, like roller reefing around a boom. But because of the way curvature is cut into a jib, a partially roller-furled headsail may not set properly.

Roller furling is also available for mainsails. The sail in these cases is rolled up on the boom. Contrary to the case of the roller-furled jib, roller furling is often an effective way of reducing mainsail area.

Since main and jib must be balanced to each other, reefing the main, by whatever means, usually means switching to a smaller jib to maintain balance.

Fig. 6-25  Sailing With Mainsail Jiffy
Reefed

Fig. 6-26  Jib Being Roller Furled

It is possible to reduce sail in a hurry simply by striking one sail or another, and furling it tightly. Which sail you choose will depend on how your boat balances and what point of sailing you are on.

In heavy weather, when you're not too sure of yourself or the boat, it's a good idea to put the boat on a reach first of all, before you attempt other points of sailing. A reach is not only the fastest point of sail, it's usually the safest as well--the boat is relatively stable and can head up into the wind, spilling the breeze's force from the sails, or head away as required, without changing tacks.

If both sails are up, try sailing first with a full jib and a mainsail eased slightly so that it begins to flutter or backwind along the luff. The sail will still be helping to move the boat, but the heeling force of the wind will be considerably eased.

Fig. 6-28  Sailing Under Jib Alone

Fig. 6-27  Full Jib—Mainsail Eased

Now try sailing under jib alone, with the main tightly furled around its boom and the boom carefully lashed to prevent its breaking free. In a case where the main and working jib are approximately equal in size--the boat will probably

maneuver well under the jib by itself, and you will be spared the worry of dealing with a swinging main boom in heavy winds.

On the other hand, boats with mainsails that are much larger than the jib will probably balance better if the main is left raised and the jib lowered, unsnapped and bagged (don't leave it on the deck, even tied down--it may easily escape over the side to act as an unwanted drag).

The only way to find which sail combination works best for your boat is to take her out and try the several variations open to you. The important thing is to try, where possible, to keep the proportion of sail areas ahead of and aft of the mast approximately the same. As the wind gets stronger, the relative amount of sail area forward of the mast may increase--the boat will probably balance better for it, a fact which will be reflected in the amount of _helm_--the pull felt by the person holding the tiller.

Fig. 6-29  Sailing Under Mainsail Alone

## Knockdown and Capsize

When a boat is temporarily overpowered by the wind and heeled over till its mast is nearly level with the water, it is said to be knocked down. When a boat is laid over and has shipped so much water that it can't right itself, it is capsized. Many of today's small centerboard sailboats are designed to right themselves from a knockdown, even if there's a substantial amount of water in the cockpit. You can aid the process by releasing the sheets and using your weight to bring the boat back up.

In the case of a genuine capsize, especially with a non-self-righting boat, the situation may be more serious. Several steps should not only be followed by the skipper, but they should also be thoroughly drilled into the crew.

Fig. 6-30  Beginning a Knock Down

Fig. 6-31  Capsized

1. Immediately after the capsize, count heads: make sure all the crew have surfaced and swum free from the boat.

Fig. 6-32    Righting a Small Boat—
             Climbing on the
             Center/Dagger Board

Fig. 6-33    Righting a Small Boat—
             Coming Up

2. Stay with the boat as long as it is floating, and put on PFDs, if you haven't already done so. If you are in this situation you should have already insisted that the crew don PFDs.

3. Recover the loose gear that will be floating around the boat. Stuff it into a sailbag and tie the sailbag to the boat.

4. Get the sails down and off--at least down. This should allow the boat to come upright by itself. You may need to have some one help by pushing upward on the mast while you stand on the centerboard.

5. Once the boat is upright, lower the centerboard, plug the top of the centerboard trunk if it's open and bail the boat. You may have to swim alongside and scoop water out until the level is low enough for one crew-member--the lightest--to ease aboard by the stern and finish the job.

   If after a couple of tries you see that it will be impossible to empty the boat and sail away, don't use up your energy and body heat by repeated attempts. Turn your attention to signaling for help. Continuous sounding of the fog horn, a

Fig. 6-34    Righting a Small Boat—
             Climbing Aboard

smoke signal by day or a flare by night, an International Orange distress flag—all are recognized signals of distress, and all can be purchased in any marine supply store and carried in a waterproof bag (most are sold that way) in even the smallest daysailer. Many skippers equip each PFD with a mouth operated whistle attached by about 10 inches of lanyard.

If your boat must be towed home while full of water, make sure the towing vessel pulls your boat very slowly--two or three miles per hour, at the maximum. Not only are water-filled boats very unstable, but the water sloshing back and forth can easily gain such momentum it knocks the transom out. Make sure your boat has an extra-strong cleat or eye bolt on the foredeck, one that is bolted through the deck and through a backing board beneath. This kind of hardware will stand the great stresses of towing. One crewmember should stay aboard the swamped boat to bail, steer, and to keep weight aft so she will ride better.

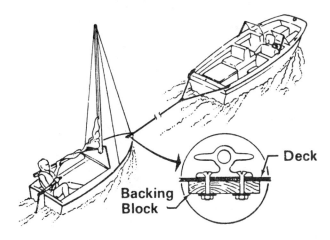

**Fig. 6-35   Backing the Bow Cleat with a Backing Block. If the Boat is Full of Water Have it Towed Very Slowly**

### Man Overboard

When you have lost someone overboard you have a possible life/death situation on your hands. These are the things you must do or have your crew do at once, not necessarily in the sequence given but at once. (See Fig 6-36)

1. Don't lose sight of the victim. Give the cry: "Man Overboard." Point toward the victim, and KEEP POINTING!

2. Heave a throwable personal flotation device (Type IV PFD) as close to the victim as possible without hitting him or her with it. One of a bright color (e.g., International Orange) is desira-

ble. A soft PFD is not likely to injure. The PFD will help the victim to float; if the victim has sunk, the PFD will mark the location. An observer should keep the victim in sight, and point continuously toward the victim so the skipper knows where to head.

3. If the boat is under power, stop the propeller (disengage the gear or, if necessary, shut down the engine) until you are sure the rotating propeller will not strike the victim.

4. Get the boat under control. All too often someone goes overboard because the boat is out of control. It is a mistake to attempt a rescue before getting matters in hand on deck. Despite the urgent temptation to turn back instantly, be sure all the crew are on deck and know what's to be done, and that all the sailing gear is in control before making a rescue attempt. Don't take too long to do this.

5. Put the boat around to pick up the victim. Under nearly all circumstances it is better to jibe around than tack. Luff the boat up into the wind alongside of the victim, as close as you can get without endangering him or her.

Now, before attempting to recover the victim, secure him or her. At the moment of rescue many people have ceased trying to keep afloat and have sunk before the eyes of their rescuers. Get a line under the victim's arms and secure it to the boat. Unless the person is injured, no other person should go over the side to help—you can almost always help better from the boat. The victim will be exhausted, scared, and probably so weighted down by clothing that he or she will be virtually helpless. In cold water areas the danger of hypothermia, the potentially fatal loss of body heat, makes it important to get the person aboard as quickly as possible. Ease the victim gently over the gunwale: usually the best

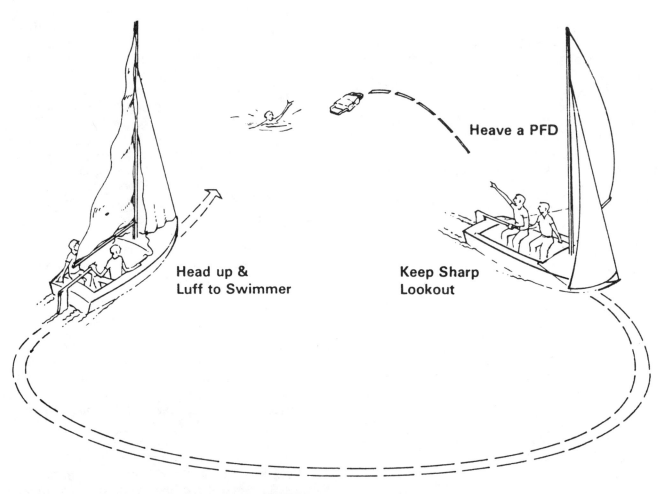

Heave a PFD

Head up &
Luff to Swimmer

Keep Sharp
Lookout

Fig. 6-36     MAN OVERBOARD–Heave a PFD, Keep
a Sharp Watch on the Victim,
Head Up and Luff to Him

Fig. 6-37   Assisting Overboard Victim

way is to get the torso up over the side and secured, then to grab a leg and to heave it up onto the deck.

Remember that a sailboat has all kinds of gear to give you leverage if the victim's weight makes it impossible to bring him or her aboard unaided: winches, halyards, the boom, a sail lowered into the water to form a sling to contain the victim and then winched aboard.

Practice. Have "Man Overboard Drills" on your boat frequently. Unexpectedly throw a floating object (the "victim") over the side and call, "Man overboard." Time yourselves from man overboard to recovery and then try to beat your time on the next try. You and your crew will become trained, experienced, and increasingly proficient.

## Disabled Rudder

If you lose your rudder or it becomes jammed, either because of bad weather conditions or a grounding, you can still get home under sail if you fly two or more sails. Naturally, you will want to stop and repair your rudder if you can, but if that is not possible, all is not lost. You can apply the principles of balancing your helm to make your boat sail with a disabled steering system.

Earlier in this chapter we found that your boat will want to head up into the wind if you sheet in the main and let the jib fly. If you sheet in the jib and let the main go, your boat will fall off. Through a series of adjustments to both sails-- trimming the jib and slacking the main if you start to sail above the course you want; doing the opposite if you fall below your desired course--you can keep going in nearly any direction you choose.

Sailing without a rudder is certainly not as easy as sailing with one. Your boat will be far less nimble and more time and sea room will be needed for any

maneuver. You may have to back your jib to come about. Jibing your boat may be difficult because the main can only go out as far as the shrouds. This constraint creates enough of a weather helm on a dead run to prevent an intentional jibe without a rudder. If your boat is small enough you can shift your crew's weight to leeward to overcome this weather helm, otherwise you may want to sail up into the wind and come about.

A paddle can make a substitute rudder. Or a bucket can be trailed on a line over the stern. Moving the bucket to one side or the other will steer the boat in an emergency.

Crew weight can also be used to increase or decrease the helm when you are trying to maintain a steady course without a rudder. When your boat is out of trim (all the crew are on one side) the boat will heel. The additional heeling creates more friction between the boat and the water on that side, causing the boat to turn toward the side the weight is on.

You can try out the principles of rudderless sailing by lashing your tiller amidships on a nice day. A little such practice can be a great ego booster. All that theory soon becomes a reality, and you become a more competent skipper.

No sailor is really competent until he or she has faced and matched heavy weather. While it is foolish to take chances, neither should you underestimate yourself or your boat. The best way to find out what heavy weather is all about is to hitch a ride aboard the boat of someone you know to be a top skipper and observe what he or she does. Ask questions anytime the actions aren't obvious. Sooner than you think you should arrive at the point where you have a healthy respect for the awesome force of the sea, but not an irrational fear of it.

# Chapter 7

# Navigation Rules

## History and Background

The danger of collision at sea has existed ever since the world's second boat was built. The Navigation Rules, or the "Rules of the Road" as they were formerly called, exist for one reason — to prevent collisions between vessels. Just as we need driving rules to govern how we drive our cars on the highway, we need "driving rules" to govern how we maneuver our vessels on the waterways.

The Navigation Rules serve that purpose. They establish responsibility for actions, a priority or precedence among vessels, specific actions to be taken in specific situations, and mechanisms for communicating needs and intentions.

During the late 1800's, the Congress of the United States enacted special rules "relating to the navigation of any harbors, rivers, or inland waters." In the years since that time the rules have grown in complexity. Most recently, the United States has adopted the International Regulations for Preventing Collisions at Sea, 1972. These are commonly called the International Rules or the 72 COLREGS.

The Inland Navigational Rules Act of 1980 became effective in most applicable waters on Dec. 24, 1981. This new set of Inland Rules supersedes the old Inland Rules, the Western Rivers Rules, the Great Lakes Rules and parts of the Motorboat Act of 1940.

Navigation Rules, International — Inland (COMDTINST M16672.2), published by the U. S. Government Printing Office for purchase, contains both sets of rules, including annexes, which are additional sections containing various technical details.

This chapter is a summary overview of the Navigation Rules. While it is believed to be accurate and to contain practically everything a recreational boater should know, it is not a substitute for the actual rules. You should get a copy of those rules and study them thoroughly, and keep it available for further reference.

Why are there two sets of rules? Just as most states have general traffic codes with special regulations for local conditions, so it is with the two sets of navigation rules. The International Rules (72 COLREGS) are designed for use on 7-3 the high seas and similar bodies of water. The Inland Rules provide special regulations for crowded waterways, rivers, Vessel Traffic Services, lakes and busy harbors and other areas where the International Rules do not apply.

The Commandant of the U. S. Coast Guard establishes demarcation lines which 7-4 mark the boundaries between waters which are governed by the International Rules and those waters which are governed by the Inland Rules. Demarcation lines are printed on charts and are also included in "Navigation Rules, International -- Inland."

## Organization of the Navigation Rules

The International and Inland Rules parallel one another, but there are important differences. In this chapter, the Rules are presented as though they were one. When there are substantial differences, they will be pointed out.

The Navigation Rules are divided into 5 major sections: (A) General; (B) Steering and Sailing Rules; (C) Lights and Shapes; (D) Sound and Light Signals; and (E) Exemptions.

The Steering and Sailing Rules govern conduct when vessels are approaching each other so as to involve risk of collision. This section comprises the "driving rules."

Lights and Shapes and Sound and Light Signals describe lights and shapes used to mark vessels and indicate special conditions, and maneuvering signals. These sections constitute a "nautical communication system."

In this chapter we will discuss the "driving rules" and the "nautical communication system" together — vessel action first, and then communications.

### General Principles

The purpose of the Navigation Rules is to prevent collisions at sea. The Navigation Rules apply to all vessels, with the Steering and Sailing Rules coming into play when vessels approach each other so as to involve risk of collision.

It is necessary to understand the following definitions in order to understand the Navigation Rules.

A power driven vessel means any vessel propelled by machinery.

A sailing vessel means any vessel under sail, provided that propelling machinery, if fitted, is not being used. A sailboat is a "power-driven vessel" if the engine is in use. All rules for power-driven vessels (maneuvering, sound signals, lights) apply to sailboats using their engines.

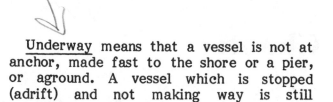

Underway means that a vessel is not at anchor, made fast to the shore or a pier, or aground. A vessel which is stopped (adrift) and not making way is still considered to be underway.

Restricted visibility means any condition in which visibility is restricted by fog, mist, falling snow, heavy rainstorms, sandstorms or other similar causes.

### Conduct in Any Condition of Visibility

Every vessel must maintain a proper lookout and always proceed at a safe speed so that she can take proper and effective action to avoid collision. To determine safe speed, consider such things as the state of visibility; traffic density, including concentration of fishing vessels, etc.; background lights (at night); the state of wind, sea and current; the proximity of navigational hazards; the vessel's draft in relation to the available depth of water; and any other factors that may apply (availability of radar, etc.).

Every vessel must use all available means to determine if risk of collision exists. Such a risk exists if the relative bearing of an approaching vessel does not change appreciably. Therefore, if the direction to an approaching vessel stays the same, or nearly so, as the vessel gets closer, there will be a collision unless someone takes positive action. For example, if you sight a vessel directly over a cleat or in line with a radio antenna on your boat, and the vessel's position with respect to the cleat or antenna doesn't change, but the vessel keeps getting closer, it is in danger of collision with your vessel. Mariners call this a "constant bearing and decreasing range," and recognize it as critical to their vessels' safety.

When you take action to avoid collision, any alteration of course or speed you make should be large enough (at least a 60° change in course) to be readily apparent to another vessel. Avoid small alterations of course and speed; it is difficult to detect them from a distance and the other skipper might misunderstand, a situation which is dangerous.

International and Inland Rules differ slightly on the subject of Narrow Channels (overtaking sound signals, and downbound right-of-way — Inland). Both sets of rules state that vessels proceeding along a narrow channel or fairway must keep to the starboard side of the channel. Vessels of less than 20 meters in length or sailing vessels, which might otherwise have the "right-of-way", must not impede the passage of a vessel which can safely navigate only within a narrow channel or fairway. No vessel may cross a narrow channel or fairway if doing so impedes the passage of a vessel which can safely navigate only within that channel or fairway. All vessels must avoid anchoring in narrow channels, if circumstances permit.

Another difference between Inland and International Rules has to do with vessels operating in a current. Under the Inland Rules a power-driven vessel on the Great Lakes, Western Rivers, or other specified waters and proceeding downbound with the current has the "right-of-way" over a vessel traveling against the current. This is because downbound vessels are carried along by the current and have less control than vessels which are making their way against the current. The downbound vessel shall propose the manner of passage and must initiate the exchange of whistle signals prescribed by the Navigation Rules.

**Traffic Separation Schemes**
Traffic Separation schemes are covered under Rule 10 of the 72 COLREGS. A vessel of less than 20 meters in length or a sailing vessel must not impede the safe passage of a power-driven vessel following a traffic lane.

**Vessel Traffic Services**
Vessel Traffic Services (VTS) have been established in the ports of New York, New Orleans, Houston/Galveston, San Francisco, Valdez, and in Puget Sound and its approaches. Some Canadian waters used frequently by American yachts also

operate VTS's, most notably on the St. Lawrence River and in Vancouver, B.C.

Other Vessel Traffic Services are located at St. Mary's River, Michigan; Berwick Bay, Louisiana; and Louisville, Kentucky.

Vessel Traffic Services have been established by the Coast Guard to reduce danger of collision in certain areas where ship traffic is heavy. VTS consists of one or more of three distinct components, depending on the area: (1) all have a Vessel Movement Reporting System (communications); (2) some have a Traffic Separation Scheme (TSS); and (3) some have Radar and/or Closed Circuit Television (CCTV) Monitoring (surveillance) of selected areas.

"Each vessel required by regulation to participate in a vessel traffic service shall comply with the applicable regulations," says Rule 10 in the first statement ever in any rule dealing with vessel traffic services. It would be unusual to find pleasure craft participating in a vessel traffic service; it is most important, however, to understand the Coast Guard's system for monitoring ship traffic.

If you are sailing in waters where there is a VTS you must learn its location and be able to recognize the buoys marking a traffic separation scheme, if any. You should never travel the "wrong way" in any one-way lane or anchor in a traffic lane. If you must cross a lane, do so at right angles to it. Realize that you are sailing where a ship is most likely to pass.

It is a good idea to listen to the radio communications between ships in the system and the Coast Guard's Vessel Traffic Communications Center for information about any ship in your proximity. VTS does not normally invite radio communications from pleasure boats except in cases of distress or emergency. **Any contact with the Coast Guard is normally made on Channel 16.** (See Chapter 12, Radiotelephone.)

# TABLE 7-I. VTS COMMUNICATIONS CHANNELS

| VTS LOCATION | VHF CHANNELS | | | | | | | | | |
|---|---|---|---|---|---|---|---|---|---|---|
| | 5 | 6 | 11 | 12 | 13* | 14 | 16 | 18 | 22 | 67* |
| HOUSTON/ GALVESTON ⓐ | | | ♦ | ♦ | ● | | ● | | | |
| NEW ORLEANS ⓑ | | | ♦ | ♦ | | ♦ | ● | | | ● |
| NEW YORK | | | | ♦ | ● | ♦ | ● | | | |
| SAN FRANCISCO ⓒ | | | | | ♦ | ♦ | ● | | | |
| PUGET SOUND | | | | | ● | ♦ | ● | | | |
| VALDEZ | | | | | | ♦ | ● | | | |

*Channel 13 is the Bridge-to-Bridge frequency in all areas except New Orleans and the Intracoastal Waterway, which use Channel 67.

LEGEND
♦ = VTS WORKING FREQUENCY
● = VTS-MONITORED FREQUENCY

Notes:   ⓐ   Houston, Channel 11, Galveston, Channel 12, boundary of separation, Exxon Baytown.

⓫   ⓑ   Channel 12: Southwest Pass to mile 75.5, Above Head of Pass (AHP); Mississippi River Gulf Outlet (MRGO) to mile 50.7 MRGO; and mile 113.0 AHP to mile 159.5 AHP. Channel 11: mile 75.5 AHP to mile 113.0 AHP; and light "114" to mile 60.0 MRGO and westerly along GIWW and IHNC. Channel 14: mile 159.5 AHP to mile 242.4 AHP.

ⓒ   Channel 12: Offshore approaches to Large Navigational Buoy. Channel 13: Remainder of VTS area.

## Conduct of Vessels in Sight of One Another — Sound and Light Signals

There are three situations which involve risk of collision: overtaking, meeting head-on, and crossing. The rules for head-on and crossing situations are different for power-driven vessels and sailing vessels, as will be discussed later. Two important definitions must now be understood. In the above situations, one vessel will be the "stand-on" vessel; and one will be the "give-way" vessel. The rules point out which is the stand-on vessel and which is the give-way vessel in each encounter.

When one of two vessels is to keep out of the way, the other, the stand-on vessel, must maintain course and speed; but the stand-on vessel must take avoiding action as soon as it becomes apparent that the vessel required to give way is not taking appropriate action. All vessels are required to take whatever action is necessary to avoid collision.

If the give-way vessel does not take appropriate action, however, the stand-on vessel must take avoiding action as soon as it becomes apparent that the vessel required to give way is not doing so.

The give-way vessel must, under the rules, take whatever action necessary to keep well clear, and do so early and obviously. If a collision occurs, it is not enough to say that you followed the rule, for the rule requires that you take whatever action necessary to avoid a collision. This means that if the give-way vessel fails to act appropriately, the stand-on vessel may actually be required to violate the rules, if that is what it takes to avoid a collision.

## Inland and International Rules for Sailing Vessels

When two sailing vessels are approaching one another so as to involve risk of collision, one of them shall keep out of the way of the other as follows:
1. When each has the wind on a different side, the vessel which has the wind on the port side shall keep out of the way of the other. (See Fig. 7-2.)
2. When both have the wind on the same side, the vessel which is to windward

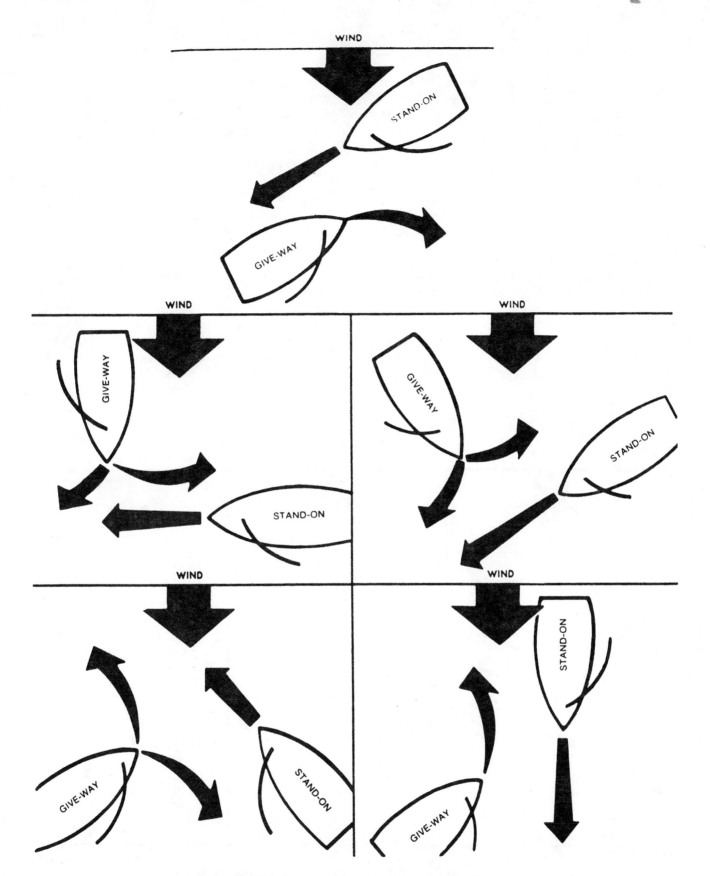

**Fig. 7-2 International and Inland Rules for Sailing Vessels**
(Wind on Different Sides – Boat with Wind on Port Side Gives Way)

shall keep out of the way of the vessel which is to leeward. (See Fig. 7-3.)

3. If a vessel with the wind on the port side sees a vessel to windward and cannot determine with certainty whether the other vessel has the wind on the port or on the starboard side, she shall keep out of the way of the other.

4. For the purposes of these rules the windward side shall be deemed to be the side opposite to that on which the mainsail is carried. On square-rigged vessels, it shall be deemed to be the side opposite to that on which the largest fore-and-aft sail is carried.

The following simplified "pecking order" may be used as a memory aid. Any vessel in the list is stand on to any vessel below it on the list.

1. Overtaken Vessel (top priority).
2. Vessel not under command.
3. Vessel restricted in its ability to maneuver.
4. Vessel constrained by its draft.
5. Fishing vessel (fishing or trawling, but not trolling).
6. Sailing vessel.
7. Power-driven vessel.

## Sound Signals — General Principles

Sound signals described in both sets of rules are normally made by whistles and bells (and sometimes gongs). Historically, power-driven vessels were "steam vessels" with steam whistles. Sailing vessels, of course, did not have steam whistles, consequently there are no maneuvering whistle signals for sailing vessels. There are, however, sound signals for all vessels, whether underway or at anchor, in or near areas of restricted visibility.

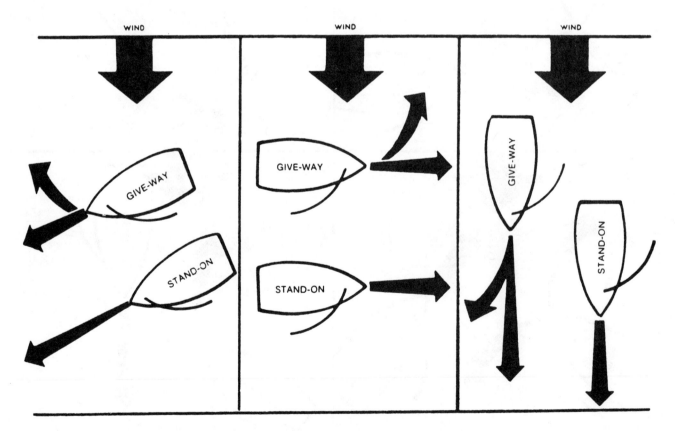

**Fig. 7-3 International and Inland Rules for Sailing Vessels (Wind on Same Side - Windward Gives Way to Leeward)**

The term short blast means a blast of one second duration.

The term prolonged blast means a blast of 4 to 6 seconds.

A vessel 12 meters or more in length must be provided with a whistle and a bell, and a vessel of 100 meters or more in length shall, in addition, be provided with a gong. A vessel of less than 12 meters in length is not obliged to carry such sound signaling appliances but must be provided with some other means of making an efficient sound signal. [Note that these are requirements of the Navigation Rules and that other rules may apply. Vessels under 12 meters in length are required to have a whistle (horn) under Federal equipment requirements. (See Chapter 4.)]

Rules governing sound signals for maneuvering are different under each set of rules. Sound signals under the 72 COLREGS for head-on, crossing and overtaking (except in narrow channels) situations are signals of action. Only the vessel actually altering course sounds a signal and the vessel not altering course does not answer. Sound signals under the Inland Rules for head-on, crossing and overtaking situations are signals of intent; one vessel signals intended action and the other responds.

## Maneuvering and Warning Signals — Danger/Doubt Signal — Both International and Inland Rules

When vessels in sight of one another are approaching each other and for any reason either vessel fails to understand the intentions or actions of the other, the vessel in doubt must immediately signal his doubt by giving five or more short and rapid blasts on the whistle. The doubt signal is sometimes called the danger signal, and it may be used to announce danger whenever necessary.

## Maneuvering and Warning Signals Under the International Rules:
- one short blast means, "I am altering my course to starboard."
- two short blasts mean, "I am altering my course to port."
- three short blasts mean, "I am operating astern propulsion."

These signals are sounded only when the action is being taken.

## Maneuvering and Warning Signals Under the Inland Rules:
- one short blast means, "I intend to leave you on my port side."
- two short blasts mean, "I intend to leave you on my starboard side."
- three short blasts mean, "I am operating astern propulsion."

Under the Inland Rules, the vessel hearing the signal of the other vessel must, if in agreement, sound the same whistle signal and take steps to effect a safe passing. "Cross signals" are not permitted under the rules. (Two blasts are never answered with one blast, for example.) If in disagreement or doubt, the only allowed response is the doubt signal (5 or more short and rapid blasts).

## The Overtaking Situation

Any vessel overtaking any other must keep out of the way of the vessel being overtaken. (Notice that this includes sailboats which are overtaking.) (See Fig. 7-4.)

A vessel is deemed to be overtaking when coming up with another vessel from a direction more than 22.5 degrees abaft (behind) her beam. At night only the sternlight of a vessel being overtaken would be visible and neither of the sidelights would be seen. If in doubt about whether it is an overtaking situation, the vessel should assume that it is and act accordingly.

The International Rules, in effect, give consideration to two types of overtaking, according to whether (1) maneuvering in a narrow channel or fairway (as explained below); or (2) maneuvering elsewhere (when the usual signals of action explained above are used).

Under the International Rules vessels in

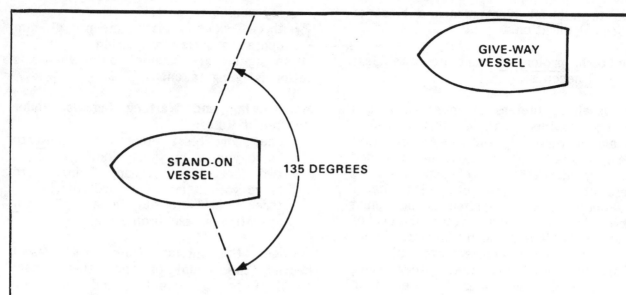

**Fig 7-4 Overtaking Situation Under International Rules (All Vessels)**

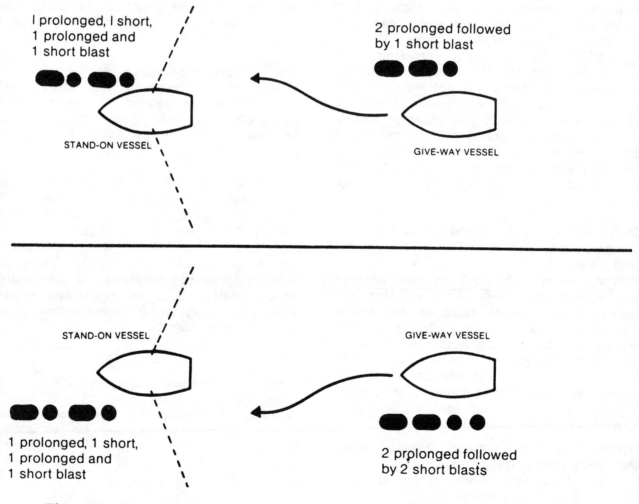

**Fig. 7-5 Overtaking Situation Under International Rules, Narrow Channels.**

sight of one another in a narrow channel or fairway must use these signals in the overtaking situation whenever the vessel ahead must take action to permit safe passing. (See Fig. 7-5.)

A vessel overtaking indicates intention by the following whistle signals:
- two prolonged blasts followed by one short blast to mean, "I intend to overtake you on your starboard side."
- two prolonged blasts followed by two short blasts to mean, "I intend to overtake you on your port side."

The two prolonged blasts, in both cases, serve as a preliminary "wake-up" signal to the vessel being overtaken.

The vessel about to be overtaken indicates agreement by:

one prolonged, one short, one prolonged and one short blast, in that order (Morse code "C").

When either vessel fails to understand the intentions of the other, or doubts whether sufficient action is being taken by the other to avoid collision, or the overtaken vessel deems the overtaking action to be unsafe, the vessel in doubt must give the doubt (danger) signal.

Under the Inland Rules, a power-driven vessel intending to overtake another power-driven vessel indicates intention by whistle signals (see Fig. 4-6):
- one short blast means, "I intend to overtake you on your starboard side."
- two short blasts mean, "I intend to overtake you on your port side."

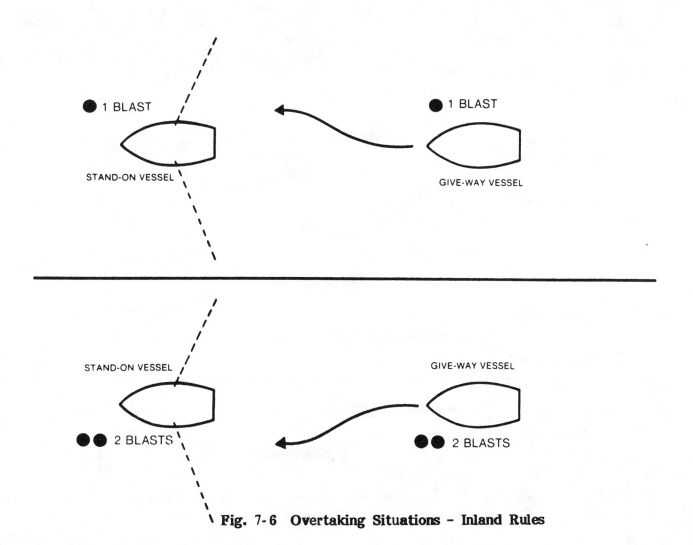

**Fig. 7-6 Overtaking Situations - Inland Rules**

7-9

The power-driven vessel about to be overtaken shall, if in agreement, sound a similar signal or, if in doubt, sound the danger signal (at least five short and rapid blasts on the whistle).

Vessels being overtaken may be passed on either side, as long as all concerned understand what is being planned and agree to it.

### The Head-on (Meeting) Situation

Vessels which approach one another on a reciprocal (opposite) or near-reciprocal course are said to be meeting, or head-on. At night it is considered to be a head-on situation when a vessel sees the other vessel's (white) masthead lights in a line or nearly in a line or sees both (red and green) sidelights simultaneously. It may not be so easy to be certain of a reciprocal course in daylight.

If there is any doubt whether a head-on situation exists, assume that it does exist and act accordingly.

A small vessel running in a heavy chop or ground swell will often yaw (move from side to side, off course). Occasionally its red light will be visible; then both red and green will be seen; and then only the green light will be seen. When you observe this sequence of light changes you must assume you have a head-on situation.

The International and Inland Rules for maneuvering in a meeting situation are identical in wording, but the whistle signals are different. See Figures 7-7 and 7-8.

Each vessel in a meeting situation must alter course to starboard so that each will pass on the port side of the other. (Note that if danger of collision exists, a port-to-port passage is required.) Neither vessel has the "right-of-way" in a meeting situation, and both are equally responsible for avoiding collision.

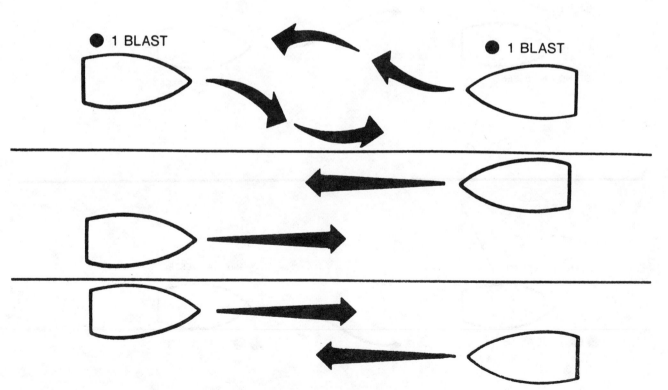

Fig. 7-7  Meeting Under International Rules (Power-driven Vessels)
Neither Vessel Has The Right-Of-Way

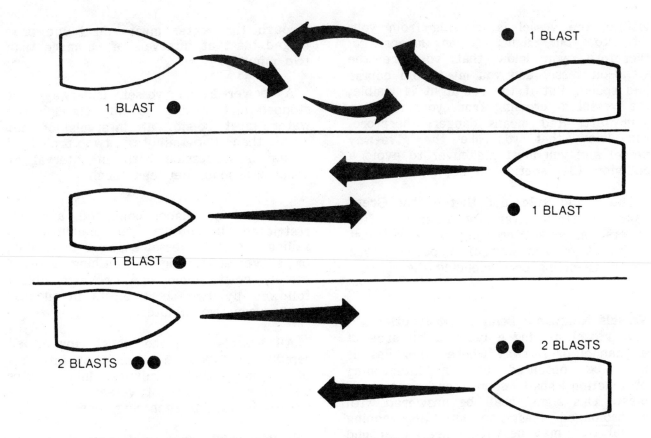

Fig. 7-8 Meeting Sound Signals for Power-driven Vessels Under Inland Rules

## The Crossing Situation

Both International and Inland Rules state that when two power-driven vessels are crossing so as to involve risk of collision, the vessel which has the other on her starboard side must keep out of the way and, if circumstances permit, cross behind the other vessel. See Fig. 7-9.

At times there may be some doubt whether the situation is a crossing or a head-on meeting. In case of doubt, you should assume that it is a meeting situation, in which neither vessel has a clear-cut "right-of-way", and each must act to avoid the other.

At night when it is difficult to see vessels and know their speed and direction, their lights convey important information. It is a crossing situation when only one of the other vessel's colored lights is visible. If the green light is

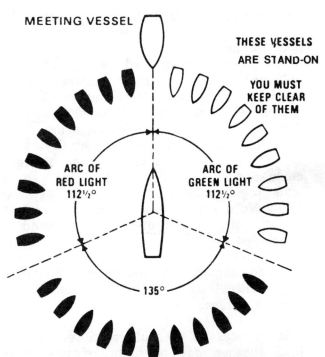

Fig. 7-9 Stand-on and Give-way in a Crossing Situation (Power-driven Vessels)

visible, the vessel is crossing from your left to your right. Green means go; therefore, you know that you are the stand-on vessel and you must hold course and speed. But if the red light is visible, the vessel is crossing from your right to your left. Red means danger; therefore, you know that you are the give-way vessel and you must maneuver to avoid a collision. (See section on Lights, below.)

The Inland Rules add that on the Great Lakes, Western Rivers, or other specified waters, a vessel crossing a river must keep out of the way of a power-driven vessel ascending or descending the river.

### Vessels Nearing a Bend or Obstruction

A vessel nearing a bend or an area of a channel or fairway where other vessels may be obscured by an intervening obstruction shall sound one prolonged blast. This signal shall be answered with a prolonged blast by any approaching vessel that may be within hearing around the bend or behind the intervening obstruction. (International and Inland Rules)

### Conduct of Vessels in Restricted Visibility

### Sound Signals

The term "restricted visibility" was defined earlier in this chapter. It is important to realize that this section of the rules applies to all vessels not in sight of each other when navigating in or near an area of restricted visibility. Why "near"? Because a vessel in broad daylight could be surprised by a large ship's emerging suddenly from a nearby fog bank. Note - the sound signals for vessels within sight of each other are not used in restricted visibility.

Sound Signals in Restricted Visibility are identical under both Inland and International Rules.

In or near an area of restricted visibility, whether day or night, signals must be used as follows:

A power-driven vessel making way through the water must sound one prolonged blast at intervals of no more than two minutes.

A power-driven vessel underway but stopped and making no way through the water must sound, at intervals of not more than two minutes, two prolonged blasts in succession with an interval of about 2 seconds between them.

A vessel not under command, a vessel restricted in ability to maneuver, a sailing vessel, a vessel engaged in fishing, or a vessel towing or pushing another vessel, must sound one prolonged blast followed by two short blasts in succession, every two minutes.

All vessels at anchor must ring a bell rapidly for about 5 seconds at intervals of not more than 1 minute. (Inland Rules do not require this of vessels 20 meters or less in special anchoring areas.)

It is helpful for a small boat skipper to know that a vessel of 100 meters or more in length sounds a bell in the forepart of the vessel and, immediately following this, sounds a gong in the after part of the vessel.

A vessel at anchor may, in addition, sound one short, one prolonged and one short blast in succession to give warning to an approaching vessel of her position and of the possibility of collision.

A vessel aground must give the bell signal (and, if required, the gong signal) given by a vessel at anchor, and in addition, give three separate and distinct strokes on the bell immediately before and after the rapid ringing of the bell.

A vessel of less than 12 meters in length is not obliged to give the above-mentioned signals but, if she does not give them, she is obliged to make some other efficient sound signal at intervals of not more than 2 minutes.

It's important to understand the signals which are used when visibility is restrict-

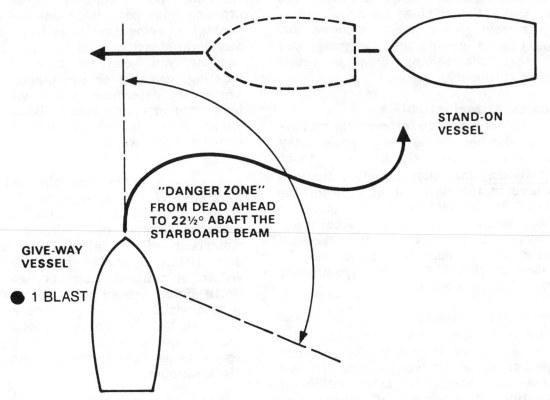

STAND-ON VESSEL

"DANGER ZONE" FROM DEAD AHEAD TO 22½° ABAFT THE STARBOARD BEAM

GIVE-WAY VESSEL

● 1 BLAST

Fig. 7-10   Crossing Situation Under International Rules (Power-driven Vessels)

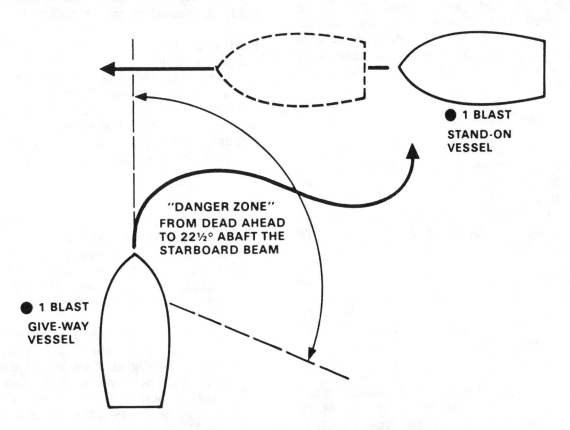

● 1 BLAST
STAND-ON VESSEL

"DANGER ZONE" FROM DEAD AHEAD TO 22½° ABAFT THE STARBOARD BEAM

● 1 BLAST
GIVE-WAY VESSEL

Fig. 7-11   Crossing Situation Under Inland Rules (Power-driven Vessels Passing Port To Port)

ed. If you hear a whistle or horn, you know that it's coming from a vessel which is moving or is about to move. But if you hear a vessel's bell or gong, you know that it's coming from a vessel which is stationary.

## Signals to Attract Attention

If it is necessary to attract the attention of another vessel, any vessel may make light or sound signals that <u>cannot be mistaken</u> for any signal authorized elsewhere in the rules, or may direct the beam of her searchlight in the direction of the danger. One should take care, however, not to blind another vessel's operator by shining the light at the steering station. This is specifically prohibited by the rules.

## Radar-equipped Vessels

There is a special provision in the rules for the vessel which detects the presence of another vessel by radar alone. The law requires this vessel to take action in ample time if a change of course becomes necessary. If the other vessel is forward of the beam (and not being overtaken) the change of course should not be to port. If the other vessel is abeam or abaft the beam, the change of course should not be toward the other vessel.

## Lights and Shapes

The rules concerning lights apply from sunset to sunrise in all weathers and in periods of restricted visibility. When navigation lights are on, no other lights may be shown if they can be confused with navigation lights or if they interfere with the keeping of a proper lookout.

Lights on a boat (with the obvious exception of a searchlight) are different from those on an automobile. They are not designed to assist you in seeing ahead of the boat. Boat lights are made to be seen.

By observing the lights on another boat at night you can determine if the other boat is headed directly for you (meeting

head-on, both colored lights visible), crossing your path (only one colored light visible) or being overtaken (only the white sternlight visible). This is important because you need to know if you are meeting, crossing or overtaking the other vessel to determine which vessel is to hold course and speed (stand-on) and which vessel is to maneuver to avoid a collision (give-way).

A vessel's lights may also help you to determine if the other vessel is a power-driven vessel or a sailing vessel. A properly lighted power-driven vessel or motorboat will have at least one white light visible whenever a colored light is visible. A sailboat, however, will have no white lights visible when a colored light is also visible. So, if you see a red light or green light on another vessel at night, and you see no white light, and it's not a vessel being towed, the chances are that it's a sailboat.

## Specifications of Lights

Following are the specifications of lights discussed in this chapter:

## Masthead Light

a white light,
placed over the fore and aft centerline,
showing an unbroken light,
over an arc of the horizon 225 degrees so as to show the light,
from right ahead to 22.5 degrees abaft (behind) the beam on either side of the boat.

## Sidelights

a green light on the starboard side,
a red light on the port side,
each showing an unbroken arc of light,
over an arc of the horizon of 112.5 degrees so as to show the light from right ahead to 22.5 degrees abaft the beam,
on the respective side of the boat.
(On boats less than 20 meters in length, sidelights may be combined in one lantern. When combined, they must be placed as nearly as practicable to the boat's fore and aft centerline.)

**Sternlight**
a white light,
at the stern,
showing an unbroken light,
over an arc of the horizon of 135 degrees,
so as to show the light 67.5 degrees from right aft on each side of the boat.

**Towing light**
a yellow light with the same characteristics as the sternlight.

**All-round light**
a white light showing in an unbroken arc of 360 degrees.

**Flashing light**
a light flashing at regular intervals of 120 or more flashes per minute.

**Special flashing light (Inland Rules)**
a yellow light,
flashing at regular intervals,
of 50 to 70 flashes per minute,
placed forward on the fore and aft centerline of a tow,
showing an unbroken arc of the horizon of not less than 180 nor more than 225 degrees,
to show from right ahead,
to abeam and no more than 22.5 degrees abaft the beam,
on either side of the vessel.

The positioning and technical details of lights and shapes are in Annex I of each set of Rules. Technical data are not within the scope of this course.

The intensity of prescribed lights must be such that they be visible from the minimum distances in nautical miles as shown in Fig. 7-12.

Lights must be exhibited from sunset to sunrise and otherwise in restricted visibility.

| LIGHT TYPE | VISIBILITY MIN DISTANCE — MILES | | | |
|---|---|---|---|---|
| | 1 | 2 | 3 | 5 |
| MASTHEAD | | ● | ▲ | ◆ |
| SIDE | ● | ▲◆ | | |
| STERN | | ●▲◆ | | |
| ALL-ROUND | | ●▲◆ | | |
| TOWING | | ●▲◆ | | |
| SPECIAL FLASHING (Inland Rules Only) | | ●▲◆ | | |

**VESSEL LENGTH**
● Less than 12 Meters
▲ 12 Meters but Less than 20 Meters
◆ 20 Meters but Less than 50 Meters

**Fig. 7-12 Light Visibility Required**

**Lights for Sailing Vessels Under Sail Only and Vessels Under Oars**
Lights for sailing vessels are the same under both sets of rules.

A sailing vessel must exhibit sidelights and a sternlight.

However, a sailing vessel less than 20 meters in length may combine the sidelights and sternlight in one lantern carried at or near the top of the mast where it can best be seen. This light cannot be used under power or sail and power; regular sidelights and forward-looking white lights must be fitted for use in such circumstances.

A sailing vessel underway may, in addition to the sidelights and sternlight, exhibit at or near the top of the mast, where best seen, two all-round lights in a vertical line, the upper red, the lower green; these may not be used in conjunction with the combined three-color lantern described in the preceding paragraph.

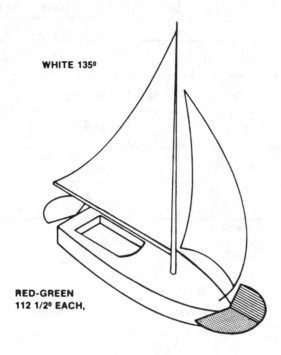

WHITE 135°

RED-GREEN
112 1/2° EACH,

Fig. 7-13    Sailing Vessel Under 20
Meters in Length, Inland and
International Rules (Option 1)

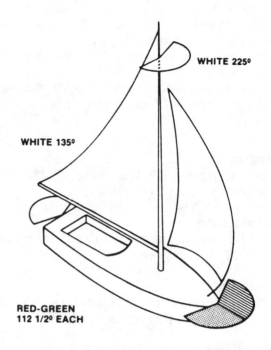

WHITE 225°

WHITE 135°

RED-GREEN
112 1/2° EACH

Fig. 7-14    Auxiliaries Under 20 Meters
in Length Using Both Sail and
Power, Inland and
International Rules (Option 1)

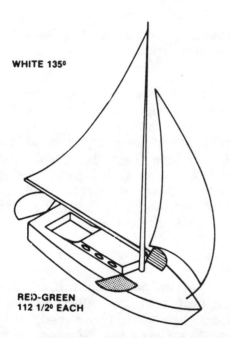

WHITE 135°

RED-GREEN
112 1/2° EACH

Fig. 7-15    Sailing Vessel Under 20
Meters in Length, Inland and
International Rules (Option 2)

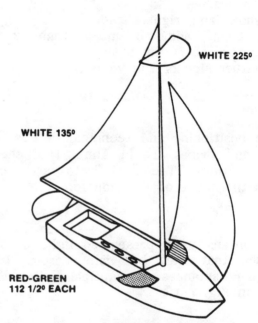

WHITE 225°

WHITE 135°

RED-GREEN
112 1/2° EACH

Fig. 7-16    Auxiliaries Under 20 Meters
in Length Using Both Sail and
Power, Inland and
International Rules (Option 2)

A sailing vessel less than 7 meters in length must, if practicable, exhibit sidelights and a sternlight, but if she does not, must have ready at hand an electric torch or lighted lantern showing a white light to be exhibited soon enough to prevent collision.

A vessel under oars may exhibit the lights described for sailing vessels.

A reminder — sailboats with propulsion machinery in use must comply with the requirements for power-driven vessels.

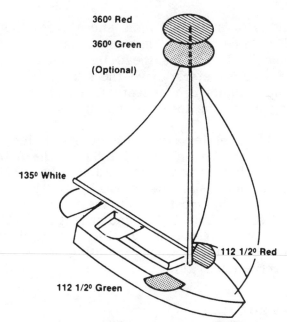

Fig. 7-18    Optional Sailboat Light Configuration, Inland and International Rules. Side Lights may be combined if desired.

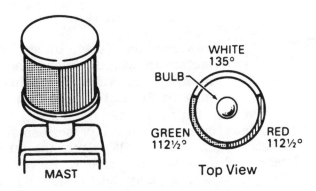

Fig. 7-17    Combination Tri-Color Light for Sailboats Under 20 Meters, Inland and International Rules

## Lights for Power-Driven Vessels Underway

The lighting configuration on a power-driven vessel depends on its length, its area of operation, and, in some cases, its date of construction.

Lighting configurations described in the International Rules differ slightly from those described in the Inland Rules. However, lights in accordance with the International Rules are acceptable in all waters of the United States.

Navigation lights may appear to be complex because of the many different configurations used. However, you will find that only one or two of the possible configurations are applicable to your vessel.

**Lights for power-driven vessels less than 20 meters in length, operating under the International Rules:**

When operating under the International Rules, a power-driven vessel less than 20 meters in length must carry side lights, a masthead light and a stern light. The side lights may be separate or combined. If the vessel is 12 meters or more in length, its masthead light must be at least 2.5 meters above the gunwale. If the vessel is less than 12 meters in length, its masthead light must be at least one meter above the side lights.

A vessel less than 12 meters in length may carry an all-round light instead of the masthead light and the stern light. (This all-round light would best be placed in the after part of the vessel.)

**Lights for power-driven vessels, less than 20 meters in length, operating under the Inland Rules:**

Power-driven vessels less than 20 meters in length built on or after December 24, 1980, and operating under the Inland Navigational Rules must carry side lights, a masthead light and a stern light. The side lights may be separate or combined. The masthead light must be at least 2.5 meters above the gunwale. Note: These lights are acceptable when operating under the International Rules.

A vessel less than 12 meters in length may carry an all-round light in the after part of the vessel instead of the masthead light and the stern light. The all-round light must be at least one meter above the side lights and may be off the centerline if necessary. Note: These lights are acceptable when operating under the International Rules.

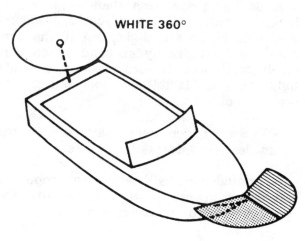

Fig. 7-21   Power-driven Vessel Under 12 Meters in Length, Inland and International Rules. Sidelights may be Separate if Desired

A vessel built before December 24, 1980, may carry the lights prescribed for vessels which were built after the new Inland Rules came into effect. However, if it does not, it may carry side lights and an all-round light which is located in the after part of the vessel. The side lights may be separate or combined. Please note, however, that the use of side lights and an all-round light on a vessel 12 meters or more in length is not acceptable under the International Rules.

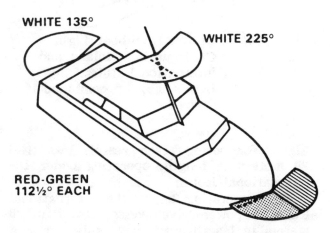

Fig.  7-19   Power-driven Vessel Under 20 Meters in Length, Inland and International Rules (Option 1)

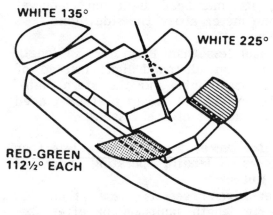

Fig.  7-20   Power-driven Vessel Under 20 Meters in Length, Inland and International Rules (Option 2)

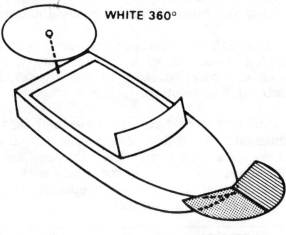

Fig.  7-22   Power-driven Vessel Under 20 Meters in Length and Built Before Dec. 24, 1980. Inland Rules (Option 1)

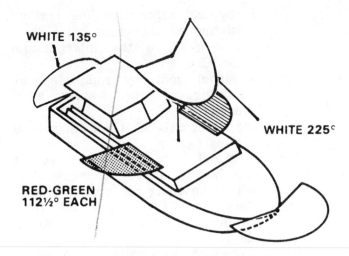

WHITE 135°

WHITE 225°

RED-GREEN 112½° EACH

**Fig. 7-23    Power-driven Vessel Under 20 Meters in Length Inland Rules (Option 2)**

The use of a masthead light forward and an all-round light aft is permitted only on the Great Lakes. Therefore, those vessels from 26 feet to 65 feet in length which display lights acceptable under the old Motorboat Act (sidelights, 225-degree white bow lights and all-round white lights), must extinguish their bow lights or convert their all-round lights to sternlights in order to comply with the new rules. However, no changes are necessary if the vessels are operating on the Great Lakes.

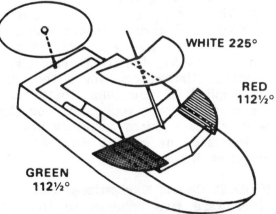

WHITE 360°

WHITE 225°

RED 112½°

GREEN 112½°

**Fig. 7-24    Power-driven Vessel, Inland Rules Optional on Great Lakes only.**

## Fishing Vessels — Lights and Shapes

A fishing vessel underway must display (in addition to the side lights and stern light for sailing and power-driven vessels described above):

Fishing vessel trawling (dragging): 2 all-round lights in a vertical line, upper green, lower white.

Fishing vessel other than trawling (but not trolling): 2 all-round lights in a vertical line, upper red, lower white.

A fishing vessel within the meaning of the Navigation Rules must display, in addition to the lights prescribed in the Rules, a shape consisting of two black cones in a vertical line, one above the other, point to point. A vessel of less than 20 meters may display a basket instead. (International and Inland Rules.)

## Other Lights — Special Vessels

Here are some other lights you should recognize. These lights are shown in addition to the sidelights and sternlight for sailing and power-driven vessels described above if underway:

Power driven vessel towing astern: 2 masthead lights (in a vertical line) instead of one (3 if tow exceeds 200 meters), plus a yellow towing light above the sternlight.

Vessel restricted in its ability to maneuver: 3 lights vertically, red-white-red, plus masthead light or anchor light as appropriate.

Vessel not under command: 2 all-round red lights in a vertical line.

Vessel constrained by her draft (72 COLREGS only): 3 all-round red lights in a vertical line.

Pilot vessel (pilot aboard): a white all-round light over a red all-round light, displayed in a vertical line.

Law enforcement vessel engaged in necessary duties: a flashing blue light.

## Anchor Lights, Inland and International Rules

An anchored vessel less than 50 meters in length must display one all-round light where it can best be seen. In daytime, a black ball must be displayed instead.

A vessel less than 7 meters in length at anchor, not in or near a narrow channel, fairway, anchorage, or where other vessels normally navigate, is not required to display anchor lights.

Under the Inland Rules, a vessel less than 20 meters in length anchored in a specially designated anchorage area is not required to display an anchor light. A list of specially designated anchorage areas appears in Title 33, Code of Federal Regulations, Part 110.

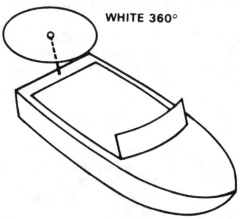

**WHITE 360°**

**Fig. 7-25    Vessel at Anchor**

## Distress Signals

When a vessel is in distress and requires assistance, signals to be used or exhibited are listed in the Annex IV of each set of Rules.

These signals include:
(a)  A gun or other explosive signal fired at intervals of about a minute;
(b)  A continuous sounding with any fog-signaling apparatus;
(c)  Rockets or shells, throwing red stars one at a time at short intervals;
(d)  A signal made by radiotelegraphy or by any other signaling method consisting of the group . . . - - - . . . (SOS in the International Morse Code);
(e)  A signal sent by radiotelephony consisting of the spoken word "Mayday";
(f)  The International Code Signal of distress (N.C.);
(g)  A signal consisting of a square flag having above or below it a ball or anything resembling a ball;
(h)  Flames on the vessel (as from burning tar barrel, oil barrel, etc.);
(i)  A rocket parachute flare or a hand flare showing a red light;
(j)  A smoke signal giving off orange-colored smoke;
(k)  Slowly and repeatedly raising and lowering arms outstretched to each side;
(l)  The radiotelegraph alarm signal;
(m)  The radiotelephone alarm signal;
(n)  Signals transmitted by emergency position-indicating radio beacons;
(o)  A high intensity white light flashing at regular intervals from 50 to 70 times per minute (Inland Rules only).

## Exemptions (Inland Rules)

Many boats carry lights in conformity with the Rules which were superseded by the Inland Navigational Rules Act of 1980. Therefore, many (not all) boats of less than 20 meters in length whose keel was laid before December 24, 1980, are permanently exempted from being changed if used in the waters where the former rules applied. If you think these exemptions may apply to your boat, you should ask your Coast Guard Auxiliary Instructor for assistance or consult Rule 38 of the Navigation Rules.

## ANNEXES (Inland Navigational Rules)

There are five annexes to the Inland Navigational Rules Act of 1980. Annexes I through III contain technical information. Annex IV and Annex V contain new requirements as follows:

ANNEX IV adds to the list of DISTRESS SIGNALS a high intensity white light flashing at intervals from 50 to 70 times per minute.

ANNEX V (Pilot Rules) requires the operator of each self-propelled vessel 12 meters or more in length to carry on board and maintain for ready reference a copy of the Inland Navigational Rules.

## PENALTIES (Inland Navigational Rules)

Whoever operates a vessel in violation of the Inland Navigational Rules Act of 1980 is liable to a civil penalty of not more than $5000 for each violation. (Notice that the operator, not the owner, is named responsible if they are not one and the same. It follows that an operator chartering a boat is held liable under the law, not the chartering firm which owns the boat.)

## International Rules' Requirements Legal Where Inland Rules Apply

All vessels complying with the construction and equipment requirements of the International Regulations are considered to be in compliance with the Inland Rules.

## A Final Note

Certain things should be noted because they are not mentioned in the Rules. Nothing in the Rules ever imposes a requirement to place your own vessel in danger. If any action called for under the Rules seems to do so, remember that the Responsibility Rule provides for a departure from the Rules to avoid immediate danger. In such circumstances you would have to decide whether the danger/doubt signal and/or a course change would be appropriate.

# Chapter 8

# Marlinspike Seamanship

## Introduction

Marlinspike seamanship is the art of handling and working all kinds of fiber, synthetic and wire rope. It includes every variety of knotting, splicing, worming, parceling, serving and fancywork. The term originates from the name of a tapered metal tool, a marlinspike, that is used in working rope, especially for splicing. In this chapter the term marlinspike seamanship is expanded to include not only handling and working rope, but also the composition, use, care and selection of various types of rope for specific uses, and the hardware associated with those uses.

The term "rope" is seldom used on a boat. Mariners generally refer to rope as "line," although in many cases rope is named for its specific use. For example, a stay is a rope (usually wire) that supports a mast; a sheet is a rope that controls a sail; an anchor line of any material is called a rode; and the line securing a dinghy is a painter. There are a few exceptions when a rope is still called a rope, such as bell ropes, boltropes and manropes, among others. However, to call a mariner's mooring lines "ropes" is to brand yourself as a landlubber.

## Rope Material

Natural fibers used may be of many types, such as Manila, sisal, hemp, jute, cotton or flax. Of the natural fibers, the best for all around use is Manila. It can be used for mooring lines, anchor lines and running rigging such as sheets to control sails and halyards to raise and lower sails. Manila is noted for its strength and durability with a minimum of stretch. Sisal is less expensive than Manila; so it is sometimes used as a substitute, although it is inferior in many ways. The other natural fibers are used mostly for small lines such as lead lines and flag halyards.

Unfortunately, all common natural fiber lines shrink when they get wet and will rot if stowed wet. They are also weaker, size for size, than rope manufactured from synthetic materials.

Today, most boat owners prefer rope made from synthetic materials that have good strength, both wet and dry, and resist water, mildew and rot. Nylon rope is the strongest, size for size, of the synthetic fiber ropes. It also resists chafe or rubbing very well. Nylon stretches more than other synthetic or natural fiber ropes without permanent damage to its fibers or construction. This feature can make nylon rope dangerous if it breaks under strain. Nylon rope can also shrink up to 10% of its length under some circumstances, but it does not shrink when wet, like Manila. It is best suited for use where stretch is a help. For example, the stretch in a nylon anchor rode will absorb surges that may otherwise pull the anchor loose. Nylon is also suitable for dock lines which do not need to be pulled taut.

Polyester fiber rope, sold under trade names such as Dacron or Terylene, is about 10% weaker than nylon rope, but not nearly as stretchy. It is acid and alkali resistant. Nylon and polyester lines look somewhat alike but polyester is easier and smoother to handle than nylon. Polyester line costs more than nylon. It is used for running rigging such as sheets and halyards which should not stretch under changing conditions. A polyester line under tension chafes easily and must be protected.

Polypropylene rope is the least costly of the common synthetic ropes. Its major advantage is that it floats. However, it deteriorates rapidly from sunlight and, under a load, its hard texture allows it to slip on cleats and to cut a person's hands. Polypropylene rope is most suited for use where its buoyancy is a major factor, such as for water-ski tow ropes. It is suitable as a dinghy painter, the line attached to a dinghy's bow, because it will not sink and foul the propeller of the boat towing the dinghy.

bing holds knots so well, it is frequently used as sail stops, which are ties used to hold a lowered sail to its boom.

## How Rope is Made and Measured

In the manufacture of fiber rope, fibers are twisted together in one direction to form yarns, and the yarns are twisted together in the opposite direction to form strands. The strands are then twisted together in the original direction to form the finished rope. The direction in which the strands are twisted is known as the lay of the rope. Rope is described as either right-laid or left-laid. Most laid line used on boats is made of three strands twisted clockwise in a right-hand lay as shown in Fig. 8-1.

Rope may also be braided, with the fibers interwoven individually or in three or four strands. Braided rope is smooth like clothesline and is easier on the hands

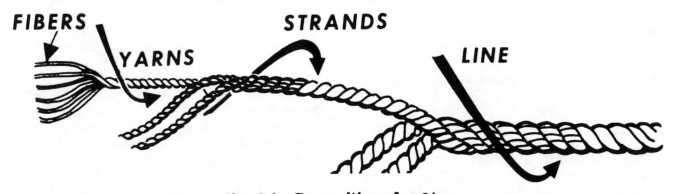

**FIBERS**  **YARNS**  **STRANDS**  **LINE**

Fig. 8-1  Composition of a Line

Other forms of flexible materials are also used on boats to serve the same purposes as rope. These include Shock cord, a multi-strand rubber line with a synthetic cover that can stretch up to twice its own length. It is used to hold things in place and to prevent halyards from slapping against the mast of a moored boat. Shock cord is often sold with hooks or eyes at each end to facilitate connections. It cannot be spliced. Webbing of woven nylon or polyester is very strong. It can be either single or double (two flat layers with a hollow center). Webbing can be used to tie down a dinghy on a larger boat or hold down a boat on a trailer. Because web-

than laid rope. Small sizes of single braided rope, up to 1/4 inch, are used for sail bag ties, flag halyards and similar special purposes. However, most synthetic braided rope used on boats is double-braid or two-in-one line. It is formed of an outer braided cover and a separate inner braided core as shown in Fig. 8-2. Double-braided rope is stronger than laid rope of the same size, in part because of the friction between the two layers. Single-braided rope is comparable in strength to the same size laid rope, but is more costly to make.

Fiber rope is correctly measured by its circumference (the distance around the rope). However, most marine suppliers measure it by its diameter, especially in smaller sizes. Most sailors also follow this practice. Small diameter fiber rope is known as <u>small stuff</u> and is designated by size according to the number of yarns it contains. Yarns are called threads when referring to small stuff. For example, six-thread small stuff is made up of six yarns of fiber twisted together. Small stuff is frequently used for whipping or wrapping the end of a larger piece of rope to prevent it from fraying.

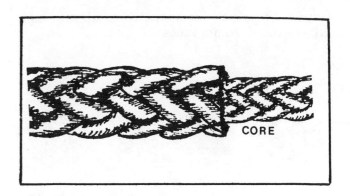

**Fig. 8-2  Braided Line.**

YACHTING ROPES – WEIGHT AND STRENGTH COMPARISON

| SIZE Diameter | NYLON (lbs) Weight per 100 ft | lbs Breaking Strength | "DACRON" (lbs) Weight per 100 ft | Lbs Breaking Strength | MANILA (lbs) Weight per 100 ft | Lbs Breaking Strength |
|---|---|---|---|---|---|---|
| ¼" | 1.7 | 1,750 | 2.2 | 1,300 | 2.0 | 600 |
| ⅜" | 3.5 | 3,200 | 4.5 | 2,850 | 4.0 | 1,350 |
| ½" | 6.6 | 6,600 | 7.6 | 4,900 | 6.1 | 2,650 |
| ⅝" | 10.5 | 10,200 | 12.4 | 7,800 | 13.1 | 4,400 |
| ¾" | 15.0 | 13,500 | 19.3 | 10,780 | 16.3 | 5,400 |
| ⅞" | 20.5 | 18,500 | 23.5 | 14,000 | 22.0 | 7,700 |
| 1" | 27.0 | 24,000 | 31.3 | 17,500 | 26.5 | 9,000 |
| 1⅛" | 34.5 | 32,000 | 40.4 | 23,500 | 35.2 | 12,000 |

**Table 8-1**

Steel wire is used where maximum strength and minimum stretch are vital, such as for standing or permanent rigging and halyards for hoisting sails. Wire for <u>standing rigging</u> is called <u>1x19</u> (spoken as "one by nineteen"), which means that it consists of 19 equal elements wound around each other. It is strong, but not particularly flexible. Wire rope for <u>running rigging</u> such as halyards is called <u>7x19</u> (seven elements, each composed of 19 individual strands) or <u>7x7</u> (seven strands, seven elements each). Running rigging wire rope is slightly weaker than standing rigging of the same diameter, but it is a great deal more flexible. Nearly all wire rope used on boats is made from stainless steel.

**Rope Selection**

You should purchase each line for its specific purpose. Strength; stretch; resistance to chafing, slipping and sunlight; buoyancy; handling ease and storage conditions are all considerations. Small lines may be suitable for securing small items,

but most people have trouble holding on to a loaded line smaller than about 3/8 inch diameter. You should choose larger-size lines for sheets, halyards and anchor lines for any but the smallest boats.

Other benefits from choosing a larger line include less stretch for an equal load and fewer turns required around a winch. Winches are used to supply a mechanical advantage for tightening running rigging and hauling in anchor lines. Larger lines offer more friction per turn around a winch.

Sailing gloves, which have palms but no fingers, are useful if you have to handle a rough line and have soft hands.

The disadvantage of a larger line is the cost, not only of the line itself, but also of the blocks or pulleys and cleats associated with the larger-line diameter. One way to determine the proper match between a fiber line and a block is to measure the block itself. The diameter of the sheave (pronounced "shiv") or pulley wheel, should be about twice the circumference of the line. The diameter of the block itself, measured along its longest axis, should be about three times the circumference of the line. For example, the circumference of 1/2-inch diameter fiber rope is 1-1/2 inches; therefore, the sheave diameter should be about 3 inches and the block diameter about 4-1/2 inches. If you want to replace an existing line that has been lost, you can reverse the procedure to find the size fiber line you should buy. Table 8-1 will give some idea of the comparative sizes and strength of some types of line.

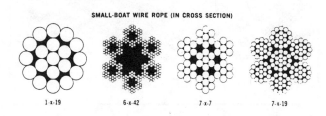

SMALL-BOAT WIRE ROPE (IN CROSS SECTION)

1-x-19    6-x-42    7-x-7    7-x-19

**Fig. 8-3   Wire Rope Has an Important Place in the Marine World.**

### Care of Fiber Line

Your efforts in caring for fiber line aboard your boat will be repaid in greater safety and longer line life. Proper care begins as soon as the rope is purchased. If a coil of new rope is opened without care, it can easily tangle and kink, forming "hockles." This makes handling the rope more difficult and can possibly weaken the fiber. There is a procedure you can follow that will avoid making kinks in the rope. If the rope is coiled, place the coil upright so that the end of the rope inside the hole in the coil is at the bottom of the hole. Take the end up through the hole and draw off the desired quantity of rope. Normally, synthetic rope is received on a reel and should be rolled off, not uncoiled. If these procedures are

**Uncoiling Fiber Rope**

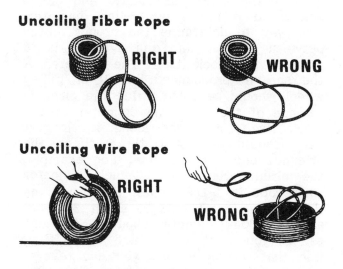

RIGHT          WRONG

**Uncoiling Wire Rope**

RIGHT          WRONG

**Fig. 8-4 Uncoiling Rope.**

not followed, there will be a kink in the rope for each turn taken off the coil or reel. Kinks should always be taken out of a rope whenever they occur. By putting a strain on the rope, a kink can be made to disappear but the rope will be badly weakened by the breaking down of the fibers at the point where the kink occurred.

For easy, seaman-like handling, each length of rope should be taped temporarily at both ends with marine tape when cut from the original coil or reel and more permanently whipped at the earliest opportunity. Rope that is not being used should be stowed in a dry, well-ventilated place to prevent accumulation of moisture and resultant rot. Lines should be stowed on shelves or gratings off the deck and other material should not be stowed on top of them. Natural fiber lines are most susceptible to damage from moisture. Manila line, for instance, should be washed off with fresh water after salt-water use and thoroughly dried before being stowed. Synthetic fiber lines such as nylon may be stowed when wet, but this practice introduces unpleasant dampness below. All lines should be kept away from exhaust pipes (and other sources of heat) and battery acids.

A fiber line should never be over-worked or overstrained. Although it may not show it, the line may be seriously weakened because of breakdown of the fibers. A good way of checking for deterioration of a line is to look at the inside of the line. If there is a noticeable accumulation of grayish, powdery material, the line should be replaced. Another indication is a decrease in the diameter of a weakened line.

Natural fiber lines will contract if they become wet or damp. A line secured at both ends will become taut during rainy weather and may become badly over-strained unless the line is loosened. This is particularly true of mooring lines and flag halyards, which should be slacked off if they become taut because of rain or dampness.

It is good practice to wrap your mooring lines with canvas chafing gear where they pass through chocks. Anchor line, too, should be protected from chafing and rubbing.

To obtain the maximum use of a line and at the same time maintain safety, it is a good idea to turn a line end-for-end periodically. Anchor rodes or boat falls, used to haul small boats out of the water, where one end of the line usually has all the strain put on it, are good examples of lines which should be reversed from time to time.

Never leave the end of a line dangling loose without a whipping to prevent it from unlaying. Unless protected, it will begin to unlay of its own accord. To prevent fraying, a temporary plain whipping can be put on with anything, even a rope yarn or a piece of friction tape.

### Whipping and Finishing

Some of the most unattractive and unseamanlike things visible on many boats are the tattered, frayed ends of line with overhand knots tied in the ends to keep further unlaying at bay. The end of every line aboard your boat should be neatly finished off, both to preserve the line itself and to make it easier for the rope to run through tight places like chocks and blocks.

There are several ways to finish the end of a nylon or Dacron line, but the easiest with lines of 3/8" diameter or less

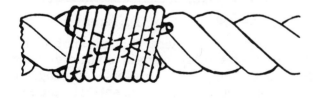

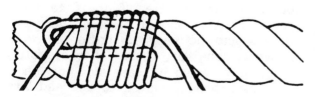

**Fig. 8-5   Temporary Whipping**

is simply to hold a match to the end until the fibers melt and fuse. Use a freshly-cut end for a neat job.

For a temporary end, simply take four to five tight turns of waterproof tape, or buy one of the many commercial products and treat the end – usually by dipping into a plastic liquid that hardens.

Another temporary whipping using small stuff is shown in Fig. 8-5. For a more permanent and dependable whipping, the method shown in Fig. 8-6 may be used.

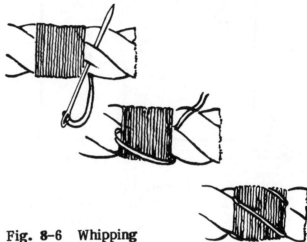

**Fig. 8-6   Whipping**

With Dacron or nylon thread, lay a series of tight turns around the end of the main rope, about half or three-eighths of an inch from the very end of the fibers.

When the whipping turns form a lashing about equal in length to the diameter of the main rope, sew through the strands. Lay the thread in the spiral groove formed by the strands of laid line, or diagonally along braid.

After making three sewed retaining threads, as shown, tie off the end of the thread. Besides being decorative, a whipping like this is very functional.

### Making Up Line

All line on board your boat should be stowed neatly when not in use. How you stow the line depends on its ultimate use. There are three methods of making up line - <u>coiling</u>, <u>faking</u> and <u>flemishing</u>. Line that is to be stowed in a compartment or locker should be coiled and made up, or stopped off with small stuff. Right-laid rope should be coiled right-handed (clockwise) and left-laid rope should be coiled left-handed (counterclockwise).

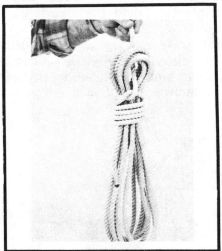

**Fig. 8-7  Line Ready for Stowing**

Lines that are made up for a fast run-off, such as mooring lines, heaving lines, and running rigging, may be faked down if there is sufficient room. Faking down consists of laying the line in coils either in a figure eight fashion or with each fake lying clear of the next. Faking down leaves the line in the most advantageous position for running out without fouling or kinking.

Some boatmen like to leave their line on the deck when not in use. To give it a neat, ornamental look, it can be flemished. The line is laid on the deck like a spring, each coil circling the one preceding it. Right-laid line should be coiled clockwise, and left-laid line should be coiled counterclockwise. To tighten the coils when you are finished, lay both hands flat on the line at the center and twist in the direction the coils are laid, thus forming a tight mat. It should be noted here that a beautifully flemished line should not be left on a varnished surface for any length of time, especially overnight. The trapped moisture will spoil a good varnished finish.

## Knots, Bends and Hitches

A line by itself is of very little use on a boat. Line is used for pulling, holding, lifting and lowering, but it must be fastened to something before it can serve those purposes. The way you fasten a line depends on purpose you have in mind. Among sailors, the landsman's all-inclusive term <u>knot</u> is broken down into more specific terms. The proper use of the term <u>knot</u> on a boat is limited to those alterations to the line that do not include any other object. A line is tied to itself with a knot. The term <u>bend</u> is used to describe methods of fastening one line to another, or to an object while the term <u>hitch</u> describes methods of attaching a line to another object, usually with the implication that it can be undone easily. Regardless of the terminology, all knots depend on friction created by turns in the line. This friction weakens the line. Splices also weaken a line because they depend on friction. Therefore a splice can be considered a variation of a knot when its impact on a rope's strength is tabulated as in Fig. 8-8.

**How Knots and Splices reduce strength of rope**

| | %EFF |
|---|---|
| Normal rope | 100% |
| KNOTS | |
| Anchor or Fisherman's bend | 76 |
| Timber hitch | 70-65 |
| Round turn | 70-65 |
| Two half-hitches | 70-65 |
| Bowline | 60 |
| Clove hitch | 60 |
| Sheet bend or Weaver's knot | 55 |
| Square or Reef knot | 45 |
| SPLICES | |
| Eye splice (over thimble) | 95-90 |
| Long splice | 87 |
| Short splice | 85 |

**Fig. 8-8 Strength of Different Knots·**

To meet your needs a good knot (bend, hitch) must display certain characteristics. It must hold well without slipping. It must be used for a practical purpose rather than serve as an ornament. It should be easy to tie. If it is to be a superior knot it should possess these advantages and be easy to untie, as well. However, none of these characteristics are of any value if you do not know which knot, bend or hitch to use and how to tie it.

Before you can learn to tie knots, it is helpful to know some terminology. The standing part is that section of the line between you and the other end of the line; it is the main part of the line. A bight is a U-section that you make in the standing part of the line, and a loop is a small circle in the standing part. It is possible to use these terms to describe scores of knots, bends and hitches, but by far the best way to learn knots is to be shown by someone who knows how to tie them.

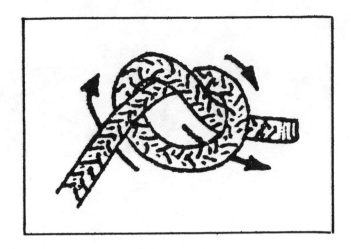

Fig 8-10 Overhand Knot

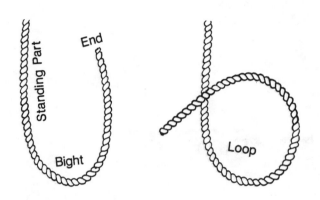

Fig. 8-9   Parts of a Line.

However, it is far better to have a good knowledge of a few commonly used knots for the normal operation of your boat than to have a superficial knowledge of a great number of seldom-used knots. The knots, bends and hitches illustrated here are functional, will serve almost every purpose, and, except as noted, are as easy to untie as they are to tie. Synthetic line is "slick" and some knots can and do pull out unless you leave an extra amount of line projecting and pull the knot tight.

Overhand Knot (Fig. 8-10). This knot is used for temporarily preventing a freshly cut rope from unlaying or unraveling. It can be used as a stopper which prevents a line from running all the way through a block or pulley. It will jam under tension and becomes very difficult to untie. It is tied by passing the bitter end through a loop in the standing part of the line.

Figure Eight Knot (Fig. 8-11). This knot is used as a stopper when heavy loads may occur. It is far superior to an overhand knot because it can be untied after being jammed. These knots should be used on every line on a sailboat except spinnaker sheets, which should always be free to run in an emergency. The knot is tied by forming a loop and passing the end around the standing part before putting it back through the loop.

Fig. 8-11   Figure Eight Knot

Fig. 8-12  Square Knot

Fig. 8-13  Sheet Bend or Becket Bend, Double Sheet Bend and Slippery Sheet Bend.

Square Knot (Fig. 8-12). This knot is also called a reef knot because it is used when securing a reefed sail to a boom. It can be used to fasten two lines of equal size or two ends of the same line. However, it is useful only when no great load is anticipated, such as in tying packages. If used to bend two lines of unequal size together, it will slip. When jammed, it is very difficult to untie. If unequal tension is applied, such as a jerk on one side, the knot is apt to turn into two half hitches. It is tied by first passing the left-hand end over and under the right-hand standing part and then returning the same end back over and under the other end. It should look like Fig. 8-12 with both ends on the same side or you have tied a "thief's knot," which will slip under tension.

Sheet Bend or Becket Bend (Fig. 8-13[a]). This bend is used to tie equal-sized or different-sized lines together. It is comparatively easy to untie even after being subjected to heavy strain for long periods of time. When used on a tow line, the ends should be tied down with small stuff for maximum security. It is tied by forming a bight in the bigger line and passing the smaller line's end up from under the bight, around behind the bigger line, and back under itself.

The double sheet bend (Fig. 8-13[b]) offers more security when one line is considerably larger than the other. It is tied by first forming a bight in the bigger line and passing the smaller line's end up from under the bight, then passing the smaller line around behind that bight and under itself twice. The slippery sheet bend (Fig. 8-13[c]) is a variation of the single sheet bend that is easier to untie. (The term "slippery" is applied to any knot when one of the ends is returned as a loop to make the knot easier to untie under tension.)

Clove Hitch (Fig. 8-14). This hitch is used to tie a line to a piling or to tie a fender to a railing. It is easy to adjust

**AROUND ONCE,**  **AND OVER AND AROUND AGAIN,**  **BACK DOWN AND THRU**

**DROP OVER BITT**

Fig. 8-14  Clove Hitch

the length of the standing part of a line tied with a clove hitch but the knot will slip if it is not under constant tension. While this feature makes a clove hitch easy to untie when it is not under tension, it can lead to trouble if the hitch comes untied by itself; so a clove hitch is considered a temporary knot. A clove hitch jams under a load; therefore, it is very difficult to untie if the load cannot be relieved. It is tied by looping the end of the line around the object twice in the same direction, once below, and once above, the standing part. The second loop is finished by passing the end between the second loop and the standing part.

A clove hitch can also be tied by making two loops in a row in the standing part, each with the end passing under the standing part. The loop nearest the end is then placed on top of the second loop before placing both loops over the

top of a piling. The clove hitch can be made more secure after it is pulled tight if the end is carried around the standing part and under itself, forming a knot called a half hitch.

Fig. 8-15  Two Half Hitches

Two Half Hitches (Fig. 8-15). This hitch is really a clove hitch tied around the standing part of a line after first forming a loop. It is used to tie a line to a ring, spar, pile, post or a grommet in the corner of an awning. It is a slip knot in the sense that the loop tightens under tension. Two half hitches are easier to untie than a clove hitch under tension and are considered a more permanent knot than a clove hitch. The knot is tied by first passing the end around the object and under the standing part. The end is then passed around the standing part and under itself. This forms the first half hitch. The second hitch is formed in exactly the same way, under the standing part from the same side, around the standing part and back under itself.

Anchor Bend or Fisherman's Bend (Fig. 8-16). This bend is one of the most secure knots for bending a line to an object. It develops considerable internal friction, reduces line chafe and weakens the line less than comparable knots. It can be difficult but not impossible to untie. As its name implies, it is often used to attach a fiber anchor rode to an anchor fitting or a fishing line or leader to the eye of a fishhook. The knot is begun by passing the end around the object twice. The end is then passed around the standing part and through the two loops previously made around the object.

ANCHOR BEND          ANCHOR BOWLINE

Fig. 8-16  Anchor Bend

The end is again passed by the same side of the standing part in the same direction, around the standing part and between the standing part and itself. The end is often tied to the standing part of a completed anchor bend with twine as added insurance that the knot will not work loose.

Rolling Hitch (Fig. 8-17). This hitch is used to tie one line to the middle of another so that it will not slip under strain. It can be used to hold a jib sheet while riding turns are removed from a winch or a block is relocated. When used to form a loop, it is adjustable, sliding easily to increase the loop size and retaining that loop size when tension is applied. It can be used to adjust fender lines and awning tie-downs. It must be tied with the double roll in the direction from which the standing part will be tensioned. The double roll must therefore be toward the inside of a loop for the knot to work. The knot is tied by passing the end around the line once, crossing over the loop and making a second turn with the end again passing the standing part on the same side, then making a third turn around the line on the other side of the standing part. The end is then passed between the standing part and the third turn to form a half hitch.

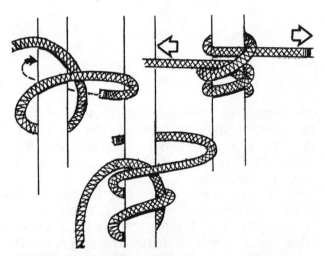

Fig. 8-17  Rolling Hitch

Bowline (Fig. 8-18). This knot is used to form a temporary but fixed size loop at the end of a line. It is often called the "King of Knots" because of its many everyday uses on a boat. Bowlines are easy to untie even after being under a load by pushing against the small bight around the standing part. They are used to tie jib sheets to the clew of the jib, to tie lines to fittings, to tie lines of equal or unequal size together and to attach a rode to an anchor. The knot is

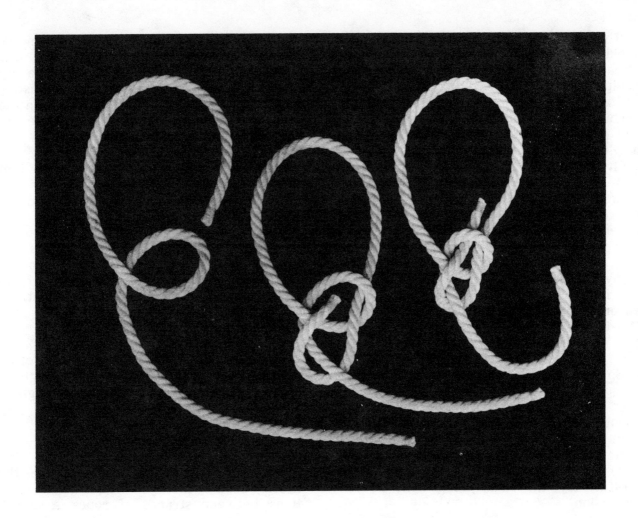

**Fig. 8–18  Bowline**

begun by forming a loop in the standing part with the end side of the loop on top. The end is then passed up through the loop, around behind the standing part and back down through the loop.

**Splices**

Splices are used when you want to join two sections of the same size line together permanently. An eye splice is used to form a permanent loop in a line. Either a short splice or a long splice can be used to join two pieces of laid line together (Fig. 8-19). Only a long splice will pass through a block or pulley. A back splice is used to prevent a fiber stranded line from unraveling.

EYE SPLICE

SHORT SPLICE

LONG SPLICE

**Fig. 8–19  Splices**

The average boat owner usually buys docking lines and anchor rode that are already spliced. Sail makers or marine equipment suppliers usually provide sheets or halyards with custom splices. Splicing double braided line requires more time and practice than the average boat owner has to dedicate to such a seldom-needed skill. However the principle of splicing laid line is simple: three strands are tucked over and under so that they interweave with three other strands. If you understand the rudiments of splicing laid line you will be a wiser customer and you will be able to make emergency repairs. Many boating enthusiasts find great pleasure in knowing how to splice and find it an enjoyable off-season pastime. The ability to splice line is usually taken as a sign of a competent seaman.

Splicing Fundamentals. When learning to splice, it's a good idea to equip yourself with a length or two of Manila line about 3/8" in diameter. Manila is stiffer than nylon or Dacron and holds its construction better during the twists and pulls of splicing. As you become more skillful, try the same thing with Dacron and nylon.

You'll also need some waterproof tape - electrician's tape will serve - but you should carry a roll of sailor's waterproof tape in your ditty bag as well. If you're working with new, stiff rope, a fid (a sailor's tool for separating strands of rope similar to a marlinspike, but generally made of wood or plastic) will also be handy. Now you're ready to make a short splice.

Unlay one end of your rope several inches. This means undoing the line into its three component strands. Tape the end of each strand to keep it from untwisting and tape the point at which you want to stop the unlaying. Now do the same for the other end of the rope.

"Marry" the two untwisted ends so that one strand of rope A alternates with one of rope B. Tape one set of strands in place.

Now take one of the loose strands and lead it over the taped neck of the opposite rope. Open a space between strands of the opposite rope and push the strand through as far as it will go - but don't pull it tight just yet.

Now do the same thing with the other two strands, working each one through an adjoining opening and pulling it through.

Pull all three tucked strands tight, one by one.

Make a second set of tucks like the first. Be sure that you keep the alternations between strands of ropes A and B even.

Make a third set of tucks and pull them tight.

Untape the free set of strands and perform the same three-tuck operation with them.

When you're done, cut off the ends of the strands to within about a quarter-inch

A.—First step is to unlay the end of the rope for a short distance. Form the desired size loop. Take middle strand of unlayed end "1" and tuck through any strand of the "standing" part of the rope.

B.—Take adjacent strand marked "2" in picture. Pass over strand under which "1" is tucked, then pass under adjacent strand of the "standing" part.

C.—Tuck remaining strand through last strand of the "standing" part of the rope, on other side.

D.—Tuck each strand alternately over and under, working against the lay of the rope. Taper off by halving the yarns on the last two tucks.

E.—Pound and roll. Then cut off remaining strands close to the rope.

**Fig. 8-20   Making an Eye Splice**

of the main rope. Roll the completed splice between your palms or under your foot.

With practice, you'll find you can achieve great neatness and speed, but it does take time.

The eye splice is basically the same idea as a short splice, except you're making the tucks back into the standing part of the original rope. Unlay and tape the line as before. Now form the eye to the size you'll want (usually just large enough to be pulled over a cleat one arm at a time) and lay the unlaid end along the standing part with one of the strands arbitrarily chosen to be the first tuck.

Open the strands of the standing part (a fid may be useful here, or use your fingers) and insert the first strand, pulling it through.

Take the next strand to the right of the first, as shown, and insert that under the next strand to the right of the one you tucked the first strand under, pulling it through.

Turn the whole splice over - this is very important - and lead the remaining strand between the only two standing part- strands left. When you have completed the first series of tucks the ends of the strands will be tucked evenly around the standing part, ready to begin the second series of tucks.

Now continue with the next set of tucks by carrying any one of the loose strands over the next strand of the standing part and under the second. Repeat that process for the other strand. After you have completed three or four sets of tucks, you are ready to trim the ends of the strand, tuck them in or seize them (see below), and use your new eye splice.

When you splice artificial fiber line, which has less friction among the strands than does natural fiber line, you should take five full series of tucks instead of three. This makes a somewhat lumpy-looking splice, but one with maximum strength, which is, of course, the most important thing.

Fig. 8-21    An Eye Splice Should be Sized To Just Fit the Cleat.

Seizing. As you can tell from reading these instructions and looking at the illustrations, this kind of splice can be made only in laid line. To splice braided line, one substitutes core for core and cover for cover. It's not really necessary, however, as one may form a semi-permanent loop by the technique of seizing (binding or lashing) the two parts of the line together.

To do this, you need a sailmaker's palm - a kind of super-thimble - large needle and thread of the same material as the line you are seizing.

Form the loop to the size desired. Now lay a series of tight, even turns of thread, lashing the two parts of the line together.

When the turns of thread have formed a lashing about equal in length to the diameter of the rope being used, sew the thread through the two parts of the line two or three times.

Now make a second series of turns with the thread between the two parts of the main rope. Draw these turns as tight as possible.

Sew through the main part of the rope, tie a figure eight in the end of the thread and cut it off.

Although not quite so neat as a splice, a seizing is very strong and can be unmade. It can also be done with laid line.

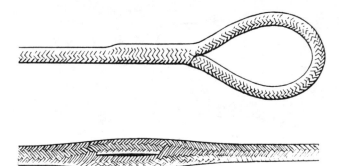

**Fig. 8-22 Braided Lines Can Also be Spliced.**

"Whipping" can also be used with laid line to finish the ends where a figure 8 knot is too bulky or tape will not hold, or to secure the loose strand ends of a splice. Begin by making a loop of small stuff and placing it alongside the end of the line to be seized. Hold the doubled portion of the loop in place and wrap the remainder tightly around the line. When a length of line approximately equal to its diameter has been wrapped, pull on both loose ends at once to tighten the wraps, then cut off the loose ends.

**Securing Lines**

There are many special fittings or pieces of hardware that can be used for securing lines on a boat. Typically, sailboats have a variety of special-purpose fittings, power boats have a more basic set of deck hardware.

A shackle, which is a "U" shaped connector with a pin or bolt across the open end, can be used to attach line to many types of equipment, including anchors.

Other than shackles, hardware for securing lines to your boat are attached to its hull or spars. All deck fittings should

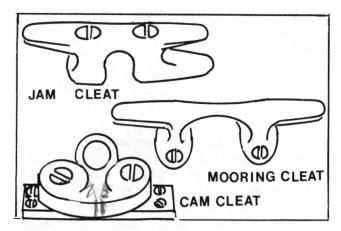

**Fig. 8-23 Typical Hardware for Attaching Lines.**

be bolted through the deck rather than screwed to it since you are going to rely on this hardware to protect your investment. On all but the smallest boats, the under side of the bolts should go through a backing plate rather than washers to prevent the bolts from pulling through the deck under heavy use. Remember that it is easier to replace a line than to patch a deck after a fitting has been pulled out of it.

A turnbuckle is a threaded fitting that pulls two eyes together. It is used on sailboats to attach the wire rigging or stays that support the mast. It is threaded so that you can put the proper amount of tension on the shroud or stay. After you adjust the tension, you should put cotter pins or ring clips through the holes in the threaded pins in the turnbuckle so that the adjustment will not change.

A horn cleat, which is an anvil-shaped fitting, may be provided for anchor rodes, mooring or docking lines, tow lines, halyards and sheets. Cleats are the most common fittings for lines on small boats.

There are two methods for securing lines to horn cleats. The first is considered as temporary and is used when a boat is underway. In such situations, it may be necessary to remove the line from the cleat in a hurry to prevent a mishap so no hitches are taken. First, take a complete turn around the cleat,

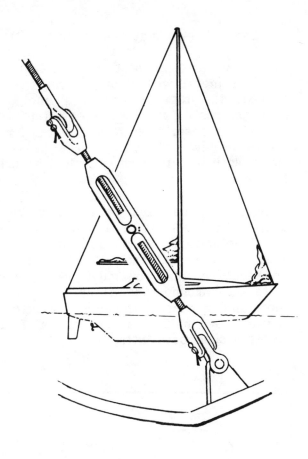

**Fig. 8-24  A Turnbuckle.**

When a line is to be belayed or tied to a horn cleat and your boat is going to be left unattended, the connection needs to be more secure. The best method is to lead the line in one round turn around the base of the cleat and then form at least one figure eight around the horns of the cleat. Finally, secure the line with a half-hitch over one of the cleat's horns. The result is really a clove hitch around the two horns of the cleat. It is important to take a full turn at the beginning, which allows you to undo the hitch while the cleated line is still under a load. One caution - be sure to have the line continue to form a figure eight when the half-hitch is made. Do not make the error of having the last loop come along the side of the cleat instead of crossing over or the knot will not develop as much friction.

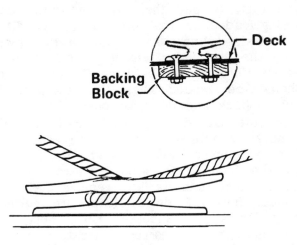

**Fig. 8-26  A Jam Cleat**

making sure that the standing end of the line leads to the end of the cleat opposite the direction of pull so that the tension will not jam the turn later. Next, lead the line over the top of the cleat and around the horn or projection to form a figure eight. Make one more figure eight and pull the line tight so that it will not slip.

A _jam cleat_ is similar to a standard cleat with one important difference. One of the horns forms a tapered slot into which the line is "jammed." This allows you to both secure and let go of the line more quickly since less than one full turn is required. Jam cleats are usually used on sailboats to secure the sheets or ropes that control the sails, and they are sometimes used to secure the centerboard pendant which controls the position or depth of the centerboard. A jam cleat must be installed so that the tapered slot is in the same direction as the standing part of the line; thus, when the line is

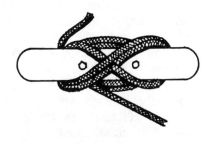

**Fig. 8-25  Belaying to a Cleat.**

first led around the base of the cleat, it will not bind. While oversized horn cleats are suitable for many purposes, a jam cleat must be sized to accommodate a specific line if it is to function properly.

Two other types of quick-action cleats are frequently found on sailboats. One is a Clam Cleat, which is a trademark name for a notched channel made of aluminum or hardened plastic into which a line is dropped. The notches grip the side of the line to hold it in place. To trim or haul in the line, simply pull back on it. To let the line go, or to free it, pull it in slightly while lifting it out of the cleat. A Clam Cleat works only with one specific size line.

The second is a Cam Cleat which has two moving, serrated cam-shaped jaws that rotate open in the direction in which you want to pull the line. The jaws are spring-loaded so that they close on different-sized lines. The teeth on the jaws hold the line under tension. A line should not be forced down between the cams but should be placed over the teeth and pulled back and down to open the cleat. The line can be trimmed or tightened simply by pulling it in; but to ease the line, you must first pull and lift to free it. The Cam Cleat is not as strong as a Clam Cleat, and its jaws require maintenance. Both of these cleats are suited only for small sailboats. They must be installed in the correct direction since they work only one way. They are hard to release when there is a heavy load on the line, the time you may most want to let the line go.

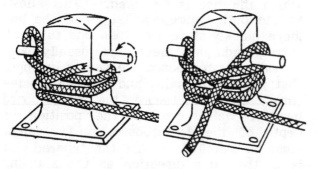

Fig. 8-27   A Sampson Post

Larger boats may be fitted with a sampson post in place of a standard cleat. A sampson post is a column of wood or metal with a pin or bar through it near the top. To secure a line to a sampson post, first take a complete turn around its base, then form several figure eights around the pins of the post and finish with a half-hitch, just like securing to a cleat.

Bow bitts may also be found on larger boats. These consist of a pair of circular metal columns on a common base, usually with a lip around the top of each post. To secure a line, you must take a complete turn around the bitt or post nearest the standing part of the line. The hitch is finished by making a number of figure eights around both bitts.

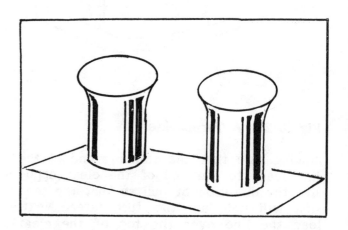

Fig. 8-28   Bow Bitts.

Mooring and towing lines that are attached to cleats undergo considerable movement and wear. In order to protect these lines from rubbing or chafing, canvas, leather, rubber or plastic hose can be fastened around the line where it passes over the rail or edge of the deck. This protective covering, called chafing gear, is usually tied on with small stuff. The line usually passes through a chock or "U" shaped fitting fastened to the boat's hull. The chock not only reduces line chafing, but also prevents hull or rail chafing as well as limiting the direction of the pull on the cleat.

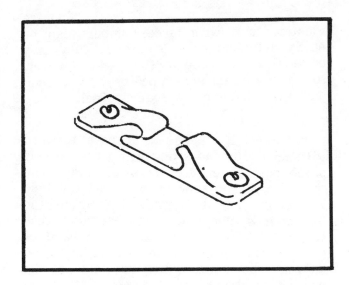

**Fig. 8-29 Chocks Protect Both Boat and Line.**

## Other Hardware Items

A <u>winch</u> provides mechanical assistance in pulling in on a loaded line such as anchor rode, sheet or halyard. It consists of a metal drum fastened to a secure base, and has a series of gears inside. An anchor winch, called a <u>windlass</u>, may be powered by an electric motor, but sailboat winches are turned by means of a winch handle. Winch drums rotate clockwise; so you must wrap the line clockwise around the drum for the winch to work. The number of wraps depends on the load on the line since the winch transmits pull by friction. Four turns are usually the most that will be required for synthetic line, while wire rope may require six. Some winches provide two gearing ranges to provide even more pulling power.

Turning the winch handle on these devices clockwise provides normal power while turning the handle counterclockwise "changes gears" and increases the pulling capability. (The drum always continues in a clockwise direction no matter which way the handle is turned when a two-speed winch is used.)

Sometimes two people are required to operate a winch on a sailboat. One person cranks the winch handle while the second collects the tail end of the line as it feeds off the winch and secures it to a cleat when the line is properly trimmed. A <u>self-tailing winch</u> solves the problem of two people working in a confined space. The top of the drum contains a notched channel which holds the line as it feeds off the winch drum, eliminating the need of a tailer and the necessity of cleating the tail. A "U" shaped fitting guides the line into the channel.

Line is always wrapped around a winch drum from the bottom up. You must be careful to see that the turns do not overlap each other and jam. Such jams are called "riding turns." You should always pull the line in by hand until it has some tension on it even if the turns are put on first. Otherwise the winch drum won't function since there will be no friction between the line and the drum. If you are using a self-tailing winch, you must be careful that the tail does not snag on anything that will pull it out of the channel while you are tightening the line. When you need two hands to operate the winch handle of a self-tailing winch, another person may have to tension the tail to keep it in the channel. Otherwise you must pause occasionally to pull the tail into the channel yourself.

To slack off on a line wound around a self-tailing winch, you must first remove the line from the channel. You then permit the line to slip out two or three inches at a time by simultaneously easing on the tail with one hand and braking the line by squeezing on the loops around the drum with the palm of your other hand. With regular winches, you first uncleat the tail and then ease it out as described. If you wish to completely release the line on the drum rather than ease it out, you merely pull the loops up and out, using the hand which is holding the tail. It is a good idea to check that the tail will not catch on anything before you throw the wraps off the winch drum.

Pulleys are called <u>blocks</u> on a boat. They are constructed by connecting a wheel called a sheave between two sides, called cheeks, on an axle called a pin. They are often attached at one end with a shackle. You should be familiar with the names given to different types of blocks that are used on sailboats. A single block has a single sheave and is used primarily to change the direction of a line. A double block has two sheaves, side by side, and a triple block has three side-by-side sheaves. A becket block has one, two or three sheaves side-by-side and an eye or becket at the end opposite the shackle connection. The becket permits you to tie the end of a line to the block. A snatch block has a hinged cheek so that you can insert the standing part of a line rather than feed it through from the end. A foot block is a single or double block with one side screwed or bolted to the deck of a sailboat. It is used to change the direction of the lines that control the sails. When the same block is screwed or bolted to a spar, it is called a cheek block. Sheaves built into the top of a mast also function as pulleys to change the direction of the halyards, but since the mast itself replaces the cheeks, the pulley is known as a halyard sheave.

### Special Lines

Among specific lines on a sail boat are wire stays to hold a mast in place, sheets to control the set of the sails and halyards to raise and lower the sails. Halyards quite frequently are made up of a combination of wire and fiber rope. Sometimes there is a fitting on the top of the mast under which you may hook the eye on the wire section. This fitting allows your sails to remain fully raised even when a strong wind is blowing because the wire section of the halyard will not stretch as much as the fiber halyard section under a heavy load.

A lead line is sometimes used on boats, both sail and power. It is a line which has been marked in such a manner that it can be used to measure the depth of the water. The line is weighted with a "lead." This generally weighs at least five pounds, and can be used for depths of up to 100 feet. Ideally, the line should be braided cotton, 150 to 200 feet long. It can be marked by strips of tape or leather or by knots to indicate the depth.

Plastic strips with large numbers can be easily attached to a lead line. They may be difficult to read in the dark, however, so many mariners prefer traditional markings that can be read by feel.

In practice, the lead is cast forward with an underhand swing while the boat is proceeding under very slow headway. The speed should be slow enough that the lead will reach the bottom by the time the line stands vertically. The vertical distance from the waterline to the hand of the person casting the lead should be known. The mark which is held in the hand is read and the distance to the water is deducted from this figure.

Fig. 8-30 Sounding With a Lead Line.

Some leads have a hollowed-out portion on the bottom of the lead which can be "armed" with a quantity of sticky material (tallow or bedding compound) to collect a small sample of the bottom. In most cases the character of the bottom is shown on your chart. By having a sample of the bottom, you may be able to further identify your position, especially in conditions of reduced visibility when no landmarks are in sight.

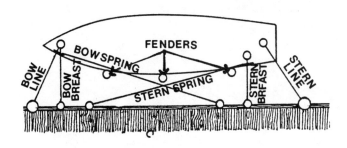

**Fig. 8-31 Special Attention is Required When Tying Up in Tidal Waters**

Other lines are docking lines or mooring lines. The most often used mooring lines are the bow line and the stern line. These are simple to employ and are usually sufficient, provided that fenders are suspended from the hull at strategic points to keep the hull from chafing against the float.

If the boat is to be left alongside a pier or float for a long time, as with a permanent mooring, or if conditions are rough, the use of breast lines and spring lines should be considered. Breast lines prevent sideways movement and spring lines limit the fore-and-aft movement of the boat. Spring lines are also extremely useful in reducing motion of a moored boat in rough conditions. If moored to a pier or wharf in tidal areas, it is important to leave sufficient slack in all lines to accommodate the rise and fall of the tide.

Spring lines may also be used in close quarters to help the boat into or out of a slip or to facilitate maneuvers alongside a wharf. If the spring line is to be handled by those aboard the boat, both ends of the line should be aboard, with the bight around a pile or a cleat on the wharf. The spring line is let go by hauling in on one end of the line. If used under these conditions, a spring line must be tended carefully to be certain that it does not become fouled on the rudder or propeller. Under no conditions should a spring line, which is being used to assist a maneuver, be tied off to a cleat or bitt aboard the boat. A half turn around the bitt or cleat is usually all that is required. The spring line should be able to be adjusted as necessary and cast off quickly when no longer needed.

Sometimes at busy docks, two lines with eye splices must be placed over one piling. If the two eyes are simply dropped over the top of the pile, it may be impossible to remove the first line before the second one has been taken off. To avoid this problem, you can follow a technique called "dipping the eye." Simply bring the end of the eye of the second line up through the eye of the first line and then drop it over the piling. Then either line may be removed first with no problem developing.

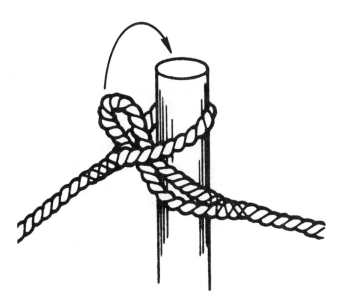

**Fig. 8-32 Dipping the Eye.**

# Chapter 9

# Engines For Sailboats

## Why a Sailboat is a Poor Powerboat

Most sailboats handle poorly under power. The sailboat engine is usually described as an auxiliary—the main power-plant is the sailing rig.

Compared to a powerboat of equal displacement, or weight, a sailboat generally has a very small engine. A cruising ketch 30 feet long, with a displacement of 10,000 lb., will probably carry an auxiliary of 30 hp. A powerboat of similar size will have an engine three times as powerful, and even larger if it's a high-speed planing boat.

## Outboard Engines

Most small engine-equipped sailboats are pushed by outboard motors. The standard outboard designed for high-speed operation is ill-suited for sailboat operation. Sailboats work most efficiently with slower-turning, high-torque propellers. They may also need a long shaft on an outboard, simply to reach the water from the transom mounting position. Outboard motors designed for sailboat applications work very well, and can push displacement hull sailboats at hull speed.

Outboard engines are normally found powering sailboats from the smallest up to about 27 or 28 feet (and light-weight multihulls considerably larger). As a general rule, outboards up to about five hp are adequate for daysailers' auxiliary engines, while motors from 10 to 15 hp are used for small cruisers.

Fig. 9-1 Outboard Mounted on Transom

Outboards can be mounted on sailboats' transoms, as they are on powerboats, and where a sailboat's design permits this location, it offers several advantages. First, the engine, which of course incorporates its own steering, is easy to operate from a transom mount, having been designed for it. Second, the outboard may be tilted up while sailing or when the boat is moored, which makes for sailing efficiency in the first case and for a better-maintained lower unit in the second. Third, the motor is most accessible on the transom, whether for repair or for removal.

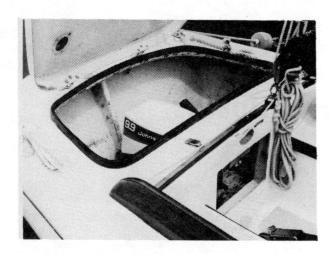

**Fig. 9-2 Outboard Mounted in Well**

On some boats, however, the shape of the stern prohibits transom mounting or makes it practically inaccessible. Such boats often have outboard wells—usually a lazarette compartment with a hole in the bottom for the outboard lower unit, and a reinforced crossbar for the motor-mounting clamps. An outboard well often looks better than a transom mount, but it frequently requires that the motor stay in the water at all times, unless the whole unit is unclamped and removed. In addition, many lazarette-type wells are rather poorly ventilated, causing the engine to run roughly and sometimes to choke on its own exhaust.

One minor inconvenience of an outboard is that it may require a fuel of gasoline and lubricating oil mixed in a fairly precise proportion. In order to be sure of having oil when it's needed, many skippers carry an extra can or two-which is fine, except that a can of oil should be mixed with an exact volume of gasoline, usually one six-gallon tank. The unlikelihood of running out of gas with the fuel dock in reach makes many skippers carry either partially full cans of oil or-better-two gas cans, both of which should be of the proper design for the engine.

Whatever the case, fuel should be stored in a well-ventilated space or on deck to prevent the accumulation of explosive vapors. Never store gasoline in an unventilated lazarette.

Until recently, only outboards of 25 hp and up were electric-start and thus provided with generators or alternators to charge the boat's battery. Recently, however, three of the four major outboard manufacturers have extended electric-start to engines of approximately 10 and 15 hp, the sizes most popular for small sailing cruisers. The generating capacity offered by these outboards is not great, but it's usually enough to keep the boat's 12-volt battery up during the season, even allowing for interior lighting and frequent use of the running lights. Self-powered anchor lights, depth sounder, spotlight and radio, RDF or Loran are still indicated, however.

An outboard's major feature is its portability. Not only can it be removed during and after sailing, but it can also be taken to a mechanic, if necessary, rather than paying for a mechanic to come to it. The modern, medium-size electric-start 10 or 15 hp motor weighs about 75 lb., exclusive of battery or fuel tank. This means that an average adult can carry it at least the length of the pier to the family car. Smaller outboards are correspondingly lighter.

Today's outboards are more reliable than the predecessors of even a few years ago, but the standard outboards are not made to push a sailboat. The special sailboat type of motor is preferred, but even they do not thrive on infrequent slow-speed use typical of sailboat operation. Two common problems with outboard auxiliary engines are spark-plug fouling at low speeds and cavitation.

Most standard outboards are made to run economically and efficiently at three-quarter throttle or better. Many sailboats achieve hull speed in calm water at about half throttle. Running a standard outboard for extended periods at half throttle or less is an invitation to fouling the spark plugs. While making the fuel-air mixture leaner (less fuel, more air) may help, a certain amount of fouling is inevitable. One answer is to get a motor that's small enough so that it needs to be run near full throttle to attain hull speed in calm water—which is when you'll be running the engine, anyway. This solution is only partial, for it means that in rough, windy conditions your engine won't be powerful enough to help the boat a great deal. But when there is wind, most sailboats are more maneuverable under sail than under power. Learn to maneuver under sail, even in adverse winds, and save the engine for getting home in flat calms.

Cavitation occurs when the propeller spins too fast, creating a partial vacuum. It can also occur if the propeller is not deep enough in the water. Since the propeller blades do not get a good "grip" on the water, the motor over speeds, causing possible damage to the engine and/or pitmarks on the propeller. Long-shaft outboard motors are marketed specifically for sailboats with high transoms. The longer shaft permits your propeller to run in deeper water while still giving you access to its controls. These outboard engines often are sold with three, four, or even five-bladed propellers for more positive bite and steering at low speeds.

**Outboard Maintenance**

The modern outboard motor requires about as little maintenance as any piece of marine equipment. Only a small amount of care is needed to keep your motor running smoothly—major accidents aside. The precise steps are detailed in your engine's owner's manual—if you've lost your copy, be sure to get another one, as it's the key to good maintenance. If you're mechanically inclined, your engine's service manual is a good buy for a small price. It will give you the complete details for your motor and will advise you on tune-up and major repairs.

While some maintenance operations for your particular outboard may be different, the following is a standard schedule for the average small engine.

Exterior Lubrication
Tilt-lock mechanism
Clamps
Throttle-to-shaft gears
Carburetor and Magneto linkages
Swivel bracket
Motor-cover latch
Gear Case
Fuel Tank
Spark Plugs

| | |
|---|---|
| Exterior Lubrication | |
| Tilt-lock mechanism | |
| Clamps | |
| Throttle-to-shaft gears | Every two months in fresh water. |
| Carburetor and Magneto linkages | Every month in |
| Swivel bracket | salt water. |
| Motor-cover latch | |
| Gear Case | Every 50 hours or once a season. |
| Fuel Tank | Grease fuel line fittings. Add fuel conditioner if tank is stored with fuel in it. |
| Spark Plugs | Replace annually or sooner as required. |

**Outboard Trouble-Shooting**

If an outboard—or any engine—breaks down on the water, you should know some basic techniques for elementary, on-the-spot repairs. These techniques don't replace regular maintenance, nor will they answer every problem. Some breakdowns require a trained mechanic and factory parts or service. All the same, it's surprising how often a little ingenuity will get your motor going again or how a knowledgeable investigation will discover a situation that's easily corrected.

**Problem—ENGINE WON'T START**
**Possible Cause/Correction**
  Fuel tank empty,
  Fuel tank vent closed (older motors),
  Fuel line improperly hooked up-check both ends,
  Engine not primed,
  Engine flooded-look for fuel overflow,
  Clogged fuel filter or line,
  Spark plug wires reversed or disconnected.

**Problem—STARTER MOTOR WON'T WORK (ELECTRIC START)**
**Possible Cause/Correction**
  Gear shift not in neutral,
  Defective starter switch—sometimes gets wet and corrodes if motor is mounted too low,
  Battery dead,
  Battery connections loose or dirty.

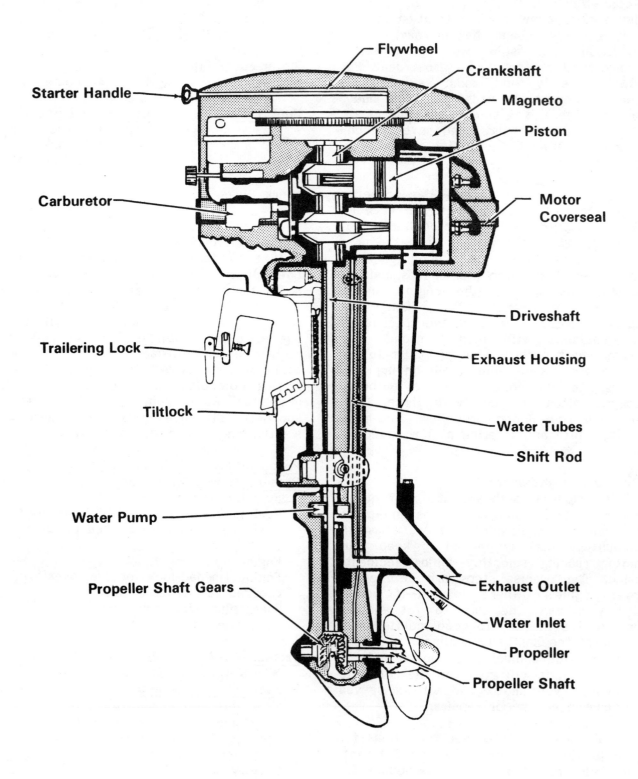

**Fig. 9-3 Cutaway of Outboard Engine**

## Problem—LOSS OF POWER
### Possible Cause/Correction
Too much oil in fuel mix,
Fuel/air mix too lean (backfires),
Fuel/air mix too rich,
Fuel hose kinked,
Slight blockage in fuel line or fuel filter,
Weed or other matter on propeller.

## Problem—MOTOR MISFIRES
### Possible Cause/Correction
Spark plug damaged,
Spark plug loose,
Spark plug incorrect.

## Problem—POOR PERFORMANCE ON BOAT
### Possible Cause/Correction
Wrong propeller,
Engine improperly tilted relative to transom,
Engine should be vertical when boat is underway,
Bent propeller—usually accompanied by high level of vibration,
Improper load distribution in boat,
Heavy marine growth on boat bottom,
Cavitation.

## Seasonal Routine Maintenance

Your outboard engine will provide reliable service over many boating seasons if you give it a few minutes' attention at the beginning and end of each season. Frequently more problems will occur during the off-season than when the engine is being used regularly unless a few simple steps are taken to protect your equipment.

Pre-Season Routine Maintenance-Outboards
1. IGNITION SYSTEM. Go over the spark plugs and points. Regap, clean, and reinstall or replace if badly worn or pitted. Check the battery with a hydrometer to ensure that it has a full charge. Clean and inspect the battery cables. Check the polarity before connecting the cables to the terminals. Clean and lubricate electric-starter drive mechanisms.

2. LUBE OIL SYSTEM. Remove the oil-level plug on the lower-unit gear case and check for the proper oil level. If the oil is dirty, change it. Remove and clean fuel filter. Clean the exterior of the carburetor.
3. METAL SURFACES. Wipe off all surfaces with a clean cloth. Check surfaces for water leaks. When run for the first time, check the operation of the engine's cooling system.

Post-Season Routine Maintenance--Outboards
1. FUEL SYSTEM. With engine operating in fresh water, put oil into the carburetor air intake(s) until the engine starts to smoke heavily. As soon as this happens, stop the engine. Drain the float chamber on the carburetor. Remove and clean the fuel-filter bowl. Drain and clean the filter elements. Check all gaskets carefully for wear, breaks, or enlarged cutouts. If in doubt, replace the gasket. Empty and clean the fuel tank.

2. IGNITION SYSTEM. Remove the spark plugs; push the throttle all the way to the stop position. Turn the flywheel over a couple of times manually to pump out any residual water in the cooling system. Clean and lubricate the electric starter. It is recommended that the battery be removed and stored in a dry place. During lay-up, the battery should be charged about once a month. Don't leave it on a constant trickle charge. If the battery is not removed, leave the spark plug terminals disconnected for the winter; this may avoid someone's accidentally trying to start the engine. Go over the points; if badly worn, replace them. If they are not too badly pitted or worn, then file even, regap, and secure.

3. METAL SURFACES. Wipe all metal surfaces with a lightly oiled rag. This will keep the surfaces from rusting during the winter months. Remove the propeller and lubricate the propeller shaft.

4. LUBRICATION. Drain the lower-unit gear case and refill with the lubricant specified by the manufacturer. Consult the owner's manual for other required lubrication.

## Requirements of an Inboard Auxiliary Engine

Ideally, a sailboat engine should meet certain criteria, but only recently have small internal combustion engines been developed that perform reasonably well for this purpose.

A primary requirement is that a sailboat engine should be compact, using up--with its fuel tank, battery, and wiring system—as little space as possible. In a daysailer, the engine should be light in weight, as it should be in any unballasted boat. It should still, however, be unobtrusive, as the average sailor is hardly fond of an engine and wants to hear from it only when it is needed.

Most sailboats have very primitive electrical systems, at least until one considers vessels in the 26-foot-and-over range. The engine itself is the primary source of a boat's electrical power, there being no separate generator. Thus, the auxiliary should be capable of turning out sufficient extra electricity to light the running lights, anchor light, interior lighting system, and perhaps to operate a radiotelephone, depth sounder, Loran or radio direction finder.

## Gasoline-Powered Inboard Engines

Compared to powerboat skippers, sailors are frequently not interested in, or attentive to, their boats' motors. Therefore, a sailboat auxiliary must be very reliable, as it will get little attention and will often by installed in a compartment too damp and inaccessible for anything else. Dampness is, of course, the major enemy of internal combustion engines, especially those gasoline engines with complex electrical systems. Many of the best inboard engines aboard sailboats are derived from the power plants used to push small agricultural equipment, such as

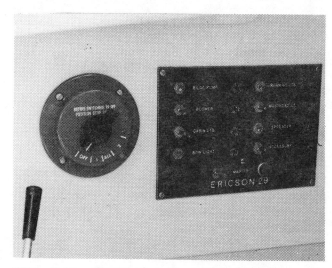

**Fig. 9-4    Spark-Proof Main Switch and Switch Panel**

tractors, where slow-turning motors with simple, rugged construction are desirable.

Above all, a sailboat engine must be safe. Because of the properties of the fuel it uses, no gasoline engine is safe in and of itself. Sailboat engines cannot be made rugged enough and foolproof enough to forestall the accidents that arise from neglect. More and more owners of larger sailing craft are turning to diesel power. In large part, this movement is happening because of the evolution of the diesel into a relatively lightweight engine, but probably the majority of skippers going to diesel power do so because of the relative safety of diesel fuel. Still, there is a sizable number of skippers who prefer inboard gasoline engines, whether because of their familiarity or because of the unpleasant smell frequently associated with diesels--a smell that can be minimized or eliminated in a proper fuel installation, properly maintained.

The standard small inboard gasoline engine used in sailing craft has a number of characteristics you can count on--some good, some bad. To begin with, most of these small engines in the 5-50 hp size range operate at relatively slow speeds and provide good power and reasonable economy. A 30-hp inboard's gasoline consumption will normally equal that of a 10-hp outboard, not even counting the oil.

Although inboard engines aren't usually seen in boats under 26 feet overall, very small gasoline-powered engines--single-cylinder, five-hp models--do exist. A single-cylinder inboard, whether gasoline or diesel, is often a noisy and vibratory engine, and unless it is a question of a special installation, a two-cylinder outboard of the same horsepower will generally be more reliable and a good deal lighter.

## Ventilation

The installation of a gasoline engine and fuel system is of vital importance, both for safety and efficiency. The accompanying illustrations detail the ventilation arrangements approved for auxiliary engines using gasoline as a fuel—these ventilation requirements apply to fuel tanks when electrical wiring is installed in the same compartment. In most cases, a sailboat's engine and gas tank will be in essentially the same compartment; so a common set of ventilators can be used.

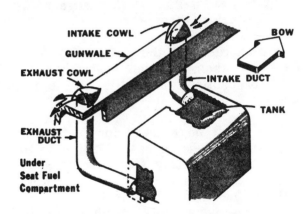

**Fig. 9-5 Example of Ventilation Arrangement for Small Boats Built Before July 31, 1980**

The minimum acceptable ventilation system to meet Coast Guard regulations calls for one intake and one exhaust ventilator for each engine/fuel compartment. A normal safe practice is that the intake vent must be so positioned that its cowl or scoop faces forward, in clear air, and that its ducting, which should be of sturdy, temperature-resistant tubing, is at least two inches in diameter, and extends downward, without kinks or obstructions.

The exhaust vent, with its cowl facing aft, should be of similar construction and size. Its ducting should extend to the lowest portion of the bilge, except that in boats--keel boats for the most part--fitted with bilge pumps, the ducting should not go so far down that its opening will be obstructed by normal accumulations of bilge water.

Obviously, the ducts should be so located that vapors from the exhaust duct cannot flow back into the intake. On a sailboat, it is wise to use removable vent cowls that can be capped in rough weather. The cowls are best mounted--all other things being equal--on the cabin top, free if possible from where they will be caught by sheets or other lines. There should be no narrowing or obstruction anywhere in the system; but it is also a good idea to install, if possible, a mechanical blower in the exhaust line. This makes it possible to ventilate the engine and fuel compartment before starting the engine on windless days, and a properly installed blower will not block the duct for normal, natural ventilation.

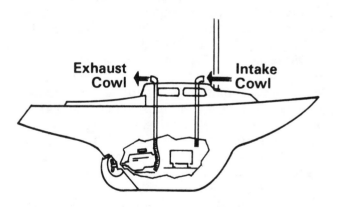

**Fig. 9-6 Example of Ventilation Ducts**

Ventilation Systems--Boats Built after July 31, 1980

Both (1) powered and (2) natural ventilation requirements have been in effect since July 31, 1980, for boats built since that date. Some boat builders have been in compliance since July 31, 1978. If you are building a boat, check with the Coast Guard for details.

1. Any compartment on a boat containing a permanently installed gasoline engine with a "cranking motor" (e.g., starter) must have a power ventilation system and a label close to the ignition switch and in plain view of the operator: WARNING—GASOLINE VAPORS CAN EXPLODE. BEFORE STARTING ENGINE OPERATE BLOWER FOR FOUR MINUTES AND CHECK ENGINE COMPARTMENT BILGE FOR GASOLINE VAPORS.

2. Other engine and/or fuel compartments may require natural ventilation.

All ventilation regulations, as in the past, require the operator to maintain them.

Boats with gasoline engines not under these newer regulations must comply with the requirements discussed previously.

### Fueling

Extremely hazardous conditions are encountered when fueling with gasoline. Safety rules should be rigidly observed. When taking on gasoline, all engines should be stopped, galley flames extinguished, hatches, windows and ports secured, and electrical devices shut off. Smoking must be forbidden. Crew, guests, etc. should get off the boat. Diesel fuel, being less flammable, is not so hazardous as gasoline; however, observing the same safety rules is advisable and should contribute to development of "the safety habit." Have unnecessary crew go ashore while you take on fuel, if possible.

The gasoline nozzle must contact the filler-pipe deck flange at all times during fueling. This prevents the possibility of explosion caused by the discharge of static electricity. (Similar precautions should be observed when fueling tanks used with outboards.) The filler-pipe deck flange must be connected to the boat's ground system. Static electricity is generated internally throughout the length of the gas hose by the flow of gasoline and by atmospheric conditions. Modern fuel-pump equipment has been designed to prevent

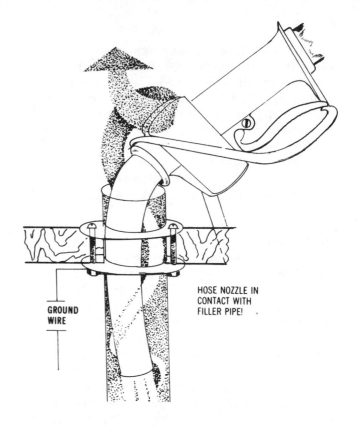

GROUND WIRE

HOSE NOZZLE IN CONTACT WITH FILLER PIPE!

**Fig. 9-7   Filler-Pipe Deck Flange with Hose Nozzle**

such discharge and the danger is, therefore, less than in the past. However, safety precautions are still an absolute necessity.

Space must be allowed for fuel expansion; the tank should not be filled to capacity. Approximately five percent should be allowed, based on the average coefficient of fuel expansion. It is not necessary to mathematically compute the fuel expansion; experience can be the controlling factor.

When the fueling operation has been completed, any spillage should be wiped up immediately. Exhaust blowers should be operated for a minimum of four minutes before starting engines. This is sometimes difficult to accomplish when the dock is crowded and other boats are waiting to fuel.

Be thoroughly familiar with the dangers of handling gasoline and the necessary precautions to reduce the risk of fire.

Become acquainted with the most effective means of extinguishing a gasoline fire. Gasoline explosions and fires are the leading causes of property damage and significant causes of loss of life and injury on small boats. Gasoline is used as fuel on the majority of boats now in operation, and the boat operator constantly faces the hazards of gasoline fire or explosion.

The following Rules for Fueling are reprinted from a publication of the National Fire Protection Association and should be thoroughly learned by every boat operator:

1. Fuel tanks should be properly installed and vented overboard.
2. Fueling should be completed before dark except in emergencies.
3. Whenever a boat is moored at service dock for fueling:
   a. Do not smoke, strike matches or throw switches;
   b. Stop all engines, motors, fans and other devices liable to produce sparks;
   c. Put out all light and galley fires.
4. Before starting to fuel:
   a. See that the boat is moored securely;
   b. Close all ports, windows, doors and hatches;
   c. Ascertain definitely how much additional fuel the tanks will hold.
   d. Have a Class B fire extinguisher handy.
5. During fueling:
   a. Keep the nozzle of the hose, or can, in contact with the fill opening to guard against possible static spark;
   b. See that no fuel spillage gets into the hull or bilges.
6. After fueling is completed:
   a. Close fill openings tightly;
   b. Wipe up ALL spilled fuel;
   c. Open all ports, windows, doors and hatches;
   d. Permit boat to ventilate for at least five minutes;
   e. See that there is no odor of gasoline in the engine room or below deck before starting machinery or

lighting fire. Dangerous vapors will settle to the lowest level of the bilges;
   f. Be prepared to cast off mooring lines as soon as engine starts.
NOTE: Portable fuel tanks should never be filled in the boat. Take them ashore to be filled.

**Installation Requirements**

Other installation requirements for an inboard engine include accessible propeller shaft bearings, especially the one located where the propeller shaft goes through the hull. This bearing, called a <u>stuffing box</u>, does require occasional adjustment so that the shaft can turn easily while admitting as little water as possible. The engine should be placed as close to horizontal as possible—something that is frequently overlooked. Lubrication systems within the engine may fail or operate badly if the engine is seated with its forward or aft end too high.

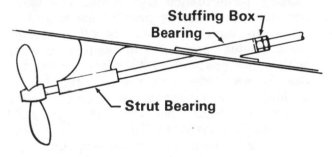

**Fig. 9-8   Stuffing Box**

The engine's accessibility is of course a matter of some importance. The more accessible the better, but an engine box in the middle of the cabin can be both a nuisance and a source of noise and smell. A prospective owner would be wise to insist on an inboard installation that allows access to the carburetor, fuel line and filter, oil fill and spark plugs—as a minimum.

Ideally, the boat should have two 12-volt batteries rated for marine service, one for starting and one for accessories, both charged by the engine's generator or alternator. The batteries should be hooked up to a master switch that allows current to be drawn from either one or both at once. Batteries should be installed as low as possible, because of their weight, yet above the level of the bilge. Batteries must be secured in their own container against the most violent heeling the boat may encounter, and they should also be protected by a cover or shield from accidental short-circuiting caused by dropping a tool across the terminals. The battery box should also be ventilated, as rapid charging builds up explosive hydrogen gas concentrations.

## Sailboat Propellers

Sailboat engines are designed—by and large—to turn a large propeller at a rather slow speed. For this reason, many auxiliary engines are geared down, so that the propeller turns at something like one-third the speed of the engine itself. The propeller may be one of several types. On cruising sailboats, where high performance under sail isn't a factor, the propeller is usually three-bladed and large. The skipper accepts the drag penalty under sail in order to have reasonably good performance under power. The sailing cruiser with some pretensions to speed under sail has a two-bladed propeller. While not so efficient for powering as a three-bladed wheel of similar diameter, the two-bladed prop can be made to lie vertically in the space just ahead of, or behind, the rudder, for minimum drag.

Racing sailboats frequently use a folding propeller. When moving through the water with the engine off, the prop folds into a flower-bud shape, but when the engine is on and in gear, centrifugal force from the spinning propeller shaft opens the blades and holds them in place, moving the boat forward. Except for boats that will be raced frequently, the folding propeller is inefficient for simple propulsion and makes close-quarters maneuvering under power difficult.

## Propeller Location

Generally speaking, a propeller forward of the rudder will steer the boat somewhat more effectively. If a fixed, two-bladed propeller is used, the propeller

Fig. 9-9   Three Blade Propeller

Fig. 9-10   Two Blade Propeller

shaft should be marked to show when the two blades are in an up-and-down position relative to the rudder. This will be the most efficient sailing position, from the viewpoint of minimizing prop drag when under sail alone.

Fig. 9-11    Folding Propeller—Closed

Fig. 9-12    Folding Propeller—Open

Nearly all inboards are installed so that the propeller shaft is in line with the rudder, and most have the propeller just forward of the rudder. Nearly all small gasoline engines are right-hand-turning. A right-hand-turning propeller, as viewed from the stern looking forward, turns in a clockwise direction to move the boat forward. This means that the

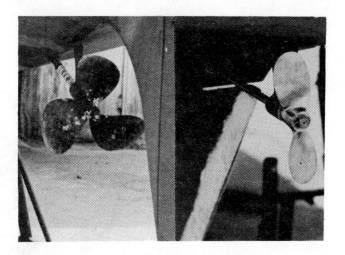

Fig. 9-13    Propeller Forward of Rudder and Propeller Aft of Rudder

boat has a tendency to edge to port when moving either ahead or astern. Going forward, the clockwise prop is more efficient on its starboard side, pulling the stern along with it and, by extension, pushing the bow to port. With the engine in reverse, the propeller turns counter-clockwise, with the same starboard effect. The stern is pulled to port as the boat backs. In many cases, this effect is very marked in reverse, and makes the boat virtually unsteerable; no matter which way the wheel or tiller is turned, the boat backs irresistibly to port. It is always most noticeable when the clutch is first engaged because the side thrust occurs before the boat begins to move forward or backward so that the rudder is temporarily ineffective.

Keep a wooden plug the size of the shaft tied nearby on a string. If it is ever necessary to remove the shaft the plug can be used to stop the hole.

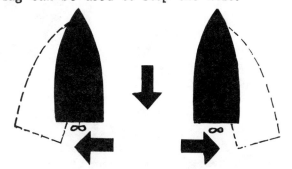

Fig.  9-14    Propeller Rotation Effect on Stern

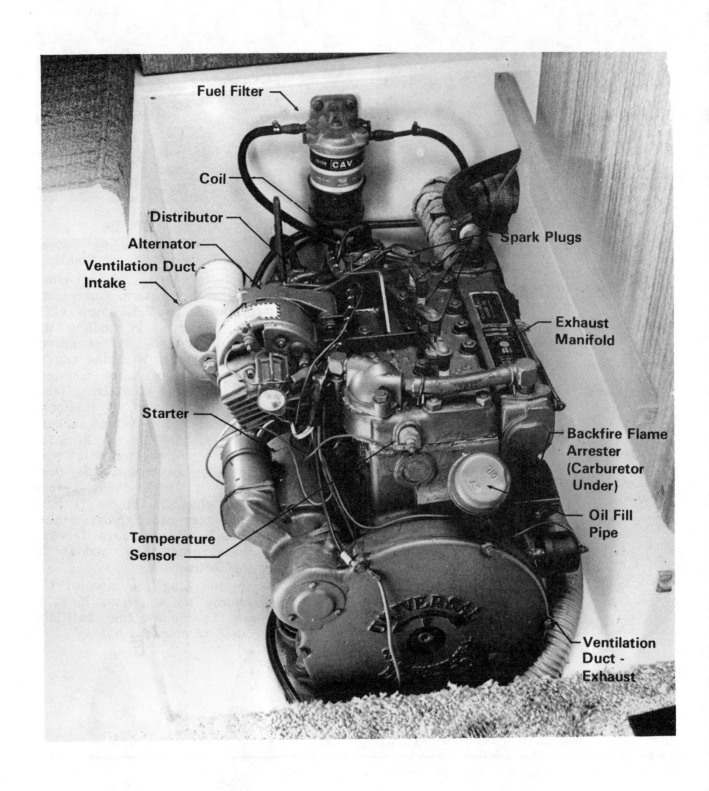

**Fig. 9-15 Inboard Gasoline Engine Mounted in its Compartment**

## Inboard Trouble-Shooting

A gasoline-fueled inboard engine is basically the same as an outboard, but it has some problems that are peculiar to its method of installation. The following suggestions should cover most engines, but it should be emphasized that your best guide for trouble-shooting and maintenance is the owner's manual.

### Problem—STARTING MOTOR WILL NOT OPERATE
**Possible Cause/Solution**
1. Low or dead battery:
   Turn off all electrical equipment and wait for about 30 minutes. While waiting for the battery to recoup enough power to turn the engine over, remove and clean the battery cable connections and then reclamp them.
2. Defective starter switch:
   Inspect connections for tightness, broken wires or bare wire touching engine. Take a test lamp (see Tools below) and place one lead to the ground post of the battery (usually the negative post, but always the one bolted to the engine frame or block) and the other lead to the primary terminal (small wire) on the distributor. When the engine is turned over, by hand or starter, the test lamp will light when the ignition switch is in the "on" position and working properly.

### Problem—STARTING MOTOR WORKS, BUT ENGINE WILL NOT START
**Possible Cause/Solution**
1. Primary electrical circuit:
   Look for corroded, dirty, damaged or loose connections in the wires from the junction box to the ignition switch, the wire to the coil and to the distributor.

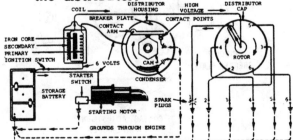

**Fig. 9-16   Battery Ignition System**

2. Secondary circuit:
   Look for broken or damaged wires to spark plugs and from the coil to the distributor cap. Check for moisture on the wires or spark plugs that would cause the spark to be grounded.
3. Ignition:
   Check distributor points to see if they open and close as the engine is cranked. In the maximum open position, the opening should be about .02 inches—about the thickness of a matchbook cover. Inspect the distributor cap to ensure that the contact button is in place and, if spring loaded, free to move so that it can touch the rotor.
4. Spark test:
   Hold a spark-plug wire about 1/4" from the engine while cranking the engine with the ignition on. (Do not hold a bare wire). The capacitor discharge ignition system utilizes an extremely high voltage which would require the use of non-conducting pliers or a testing tool which has been specifically designed for this purpose. If a spark occurs, problem is probably in the fuel system or with the plugs themselves. If there is no spark, remove the secondary wire from the distributor cap to the coil and try the spark test again. If you get a spark this time, the trouble is between the coil lead and the spark plugs--that is, the distributor cap, rotor contact, plug wires and spark plugs.

### Problem—STARTING MOTOR OPERATES, SPARK IS GOOD, BUT ENGINE WILL NOT START
**Possible Cause/Solution**
1. Out of fuel:
   Always refuel in plenty of time, preferably when tank is still one-third full. If you are planning a round trip with no fuel stops, make sure the outbound leg is one-third the boat's cruising range or less.
2. Fuel not reaching fuel pump:
   Check the fuel filter or sediment bowl. If it is not filled with fuel and if the tank is full, the gas line shut-

off may be closed or the line may be clogged.

3. <u>Fuel not reaching carburetor:</u>
Make sure the filter screen is clean. If there is an additional filter beside the fuel pump, check that, too. Disconnect the outlet line from the fuel pump to the carburetor, turn off ignition, and see if fuel flows out when the engine is cranked.
<u>CAUTION!</u> Take special care not to spill fuel where it can cause a fire or explosion risk, or where it will pollute the water.

4. <u>Fuel not reaching cylinders:</u>
Remove spark plugs and see if they are moist. If the plugs are dry, the problem may be in the carburetor. Check the main jet adjustment and open it more, if possible.

5. <u>Choke not closing properly:</u>
Operate manually.

6. <u>Engine flooded:</u>
Open the throttle all the way; put choke in non-choke position (open); turn ignition on; crank engine several times.

**Routine Check List — Inboard Engines**

When preparing to leave the dock, before casting off the lines, check the oil pressure and be sure the cooling water is circulating. If water is not circulating, determine the cause immediately, otherwise overheating may develop and substantial damage could result.

To ensure reliable operation of the engine after leaving the dock, the following check list is provided to be used before leaving dock.

1. FUEL. Top off the fuel tank; don't run out of fuel at sea.
2. OIL. Dipstick should indicate oil level is within proper operating range. Don't overfill beyond the top level indicator.
3. HYDRAULIC DRIVE TRANSMISSION. Check the oil level on the dipstick. Again, don't overfill beyond the top level indicator.

4. ALTERNATOR AND PUMP BELTS. Replace if frayed or cracked, tighten if loose. Belts should not be too tight as excessive belt and bearing wear may result.
5. WATER. Closed cooling systems--top off or fill to proper level.
6. BATTERIES. Fill with distilled water to proper level. Check to see if they are fully charged. If a hydrometer is available, each should be checked for proper specific gravity.
7. BILGE BLOWERS. Ventilate at least 4 minutes before starting the engine.
8. ALARM SYSTEMS. There are many alarm systems available for monitoring the items above; however, these systems do not eliminate the need to check the gauges or sniff in closed spaces for fuel vapors.
9. GREASE CUPS. Keep clean and filled.
10. FILTERS. Keep clean and change at frequency recommended by manufacturer's operating manual.
11. ENGINE. Permit the engine to warm up slowly. Don't get underway with a cold engine. The result may soon be a breakdown of valves, bearings, etc. It is mandatory that the proper warm-up period be followed so that oil reaches all the moving parts. It is better to warm the engine "in gear" with propeller loading rather than by prolonged idling, if this can be done without straining deck fittings, etc.

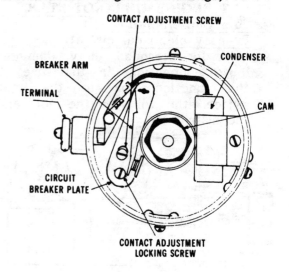

**Fig. 9-17 Distributor**

Check the flow of cooling water through the engine and exhaust.

12. FUEL PUMP. Some engines are equipped with double diaphragm fuel pumps with a small sight-glass indicator. If the sight glass contains fuel, one of the diaphragms has ruptured. The second diaphragm should continue to operate, supplying fuel to the engine, as this is a back-up feature intended for emergency situations. If a ruptured diaphragm is indicated, the fuel pump should be replaced or repaired prior to the boat's getting underway.

## Seasonal Routine Maintenance

### Pre-Season Routine Maintenance—Inboards

1. FUSE SYSTEMS. Prior to putting the boat in the water, go over the electrical system very carefully. Trace each circuit and develop a wiring diagram. Determine the fuse rating and store several spare fuses of each size in the parts kit. Don't overlook the spare fuses; the fuse box can't be "jury-rigged" without the possibility of starting a fire. Seal the wiring diagram in a plastic bag so that it won't be ruined by moisture.

2. BREAKER POINTS AND CONDENSER There are special ignition wrenches used to adjust and set the points. These wrenches aren't too expensive and represent a good investment. Before the season starts, check the points carefully for sharp points or pitting. Use a fine file to smooth off the points and then regap the points. Don't use emery boards or sandpaper on the points; emery dust or sandpaper dust or grit may contribute to difficulties in the electrical circuit. If the contact points are badly worn, replace the points and the condenser. Using the manufacturer's operating manual, set the proper gap. Then test the engine.

3. SPARK PLUGS. Before the season starts, go over the plugs carefully, clean and regap. Replace if badly worn. Refer to the trouble-shooting section and follow instructions.

4. CARBURETOR. If the boat has been laid up for the winter and all fuel was not drained, there may be a gum residue in the carburetor. There are numerous commercial carburetor cleaners in spray cans on the market that will help. Check all parts very carefully. Replace worn or broken gaskets.

5. HOLD-DOWN BOLTS. Go over the base of the engine carefully to determine if any of the bolts are loose. This can result in vibration and cause the engine to run improperly. While checking the hold-down bolts, make sure the bolts on the propeller shaft flange coupling are tight. If the boat has been out of water, this coupling was probably loosened to avoid strain. Check stuffing boxes for the propeller shaft and rudder post.

6. FLAME ARRESTERS. Clean and inspect the flame arresters.

7. GENERATOR BELTS. Check the generator belt carefully. If it is frayed or worn, replace it. If loose or too tight, adjust it according to the operator's manual.

8. COOLING SYSTEM. Inspect the water hoses thoroughly. Remove cork plugs and store for use again next winter. Check all clamps; make sure they are tight. Check for leaks. If the hoses are limp or soft, replace them. They may be about to rupture. If water pump is belt-driven, give the belt the same check as generator belt. Check the coolant level in a closed system.

9. BATTERY. Check with a hydrometer to make sure it has the proper specific gravity--that all the cells are good. Clean the terminals and cover with grease. Before connecting the battery cables, check the polarity. The cable lugs and battery terminals are marked (+) and (-) or (POS) and (NEG). Just match them.

If the battery has just been charged, allow it to sit for about 30 minutes before installing it. Hydrogen gas is

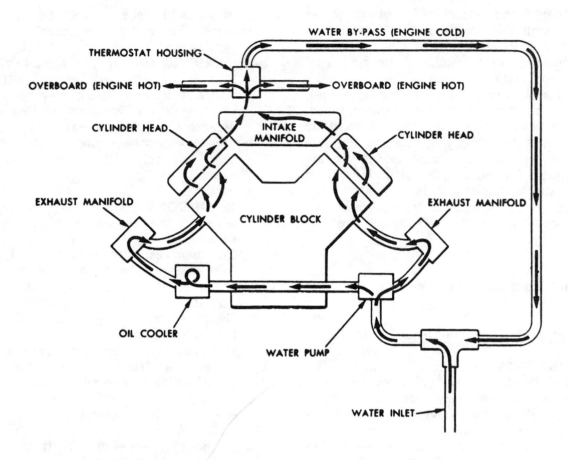

**Fig. 9-18    Water Cooling System**

generated by charging, and continues to be released for some time afterward. Hydrogen can be explosive.

When you connect the battery teminals connect the "hot" lead first, the grounded lead last.

10. LUBRICATION. If oil was changed before storage, check the oil level only. If oil was not changed, do so now, and change the filter, too. Dispose of the old oil and filter properly. Perform all other engine lubrication specified by the manufacturer. Check transmission or gear case for lubricant.

Post-Season Routine Maintenance —
Inboards

1. LUBE OIL SYSTEM. Allow the engine to operate until it is warm; then drain the oil and replace it with new oil. If the engine has a filter, change and replace it with a new one. Start the engine again and pour engine oil slowly into the carburetor air intake until the engine stalls. Fill all grease cups and lubricate all points specified by the manufacturer.

2. COOLING SYSTEM. Drain the water cooling system and, if equipped with a closed system, replace with a half and half mixture of permanent automotive-type anti-freeze and water. If raw-water cooled, flush with fresh water and drain. Check the water pump carefully for worn gaskets, leaks, cable breaks, worn hoses, etc. Plug the exhaust and cooling water lines.

3. IGNITION SYSTEM. Remove the spark plugs. While they are out for cleaning, regapping, or replacing, squirt a little oil into each cylinder and turn the engine over a few times. Replace the plugs but don't cinch them down tight. Don't turn the engine over again until next spring. Use the manufacturer's recommended lubricant on the distributor, starter, and genera-

tor. Examine the breaker points and condenser. Check the points for pitting or excess wear. Replace if badly worn or, if not worn too badly, file points until even. As previously mentioned, the points and condenser should be replaced together. Remove the battery and store.

4. FUEL SYSTEM. Drain all fuel from the carburetor and fuel lines. The removal of fuel cuts down the possibility of a fire hazard and the formation of gum or varnish in the fuel system.

5. DRIVE SYSTEM. Drain the transmission and fill it with the proper lubricant. Disconnect the propeller-shaft flange.

6. GENERAL. Wipe all the exposed metal surfaces with a lightly oiled rag. This should inhibit rusting during the winter. If the engine has a hood or cover, it should remain on the engine. But don't seal off the engine; it is mandatory that air be allowed to circulate around the engine. Do seal securely the opening at the carburetor intake with strong plastic film or other moisture-proof material. On overhead valve engines, remove valve cover and give the entire valve assembly a good oiling.

7. OLDER ENGINES. Check all rubber fuel hoses for deterioration caused by using low-lead or no-lead fuel containing alcohol.

8. FUEL SYSTEM. Fill the fuel tank(s) to the recommended maximum with fresh fuel.

## Diesel-Powered Inboard Engines

More and more owners of cruising sailboats are turning to diesel power, because of its safety, its dependability and its operating economy. Diesels are more expensive to buy than equivalent-horsepower gasoline engines, and they are heavier than equivalent gas engines. Diesel horsepower sizes are much the same as those of gasoline-powered engines, and auxiliaries in larger cruising vessels may be 60 hp or even larger. Because diesels have a dual horsepower rating, it is sometimes a little difficult to know just what to expect from a given engine. The maximum continuous horsepower is what the engine will put out hour after hour, and is the figure of most interest to the consumer. Maximum intermittent horsepower is a higher rating but can be sustained for brief periods of emergency speed.

Diesel installation and operation is much the same as for gasoline engines. Because one need not ventilate a diesel for safety reasons, many skippers do not provide the kind of venting they would for a gas engine. This is a mistake, as a diesel requires considerable quantities of fresh air to operate properly. A diesel's only great drawback, purchase price aside, is its smell--more correctly, the smell of its fuel. Many people find it considerably more unpleasant than gasoline, but a proper installation, good maintenance and careful fueling procedures can minimize odors. Most small diesels are left-hand-turning (counter-clockwise), so the stern will move to port--and the bow to starboard--when in forward gear. In reverse, the stern moves to starboard.

## Diesel Trouble-Shooting

One reason a diesel is so reliable is that it lacks the complex electrical system required to provide a timed spark to a gasoline engine. Since electricity and the dampness of the nautical environment are incompatible, a simple electrical system means fewer breakdowns.

## Fuel problems
1. Tank empty.
2. Shut-off valve closed.
3. Water in fuel: Open drain cock in bottom of fuel filter. If there is water in the filter, drain it all out and prime system with the prime pump or by cranking the engine.
4. Clogged or dirty filter(s): There are usually at least two filters in a diesel fuel system.
5. Air leak in fuel system: Check connections in the fuel lines from tank to fuel pump. Check gaskets on fuel filter and strainer housing or cap.

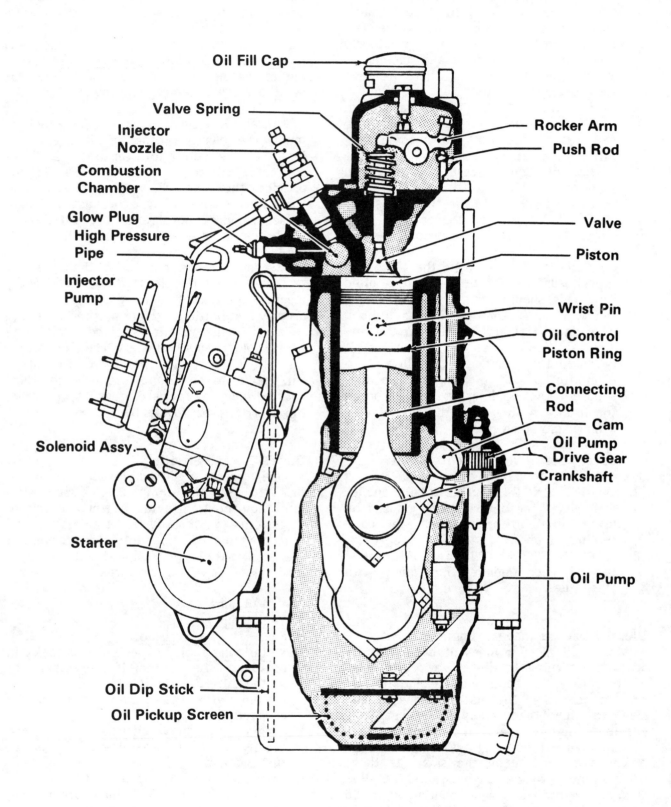

Oil Fill Cap

Valve Spring

Injector
Nozzle

Combustion
Chamber

Glow Plug
High Pressure
Pipe

Injector
Pump

Solenoid Assy.

Starter

Oil Dip Stick

Oil Pickup Screen

Rocker Arm

Push Rod

Valve

Piston

Wrist Pin

Oil Control
Piston Ring

Connecting
Rod

Cam

Oil Pump
Drive Gear

Crankshaft

Oil Pump

Fig. 9-19  Cutaway of Diesel Engine

Disconnect fuel return line and allow fuel to flow until no air bubbles show in the fuel.

6. Fuel not reaching engine: Some engines have electrical fuel shut-offs which operate when the engine is shut down. A "short" may have closed the switch. Disconnect it and try to start the engine.

7. Air in fuel lines: Use the prime pump to build up fuel pressure and try to restart.

**Electrical problems—Probably associated with starter motor.** See "Starting motor will not operate" above.

**A Basic Tool Kit**

A sailor's tools are generally associated with rigging adjustment. It is a good idea to have a separate set of tools for your boat's engine. In many cases, your owner's manual will suggest special tools for your engine, and many manufacturers offer a prepackaged set of spare parts for their engines—an extra well worth having.

Test lamp: available in hardware stores or easily made by purchasing a socket for the bulbs used aboard your boat plus two six-foot lengths of wire. Uncover about

**Fig. 9-20    Test Lamp**

one inch of each end of the wires; attach one end to the lamp socket and use the other as a test probe. Use a bulb of the same voltage as your boat's electrical system.

| | |
|---|---|
| Wrenches: | Adjustable end wrench (crescent) |
| | Pipe wrench |
| | Box-end wrench set (Metric or English, to fit the engine and other fittings.) |
| Pliers: | Slip-joint adjustable (insulated) pliers |
| | Vise grips |
| | Wire-cutting pliers |
| | Needle-nose pliers |
| Screwdrivers: | Assorted regular and Phillips head |

Hammer
Hacksaw
File

Spare Parts
    Points for distributor
    Condenser
    Coil
    Spark plugs
    Fan belt (and belts for all engine's power take-offs)
    Fuel pump
    Fuel filter for diesel engines
    Fuel injectors for diesel engines and special tools, if necessary
    Waterproof tape
    Hose clamps
    Marine water pump and wheel bearing grease.
    Waterless hand cleaner

# Chapter 10

# Trailering

The average small sailing cruiser meanders along at about four knots. Power boats average a little faster. Ten hours of cruising, given decent conditions, and you're only a few miles from where you started. Or consider the price of marina accommodation for a small boat - even assuming the berths are available. By fitting your boat with a trailer, you can start your boating vacation 500 miles from your usual cruising grounds, visit places you would normally never see, and avoid the costs and hazards of marinas. At season's end you can store your boat at home where you can work on her through the winter months as the weather allows.

Trailer boating has become increasingly popular in recent years. Of the approximately 13 million recreational boats in the United States, over 95% are trailerable.

10-1

## The Trailerable Boat

The first requirement is a suitable boat. One of the few absolute limiting factors of such a boat is its width. For trailering without a special permit, the maximum width of the boat and trailer combination is eight feet on some state roads or 8 feet 6 inches on Interstate and other Federal-aid highways with 12-foot lanes. Most manufacturers and designers make a special point to make sure that the beam falls within the trailerable limit, if the design permits. Although boats over 30 feet have been built with an eight-foot beam, the maximum length of most trailerable sailboats is under 25 feet. Boats with unusual hull shapes, and

Fig. 10-1  Trailerable  Keel–Centerboard Hull

especially sailboats, can pose special problems.

It's obvious that hull shape is also a major factor. The ideal hull from a trailering point of view is flat-bottomed or gently rounded, with no protrusions. This kind of hull is virtually required if you are going to launch at a municipal ramp or off a beach. If in doubt, get in touch with the dealer who handles your boat, and if he doesn't know, have him ask the manufacturer. Chances are that the designer had a standard brand of trailer in mind when designing the boat. Whatever the hull shape, it is essential that it be supported evenly by the trailer.

## The Trailer

Width and length aside, highway requirements for a trailer to be towed at high speeds are fairly serious. These requirements fall into two general categories - what is legally necessary, and what is derived from common sense. Legal requirements are still changing in many areas, as more and more states turn their attention to the dangers inherent in trailering. Consult your state police and your motor vehicle bureau for up-to-the-minute information.

Trailers are divided into classes based on the total weight of the trailer and its load at a standard speed. A decrease in speed will allow a slight increase in weight.

CLASS 1.  Gross weight of trailer including load not to exceed 2000 pounds.

CLASS 2.  Gross weight of trailer including load of over 2000 pounds through 3500 pounds.

CLASS 3.  Gross weight of trailer including load of over 3500 pounds through 5000 pounds.

CLASS 4.  Gross weight of trailer including load of over 5000 pounds.

Federal Law requires that all trailers have certain important capacity information displayed. The Gross Vehicle Weight Rating (GVWR) for the trailer must be displayed, which includes the trailer and all weight it is expected to carry. If the rating of the trailer is within 15% of the total weight of your boat, gear and trail-

er, it is recommended that you select the next larger capacity trailer. The Gross Axle Weight Rating (GAWR) Capacity information will show the size of tires needed to carry the load for which the trailer is rated. On multi-axle trailers, the combined Gross Axle Weight Rating (GAWR) of all axles must be equal to or greater than the Gross Vehicle Weight Rating (GVWR) for the trailer.

Your trailer will probably require license plates and lights. If possible, get a rear light and license-plate set that's demountable, so that you can remove them before backing the trailer into the water. Lights like this normally clamp to the boat's transom. No lighting system made can resist repeated immersion, despite what a manufacturer may claim. You will also need turn-indicator lights and, if your rig nears the eight-foot maximum, side lights as well.

Pay special attention to the electrical plug and socket arrangement connecting the car's lighting system to the trailer. The wiring should be under no stress, should be as weatherproof as possible, and should not sag or loop so that it can get caught in machinery or drag along the ground. Stranded wire is recommended to reduce vibration damage. A good ground is essential, and a separate ground cable between the trailer and the tow vehicle may be necessary. The addition of lights and reflectors to the rear of the boat or trailer, beyond that required by law, will significantly increase safety at night.

Brake requirements vary greatly from state to state, but the American Boat &

☐ SAFE LOADING
   CAPACITY

☐ MOTOR UP               ☐ REAR VIEW
                            MIRRORS

☐                      ☐ SAFETY CHAINS
LIGHTING        WEIGHT
EQUIPMENT   DISTRIBUTED
            EVENLY

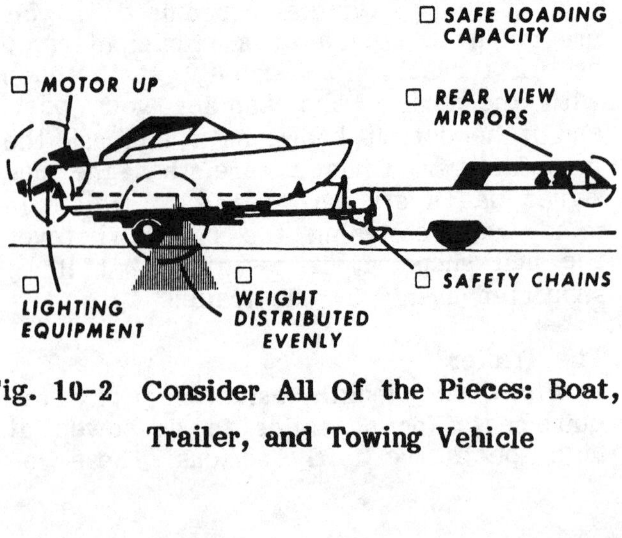

Fig. 10-2  Consider All Of the Pieces: Boat,
Trailer, and Towing Vehicle

Fig. 10-3  Typical Electrical Connector

Yacht Council recommends that trailer manufacturers offer brakes of some sort for all wheels of trailers designed for a gross weight of 1,500 lbs. or more. Legal requirements can be met by any one of the three common brake systems—electrical, hydraulic or surge. The first two are integrated into the tow vehicle's own brake system; the surge brake is activated by the trailer's own momentum. Your trailer's brakes should operate automatically when the towing car's service brakes are applied, and should continue to operate even if the trailer separates from the tow car.

## The Hitch

Choosing the proper class of hitch for the weight of the trailer being towed is very important. There are two basic types of hitch, the weight-carrying hitch and the weight-distribution (or load-equalizer) hitch.

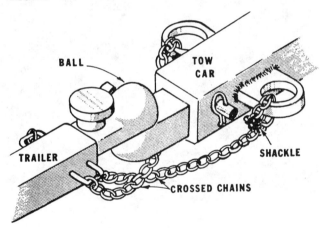

Fig. 10-4   Trailer Hitch

The class of hitch required depends on the gross trailer weight and its tongue weight. The dealer that supplied the towing vehicle can normally provide guidance in purchasing a suitable hitch.

## Weight-Carrying Hitches

The simplest and most inexpensive weight hitch is the so-called "bumper hitch," which is mounted on the rear bumper of the car. While it may be adequate for very light trailers, it is not recommended, and is banned in several states. (The "step-bumper" hitch mounted on many light trucks is not considered a bumper hitch and may be acceptable.)

Weight-carrying hitches come in various sizes and configurations depending upon the gross trailer weight, the tongue weight and the tow vehicle characteristics. As the name implies, the weight-carrying hitch holds the trailer's entire tongue weight.

Fig. 10-5   Front Hitch

## Weight-Distribution Hitch

The rear of a tow vehicle is generally loaded with luggage, gear, and, sometimes a back seat full of kids. When you add the tongue weight of a loaded trailer, you can place heavy strain on the rear tires, shocks and springs of the tow vehicle. There may be so much weight on the rear of the car that some of the weight on the front wheels is removed, making it difficult to control the car. A weight-distribution hitch redistributes much of this weight to all four wheels of the tow vehicle as well as the wheels of the trailer, resulting in better handling, safer operation and less wear on the tow vehicle. Some weight-distribution hitches are also equipped with anti-sway bars, which help control trailer sway and improve control.

## Coupler and Ball

The coupler is the mechanism which

attaches the trailer to the hitch. It is generally one of two basic types, the latch or the screw type.

The coupler must be of a size which matches the ball. The size of the ball is determined by the Gross Vehicle Weight Rating (GVWR). All couplers manufactured after 1973 have the Gross Vehicle Weight Rating stamped on them.

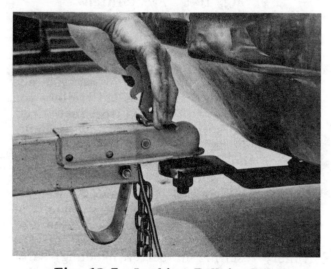

**Fig. 10-7 Locking Ball in Cup**

Among your trailer-gear spares, you should carry an extra ball, in case wear or turning stresses force yours out of roundness. Like all trailer bolt fittings, the ball should be secured by a lock nut.

## Safety Chains

The final legal requirement in most states is safety chains. These consist simply of a pair of chains running from the tongue of the trailer to the towing hitch. The chains are crossed under the hitch in such a way that if the ball and coupler should fail, the trailer tongue won't hit the ground, dig in and cause the trailer to somersault. The chains should be just long enough to permit free turning and should be fastened securely to the vehicle. If S-hooks are used, they should be hooked with the S facing back toward the trailer to prevent their jumping free. Although S-hooks are acceptable, it is a safer practice to use a shackle and safety wire in place of the S-hook.

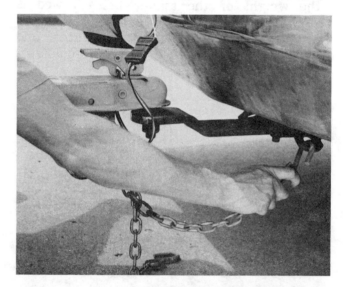

**10-9 Crossing Second Chain Under First**

**10-10 Hookup Complete**

The chains themselves should be of welded steel, with a working test-load equivalent to the trailer's recommended gross weight, which is marked on the trailer itself. Although a single length of safety chain, looping through the eyes on the trailer tongue, may be used, individually attached chains provide an extra safety factor. The chains should never be made fast to a fitting common with the ball, but to some separate solid attachment point.

**Fig. 10-11  Outboard Chained to Transom and Drain Plug in Place**

## Support Points

After safety considerations, the most important thing about a trailer is its sup-

port of your boat's hull. Even sturdy fiberglass boats can be badly wrenched out of shape if they're not braced at critical points. The problem is that no roller-supporting system can support a hull on all points as evenly as water. All hull support systems are a compromise, and there are a few key things to watch out for.

For most hulls, vital support points are the forefoot, the keel, the turn of the bilge (especially where interior weights are concentrated) and the transom. Any other spot where a specially heavy downward force is exerted on the hull should also be braced from below when the hull is fully seated on the trailer. In the general category of concentrated weights you can include retractable keels or weighted centerboards on sailboats, water and fuel tanks, batteries, and engines. If your boat has an inboard engine, this is an absolutely overriding weight concentration that must be carefully braced beneath the engine bed stringers.

On most commercial trailers, the rollers and bolsters are adjustable, both up and down and fore an aft, and the winch column and wheel assemblies can also be moved along the frame. Given a trailer of adequate length and width, therefore, it should be possible to adjust the various elements of the frame and the supports to match the boat with some precision. Remember to be careful when adjusting any element that has a matching component on the boat's other side. An inch or so of fore-and-aft difference between the rollers can make a serious riding problem for the whole rig.

**Fig. 10-12  Roller Supporting System**

## Tires

A trailer's tires and wheels undergo far more strain than do those on your car. Not only are a trailer's wheels often smaller to begin with, turning at higher speeds, but they are also subject to immersion, often in corrosive salt water. Maximum tire-load capacity and pressure are marked on the tire itself. These pressures are considerably higher than those of the tires on your family car. You should carry a suitable tire-pressure gauge and check your trailer's tires frequently. If you err, it should be on the side of more air in the tires, not less. Low air pressure in small, high-speed tires causes them to heat up faster and fail sooner.

## The Winch

Under way on the open road, a trailered boat is subject to a type of motion that it will never encounter on the water. Every unattached piece of gear in the trailered boat should be firmly secured, and the boat itself should be firmly lashed in place.

The primary point of attachment is forward, at the trailer winch. If you plan to launch and recover off the trailer with some frequency, this winch is an especially important piece of equipment. It is usually an extra-cost option, so you have some choice as to type.

Your winch should have an anti-reverse gear so that the boat cannot slide backwards, and unless the boat is very light, the standard rope on the winch drum should be replaced with stainless steel wire. For larger boats, geared winches and electrical winches running off the towing vehicle's battery are available. The winch drum should be mounted, if possible, approximately on a line with the towing eye on your boat's bow when the boat is fully cradled. If there is no towing eye, the angle of pull from the bow chocks should be slightly downward.

Do not expect the winch alone to hold the bow in place. An additional wire cable, preferably with a turnbuckle, should

**Fig. 10-13 Winch Cable Hooked to Eye of Stem**

connect the boat's stem to the winch pillar. There should also be a non-stretching strap across the after part of the boat. Webbing like that used for auto seat belts or sailboat hiking straps will do well enough, but pad the hull or wood trim directly under the strap with old carpeting to preserve gel coat and varnish. A pair of spring lines (these can be your boat's dock lines) should be run aft from the bow cleat to the trailer frame about even with the wheels.

Important extras, after a winch and brakes, include the following: spare trailer wheel, bearing grease and a complete set of wheel bearings, bulbs for the trailer's lights, a jack that suits the trailer's frame and can lift the trailer and boat, a set of long-handled wrenches for tightening the various body bolts regularly, outside mirrors for the towing vehicle, flares, trouble flag and trouble light.

## The Tow Vehicle

The average passenger car is designed to carry only people. You will need to beef it up if you want to tow anything but the lightest of trailers. The advent of front-wheel drive makes the load distribu-

**Fig. 10-14 Trailer Tongue Jack and Dolly Wheel**

tion between the front and rear axles even more important than it was on the older, heavier cars. Both steering and traction now depend on sufficient weight on the front axle. The owner's manual of a typical front-wheel drive car with a gross vehicle weight of 2800 pounds indicates that the permissible trailer gross weight without brakes is only 885 pounds. The same car can tow a 2200 GVW trailer with brakes, but only on hills with less than a 12% gradient if the car has a manual transmission, or less than 16% with an automatic transmission. Trailer-tongue loading is limited in all cases, often to as little as 110 pounds.

Except for specially equipped utility vehicles, you should not tow a trailer heavier than your car. Many manufacturers sell towing packages including items such as a non-slip differential, heavy-duty cooling system, heavy-duty flashers, over-size battery and alternator, heavy-duty suspension, special wiring, special rear-axle ratio, and larger tires and wheels. Such packages are suitable when included in an order for a new car but are not a viable addition to the car you already own.

The essentials for a towing vehicle include:

Adequate Power - The tow vehicle must have enough power to merge safely with highway traffic when towing maximum load. It must also be able to climb commonly encountered hills without losing speed; therefore, get the largest engine available.

Cooling - For cooling, the engine may need a heavy-duty, high-capacity radiator with more core tubes to speed heat release, possibly a special fan shroud, and a coolant-recovery unit. A thermostat-operated spray-coolant unit to spray cool water on the radiator core tubes when the temperature of the coolant goes too high is also available.

Transmission - Towing a trailer places an extra load on the transmission. This may generate enough heat to thin out the transmission fluid and damage the transmission. To prevent this, it may be necessary to install a small radiator to cool the transmission fluid. The driver of a towing vehicle must always be on the a-lert for transmission leaks, slippage or rough shifting, all of which are indicative of transmission problems.

Brakes - Cars ordered with a towing option have oversized drums and/or special heavy-duty brake linings. Standard auto brakes are undersized for towing all but very light trailers. Brakes should have premium linings, especially on the rear, as the tongue weight keeps wheels in tighter contact with the pavement.

Suspension System - 100 pounds of tongue weight 4 feet behind the rear axle have the same effect as 400 pounds added to the trunk of the car. To avoid excessive sagging and "bottoming out," the suspension should be beefed up with heavy-duty springs, air shocks, or air bags. Heavy-duty shock absorbers are necessary to control the added weight. This will allow the vehicle to ride in a nearly normal attitude and improve visibility and handling.

**Proper Loading**
Balancing the load on your trailer is really the key to successful towing. What it amounts to is adjusting the boat's gross weight - the boat and its contents - so that the load on the trailer tongue is somewhere between five and seven percent of the total gross weight of the

tow: boat + contents + trailer. For the average small passenger car, the weight at the tongue shouldn't be much more than 100 lb. Working backward, that indicates a gross weight of 2,000 lb. as the maximum an ordinary sedan should be asked to pull. If you're in doubt about the towing capabilities of your car, check with the dealer.

To measure tongue weight, load the boat (which is on the trailer) with the gear she would normally carry on the road. Then stack two or three cinder blocks under a set of bathroom scales and ease the trailer's tongue down on this platform. If the weight involved is over about 75 lb., consider fixing an accessory jack and caster to the tongue. The jack-and-caster assembly was developed to facilitate the mating of heavy trailers to the trailer hitch. It allows raising and lowering the trailer tongue and facilitates moving the trailer for parking and other purposes. Raising the trailer tongue will also tilt the boat to allow for drainage when the boat is stored.

If the weight at the trailer tongue is much more than the recommended maximum, the tow car will have too much load behind and be hard to handle at speed. If the tongue weight is too little, the trailer is likely to fishtail. What you want, then, is the happy medium. If you're pulling a load over about 4,000 pounds, by the way, you'll want a tandem, or four-wheel, trailer as well as a special towing vehicle.

You can determine the gross vehicle (trailer) weight by loading the trailer with everything that normally would be on it during transportation and taking the rig to the nearest scales with a platform (highway weighing station, building supply company, trucking company, junk yard, etc.). Weigh the trailer by itself, unhitched and supported on the jack. This will give the gross trailer weight. It is important that the gross trailer weight (Gross Vehicle Weight) does not exceed the Gross Vehicle Weight Rating as shown on the capacity label. Keep the trailer in

a level attitude by adjusting the jack-caster assembly.

Even before loading a new trailer for the first time, it might be wise to consider what might happen if you get a flat tire after the trailer is loaded. Check the wheel nuts for tightness. Factories tend to install wheelnuts with air wrenches; the nuts may be too tight for you to loosen with a tire iron. You might also let the air out of a tire to make sure your jack will fit under the axle when you really need to use it.

### Pre-Departure Checks

Before setting out, you should check the items loaded in the boat to be sure they are properly secured in place. Make certain that no one has tossed in last-minute items that can significantly alter the trailer's balance. Check also that the trailer's bolts are all tightened up. They can work loose slowly and insidiously. Check boat tie-downs, trailer lights and brakes. Spare a moment to make certain that the car-to-trailer umbilicals will stay secured when under way.

If you trailer a sailboat, the mast and boom should be firmly lashed down, preferably in a padded rack. Some trailerable-boat manufacturers supply just such a fitting, but you can usually rig one yourself. The standing and running rigging should be bundled together and tied to

**Fig. 10-15    Mast Padded at the Rack and Transom**

the spar at intervals so that it can't work loose. If you travel rough roads or long distances, consider a covering for at least the winch cluster at the base of the spar and the sheave arrangement at the masthead, just to keep out highway dirt. If the mast protrudes aft, it should have a red flag lashed to its end.

The rudder of a sailboat should be removed before trailering, if it's removable. A bracket-mounted outboard can stay on the boat as long as the transom is supported directly beneath the motor. Protect the motor (or lower unit, if an I/O) from excessive and uncontrolled swinging or bouncing. Avoid supports which concentrate stress in fragile castings, or which rely on hydraulic cylinders, which may suffer damaged seals.

If your sailboat has a swing-keel or a weighted centerboard, it should be lowered until it rests on a frame cross-member. This will save much wear on the centerboard pennant (the wire rope used to raise the centerboard) and a certain amount of stress on the hull, as well.

Underway, remember that you've got a long, heavy, awkward tail behind you. This sounds very obvious, until you see someone pulling a trailer cut in ahead of you, oblivious to the fact that his vehicle is 20 or 25 feet longer than normal.

Start your towing car slowly, in low gear, and take it up through the speeds gently and smoothly. Think twice about passing other cars, but if you decide to pass, pick a spot and go - don't hesitate. When rounding corners, swing wide, after having checked traffic just behind and alongside you. Give plenty of warning with your turn signal.

Remain sensitive to any unusual sounds or handling factors, and if you notice anything at all out of the ordinary, pull over at once and check. In fact, you should get off the road and check out the entire rig every hour or so - look for high temperatures in the wheel bearings,

loosening tie-downs, slacked-off bolts, brake and turn lights, tire pressure and car-engine temperature.

Heavy-duty flashers can slow down the blinking of your turn signal to a "normal" rate, but they have the disadvantage of not revealing a burned-out bulb by failing to flash. If you have them, you should turn on your parking lights and hazard flashers every time you stop and walk around to make sure that all the bulbs are working. This problem exists even if you are not towing your trailer as long as the heavy-duty flasher is installed.

## Launching

Before you attempt a real launching, put in a couple of hours some Sunday in an empty parking lot learning how to line up and back the trailer effectively. Have someone help you by acting as a guide, and develop a set of simple hand signals. Backing a trailer is much easier than docking, but it does take practice. If you have an exceptionally heavy or unwieldy rig, consider buying a front bumper hitch. With this accessory, you can make the launch while moving the towing vehicle forward, and close-quarters maneuvering will be simpler.

When launching, try to avoid getting the trailer hubs in the water. If you can't avoid immersing them, at least let them cool off first, or the heat will simply suck the bearing full of water.

One way to pass the time while waiting for the trailer wheels to cool down from highway temperatures is by preparing the boat. If you have a sailboat, one thing you must do is step the mast. Before you try this, check to be sure that there are no low power lines or other overhead obstructions between you and the launching ramp. Many municipal ramps were laid out for outboard skiffs, not masted vessels. Be certain that no matter how the mast could fall, there are no overhead obstructions that it could hit, especially wire.

## Sailboat Trailering - Raising the Mast

Many sailboats have some form of

**Fig. 10-16   Mast Step on Hinge**

tabernacle for raising the mast. This is essentially a mast stepped on a hinge, and most of them are so arranged that the mast swings up from astern. Smaller boats, of course, don't require this kind of fancy gear, and the mast goes into the normal step guided by a crewmember, as described earlier in this book.

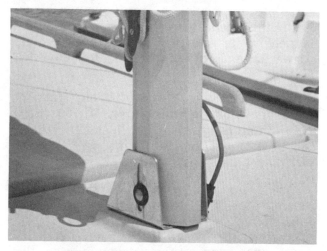

**Fig. 10-17   Mast Tabernacle**

Before beginning to raise the mast, check overhead for wires and obstructions. Check too, that there is a clear overhead path from the set-up area to the actual launching area and beyond.

Masts that pivot up and forward are simple to raise but require a fair amount of muscle power from the crew. With the mast in its hinged tabernacle, attach the upper shrouds and the backstay and tie a

pulling line - a good, thick one, comfortable to the hand - to the forestay just above the turnbuckle. As one person stands in the cockpit and raises the spar, the other crewmember at the bow, who should be the stronger of the two, pulls on the forestay extension.

If the boat is very small and light, the person raising the spar should stay out of the boat while doing it, since the unsupported hull might be damaged by the weight of the person inside. As the mast approaches the point where the person aft can exert no more lift, it may be necessary to tie off the forestay extension until the cockpit hand can get around forward to help pull. Until you're used to the stresses involved, don't take anything for granted: even a light mast can exert an enormous pull at certain acute angles.

The mast may, in some cases, swing up and aft from the bow. The spar thus lies flat over the foredeck after being made fast in its tabernacle. In this case, first make fast the upper shrouds and the forestay. Then attach the boom to its gooseneck at right angles to the mast, holding it in place with the topping lift and temporary guys to the deck at either side. To raise the mast, you simply employ the four- or five-part mechanical advantage of the mainsheet tackle system, amplified if necessary by the genoa sheet winch.

**Launching and Recovery**

Before launching (or recovery) make sure that there is nothing protruding down from the boat to snag on the trailer frame. The outboard should be raised and locked, and the sailboat's centerboard or swing keel should be pulled all the way into its well and the pennant lashed. Don't forget to release the tiedowns and disconnect or remove the trailer's stop and directional lights, and make one last check to see to it that all drain plugs, etc., are in place.

Make sure you NEVER, NEVER cast off all the lines from the boat before launching. Someone on shore must have a

Fig. 10-18   Backing Down the Launch Ramp

line that is made fast to the boat. The line makes it easy to shove the boat off the trailer and then pull the boat to a dock or boarding platform or back to the trailer at a wide, busy launching ramp.

Back the trailer slowly down the ramp until the boat's stern is afloat, then ease it off the trailer. A person ashore should hold a bow line while this is being done. If you can remain in the car, it is a good idea not to turn the engine off so that the car won't roll back into the water when you try to start it again. Put an automatic transmission in "park" and keep a foot on the brake. If you are driving a manual shift vehicle, put the gearshift in first gear and keep your feet on both the clutch and the brake. Remember that the trailer's brakes do not operate from your parking brake lever, and that surge brakes do not work in reverse in any event.

If you must get out of your car to assist in the launching, it is not a good idea to leave your engine running. An

Fig. 10-20   Launched

automatic transmission can slip out of park into reverse with obvious results. If you leave your manual shift in neutral, you are depending entirely on your parking brake. How many times have you backed down your driveway and then shifted into a forward gear before you discovered you had forgotten to release your parking brake? The safest course of action is to set your automatic transmission in park, let up on the footbrake to make sure the transmission is locked,

Fig. 10-19   Releasing the Stem Hook

Fig. 10-21   Beginning Recovery Process

10-11

**Fig. 10-22  Boat Recovered and on Trailer**

then put on the parking brake and shut off the engine. A standard transmission should be left in first gear with the parking brake set and the engine off.

Today, many trailers have special bearings that resist moisture if they are not hot when they are immersed in water. If your trailer does not have immersible bearings and the wheels get wetted down, repack the bearings with grease. It doesn't take long and is easier than changing a burnt-out bearing on the road home.

### Trailer Storage
When the boat is on her trailer for any length of time, get the weight off the trailer suspension and wheels. Jack up the trailer frame and support it with cinder blocks, shimmed up if necessary with pieces of planking. Once the frame is fully jacked up, check underneath to be sure the boat is still evenly supported – the frame can be easily and imperceptibly

wrenched out of shape during the jacking process.

### Boat Covers
Your boat cover should be tailored to your specific boat to stay in place under a variety of conditions. A top drawstring allows for pulling the cover high enough to shed water. Remember that puddling of water must be prevented since rain weighs about 8.3 pounds per gallon. The weight of collected water stretches the cover, allowing the puddle to grow larger until the cover rips or the bottom edge comes up, allowing the water to funnel into the boat. The bottom drawstring and tiedowns, which go under the boat, are handy to prevent the cover from whipping while trailering. Sandbags or other weights sewn into pockets along the bottom drawstring will help keep the cover in place. A tire cover for storage extends tire life by eliminating harmful sun rays.

# Chapter 11

# Weather

## Introduction

Boating people are, as a group, directly concerned with weather. Boaters have a special need to know about sea and wind conditions. Although many sailors tend to regard wind as synonymous with weather, the first is but one aspect of the second. Weather also includes temperature, pressure and moisture, all of which affect the condition of the atmosphere. This chapter will deal with the essentials of weather on two levels, systemic and local. The weather system information here won't make you a meteorologist. But it should help, with practice, in making you aware of what weather to expect before you set out. Weather can turn nasty during an afternoon's outing. Knowing what to expect from local weather signs can reduce your chance of being caught unprepared.

## What Makes Weather Work

All weather is ultimately brought about by heat from the sun within the shallow envelope of gas we call the atmosphere. And all weather change is brought about by rising or falling temperature.

In very simplified terms, the large-scale movement of air around the earth is caused by the air becoming heated from contact with the ground or ocean near the Equator. The heated air rises and spreads around the globe while colder air from the north and south replaces it. If the world didn't rotate, air circulation around it would be much simpler. Because of the earth's rotation, the basic wind patterns are as shown, with prevailing winds that are generally quite reliable. In the continental United States, most of which is located between Latitudes 30° and 60° North, the prevailing winds are

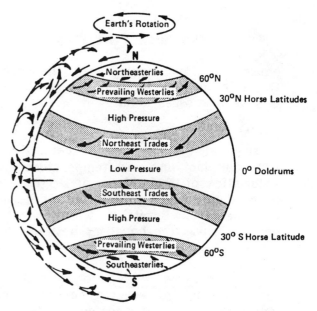

**Fig. 11-1  Global Atmospheric Circulation**

from the west--a fact that influences not only boating habits, but also marina and harbor layouts.

Although the majority of winds across our country blow from a generally westerly direction, there are many days when this isn't the case. Seasonal changes, differences in heat distribution over water and land, geographic features, uneven local heating—all contribute to making weather variable. In the United States, the position of the **Polar Front**, the boundary between the polar easterlies and our prevailing westerlies, normally lies around 60° North. But when the cold polar air moves south, violent weather is sometimes the result.

Another major influence on weather change is the Rocky Mountains, which

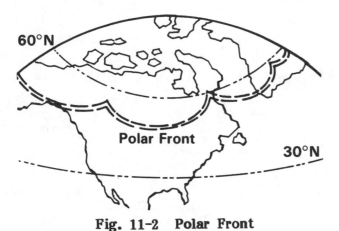

Fig. 11-2 Polar Front

cause the air moving off the Pacific Ocean to change many of its characteristics as it crosses them.

**Air Masses and Fronts**

Huge air masses, which retain for a time the moisture and temperature characteristics of their place of origin, move over the earth's surface, and determine our weather. Unsettled weather regions develop along the boundary between these masses.

High pressure areas are formed when air (for any of several reasons) cools, becomes more compressed, and consequently sinks. In the northern hemisphere the circulation of air is clockwise around a high and the wind directions are both

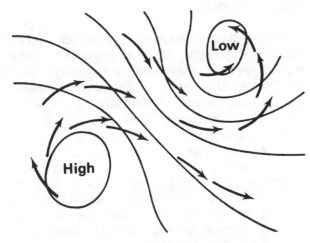

Fig. 11-3 Air Circulation—Clockwise Around Highs, Counterclockwise Around Lows in the Northern Hemisphere

clockwise and outward from the high's center, as shown in Fig. 11-3. High pressure areas may cover immense stretches of the earth's surface--half the United States, under certain conditions--but they are usually a few hundred miles in diameter. Highs originating in the polar area move south and east. Cool, dry air and fair weather is generally characteristic of a high, as are light winds and steady temperatures.

Low pressure areas, in most respects, are the opposite of highs. A low's center is constantly being filled with air moving into it in a generally counterclockwise direction (in the Northern Hemisphere). Winds are strong, but lows, like highs, generally move from west to east across our continent.

There are, however, semi-permanent high and low pressure areas. Off the West Coast of the United States is the **Pacific High**, somewhat larger in summer than in winter. The **Azores High**, over the Atlantic, shows the same seasonal changes in size. In winter, a low frequently exists in the Aleutians, while in summer there is a low that extends from northeast Africa all the way to Indochina. The semi-permanent highs form largely over water, when the sea is cooler than the land.

Localized low pressure areas may also form under a thundercloud formation, where air is rising with great speed, or over very hot areas into which the cooler air flows as the heated air is elevated.

It can be useful to know where a low pressure area is in relation to you, since lows are usually the source of bad boating weather. In the northern hemisphere, stand with your back to the present surface wind, then turn 45° or so to the right. This aligns you with the existing wind aloft, which blows in a somewhat different direction than the breeze at ground level. Under normal circumstances, where the true wind is not affected by highly localized conditions, the high pressure center is now to your right, the low center to your left. The pressure area to

11-2

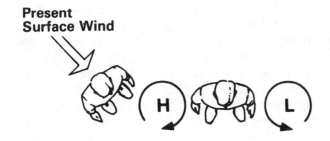

**Present Surface Wind**

**Fig. 11-4 Buys-Ballot's Law for Determining Low Pressure Area**

the west of you is, generally speaking, the one that will reach you, while weather to the east has already passed.

Besides highs and lows, it is useful to consider the great air masses, bodies of air in which conditions of temperature and moisture are the same or similar from one side to the other. Air masses take their names from their characteristics, and the masses which cross our country can be very different.

Although air masses change somewhat according to the surfaces they cross, they remain essentially the same. In the United States, there are two origins of such masses, called **Tropical** and **Polar**. Obviously the former comes from southern latitudes, while the latter originates in the north. But each may be further defined as **continental**—having formed over land—or **maritime**, having formed over the sea.

The air masses that affect us are:

Continental Polar (cP)—cold and dry

Maritime Polar (mP)—cold or warm, but moist

Maritime Tropical (mT)—warm and moist

Fronts form when air masses of different characteristics collide—the front being the boundary between two such masses. The front takes its name from the type of air which is arriving. That is, when an eastward-moving mass of cold air catches up with warm air, also moving east, but

not so quickly, a cold front is formed. Cold air, being more compact and heavier, pushes under the warm air mass and lifts it. This lifting causes unsettled or stormy weather along the front. The same thing happens with warm fronts, but in this case the warm air rides up and over the cold, and the storms which accompany a warm front are not so severe as those characteristic of a cold front. In either case, however, the weather along the front is not good.

**Cold Fronts**

Cold fronts move at speeds from 10 to 50 knots, depending on the time of year—they are two or three times as fast in winter as in summer. If a cold front is moving fast, it may be preceded by a **squall line**, a roll of black, towering clouds that may reach heights of 40,000 feet, with violent storms and even tornadoes. Wind shifts along the front will be sudden and velocities will increase dramatically. Behind the squall line are heavy rains, followed by clearing.

About 150 miles ahead of the usual cold front are high sheets of Altocumulus cloud, followed by lowering, thickening Nimbostratus, a low cloud with rain and wind. The barometer falls, sometimes very fast, and the wind becomes gusty. As the actual front passes overhead, the winds increase and the barometer contin-

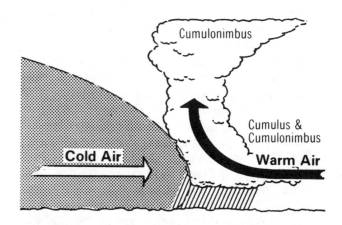

**Fig. 11-5 Collision of Cold and Warm Fronts Results in Bad Weather for the Boater**

ues to drop, then as the barometer hits bottom, the wind direction shifts abruptly clockwise, continuing gusty, and the barometer begins to rise quickly as the temperature falls.

A cold front is normally followed by some heavy rain, then clearing and gusty winds from west or northwest. At least a couple of days of clear, cool weather, often with excellent sailing winds, are in prospect.

## Warm Fronts

The warm front is a different creature. Its cloud warnings--high, thin Cirrus--extend as much as 1,000 miles ahead, clouds representing warm air that has climbed up and over the retreating cold

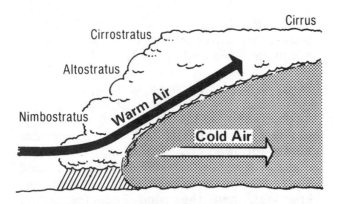

Fig. 11-6  **Warm Front Storm**

air mass. As the front slowly advances, clouds thicken and lower. The barometer starts a steady fall and the winds pick up. High-level **Cirrostratus** clouds become mid-level **Altostratus** clouds and rain or snow begins to fall, continuing until after the front passes. As this occurs, the winds shift clockwise and decrease. The temperature begins to rise and visibility is often poor. Behind the front are some **Stratus** clouds and perhaps a little more rain. The barometer may rise and then fall slightly. After the front has completely passed, the skies will clear and winds will normally be from the southwest. Unfortunately, cold fronts frequently follow hard on the heels of warm fronts, so the duration of good weather may be short.

It's very useful to know these normal sequences of weather as fronts pass through. Although the time it takes for an individual front to pass through an area will vary, it's possible to predict the actual weather sequence with considerable accuracy. Weather fronts are accompanied by specific cloud formations which are developed by the front itself, as you saw in Figures 11-5 and 11-6. If you learn to recognize these cloud formations you can relate the approaching weather pattern with the clouds you can see overhead.

## Clouds

As indicated earlier, weather changes are caused by changing temperatures. When air cools below its saturation point, the water vapor in the air condenses and forms clouds. The two basic cloud types are called **Cumulus**, which are fluffy,

Fig. 11-7    **Scattered Cumulus Clouds— Good Weather**

piled up clouds (Fig. 11-7), and **Stratus**, which are flat and frequently layered (Fig. 11-8).

Specific cloud names include a description of the altitude where the clouds form. Three types of high clouds exist. **Cirrus** are thin, wispy high clouds that sometimes stretch right up to the lower

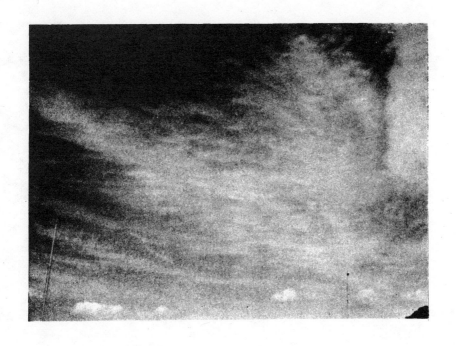

Fig. 11-8     Stratus Clouds— Overcast
Sky

Fig. 11-9     Cirrostratus Clouds—Cause
Sun and Moon Halo—Maybe
Rain

Fig. 11-10     Altostratus Clouds—
              Overcast Sky or Rain

Fig. 11-11   Altocumulus Clouds

level of the stratosphere. They are composed entirely of ice crystals and are often called "mares tails." The second type of high cloud is called **cirrocumulus**. It often appears as faint ripples like those on windblown sand, sometimes called a mackerel sky. The **cirrostratus** (Fig. 11-9) is the lowest of the high clouds, although it may be as much as four or five miles up. It is veil-like, causing the sky to look milky and causing those rings or halos around the sun or moon that are said to forecast approaching rain.

The middle clouds, averaging 10,000 feet in altitude, contain the prefix "alto." **Altostratus** have a fibrous, frosted appearance (Fig. 11-10); **altocumulus** resemble them except they are puffier (Fig. 11-11).

Of the three types of low clouds, ranging from ground level to 6,500 feet, the **nimbostratus** is the typical rain cloud

through. It sometimes looks like a high bank of fog and causes only drizzle. The atmosphere below a sheet of stratus is often very clear and distant objects look to be quite close. **Stratocumulus** appears as a layer or patches of globular cloud masses, regularly arranged. The smallest are quite large, and are mostly soft and grey, with some darker parts (Fig. 11-13). While they may indicate rain is on the way, they are not rain clouds.

Fig. 11-13   Stratocumulus Clouds—Rain Warning

Fig. 11-12   Nimbostratus Clouds—Rain or Snow

(Fig. 11-12). At a low altitude, it is a dark grey color and nearly uniform. Low **stratus** cloud, on the other hand, consists of an even, continuous layer all the way

There are also two types of clouds that form vertically, including the **cumulus**. These cauliflower-like puffs mean fair weather and can form at any altitude (Fig. 11-7). The second is the **cumulonimbus**, the common thunderhead which can grow to 50,000 feet and develop an anvil top where the cloud reaches the high altitude "jet-stream" winds (Fig. 11-14).

**Fig. 11-14    Cumulonimbus Clouds—Note Anvil Shaped Cirroform Cap**

### Weather Clues from the Clouds

Clouds not only tell you where you are in relation to an approaching front, but also indicate something about the weather in general. When you see clouds moving leisurely across the sky, you can anticipate continued fair weather. You can look for wind and rain when they scud rapidly overhead. When small clouds decrease or melt away towards sunset, fair weather can be expected, but increasing clouds indicate unsettled weather ahead. Near the end of a long spell of good weather, clouds sometimes begin to form high in the sky. This is said to indicate that the change in weather will be gradual with the bad weather as much as two days away. It can also mean that the bad weather will be around for awhile. When the higher clouds are moving in a different direction than the lower prevailing wind, or the lower clouds, it means that a general change of wind direction to the direction of the higher clouds is coming.

Even the color of the sky can be revealing since moisture in the atmosphere can act like a prism to break up the sunlight. On a good day when little moisture is present, the blue rays are not scattered.

As the moisture increases, the blue rays are turned aside and the long-wave reds and yellows dominate. Yellow is often the forerunner of heavy rain and wind within the next day and a half.

A red glow over the western sky at sunset, or in long narrow streaks of high cloud showing across the setting sun, means fine weather tomorrow. But red reflecting over lowering masses of ragged clouds at sunset indicates stormy weather ahead. Red is also a bad sign in the eastern sky at dawn because it indicates the approach of clouds. The red is caused by high thin clouds that are often otherwise invisible.

Green appearing sky in the clearing areas between showers indicates the upper atmosphere is very moist and intermittent showers will continue, interspersed with sunshine. A soft light blue sky means settled weather, but very dark blue sky that sharply outlines the clouds means a storm is coming.

### Thunderstorms

The localized thundersquall is probably the one kind of weather most feared by experienced boaters. It need not be associated with major weather systems, as it can arise in a very short time, or it may lurk concealed in a hazy sky, and it can produce winds of shattering force. Add to that the fearful and often dangerous effect of lightning, and you have a natural demonstration that should inspire respect in any seafarer.

Causes of thunderstorms vary, but they are all characterized by a violent uplifting of air, sometimes to heights of 75,000 feet. There are usually three stages in the life cycle of an average thunderstorm. The early, or cumulus, stage occurs when a **cumulus cloud**--the detached,

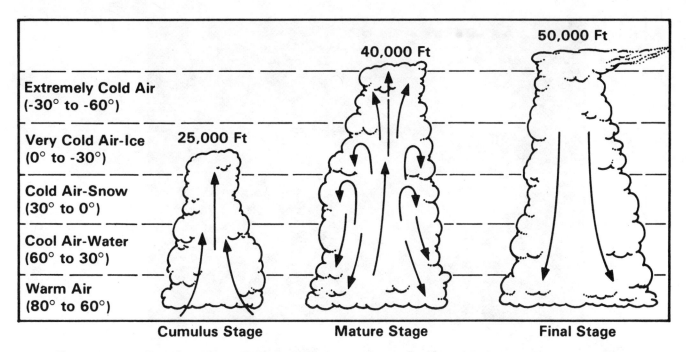

| | |
|---|---|
| **Extremely Cold Air** (-30° to -60°) | |
| **Very Cold Air-Ice** (0° to -30°) | 25,000 Ft |
| **Cold Air-Snow** (30° to 0°) | |
| **Cool Air-Water** (60° to 30°) | |
| **Warm Air** (80° to 60°) | |

40,000 Ft

50,000 Ft

Cumulus Stage          Mature Stage          Final Stage

Fig. 11-15   Thunderstorm Development

puffy cloud of summer fair weather--develops vertically from 15,000 to 25,000 feet. This means that the rising air currents within it may be cooled as much as 80° while ascending, to well below freezing at the cloud's top. The air in the cloud is still warmer than the air outside.

In the second stage, when the cloud reaches a height of approximately 40,000 feet, its full vertical development, precipitation occurs and falling rain or hail cools the air inside, creating downdrafts and heavy rains. In the terminal third stage, the entire cloud becomes sinking air. With no ascending air to be cooled, rain stops. At this point, the cloud at the top of the thunderhead has been blown into the familiar anvil shape--the sign of an aging storm.

On most summer days, the cumulus clouds of afternoon have at least some potential for becoming thunderheads. As long as you keep an eye on them, you can usually make for safety long before there's any danger. On the other hand, when visibility is limited by haze, as it sometimes is during ideal thunderstorm conditions, the formation of the towering,

sharp-edged cloud—called **cumulonimbus**—typical of thunderstorms, may be veiled by haze.

On such hot, muggy, hazy afternoons, you should be alert for static on AM (not FM) radios, the sound of distant thunder, or the flicker of lightning. You should stay close to port, as the wind may die shortly before the storm itself begins. Anytime there is a threat of bad weather all hands should don their PFDs.

Once you can see the cumulonimbus cloud, you can estimate your distance from the thunderstorm. Since thunder and lightning occur simultaneously at the point of the lightning discharge, you see the lightning flash before you hear the thunder unless it is directly overhead. The sound takes approximately five seconds to travel one statute mile. Therefore if you slowly count one thousand, two thousand, ...., every five counts indicates the lightning is one mile away. You must take care that you relate the sound to its appropriate flash, a difficult task if the lightning is nearly continuous.

Fig. 11-16   Squall Line—Heavy Wind, Rain, and Thunderstorm Ahead

## Squall Lines

Squall lines may precede fast-moving cold fronts. They are an unbroken line of black, ominous clouds, towering 40,000 feet or more into the sky, including thunderstorms of almost incredible violence and occasional tornadoes. Such squall lines are extremely turbulent, sometimes more so than a typical hurricane. From the water, a squall line looks like a wall of rolling, boiling black fog. Winds shift and sharpen suddenly with the approach of the squall line, and downward-pouring rain may carry the cloud clear to the water in sharp, vertical bands. Torrential rains fall behind the leading edge of the squall line.

Squall lines occur when winds above a cold front, moving in the same direction as the front's advance, prevent the lifting of a warm air mass. This is why little bad weather occurs right at the surface front. But miles ahead of the front the strong winds force up the warm air with almost explosive violence, producing the squall line.

## Tornadoes

When numerous thunderstorms occur along a single cold front, they are often organized into a long, narrow band. The front of this band is usually marked by a squall line. The cold downdrafts from the thunderstorms meet the warm air along these squall lines, causing the wind direction to change suddenly in strong gusts. The temperature also drops suddenly. Such conditions often spawn tornadoes. The tornadoes formed at squall lines often occur in families and move with the prevailing wind in the warm sector ahead of the cold front. This is usually a southwest wind which moves the tornadoes in a northeast direction.

A **tornado** is a whirlpool of air of relatively small diameter which extends downward from a cumulonimbus cloud. It has a funnel-like appearance, the average diameter of the visible funnel is about 750 feet. The destructive effects of the whirling winds associated with the funnel may extend as much as one-half mile on each side of the center. Wind speed near the tornado's center has been estimated in excess of 200 knots. Tornadoes occur in boating areas along the Atlantic and Gulf of Mexico coasts and in all inland boating areas east of the Rocky Mountains.

## Microbursts

In 1976 the U. S. Government first identified the microburst phenomenon as a possible hazard to landing aircraft and to pleasure boats. The downdrafts from a single thunderstorm act in the same manner as the downdrafts in front of a squall line, meeting the warm air and causing the wind direction to change suddenly in the form of strong gusts. These gusts usually flow radially from the point where the downdraft hits the surface and are strongest in the direction in which the thundercloud is moving. Such microburst winds have been estimated to exceed 100 knots.

Microbursts may occur even when no rain is apparent below the thunder-cloud since within the cloud there may be rainfall which evaporates before it reaches the surface. This phenomenon is known as a dry microburst. The gusts of wind associated with microbursts are called "windshear." Because there is no visible indication of windshear, it is very difficult to forecast. Microbursts can occur several miles away from an associated squall line, so you should be alert to the possibility of strong gusts from a different direction than the prevailing wind whenever you are sailing near a thunderstorm area, whether it is raining or not.

## Waterspouts

A **waterspout** is the marine equivalent of a tornado. It forms under the same conditions and may have a diameter of from 20 to 200 feet. Waterspouts begin as a funnel-shaped protuberance at the base of a cumulonimbus cloud and grow downward toward the sea. A cloud of spray forms below the funnel where the water surface is agitated. The funnel-like cloud descends until it merges with the spray, then the water spout appears as a tube reaching from the sea to the cloud. Although waterspouts are less violent than tornadoes, they are still a real danger to pleasure boats. They are more common to the tropics than to the middle latitudes and may last from ten minutes to a half an hour before the tube breaks and the "spout" at the water surface subsides.

## Hurricanes

A hurricane is not related to warm or cold fronts. It is a storm that originates in the tropics and is characterized by its counterclockwise circulation. A hurricane begins as a **tropical depression.** Once its winds reach 33 knots, it becomes a **tropical storm.** It is classified as a **hurricane** when it reaches sustained speeds of 64 knots. Hurricanes are a form of a **Tropical Cyclone** as are the **Typhoons** which occur in the western Pacific Ocean. Typhoons are often larger and more intense than hurricanes because of the greater expanse of the Pacific Ocean.

A well developed hurricane may average 400 miles in diameter. Its center or eye is a low pressure area (which accounts for the hurricane's counterclockwise circulation) and may be 15 to 25 miles in diameter. While hurricane winds, by definition, are more than 64 knots, the winds in the eye seldom reach 15 knots, although seas within the eye are heavy and confused.

The Atlantic Ocean hurricane season is June through November, August through October is the season of greatest hurricane frequency. Hurricanes usually mature near the West Indies and move westward toward the Gulf of Mexico. They often follow a route around the semi-permanent Azores-Bermuda high-pressure area and track northward. However, their exact route over the water can be erratic and unpredictable.

Hurricanes move at around 15 knots while they are traveling westward in the low latitudes. After they have finished their turn to a northerly direction, they usually pick up speed, traveling at 25 knots or better, sometimes as fast as 50 or 60 knots if they remain over open water. They lose their intensity as they move over the cooler waters in the middle and upper latitudes or when they move over land.

Since the government has an imperfect record of forecasting the movement of specific hurricanes, you should not try to outguess either the hurricane or the forecasters, and should stay ashore if a hurricane threatens. While you should take every precaution to secure your boat properly before a hurricane arrives, you should not try to "ride out" a hurricane on your boat. No boat is worth the loss of a life in order to protect it.

## Fog

One weather feature that is of particular concern to boaters is fog. **Fog** is formed when air at the surface is cooled to the point (dew point) where its moisture condenses into very small droplets. This is similar to the way a cloud forms. Fog is really a cloud that is on, or near the ground.

To understand more about fog, let's review some facts we discussed earlier. Cool air cannot hold as much moisture as warm. Thus, if air that is already moist is made cooler, fog will form. This occurs in several ways.

On land, if the air is very humid at sunset, the land, and the air close to it, will cool off and fog may form. This is known as **radiation** fog. When the sun rises the following morning, it will warm the air a few degrees. The condensed moisture will disappear and the fog will dissipate ("burn off").

The fog most common to boaters is caused by moist air moving over a cool surface. An example of this is warm moist air from land blowing over cold coastal waters. This is called **advection** fog because the temperature change is brought on by air moving to a cooler location. It is a particular hazard to boaters because it commonly occurs on coastal waters especially in cold seasons, and it moves in a "bank" that can overtake and surprise the unwary boater. The fog will usually be concentrated close to the water's surface and may be absent at a height of 50 feet. This is because the water is the cooling agent.

Fog is likely wherever an area of cold water exists; as for example, on the Pacific coast, where upwelling brings cold water to the surface. For this same reason, fog can form on rivers where cold water flows through areas with very moist air. The cold river will cool air near the surface causing fog. Sometimes this situation occurs below dams because the water becomes cold in the deep pool behind the dam.

Fortunately, weathermen, by carefully predicting temperature change and measuring dew point (the temperature at which moisture condenses), can predict fog with high reliability. Marine weather forecasts include information about any anticipated fog. Inasmuch as the normal weather forecasts often don't give this information, wise boaters always get the marine forecast before departing.

## Sources of Weather Information

The best source of weather information is the one that is easiest for you to get and most up to date. You will, of course, want to have the very best information you can get, but you must also recognize that conditions can be very localized, and can change very quickly. You should develop the ability to analyze developing weather conditions and be prepared to change your plans as conditions dictate.

In some areas, principally large metropolitan areas, recorded telephone marine weather forecasts are available. Call while you are planning your trip, then again just before you leave, to get the latest update.

VHF-FM weather broadcasts are probably the best overall source of weather information for the boater. These broadcasts, transmitted continuously from National Weather Service stations, repeat every few minutes, and include detailed reports of conditions and forecasts for the coverage area. They are updated frequently, and may be interrupted with live updates as developing situations require.

VHF weather broadcasts draw on National Weather Service computers, reports from Coast Guard and other units in the area, and represent the best information available. Reception on suitable radios is excellent over very wide areas, since the transmitting antennas are generally located on very advantageous sites.

Most VHF-FM radiotelephones are equipped for two or more weather channels (receive only - you cannot transmit), identified as "WX-1," "WX-2," etc. (See Chapter 12, Radiotelephone.)

Scheduled weather forecasts on commercial radio and television stations are also available to you. Some of these come directly from the National Weather Service, and others augment NWS forecasts with more specific forecasts developed by consultant meteorologists.

You should understand, however, that many forecasts on commercial broadcast stations are intended for a different audience, and may lack the details, or the areas of coverage, that you as a boater may need.

Newspapers generally include weather forecast information, and may also show weather maps from which you may be able to gain a general idea of the weather patterns that are approaching your area. Use these data with caution, however, since they may be from 12 to 24 hours old by the time you see them. Outdated information can be worse than no information at all, and conditions can change very seriously over a 24-hour period.

Yachtsmen who routinely make long passages know the importance of good, up-to-date weather information, and sometimes go to great lengths to obtain it. Coded weather data are broadcast by short-wave radio, but they require a good deal of sophistication to decode, plot and develop into a forecast for your region. Facsimile weather maps and forecast information are also available from short-wave broadcasts. Special and very expensive equipment is necessary to convert these radio signals into weather maps, but

if you are caught in mid-ocean by a developing tropical storm, the cost may be negligible compared to the cost of a catastrophe.

**Pennants and Lights**
Visual warning displays may be shown by yacht clubs, marinas, and some Coast Guard facilities when conditions warrant. The most common of these is the "small craft advisory." It forecasts possible hazards to small craft, such as winds over 30 knots or scattered afternoon thunderstorms. These warnings should not be disregarded, no matter how good conditions appear to be at the time. Remember, too, that "small craft" includes some rather large boats — up to 65' in length.

Gale and storm warnings also may be shown, and indicate that even more severe weather conditions are anticipated. And, of course, the hurricane warning signals warn of the development of very serious weather, indeed.

In order for you to relate these various wind velocities to visual aids, the Beaufort Wind Scale is shown in Fig. 11-18.

Before you start out on a boating trip, whether it be an extended cruise or merely an afternoon outing on a local lake, check the weather patterns. If you anticipate a lengthy trip, you might begin watching some days in advance of the trip so you can have a feeling for the kinds of trends that develop over time.

Even more important than gathering forecast information, keep your "weather eye" peeled for the approach of conditions that suggest a storm. Dark, threatening clouds, with or without lightning, should be avoided.

Storms that are too distant to be seen or heard can sometimes be detected by listening to static, caused by lightning activity, on AM broadcast radios.

Take special note of any changes in wind direction or strength that is not expected, and watch for changes in the character or direction of waves. If you have any doubts about the weather, look for a protected anchorage. In any case, you should always have an alternative port in mind should weather conditions change suddenly and catch you unprepared.

**Local Weather**

All weather lore and forecasts aside, local weather conditions may be unique, and your ability to handle them may depend more on your knowledge--and the knowledge and experience of others--of these local conditions. This is especially true of conditions in the vicinity of mountains, islands, or even large cities. Forecast winds from a particular direction may be deflected and appear to come from a very different direction if structures and land masses intervene. Many sailors have been capsized, for instance, when they failed to note a "notch" in the shore line, or a bay entrance. The wind or waves funneled through that opening could easily upset sail trim, and could even knock the boat on her beam ends.

### SMALL CRAFT

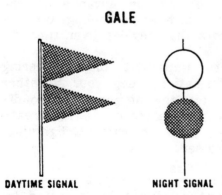

DAYTIME SIGNAL          NIGHT SIGNAL

One RED pennant displayed by day and a RED light over a WHITE light at night to indicate winds as high as 33 knots (38 m.p.h.) and/or sea conditions considered dangerous to small craft operations are forecast for the area.

### STORM

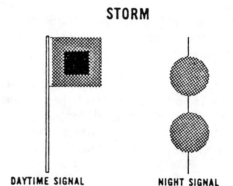

DAYTIME SIGNAL          NIGHT SIGNAL

A single square RED flag with a BLACK center displayed during daytime and two RED lights at night to indicate that winds 48 knots (55 m.p.h.) and above are forecast for the area. If the winds are associated with a tropical cyclone (hurricane), the "Storm Warning" display indicates winds 48 to 63 knots (55 to 73 m.p.h.) are forecast.

### GALE

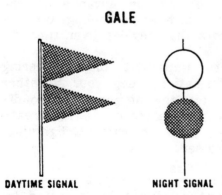

DAYTIME SIGNAL          NIGHT SIGNAL

Two RED pennants displayed by day and a WHITE light above a RED light at night to indicate winds within the range 34 to 47 knots (39 to 54 m.p.h.) are forecast for the area.

### HURRICANE

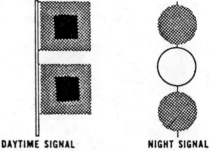

DAYTIME SIGNAL          NIGHT SIGNAL

Displayed only in connection with a tropical cyclone (hurricane). Two square RED flags with BLACK centers displayed by day and a WHITE light between two RED lights at night to indicate that winds 64 knots (74 m.p.h.) and above are forecast for the area.

**Fig. 11-17   Warning Signal Displays**

# BEAUFORT WIND SCALE

| Beaufort number | Seaman's description of wind | Velocity m. p. h. | Estimating velocities on land | Estimating velocities on sea | Probable mean height of waves in feet | Description of Sea |
|---|---|---|---|---|---|---|
| 0 | Calm ............... | Less than 1 ... | Smoke rises vertically. | Sea like a mirror .......... | ......... | Calm (glassy) |
| 1 | Light air .......... | 1-3 ................. | Smoke drifts; wind vanes unmoved. | Ripples with the appearance of scales are formed but without foam crests. | ½ ...... | Rippled |
| 2 | Light breeze .... | 4-7 ................. | Wind felt on face; leaves rustle; ordinary vane moved by wind. | Small wavelets, still short but more pronounced; crests have a glassy appearance and do not break. | 1 ....... | Smooth |
| 3 | Gentle breeze ... | 8-12 ............... | Leaves and twigs in constant motion; wind extends light flag. | Large wavelets. Crests begin to break. Foam of glassy appearance. Perhaps scattered white caps. | 2½ ..... | |
| 4 | Mod. breeze .... | 13-18 .............. | Raises dust and loose paper; small branches are moved. | Small waves, becoming longer, fairly frequent white caps. | 5 ....... | Slight |
| 5 | Fresh breeze .... | 19-24 ............. | Small trees in leaf begin to sway; crested wavelets form on inland water. | Moderate waves, taking a more pronounced long form; many white caps are formed. (Chance of some spray.) | 10 ...... | Moderate |
| 6 | Strong breeze .. | 25-31 ............. | Large branches in motion; whistling heard in telegraph wires; umbrellas used with difficulty. | Large waves begin to form; the white foam crests are more extensive everywhere. (Probably some spray.) | 15 ...... | Rough |
| 7 | Moderate gale .. | 32-38 ............. | Whole trees in motion; inconvenience felt in walking against wind. | Sea heaps up and white foam from breaking waves begins to be blown in streaks. | 20 ...... | Very rough |
| 8 | Fresh gale ....... | 39-46 ............. | Breaks twigs off trees; generally impedes progress. | Moderately high waves of greater length; edges of crests break into spindrift. The foam is blown in well-marked streaks along the direction of the wind. | 25 ...... | High |
| 9 | Strong gale ..... | 47-54 ............. | Slight structural damage occurs. | High waves. Dense streaks of foam along the direction of the wind. Sea begins to roll. Spray may affect visibility. | 30 ...... | |
| 10 | Whole gale ...... | 55-63 ............. | Trees uprooted; considerable structural damage occurs. | Very high waves with long, overhanging crests. The surface of the sea takes a white appearance. | 35 ...... | Very high |
| 11 | Storm ............. | 64-73 ............. | | The sea is completely covered with long white patches of foam lying along the direction of the wind. Everywhere edges of the wave crests are blown into froth. Visibility affected. | 40 ...... | |
| 12 | Hurricane ........ | 74-82 ............. | | The air is filled with foam and spray. Sea completely white with driving spray; visibility very seriously affected. | 45 or more .. | Phenomenal |

**Fig. 11-18  Beaufort Wind Scale**

## Weather Instruments

There are several devices used to describe the weather by measuring physical properties of the atmosphere. Unless you are planning to formulate your own forecast, having a lot of weather instruments will not be of much benefit to you. However, you may wish to purchase an inexpensive barometer. Barometers will give a rough indication of approaching fronts and low pressure systems. Leave the reading and interpreting of the highly technical instruments to the professionals.

The following definitions are intended for your general information only. An **Anemometer**, measures wind speed. A **Barometer** measures atmospheric pressure in either inches of mercury or millibars. A **Thermometer** measures degree of temperature. A **Hygrometer** measures relative humidity. A **Psychrometer** measures wet and dry bulb air temperatures.

Further explanation here might be helpful. **Relative humidity** is the ratio of water vapor in the air to the amount the air could hold at that temperature. The **dew point** is the temperature below which moisture will condense out of the air to form droplets as fog or cloud. A psychrometer is a set of two thermometers with the bulb of one enclosed in a wet gauze. The "wet bulb" thermometer will read lower because of the cooling effect of evaporation. The amount of evaporation depends on the relative humidity of the air. If the air is humid, there will be little evaporation and the "wet bulb" thermometer will not read very much lower than the "dry bulb" thermometer. In other words, the difference between the two thermometer readings varies with the relative humidity.

## Forecasting with a Barometer

Let's review the weather sequence associated with a passing cold front again, this time noting the changes in barometric pressure and wind direction which occur as the front moves through. When a **strong cold front** approaches, we first notice a sharpening of wind from the south or southwest and altocumulus clouds appear on the west or northwest horizon. The barometer begins to fall.

As the front approaches, the clouds lower and cumulonimbus clouds begin to appear overhead. Once it begins to rain, the rain increases in intensity very rapidly. The wind may increase and the barometer may fall still further. As the front passes overhead, the wind shifts (veers) rapidly to the west or north and begins to blow in strong gusts. Squall-like rains continue and the barometer reaches its lowest reading. Once the front passes, the weather improves rapidly, the barometer rises rapidly, and the temperature drops as the winds steady out of the west or northwest.

Each phase in the passing of a cold or warm front is tied to a wind direction and barometric reading. As with any type of weather instrument, a single observation is of little use. A sequence of measurements will reveal a trend—most of the time. As a general rule, the more rapid the drop in the barometer reading, the closer and more severe an approaching storm will be. Fig. 11-19 correlates wind direction and barometric tendency. With it and little else you can sometimes forecast local weather with tolerable accuracy.

Other weather indicators are more subjective, but can frequently aid you in predicting local weather patterns. Here are some that have proven quite accurate over many years, in some cases many centuries:

## Indicators of Deteriorating Weather
- Clouds lowering and thickening
- Clouds increasing in number, moving fast across the sky
- Veils or sheets of gray cloud increasing on the western horizon
- Clouds moving in different directions at different heights
- Clouds moving from east or northeast toward the south
- Barometer falling steadily or rapidly
- Static on AM radio
- Strong wind in the morning

- Wind shifts from north to east and possibly through east to south (veering wind)
- Temperatures far above or below

**Indicators of Strong Wind**
- Light scud clouds alone in a clear sky
- Sharp, clearly-defined edges to clouds
- Yellow sunset

| Wind Direction | Sea-Level Pressure | Forecast | Wind Direction | Sea-Level Pressure | Forecast |
|---|---|---|---|---|---|
| SW to NW | 30.10 to 30.20 and steady | Fair, with little temperature change, for 1 to 2 days. | E to NE | 30.10 or higher; falling slowly | In summer, with light winds, rain may not fall for 2 to 3 days. In winter, rain within 24 hours. |
| SW to NW | 30.10 to 30.20 rising rapidly | Fair, followed within 2 days by rain. | E to NE | 30.10 or higher; falling rapidly | In summer, rain probably within 12 to 24 hours. In winter, rain or snow within 12 hours and increasing winds. |
| SW to NW | 30.20 or higher and steady | Continued fair with little temperature change. | | | |
| SW to NW | 30.20 or higher; falling slowly | Fair for 2 days with slowly rising temperature. | S to SW | 30.00 or below; rising slowly | Clearing within a few hours. Then fair for several days. |
| S to SE | 30.10 to 30.20; falling slowly | Rain within 24 hours. | S to E | 29.80 or below; falling rapidly | Severe storm within a few hours. Then clearing within 24 hours- followed by colder in winter. |
| S to SE | 30.10 to 30.20; falling rapidly | Increasing winds and rain within 12 to 24 hours. | | | |
| SE to NE | 30.10 to 30.20; falling slowly | Increasing winds and rain within 12 to 18 hours. | E to N | 29.80 or below; falling rapidly | Severe storm (typical nor'easter) in a few hours. Heavy rains or snowstorm. Followed by a cold wave in winter. |
| SE to NE | 30.10 to 30.20; falling rapidly | Increasing winds and rain within 12 hours. | | | |
| SE to NE | 30.00 or below; falling slowly | Rain will continue 1 to 3 days, perhaps even longer. | Hauling to W | 29.80 or below; rising rapidly | End of the storm. Followed by clearing and colder. |
| SE to NE | 30.00 or below; falling rapidly | Rain with high winds in a few hours. Clearing within 36 hours- becoming colder in winter. | NOTE: **Falling** or **rising rapidly** means a pressure change of .24 inches or greater within three hours. **Falling** or **rising slowly** means a change of approximately .09 inches or less in a three-hour period. | | |

**Fig. 11-19 Wind/Barometer Table (Eastern United States)**

## Indicators of Impending Precipitation
- Distant objects seem to stand above the horizon
- Sounds are very clear and heard for great distances
- Transparent, veil-like clouds thickening and lowering
- Halo around sun or moon
- Increasing south wind, with clouds moving from the west
- Wind (especially north wind) shifts to west and then to south (backing wind)
- Steadily falling barometer
- Pale sunset
- Red sky at dawn
- No dew after a hot day.

## Indicators of Clearing Weather
- Cloud bases rise
- Wind shifts to west, especially from east through south
- Barometer rises quickly
- Gray early morning
- Morning fog or dew.

## Indicators of Continuing Fair Weather
- Early morning fog that clears
- Gentle wind from west or northwest
- Barometer steady or rising slightly
- Red sunset
- Bright moon and light breeze
- Heavy dew or frost
- Clear blue morning sky
- Dull hearing, short range of sound.

# Chapter 12

# Radiotelephone

The marine radiotelephone system exists to (1) provide monitored distress and safety frequencies, (2) allow exchange of information pertaining to navigation, movement or management of vessels, (3) allow communication between private vessels and local and Federal agencies, (4) provide communications for stations and vessels engaged in commerce, (5) allow common-carrier (telephone) service to vessels afloat, and (6) provide for the communications needs of recreational boaters.

Recreational boats are not required by law to be equipped with radiotelephone equipment, as certain types of commercial vessels are, but many people find a marine radiotelephone to be an enormous convenience. And there is no doubt that it can be an important safety factor in emergencies.

Boats carrying more than six passengers for hire, as well as many other commercial craft, are required to carry radio equipment. If you operate any type of commercial vessel, consult your nearest FCC office to determine the requirements which may apply to you and your boat.

To provide these services, special frequency bands have been set aside in the high frequency (HF) and very high frequency (VHF) portions of the radio spectrum. Most marine radiotelephone service is provided in the VHF band, where the assigned frequencies are identified as "channels." Certain other services (such as very long-distance communications, for instance) can only be provided in the HF band, due to technical limitations.

The VHF system is essentially a line-of-sight system, limited in range to only a little beyond the horizon. This is sufficient for the vast majority of important marine communications, especially since important land stations have very high antennas, and therefore have very wide horizons.

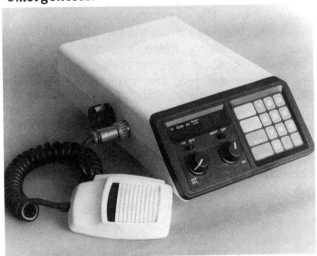

Fig. 12-1 Radiotelephone Set.

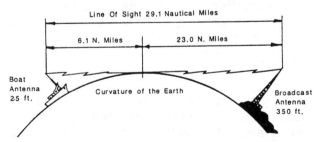

Fig. 12-2 Line of Sight Distances for Radio

The long-range characteristics of the HF system are an advantage for vessels that typically cross oceans or cruise several hundred miles offshore.

Marine radiotelephones require a license from the FCC.

The station license is obtained by submitting forms obtained from the FCC. Many manufacturers include copies of the necessary forms in the package with a new marine radiotelephone.

Typically, it takes several weeks for a license application to be processed and a license issued. The FCC has made provisions for a temporary station license for use while the actual license application is pending.

With the station license comes a call sign. The call sign, which is a combination of letters and numbers, identifies your station uniquely, and must be given at prescribed times during a series of transmissions. (See Operating Procedures, below.)

The station license covers all transmitting radio equipment aboard used in the marine radio service. That is, it covers VHF and HF radiotelephones, radar, or an Emergency Position Indicating Radio Beacon (EPIRB), if the license so states. It does not cover receiving equipment, such as receivers for broadcast stations, radio direction-finding receivers, LORAN navigation receivers, etc., which do not need to be licensed. It also does not cover amateur (ham) radio transmitters or Citizens' Band (CB) transmitters, which are covered by a different set of licensing regulations, or mobile (cellular) telephones, which are licensed under the common carrier which provides the connecting service.

If you have an existing license and you add one of these covered pieces of equipment, the FCC must be notified and the license must be modified to cover the new equipment.

Modern radiotelephone equipment is reliable, generally reasonable in cost, available with a broad array of features, and simple to use.

All marine radiotelephone transmitters are "type accepted" by the FCC. That is. the design of the equipment is such tha it meets certain minimum technical standards, and cannot be operated on frequencies outside the marine channels. The owner/operator of the equipment is not permitted to make any internal adjustments to the set that could alter its transmitting characteristics, and repairs must generally be carried out by licensed technicians specially qualified to work on marine radio equipment.

Installation can be performed by the owner, however, but you should be aware that improper power and antenna connections can seriously impede performance, and can result in damage to the equipment.

The units used in recreational craft are typically combined transmitter and receiver units, called "transceivers." The controls are simple: a channel selector knob, a volume control (which usually is also the on-off switch), a "squelch control," and a high power-low power switch.

The volume control controls the loudness of the received signal; it has no effect on the transmitted signal. The squelch control is used to eliminate the constant rushing noise which is produced by radio that is not receiving a signal. It essentially renders the radio quiet until a signal is received. Unfortunately, it is possible to set this control so high that even a strong signal will not "break squelch." This has the effect of turning the receiver off, and no signals can be heard. The squelch control should be set so that the no-signal noise just disappears, and no higher, lest important calls be missed.

The high power-low power switch is provided so that you can raise the power of your transmitter for longer range communications. It is normally kept on the low setting since many times it is necessary to communicate with a station just a short distance away, and even within sight of you, as when getting instructions from a lock master or a bridge tender, for instance. The low power setting allows you to do that without interfering with other communications a longer distance away. The high power setting is used only when necessary.

Since the radiotelephone is a "transceiver," it cannot both transmit and receive at the same time, but must be switched between transmitting and receiving. This is usually done with a switch or pushbutton on the microphone, the "push-to-talk" button.

## Adjustments of Transmitting Equipment

You are responsible for the proper technical operation of your equipment. All transmitter measurements, adjustments, or repairs that may affect the proper operation of the transmitter must be made by or under the immediate supervision and responsibility of a person holding a valid First- or Second-Class Radiotelegraph or Radiotelephone Operator License. A special license endorsement is required to service a radar set.

## Selecting a VHF Radiotelephone

Before purchasing a VHF-FM radiotelephone, you should consider your requirements carefully and select a unit that will meet these needs. You should remember that VHF communications are essentially "line of sight." The average ship-to-ship range is about 10 to 15 miles, while the normally expected ship-to-shore range is 20 to 30 miles, since the shore station typically has a much higher antenna. These figures vary depending upon transmitter power, antenna height, and terrain.

The FCC limits the transmitter power for VHF-FM to 25 watts for vessels and also requires the capability to reduce transmitter power to not more than one watt for short range communication.

No matter how powerful your transmitter is, if you can't hear the other station—you can't communicate. The receiver performance of your radiotelephone is therefore an important aspect of your communication capability.

## Antennas

The quality of the antenna and of its installation can be the largest single factor determining how well a marine radiotelephone installation works. Two design factors are vital, height and gain.

Since the VHF system is essentially a line-of-sight transmission system, it is obvious that the higher the antenna, the further it can "hear," and the further you can communicate. Sailboats with antennas mounted at the top of the mast have an advantage over small powerboats in this area, an advantage which may even outweigh the advantage that most power boats have in readily available electrical power. Some power boaters compensate by mounting the antenna at the highest point on the boat or by using extension masts made just for that purpose, but there is a limit to how many extensions one can support.

The other factor is "gain." Generally, the station to be communicated with is located somewhere toward the horizon. Energy that is radiated upward into space or downward into the water is effectively wasted energy. Some antenna designs redirect some of this wasted energy so that it is radiated outward toward the horizon, effectively boosting the output of the transmitter.

But, as with all good things, there is a limit to this, too. If a very high gain antenna is used (greater than 9dB, typically) and the boat heels or rocks, much of the signal is directed into the water or out into space. In this situation a lower gain antenna would be more effective.

## Operating Procedures

### Maintain a Watch

Whenever your radio is turned on, keep

the receiver tuned to the appropriate distress and calling frequency, 156.8 MHz. This listening watch must be maintained at all times the station is in operation and you are not actually communicating.

You should expect to do far more listening on the radiotelephone than talking. Not only is the marine radiotelephone an extremely busy "party line," with a great many users, but it is also a vitally important link for emergency communications that must not be interfered with. A general rule to follow is to listen carefully before transmitting, preferably with the squelch turned all the way off so that very weak signals can be heard. There may be an emergency condition in effect, and you must avoid interfering.

VHF Channel 16 and SSB 2182 kHz have been designated as BOTH the emergency channel and the calling channel. All calls originate on Channel 16, but ONLY call originations or emergency traffic are permitted on that channel. This ensures that virtually every vessel with a radiotelephone that is not in use on another channel will be available to hear an emergency call, since all monitor channel 16 for incoming messages.

## Operating Procedures

The operation of marine radiotelephones is governed by regulations of the Federal Communications Commission (FCC). These regulations are set forth in detail in Volume IV, Part 83, of the FCC Rules and Regulations available from the Superintendent of Documents, U. S. Government Printing Office, Washington, D. C. 20402.

The FCC has been a leader in government agencies in presenting regulations to the public in a readable form, avoiding much of the legal language that makes so many regulations difficult to understand.

There are very specific procedures (detailed below) for placing calls to other

vessels and for answering calls to your vessel. These procedures are intended, (1) to ensure clear communications with a minimum risk of confusion of intent, and (2) to tie up the limited available radio channels as little as possible.

## Choose the Correct Channel or Frequency

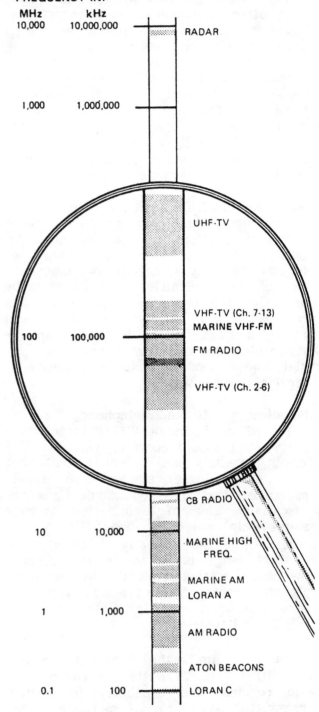

Fig. 12-3 Radio Frequency Spectrum

## TABLE 12-I

| Channel Numbers | Type of Communication | Suggested Channel Selection for Recreational Vessels 6 Ch. | 12 Ch. |
|---|---|---|---|
| 16 | DISTRESS, SAFETY & CALLING Intership & ship to coast | • | • |
| 6 | INTERSHIP SAFETY Intership. NOT to be used for non-safety intership communications | • | • |
| 22 | Communications with U. S. Coast Guard ship, coast, or aircraft stations. | 1 | 1 |
| 65, 66, 12, 73, 14, 74, 20 | PORT OPERATIONS Intership & ship to coast | | 1 |
| 13 | NAVIGATIONAL | | 1 |
| 68, 9 | NON-COMMERCIAL Intership & ship to coast | 1 | 2 |
| 69, 71, 78 | NON-COMMERCIAL Ship to coast | | 1 |
| 72 | NON-COMMERCIAL Intership | | 2 |
| 24, 84, 25, 85, 26, 86, 27, 87, 28 | PUBLIC CORRESPONDENCE Ship to public coast | 2 | 2 |
| 162.40 & 162.475 MHz 162.55 MHz | NOAA WEATHER SERVICE Ship receive only Ship receive only | •• •• •• | •• •• •• |

\* These stations are required to be installed in every ship station equipped with a VHF radio.

\*\*The weather receive channels are half-channels (receive only) one or both of which are recommended to be installed in each ship station. Many manufacturers include one or both of these channels in their sets in addition to the normal six or twelve channel capacity.

## TABLE II

### *CHANNEL USAGE*

| Channel Number | Ship Transmit | Ship Receive | Intended Use |
|---|---|---|---|
| 6 | 156.300 | 156.300 | INTERSHIP SAFETY. Required for all VHF-FM equipped vessels for intership safety purposes and search and rescue (SAR) communications with ships and aircraft of the U. S. Coast Guard. Must not be used for non-safety communications. |
| 9 | 156.450 | 156.450 | COMMERCIAL AND NON-COMMERCIAL (INTERSHIP AND SHIP-TO-COAST). Some examples of use are communications with commercial marinas and public docks to obtain supplies to schedule repairs and contacting commercial vessels about matters of common concern. |
| 12 | 156.600 | 156.600 | PORT OPERATIONS (INTERSHIP AND SHIP-TO-COAST). Available to all vessels. This is a traffic advisory channel for use by agencies directing the movement of vessels in or near ports, locks, or waterways. Messages are restricted to the operational handling, movement and safety to ships and, in emergency, to the safety of persons. It should be noted, however, in the Ports of New York and New Orleans channels 11, 12 and 14 are to be used exclusively for the Vessel Traffic System being developed by the United States Coast Guard. |
| 13 | 156.650 | 156.650 | NAVIGATIONAL — (SHIP'S) BRIDGE TO (SHIP'S) BRIDGE. This channel is available to all vessels and is required on large passenger and commercial vessels (including many tugs). Use is limited to navigational communications such as in meeting and passing situations. Abbreviated short operating procedures and 1 watt maximum power (except in certain special instances) are used on this channel for both calling and working. For recreational vessels, this channel should be used for *listening* to determine the intentions of large vessels. This is also the primary channel used at locks and bridges operated by the U. S. Army Corps of Engineers. |
| 14 | 156.700 | 156.700 | PORT OPERATIONS (INTERSHIP AND SHIP-TO-COAST). Same as channel 12. |
| 15 | 156.750 | 156.750 | ENVIRONMENTAL (RECEIVE ONLY). A receive only channel used to broadcast environmental information to ships such as weather, sea conditions, time signals for navigation, notices to mariners, etc. Most of this information is also broadcast on the weather (WX) channels. |
| 16 | 156.800 | 156.800 | DISTRESS, SAFETY AND CALLING (INTERSHIP AND SHIP-TO-COAST). Required channel for all VHF-FM equipped vessels. Must be monitored at all times station is in operation (except when actually communicating on another channel). This channel is monitored also by the Coast Guard, public coast stations and many limited coast stations. Calls to other vessels are normally initiated on this channel. Then, except in an emergency, you must switch to a working channel. For additional information see the sections on operating procedures. |
| 17 | 156.850 | 156.850 | STATE CONTROL. Available to all vessels to communicate with ships and coast stations operated by state or local governments. Messages are restricted to regulation and control, or rendering assistance. Use of low power (1 watt) setting is required by international treaty. |
| 20 | 157.000 | 161.600 | PORT OPERATIONS (SHIP-TO-COAST). Available to all vessels. This is a traffic advisory channel for use by agencies directing the movement of vessels in or near ports, locks, or waterways. Messages are restricted to the operational handling, movement and safety of ships and, in emergency, to the safety of persons. |
| 21A | 157.050 | 157.050 | U.S. GOVERNMENT ONLY. |
| 22A | 157.100 | 157.100 | COAST GUARD LIAISON. This channel is used for communications with U. S. Coast Guard ship, coast and aircraft stations after first establishing communications on channel 16. *It is strongly recommended that every VHF radiotelephone include this channel.* |
| 23A | 157.150 | 157.150 | U. S. GOVERNMENT ONLY |
| 24 | 157.200 | 161.800 | PUBLIC CORRESPONDENCE (SHIP-TO-COAST). Available to all vessels to communicate with public coast stations operated by telephone companies. Channels 26 and 28 are the primary public correspondence channels and therefore become the first choice for the cruising vessel having limited channel capacity. |
| 25 | 157.250 | 161.850 | PUBLIC CORRESPONDENCE (SHIP-TO-COAST). Same as channel 24. |
| 26 | 157.300 | 161.900 | PUBLIC CORRESPONDENCE (SHIP-TO-COAST). Same as channel 24. |
| 27 | 157.350 | 161.950 | PUBLIC CORRESPONDENCE (SHIP-TO-COAST). Same as channel 24 |

| | | | |
|---|---|---|---|
| 28 | 157.400 | 162.000 | PUBLIC CORRESPONDENCE (SHIP-TO-COAST). Same as channel 24. |
| 65A | 156.275 | 156.275 | PORT OPERATIONS (INTERSHIP AND SHIP-TO-COAST). Same as channel 12. |
| 66A | 156.325 | 156.325 | PORT OPERATIONS (INTERSHIP AND SHIP-TO-COAST). Same as channel 12. |
| 68 | 156.425 | 156.425 | NON-COMMERCIAL (INTERSHIP AND SHIP-TO-COAST). A working channel for non-commercial vessels. May be used for obtaining supplies, scheduling repairs, berthing and accommodations, etc. from yacht clubs or marinas, and intership operational communications such as piloting or arranging for rendezvous with other vessels. It should be noted that channel 68 (and channel 70 for intership only) is the most popular non-commercial channel and therefore is the first choice for vessels having limited channel capacity. |
| 69 | 156.475 | 156.475 | NON-COMMERCIAL WORKING. For pleasure boats ship-to-ship and ship-to-shore communications only |
| 72 | 156.625 | 156.625 | NON-COMMERCIAL (INTERSHIP). Same as channel 68 except limited to intership communications. |
| 73 | 156.675 | 156.675 | PORT OPERATIONS (INTERSHIP AND SHIP-TO-COAST). Same as channel 20. |
| 74 | 156.725 | 156.725 | PORT OPERATIONS (INTERSHIP AND SHIP-TO-COAST). Same as channel 20. |
| 78A | 156.925 | 156.925 | NON-COMMERCIAL WORKING. For pleasure boats ship-to-ship and ship-to-shore communications only. (Not available for pleasure boat use in Canada.) |
| 81A | 157.075 | 157.075 | U. S. GOVERNMENT ONLY. |
| 82A | 157.125 | 157.125 | U. S. GOVERNMENT ONLY. |
| 83A | 157.175 | 157.175 | U. S. GOVERNMENT ONLY. |
| 84 | 157.225 | 161.825 | PUBLIC CORRESPONDENCE (SHIP-TO-COAST). Same as channel 24. |
| 85 | 157.275 | 161.875 | PUBLIC CORRESPONDENCE (SHIP-TO-COAST). Same as channel 24. |
| 86 | 157.325 | 161.925 | PUBLIC CORRESPONDENCE (SHIP-TO-COAST). Same as channel 24. |
| 87 | 157.375 | 161.975 | PUBLIC CORRESPONDENCE (SHIP-TO-COAST). Same as channel 24. |
| WX1 | — | 162.550 | WEATHER (RECEIVE ONLY). To receive weather broadcasts of the Department of Commerce, National Oceanic and Atmospheric Administration (NOAA). |
| WX2 | — | 162.400 | WEATHER (RECEIVE ONLY). Same as WX1. |
| WX3 | — | 162.475 | WEATHER (RECEIVE ONLY). Same as WX1. |

NOTE: The addition of the letter "A" to the channel number indicates that the ship receive channel used in the United States is different from the one used by vessels and coast stations of other countries. Vessels equipped for U. S. operations only, will experience difficulty communicating with foreign ships and coast stations on these channels.

**TABLE 12-II**

Each of the marine frequencies and channels is authorized for a specific type of communication. It is therefore required that you choose the correct channel for the type of communications you wish to engage in. For example, certain channels are set aside exclusively for intership (ship-to-ship) use and may not be used for ship-to-coast communications. Channels are further classified according to the subject matter or content of the communications. For example, commercial communications are limited to matters pertaining to the commercial enterprise the vessel is engaged in.

The authorized use of each of the VHF channels is given in Table 12-II. For recreational boats, most of the communications will be limited to what is known as Non-commercial (Operational in the MF band) communications and Public Correspondence.

**Public Correspondence**

By using the channels set aside for Public Correspondence and establishing communications through the facilities of the public coast stations, you are able to make and receive calls from any telephone on shore. There is no restriction on the content of your communication and you do not have to limit your messages strictly to ship's business. Except for distress calls, public coast stations will charge for this service.

One other comment about using public correspondence channels—other people are listening! You have a private channel through the telephone lines, but the radio link between the vessel and the shore station is very public!

**Calling Intership**

Turn your radiotelephone on and listen on the appropriate distress and calling frequency, Channel 16 or 2182 kHz, to make sure it is not being used. If it is clear, put your transmitter on the air. This is usually done by depressing the "push to talk" button on the microphone.

You must release the microphone button when you are through transmitting. You cannot receive transmissions directed at you until you release the microphone button and switch your radio to "receive." It is also good practice to pause just a fraction of a second after you press the button before you begin to speak. This allows time for the receiving radio on the other end of your communication link to "break squelch," it allows the listener a fraction of a second to get ready to listen, and it also helps you to avoid the common error of rushing things and starting to talk <u>before</u> the button is pushed. Both of these factors tend to clip off the beginning of the message and make communication difficult.

Speak directly into the microphone in a normal tone of voice. Check the manufacturer's recommendation for distance to be used. Speak clearly and distinctly. Call the vessel with which you wish to communicate by using its name; then identify your vessel with its name and FCC assigned call sign. Do not add unnecessary words and phrases such as "Come in, Bob" or "Do you read me?" Limit the use of phonetics to poor transmission conditions.

This preliminary call must not exceed 30 seconds. If contact is not made, wait at least 2 minutes before repeating the call. After this time interval, make the call in the same manner. This procedure may be repeated no more than three times. If contact is not made during this period, you must wait at least 15 minutes before making your next attempt. Again, avoid unnecessary transmission, such as, "negative contact." It is unnecessary and very unprofessional.

Once you establish contact on the calling channel, you must switch to a "working channel" to carry out the rest of your business.

As a recreational boater, you have access to only a few of the many channels that your radio may have. There are 73 channels of which 55 may be used in the United States.

These remaining channels include twelve that are designated for commercial operator use only, for communication between commercial vessels and their operational headquarters, etc.

There are also several channels set aside for government use. For instance, Channel 21A is a "U. S. Government Use Only" channel, designated for the U. S. Coast Guard. There are also several channels that are designated "Public Correspondence" channels, where common carrier operators provide ship-to-shore telephone service.

All radios are equipped with Channel 16, the internationally recognized emergency and calling channel. They also are equipped with Channel 06. Thus, wherever in the world you may go where VHF radiotelephones are used, there will be at least two channels you will have in common with anyone else you may meet.

Monitor the "working" frequency you wish to use, briefly, before initiating the call on Channel 16 or 2182 kHz. This will help prevent you from interrupting other users of the channel.

All communications should be kept as brief as possible and at the end of the communication each vessel is required to give its call sign, after which, both vessels switch back to the distress and calling channel and reestablish the watch.

## Voice Operating Procedures

There are accepted and established procedures for establishing and maintaining effective communications, and it is your responsibility to learn them and use them.

These procedures are based on extensive practical experience, and are carefully thought out to give effective communication with the minimum usage of radio spectrum and time.

A key to efficient use of the radiotelephone is the use of PROCEDURE WORDS, or "prowords." They are a form of shorthand, and as long as everybody understands and uses them correctly, a great deal of time can be saved. There is a fixed amount of radio spectrum and time available; the more people who can use it, the better. The basic prowords are shown in Table 12-III.

TABLE 12-III  Procedure Words (PROWORDS) and Phonetic Alphabet.

| PROCEDURE WORD | MEANING |
| --- | --- |
| OUT | This is the end of my transmission to you and no answer is required or expected. |
| OVER | This is the end of my transmission to you and a response is necessary. Go ahead and transmit. |
| | (Note: Observe the considerable difference between "Over," used during a message exchange, and "Out," employed at the end of an exchange. "Over" should be omitted when the context of a transmission makes it clear that it is unnecessary.) |
| ROGER | I have received your last transmission satisfactorily. |
| WILCO | Your last message has been received, understood, and will be complied with. |
| THIS IS | This transmission is from the station whose name, or call sign immediately follows. |
| | (Note: Normally used at the beginning of a transmission: "BLUE DUCK — THIS IS — GIMLET — WHISKEY ZULU ECHO 3488." Sometimes omitted in transmissions between experienced operators familiar with each other's boat names.) |
| FIGURES | Figures or numbers follow. |
| | (Used when numbers occur in the middle of a message: "Vessel length is figures two three feet.") |
| SPEAK SLOWER | Your transmission is at too fast a speed, speak more slowly. |
| SAY AGAIN | Repeat. |
| WORDS TWICE | Communication is difficult — give every phrase twice. |
| I SPELL | I shall spell the next word phonetically. |
| | (Note: Often used where a proper name or unusual word is important to a message; "Boat name is *Martha*. I spell — Mike; Alfa; Romeo; Tango; Hotel; Alfa." See phonetic alphabet.) |
| MESSAGE FOLLOWS | A message that requires recording is about to follow. |
| BREAK | I separate the text from other portions of the message; or one message from one immediately following. |
| WAIT | I must pause for a few seconds; stand by for further transmission. |
| | (Note: This is normally used when a message must be interrupted by the *sender*. If, for instance, one station is asked for information not instantly available, its operator might send "WAIT" while looking up the required data. In addition, WAIT may also be used to suspend the transmission of an on-the-air test. If a station announces its intention of making such a test, another station using the channel may transmit the word "WAIT;" the test shall then be suspended.) |
| AFFIRMATIVE | You are correct, or what you have transmitted is correct. |
| NEGATIVE | No. |
| SILENCE (said three times) | Cease all transmissions immediately. Silence will be maintained until lifted. |
| | (Note: Used to clear routine business from a channel when an emergency is in progress. In this meaning *Silence* is correctly pronounced SEE LONSS.) |

| SILENCE FINI | Silence is lifted. | | 5 | FIVE | FI FE |
|---|---|---|---|---|---|
| | | | 6 | SIX | SIX |
| | (Note: Signifies the end of the emergency and the resumption of normal traffic. Correctly pronounced SEE LONSS FEE NEE.) | | 7 | SEVEN | SEVEN |
| | | | 8 | EIGHT | ATE |
| | | | 9 | NINE | NINER |

## PHONETIC ALPHABET

| Letter | Phonetic Equivalent | Pronunciation |
|---|---|---|
| A | ALFA | *AL* FAH |
| B | BRAVO | *BRAH* VOH |
| C | CHARLIE | *CHAR* LEE |
| D | DELTA | *DELL* TAH |
| E | ECHO | *ECK* OH |
| F | FOXTROT | *FOKS* TROT |
| G | GOLF | GOLF |
| H | HOTEL | HO *TELL* |
| I | INDIA | *IN* DEE AH |
| J | JULIETT | JEW LEE *ETT* |
| K | KILO | *KEY* LOH |
| L | LIMA | *LEE* MAH |
| M | MIKE | MIKE |
| N | NOVEMBER | NO *VEM* BER |
| O | OSCAR | *OSS* CAH |
| P | PAPA | PAH *PAH* |
| Q | QUEBEC | KEH *BECK* |
| R | ROMEO | *ROW* ME OH |
| S | SIERRA | SEE *AIR* RAH |
| T | TANGO | *TANG* GO |
| U | UNIFORM | *YOU* NEE FORM |
| V | VICTOR | *VIK* TAH |
| W | WHISKEY | *WISS* KEY |
| X | XRAY | *ECKS* RAY |
| Y | YANKEE | *YANG* KEY |
| Z | ZULU | *ZOO* LOO |
| 0 | ZERO | ZERO |
| 1 | ONE | WUN |
| 2 | TWO | TOO |
| 3 | THREE | THUH REE |
| 4 | FOUR | FO WER |

You should not be sensitive about using these prowords. Nobody will think you are imitating the dialog on the late movie if you say "Wilco," as long as you use it appropriately.

On the other hand, there are other words and phrases that have come into common usage that have the "flavor" of prowords, but which accomplish nothing. A recent example heard on Channel 16: Several calls to a particular boat went unanswered, whereupon the caller said, "Negative contact. This is XXXXXX, out."

We will ignore for the moment the fact that "negative contact" is meaningless. What is important is that it was obvious to anybody listening that the attempt to establish contact was fruitless, since there was no reply. The time taken to announce that obvious fact to the world was enough that someone else, more efficient, could have placed a call. Worse, the unnecessary announcement could have masked an emergency call.

**Calling Ship to Coast**
The procedures for calling coast stations are similar to those used in making intership calls with the exception that you normally initiate the call on the assigned frequency of the coast station.

**Routine Radio Check**
Radio checks may be made by calling a specific station. (General calls even for radio checks, are not permitted except for special situations.) Begin by initiating a call on Channel 16, but shift to a working channel as quickly as possible.

Listen to make sure that the Distress and Calling frequency is not busy. If it is free, put your transmitter on the air and call a specific station or vessel and include the phrase "request a radio check" in your initial call. For example, "MARY JANE - THIS IS BLUE DUCK - WHISKEY ALFA 1234 - REQUEST RADIO CHECK CHANNEL _____ (names working channel) - OVER." After the reply by Mary Jane, Blue Duck would then say "HOW DO YOU HEAR ME? - OVER."

The proper response by Mary Jane, depending on the respective conditions, would be:
"I HEAR YOU LOUD AND CLEAR," or
"I HEAR YOU WEAK BUT CLEAR," or
"YOU ARE LOUD BUT DISTORTED," etc.
Do not respond to a request for a radio check with such phrases as:
"I HEAR YOU FIVE BY FIVE," or
"I READ YOU LOUD AND CLEAR."
Figures are not a clear response as to the character of the transmission and the word "read" implies a radio check by a meter.

It is illegal to call a Coast Guard station on 156.8 MHz or 2182 kHz for a radio check. This prohibition does not apply to tests conducted during investigations by FCC representatives or when qualified radio technicians are installing equipment or correcting deficiencies in the station radiotelephone equipment.

## Radiotelephone Station Log

A radio log when used should have each page (1) be numbered; (2) bear the name of the vessel and call sign; and (3) be signed by the operator. Entries should show the time each watch begins and ends. All distress and alarm signals should be recorded as completely as possible. This applies to all related communications transmitted or intercepted, and to all urgency and safety signals and communications transmitted. A record of all installations, services, or maintenance work performed that may affect the proper operation of the station should also be entered by the licensed operator doing the work, including his address and the class, serial number, and expiration date of his license.

The 24-hour system is used in a radio log for recording time; that is, 8:45 a.m. is written as 0845 and 1:00 p.m. as 1300. Local time is normally used, but Eastern Standard Time (EST) or Universal Coordinated time (UTC) must be used throughout the Great Lakes. Vessels on international voyages use UTC exclusively. Whichever time is used, the appropriate abbreviation for the time zone must be entered at the head of the time column.

Radio logs must be retained for at least a year, and for 3 years if they contain entries concerning distress, and for longer periods if they concern communications being investigated by the FCC or against which claims or complaints have been filed.

Station logs must be made available for inspection at the request of an FCC representative.

## Secrecy of Communications

The Communications Act prohibits divulging interstate or foreign communications transmitted, received, or intercepted by wire or radio to anyone other than the addressee or his agent or attorney, or to persons necessarily involved in the handling of the communications, unless the sender authorizes the divulgence of the contents of the communication. Persons intercepting such communications or becoming acquainted with them are also prohibited from divulging the contents or using the contents for the benefit of themselves or others.

Obviously, this requirement of secrecy does not apply to radio communications relating to ships in distress, nor to radio communications transmitted by amateurs or broadcasts by others for use of the general public. It does apply, however, to all other communications. These statutory secrecy provisions cover messages addressed to a specific ship station or coast station or to a person via such station.

## Obscenity, Indecency and Profanity

When two or more ship stations are communicating with each other, they are talking over an extensive party line. Users should always bear this fact in mind and assume that many persons are listening. All users therefore have a compelling moral obligation to avoid offensive remarks. They also have a strict legal obligation inasmuch as it is a criminal offense for any person to transmit communications containing obscene, indecent, or profane words, language, or meaning. Whoever utters any obscene, indecent or profane language by radio may be fined up to $10,000 or imprisoned up to 2 years, or both.

## Crew Training

As with all other aspects of boat operation, more than one person on board should be familiar with the operation of the radiotelephone. You should be sure to check out all members of your "regular" crew on radiotelephone operation, and include a brief introduction to the basic operation of the radiotelephone as part of your familiarization tour for guests on board your boat. Finally, you should complete the form in Table 12-IV and post it in a conspicuous location near the radiotelephone so that in an emergency anyone on board will be able to summon assistance.

Some of these precautions may seem unnecessarily simple-minded, but under stress even experienced people sometimes fail to do seemingly simple tasks. An emergency broadcast that fails to summon help because the rattled operator does not turn on the power, or calls on the wrong channel, or the return call that is missed because the squelch is set too high or the operator fails to release the microphone button, is tragic.

Remember: The RMS TITANIC sank, with the loss of over 1,700 lives, while another ship sat just a few miles away, unaware of the situation. TITANIC sent out radio distress calls that were heard hundreds of miles away in New York, but

---

**MARINE DISTRESS COMMUNICATIONS FORM**

Instructions: Complete this form now (except for items 6 through 9) and post near your radiotelephone for use if you are in DISTRESS.

*********

SPEAK:  SLOWLY  —  CLEARLY  —  CALMLY

1. Make sure your radiotelephone is on.
2. Select either <u>VHF Channel 16</u> (156.8 MHz) or <u>2182 kHz.</u>
3. Press microphone button and say:  "MAYDAY—MAYDAY—MAYDAY."
4. Say: "THIS IS _____
   Your Call Sign/Boat Name repeated three times
5. Say: "MAYDAY_____."
   Your Boat Name
6. TELL WHERE YOU ARE (What navigational aids or landmarks are near?).
7. STATE THE NATURE OF YOUR DISTRESS.
8. GIVE NUMBER OF PERSONS ABOARD AND CONDITIONS OF ANY INJURED.
9. ESTIMATE PRESENT SEAWORTHINESS OF YOUR BOAT.
10. BRIEFLY DESCRIBE YOUR BOAT:_____FEET; _____; _____ HULL;
    Length ____ Type ____ Color
    _____ TRIM;_____MASTS;_____
    Color ____ Number ____ Anything else you think will help rescuers find you.
11. Say: "I WILL BE LISTENING ON CHANNEL 16/2182."
    Cross out one which does not apply
12. End Message by saying: "THIS IS _____ o . OVER"
    Your Boat Name and Call Sign
13. Release microphone button and listen: Someone should answer.
    IF THEY DO NOT, REPEAT CALL, BEGINNING AT ITEM NO. 3 ABOVE.
    If there is still no answer, switch to another channel and begin again.

**TABLE 12-IV**

the vessel nearest and best able to render assistance did not hear them because her radio was turned off!

## Operating Procedures (Distress, Urgency and Safety)

### General

If you are in distress, you may use any means at your disposal to attract attention and obtain assistance. You are by no means limited to the use of your marine radiotelephone. Often, visual signals, including flags, flares, lights, smoke, etc., or audible signals such as your boat's horn or siren, or a whistle, or megaphone will get the attention and help you need.

For boats equipped with a marine radiotelephone, help is just a radio signal away. Two marine radiotelephone channels have been set aside for use in emergencies. Channel 16 (156.8 MHz), the VHF-FM Distress, Safety and Calling frequency is the primary emergency channel in the VHF marine band. For those who have medium frequency (MF) radiotelephone also, 2182 kHz is the emergency frequency for use in that band. You are not limited to the use of these channels; you may use any other frequency channel available to you. The working frequency of the local marine operator (public telephone coast station) is a good example of a channel that is monitored.

There are other types of marine stations located ashore that are listening to Channel 16 and 2182 kHz along with the marine radio equipped vessels operating in the area. Because of this coverage, almost any kind of a call for assistance on Channel 16 (Or 2182 kHz) will probably get a response. There are times, however, when the situation demands immediate attention; when you just can't tolerate delay. These are the times when you need to know how to use (or respond to) the Distress and Urgency signals and how to respond to the Safety signal.

### Spoken Emergency Signals

There are three spoken emergency signals:

1. Distress Signal: MAYDAY
   The distress signal MAYDAY is used to indicate that a mobile station is threatened by grave and imminent danger and requests immediate assistance. MAYDAY has priority over all other communications.

2. Urgency Signal: PAN PAN (Properly pronounced PAHN PAHN)
   Used when the safety of the vessel or person is in jeopardy. "Man overboard" messages are sent with the Urgency signal. PAN PAN has priority over all other communications with the exception of distress traffic.

3. Safety Signal: SECURITY (Pronounced SAY-CURITAY)
   Used for messages concerning the safety of navigation or giving important meteorological warnings.

Any message headed by one of the emergency signals (MAYDAY, PAN PAN, or SECURITY) must be given precedence over routine communications. This means listen. Don't transmit. Be prepared to help if you can. The decision of which of these emergency signals to use is the responsibility of the person in charge of the vessel.

### Radiotelephone Alarm Signal

This signal consists of two audio frequency tones transmitted alternately. This signal is similar in sound to a two-tone siren used by some ambulances and lasts 30 seconds to 1 minute. The purpose of the signal is to attract attention of the person on watch or to actuate automatic devices giving the alarm. The radiotelephone alarm signal shall be used only with the distress signal except in two situations dealing with the Urgency Signal.

### Sending Distress Call and Message

First send the Radiotelephone Alarm Signal, if available.

1. Distress signal MAYDAY (spoken three times).

**Fig. 12-4    Coast Guard Communication Station**

2. The words THIS IS (spoken once).
3. Name of vessel in distress (spoken three times) and call sign (spoken once).

The Distress Message immediately follows the Distress Call and consists of:

4. Distress signal MAYDAY (spoken once).
5. Name of vessel (spoken once).
6. Position of vessel in distress by latitude and longitude or by bearing (true or magnetic, state which) and distance to a well-known landmark such as a navigational aid or small island, or in any terms which will assist a responding station in locating the vessel in distress.
7. Nature of distress (sinking, fire, etc.).
8. Kind of assistance desired.
9. Any other information which might facilitate rescue, such as:
   - length or tonnage of vessel,
   - number of persons on board and number needing medical attention,
   - color of hull, decks, cabin, masts, etc.
10. The word OVER.

**Acknowledgement of Distress Message**

If you hear a Distress Message from a vessel and it is not answered, then YOU must answer. If you are reasonably sure that the distressed vessel is not in your vicinity, you should wait a short time for others to acknowledge. In any event, you must log all pertinent details of the Distress Call and Message.

**Offer of Assistance**

After you acknowledge receipt of the distress message, allow a short interval of time for other stations to acknowledge receipt, if there are any in a position to assist. When you are sure of not interfering with other distress-related communications, contact the vessel in distress and advise them what assistance you can render. Make every effort to notify the Coast Guard. The offer-of-assistance message shall be sent only with permission of the person in charge of your vessel.

## Urgency Call and Message Procedures

The emergency signal PAN PAN (pronounced PAHN PAHN), spoken three times as PAN PAN, PAN PAN, PAN PAN, begins the Urgency Call. The Urgency Call and Message is transmitted on Channel 16 (or on 2182 kHz) in the same way as the Distress Call and Distress Message. The Urgency signal PAN PAN indicates that the calling person has a message concerning the safety of the vessel, or a person in jeopardy. The Urgency signal is authorized for situations like the following:
- Transmission of an urgent storm warning by an authorized shore station.
- Loss of person overboard but only when the assistance of other vessels is required.
- No steering or power in shipping lane.

## Sending Urgency Call and Message

The Urgency Call and Message usually includes the following:
1. The Urgency signal PAN PAN (spoken three times).
2. Addressee ALL STATIONS (or a particular station).
3. The words THIS IS.
4. Name of calling vessel (spoken three times) and call sign (spoken once).
5. The Urgency Message (state the urgent problem).
6. Position of vessel and any other information that will assist responding vessels. Include description of your vessel, etc.
7. The words THIS IS.
8. Name of calling vessel and radio call sign (spoken once).
9. The word OVER.

## Safety Call and Message Procedures

The Safety Call, headed with the word SECURITY (Say-curitay, spoken three times), is transmitted on the Distress and Calling frequency (Channel 16 or 2182 kHz), together with a request to shift to a working frequency where the Safety Message will be given. The Safety Message may be given on any available working frequency.

United States Coast Guard stations routinely use the Safety Call SECURITY to alert boating operators that they are preparing to broadcast a message concerning safety of navigation. The call also precedes an important meteorological warning. The Safety Message itself usually is broadcast on Coast Guard VHF/FM Channel 22 (157.1 MHz) and AM 2670 kHz. Although recreational boating operators may use the Safety Signal and Message, in many cases they would get better results by giving the information to the Coast Guard without making a formal Safety Call. The Coast Guard usually has better broadcast coverage from its shore stations and will rebroadcast the information if it is appropriate.

## Public Coast Stations

### General

By utilizing the services of Public Coast Stations, ships may make and receive telephone calls to and from any telephone with access to the nationwide telephone network, including telephones overseas and on other ships and aircraft. In effect, these coast stations extend the talking range of ship telephones almost without limit.

### Description of Public Coast Stations

Three categories of Public Coast Stations operate in different frequency bands to provide for telephone service over a wide range of situations. The following brief descriptions of these services are of interest in selecting a service appropriate for your requirements. This information is followed by some suggestions for operating ship stations on public correspondence channels.

### VHF-FM Marine Operator Service

VHF-FM service offers reliable operation with good transmission quality over relatively short distances up to 20-50 miles, using channels in the 157-162 MHz range. Channels 24, 25, 26, 27, 28, 84, 85, 86 and 87 are available for assignment to public coast stations in the United States. Channels 26 and 28 are used in more areas than any others. To obtain information on VHF-FM ship-to-shore telephone coverage in your area, call your local Marine Operator, according to instructions in your telephone directory.

In addition, in some localities not yet served by VHF-FM coast stations, ships are permitted to make telephone calls through local VHF-FM base stations operating in the land mobile radio telephone service. In these instances, a different license authorization as well as different transmitting equipment is required.

## Medium Frequency Service

The Medium Frequency Service operates over considerably greater distance ranges than VHF-FM, but ranges vary widely with time of day and a variety of other circumstances. Distances in excess of 1,000 miles are possible at certain times, but may be limited to less than 100 miles at other times.

Medium Frequency Coast Stations operate on frequencies in the 2 MHz band along the sea coasts and Gulf of Mexico. Stations serving the Great Lakes and the Mississippi River valley also operate on frequencies in the high-frequency bands.

## High Frequency

A High Seas Service using high frequencies provides long-range radiotelephone communications with suitably equipped vessels throughout the world. Service is provided via four coast stations within the United States coastal areas plus one station in the state of Hawaii. These stations operate on various radio channels in the 4 through 23 MHz HF bands and are equipped for single sideband operation.

## Registration With Your Public Coast Station

It is important for the vessel owner who plans on using the public radiotelephone service to register with the telephone company in the location

where you wish to be billed.

This registration provides all coast stations with the name and address to be used in billing for ship-originated calls. Public coast stations are supported by charges made in accordance with tariffs filed with regulatory authorities. If a ship is not registered, billing information must be passed to the coast station operator each time a call is made, with consequent expenditure of time and effort. Registration may also serve to establish the procedures under which a coast station will call the ship in completing land-originated calls. Should you encounter any problems, contact your local telephone company business office and request assistance in registering your vessel.

## Making Ship-To-Shore Calls

Use the VHF-FM Service (up to 20 to 50 miles) in preference to the Medium Frequency or High Frequency Services, if within range.

1. Select the public correspondence channel assigned to the desired shore station. Do not call on Channel 16 or on 2182 kHz except in an emergency.

2. Listen to determine if the working channel of the desired coast station is busy. A busy condition is evidenced by hearing speech, signaling tones, or a busy signal.

3. If the channel is busy, wait until it clears or switch to an alternate channel if available.

4. If the channel is not busy, press the push-to-talk button and say: (Name of the coast station) - THIS IS - (your call sign once). Do not call for more than a few seconds.

5. Listen for a reply. If none is received, repeat call after an interval of two minutes.

When the coast station operator answers, say:

THIS IS - Name of vessel, call sign, and ship's telephone or billing number (if assigned), CALLING (city, telephone number desired).

If your vessel is not registered or if the coast station operator does not have the listing, the operator will ask for additional information for billing purposes. At completion of call say:

Name of vessel - Call sign - OUT.

## Receiving Shore-to-Ship Calls

Obviously, to receive public coast station calls, a receiver must be in operation on the proper channel. When calling on VHF-FM frequencies, coast stations will call on Channel 16 unless you have selective signaling, in which case the shore station will dial your number on a working channel. When calling on SSB medium frequencies, the preferred channel is the working channel of the coast station. Commercial coast stations operating on channels in the 2 MHz band routinely call on a working channel, but will call on 2182 kHz when requested to do so by the calling party. If you are expecting calls on medium frequencies and are not planning to monitor the working channel, you should tell prospective calling parties to so advise the Marine Operator. Note: A guard must be maintained on the distress, safety and calling channel; therefore a second channel receiver capability is essential if a guard is to be maintained on a coast station working channel.

Selective signaling, of course, requires a second receiver, since monitoring of the working channel would be essential. It is illegal to send dial pulses over Channel 16 or 2182 kHz.

## Making Ship-to-Ship Calls Through a Coast Station

Although contacts between ships are normally made directly, ship-to-ship calls can be made by going through your coast station, using the same procedure as you do for the ship-to-shore calls.

## How to Place a Shore-to-Ship Call

The basic procedure that the telephone subscriber should follow in placing a telephone call to a ship station from his home or office is found in the first few pages of most telephone directories. These instructions generally consist of dialing "O" (Zero) for the Operator, and asking for the "Marine Operator."

It is further necessary to know the name of the vessel being called (not the owner's name) and the approximate location so that the marine operator may judge which coast station to place the call through.

More specific information about the vessel is often useful. For instance, the channel generally monitored for receiving calls, a selective signaling number (if applicable), and the coast station through which calls can generally be received.

Remember that the ship station generally operates using push-to-talk techniques, so that it is impossible for you to break in while the ship station is transmitting.

## Limited Coast Stations

The term **limited coast stations** includes coast stations that there to serve the operational and business needs of vessels, but are not open to public correspondence. Many, such as those operated by a harbor master coordinating the movement of vessels within a confined area, or a station at a highway bridge, serve a safety function as well. Shore stations operated by the United States Coast Guard provide a safety communications service rather than business or operational. They are classified as Government stations rather than as limited coast stations although they also are not open to public correspondence.

While limited coast stations are not new to the Marine Service, most small vessel operators are finding this service available for the first time on VHF-FM. Thus, tug companies may have a limited coast station for the purpose of dispatching their own tugs. A fleet of fishing vessels may be directed from a limited coast station operated by a fish cannery.

Yacht clubs having docking facilities, marina operators, ship chandlers, boatels, harbor masters, dock-side restaurants, marine police, and marine radio service shops are among those who maintain and operate limited coast stations as a part of their regular operations. No charge is made for the communications service, which is incidental to their business.

## How to Use the Services of Limited Coast Stations

Vessels should call limited coast stations on the limited coast station's working channel. All limited coast stations have Channel 16 plus one or more working channels. Limited coast stations, on the other hand, will call boats on Channel 16; therefore you do not need to monitor his working channel even if you are expecting a call.

As a general rule, limited coast stations operate only during their normal working hours. The calling procedure to use is the same as you would use to call another vessel except that you should initiate the call on the coast station's working channel. Be sure to give them plenty of time to answer your call as operating the radio is secondary to the operator's normal tasks. Many of these stations monitor Channel 16 as well as their working channels. If you don't know their assigned working channel, or if they don't appear to be watching their working channel, call on Channel 16.

## Other Radio Services

### CB

Citizens' Band (CB) radio is inexpensive and popular with both fixed land and land mobile stations, and in many inland areas CB radios are very common on boats, as well. In inland areas where marine radiotelephone services are not available, some boaters have only CB radio.

CB radio may be very useful for local communications, such as between boats traveling together on a river cruise, etc. As such, it can actually relieve some usage pressure on the marine VHF system.

On the other hand, there is no established standard channel which is generally monitored for marine use, and actively monitored channels vary from region to region. There are active volunteer groups which monitor CB channel 9 (the highway emergency calling channel), but in most cases the likelihood that you will be able to reach competent help in an emergency is slight. Add to this the fact that the effective range of CB radio under most conditions is limited (typically 4-5 miles) and it becomes clear that dependence on CB for emergency communications is risky.

The Coast Guard does monitor CB channel 9, but only on a "not to interfere" basis. What this means is that the CB is a secondary concern, after the VHF system. If the VHF radio requires attention, the CB will not be monitored.

In summary, then, the CB radio may be a useful addition to your boat's radio equipment, but it should not be looked on as a primary means of emergency communications except in extreme situations.

### Amateur Radio

Some boaters who plan extended long-distance cruises offshore equip their boats with amateur ("ham") radio gear. If they are already amateur radio operators and wish to combine their hobbies, or if they want to maintain contact with their ham friends at home and elsewhere, this is fine. However, if the intent is to substitute amateur radio for marine radiotelephone, it is a serious mistake.

Amateur radio and HF-SSB marine radiotelephones are superficially similar. Amateur equipment is available that operates at frequencies NEAR the marine HF frequencies. Much amateur equipment uses SSB transmissions, and similar levels of power are available. An additional inducement is that amateur equipment is available for a fraction of the cost of a typical marine HF radiotelephone.

The problems, however, are many. While there are many boaters who are also hams, there are no internationally-recognized frequencies where assistance is consistently available, and there is no watch maintained for emergency calls, let alone for routine calls.

As with CB radio, the likelihood that a boater in distress will be able to reach someone in a position to help is slim. The people who might happen to be listening to hear your call at that time and at that frequency is a random sample of all hams in the world. The very long-range nature of ham communications which makes it so seductive as an alternative could also mean that your call for distress could be heard by someone halfway around the world from you!

Then there is the issue of equipment reliability. Marine radiotelephone equipment is quite a bit more expensive than amateur equipment, and that extra expense is reflected largely in quality of construction and added reliability. Just as slim as the chance that you will be able to contact somebody nearby is the chance that the equipment will still be working during an emergency, just when you need it most.

Approved marine radiotelephone equipment is designed to be nearly fool-proof, and very easy to operate. Amateur radio gear is considerably more difficult to operate, and relatively easy to make operate improperly. If you already have an electronics hobby, this is no major concern. But if you are a boater who wants reliable communications, you may not want to have to deal with a sensitive and delicate piece of equipment.

Finally, there is the matter of licensing. Amateur radio requires a special license, which in turn requires an examination. Various technical and legal matters are covered in the examination, and you will be tested on your ability to send and receive International Morse code. Once again, this is beyond the interests of most boaters who just want to talk to the folks back home from time to time.

In summary, amateur radio is an excellent hobby, and combines well with boating, once certain technical problems are resolved. It may even serve on occasion to supplement regular marine radiotelephone communications, or in rare instances may even serve in an emergency when the marine radiotelephone has failed. However, it has no place as a complete substitute or replacement for proper marine radiotelephone, properly installed and operated.

# Chapter 13

# Inland Waterways, Locks And Dams

**River Boating**

Some of the finest boating this country offers can be found on the inland waterways of interconnected rivers and lakes. Throughout the United States there are nearly 30,000 miles of inland waterways. The Mississippi River system alone covers more than 12,000 miles. Rivers as a rule seldom offer large open expanses, but they do require unique piloting skills.

Changing conditions on the rivers put a premium on local knowledge and raise river navigation to an art. Piloting the riverways is both exciting and interesting. Although the rivers hold no dark secrets, they do have peculiarities that offer new challenges to the coastal and lake boater.

**Fig. 13-1 Dam with Double Locks.**

While the coastal boater keeps close watch on the tides and water depth, the river boater watches overhead clearance, buoys, channels, dikes, wing dams, and low water dams in back channels. Except for flooding conditions that occur following a heavy rain, the only fluctuation in river level is seasonal. In some of the navigable streams, sudden rains may raise the level several feet in a very few hours.

**Maintained Channels**

Federal waterways are maintained by the U. S. Army Corps of Engineers. They attempt to maintain a minimum channel depth and width through dredging and other maintenance activities. Minimum channel depths vary depending on the river and (to some extent) the season of the year. But like Mean Low Water in tidal waters, this is a target (reference) level, and under special conditions the water may actually be more shallow than indicated. Commercial interests plan on these minimum depths, and load their barges and plan schedules accordingly.

If changes occur in the river channel that will affect the channel depth, announcements are published in the LOCAL NOTICE TO MARINERS. Minute-to-minute updates are also available for critical situations through broadcast messages on the VHF-FM radiotelephone system from the Coast Guard. (See Chapter 12, Radiotelephone.)

**Currents**

Currents can be of great concern to the river boater. Vessels moving upstream, against the current, may make very little advance over the ground, while making considerable speed through the water and using up a substantial quantity of fuel. Some slower houseboats and sailboats may not be able to make headway upstream at all.

Movement downstream is aided by a current, and speed and fuel economy are boosted by the amount of the current flow. But this is not an unmixed blessing, as a vessel that is being carried downstream by a substantial current is to a large extent at the mercy of that current, and lacks an element of control. (It is for this reason that the Inland Navigation Rules make vessels headed downstream the "stand-on vessel," and place the burden of avoidance on those headed up, who have more control, even if they are making less headway.) [See Chapter 7.]

Currents in the river can also be complex, as they respond to changes in the channel direction and bottom configuration. Currents at various depths, too, may run contrary to one another. Deep-draft vessels may be affected by deep currents, while shallow-draft vessels may be in a current running in the opposite direction. (Needless to say, this can create some interesting situations for two vessels maneuvering alongside one another.)

Knowledgeable river boaters learn to read these currents and to take advantage of them. Vessels headed upstream may move to the inside of a bend, where currents are lessened, or may actually reverse and head upstream. This can result in significant fuel savings, which is important for recreational and commercial users alike. (Of course, the inside of the bend is usually the shallowest part of the river, so this maneuver must be used with caution.)

The rivers and the river boatmen who plied them were a vital part of commerce in the 18th and 19th Centuries, and played an important role in opening up the western territories. But much depended on the individual skill and knowledge of the river pilots, whose local knowledge was all that stood between reliable transportation and a series of groundings, wrecks and sinkings.

Those rivers that were navigable suffered from water levels that changed rapidly and often unpredictably, and wandering channels and sandbars that could open up or close the river over night.

Early efforts to control some of the rivers, to maintain a clear channel and control the random meandering of sandbars, involved the construction of "wing dams." These structures diverted the current to the center of the channel. This kept the channel scoured out and reduced shoaling. Wing dams could not control the river level, however, and spring floods were inevitably followed by late summer dry weather and shallow water.

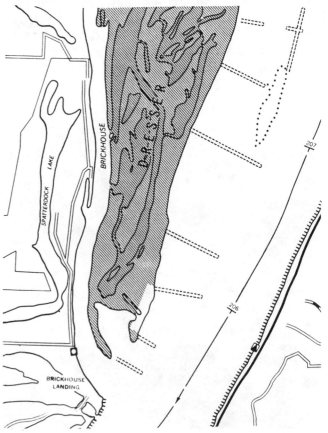

Fig. 13-2  Wing Dams On a River Chart.

Later, full dams were built that changed the rivers from a continuous flow of water from higher to lower elevation into a stepwise series of "pools." Excess water could be retained upstream of the dams and released into the lower pool as needed to maintain water depth and control shoaling.

These dams not only aided in controlling the channel, but also helped regulate the flow of water, so that the water accumulated during the spring floods can be held back and released later in the summer when the rains upstream are less plentiful.

The construction of the full dams, however, while it brought many benefits, created two new problems. The first is how to get vessels through the barriers created by the dams; the second is the wing dams, which were left in place but which are now generally under the surface and invisible.

The problem of navigation through the dams was solved by the construction of LOCKS. (See below.) The wing dams remain as a potentially serious navigation hazard for the unwary. They are clearly marked on navigational charts of the river, however, and many are further marked with warning buoys. As a result, they constitute no real problem if you are aware of them and stay in the channel or move outside the channel with care.

## Commercial Traffic (Barges & Tows)

One of the fascinating aspects of the inland waterways is the commercial traffic you encounter there. In some areas this traffic consists of ships, often from foreign ports. But in most cases the vessels are integrated collections of barges and towboats. Most generally the barges are lashed alongside the towboat or pushed ahead. All of the units are connected to one another in such a way that the whole collection can be maneuvered as one vessel, yet individual barges can be broken out and left at various intermediate locations for unloading

while the rest of the tow goes on about its business.

Fig. 13-3   View from Towboat Pilothouse.

Large tows may also be equipped with a "bowboat," sometimes specially built for the job, to assist in controlling the combination.

Tows can be 1000 feet or more in length, and comprise some of the largest vessels to be seen anywhere. They require a great deal of maneuvering room, and special attention is necessary for small boats operating in their vicinity.

These extremely large vessels may require a mile or more to stop in an emergency, and they often cannot maneuver laterally to avoid difficulty, either.

Second, since the helmsman is usually located at the after part of the tow, he has limited visibility forward. That is to say, there is a large area immediately in front of the tow that is blocked to his view. Many towboats have very high pilothouses, and other towboats that must be lower to operate under bridges, etc., have pilothouses mounted on hydraulic rams to allow them a higher vantage point whenever possible. These measures only lessen the problem, however. They do not eliminate it.

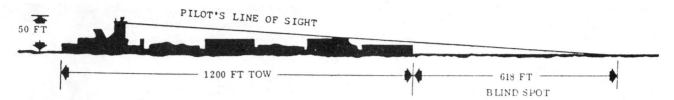

PILOT'S LINE OF SIGHT

50 FT

1200 FT TOW                    618 FT
                               BLIND SPOT

Fig. 13-4  Towboat Danger Area (Blind Spot)

The visibility problem is made even worse when the tow includes empty barges. Empties are almost always carried at the head (front) of the tow. Otherwise the whole tow becomes almost unmaneuverable. But empties ride high in the water, and block even more of the forward view.

When you are operating in the vicinity of a tow, then, be especially sensitive to the helmsman's field of view, and avoid running into his blind zone. It is tempting to move back to the center of the channel quickly after you pass a tow. But this almost invariably means that you move into the blind zone. If you were to suffer an engine failure, or strike a submerged object and become disabled at that point, the towboat operator might never know you were there, even after he had run over you. Even if he had a lookout posted on the bow, as many do in congested waters, he might not be able to stop in time to avoid hitting a stalled boat.

The third issue has to do with maneuverability outside the channel. Most towboats and barges are loaded to the maximum depth the channel will accommodate. They may have only a few inches clearance on the bottom. As a result, they do not have the ability to operate outside the buoyed channel. Most recreational boats, on the other hand, have more flexibility in this regard. It is only common courtesy and common good judgment to avoid forcing the issue.

It may be possible to feel the effects of an approaching tow in the water a considerable distance ahead and behind, as water is alternately pulled toward the tow, then pushed away behind it. Large, powerful screws acting in a narrow channel close to the bottom can create pressure waves that can be felt through the hull of a small boat and can give advance warning of the approach of a tow.

In addition to the wave action produced by the towboat's screws, the disturbance produced by its passage may cause submerged objects lying on the bottom to be stirred up to depths where they may be a hazard to small craft following behind. Waterlogged trees, sunken steel drums, even sunken barges, may be encountered this way. For this reason alone it is wise to avoid running in the wake of any deep-draft vessel on the river (including large pleasure boats).

**Dams** [View of Dam upper level]

Fig. 13-5  TAINTER GATE DAM

13-4

Dams are not simply solid walls built across the river. They may actually be very complex structures, and may incorporate hydroelectric generating plants and other structures that present a very confusing picture when viewed from water level.

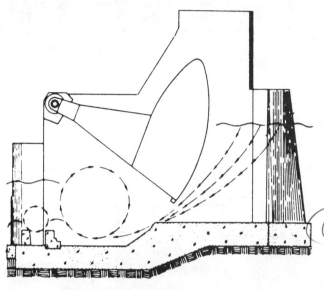

**Fig. 13-6  Tainter Gate**

Dams must make provision for allowing water to flow to the downstream pool, and for controlling that flow. To do this they have various types of "gate." So-called "tainter" gates allow water to flow downstream from the bottom of the dam. This allows accumulated sediment to be flushed downstream so it doesn't collect

**Fig. 13-7  Dam and Lock**

at the base of the dam. However, it also means that you cannot tell by looking if the dam gates are open or not. Open gates mean turbulent water, and this 'in turn means a potentially dangerous situation for small boats.

Another type of dam uses "wicket" gates, which can be lowered to lie along the bottom and which allow water to flow over the top of the wickets. The principle advantage of wicket dams is that in times of high water the wickets can be lowered completely and river traffic can pass over the dam without hinderance and without having to pass through the locks.

From the small boater's point of view, wicket dams present a potential hazard, since a small boat can be swept over a partially open wicket. A small boat caught up against the wall of a tainter dam, on the other hand, will be held there and can be rescued if it does not capsize and if the occupants stay with the boat.

### Locks

Locks are a means of passing vessels through the dam and, at the same time, raising or lowering them to the level of the next pool. A lock is a large chamber, typically 800-1200 feet long and 100-120 feet wide, and equipped with gates at each end.

A vessel headed upstream enters the lock chamber through the downstream gates, which are closed behind. Valves are then opened which permit water to enter the chamber from the upstream pool. No pumps are used; gravity powers the lock.

As the water level rises in the chamber the vessel rises with it. When the water level in the lock comes even with the level in the upstream pool the flow of water slows, then stops. The upstream gates are then opened, and the vessel moves out of the chamber and continues on its way.

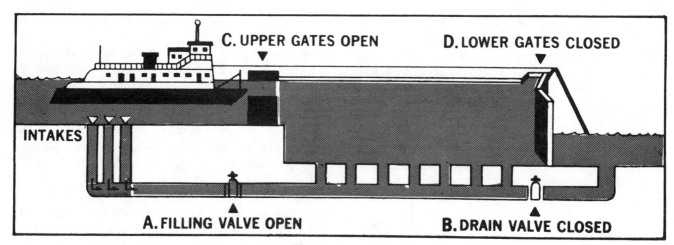

Fig. 13-8    Lock Open to Upper Pool.

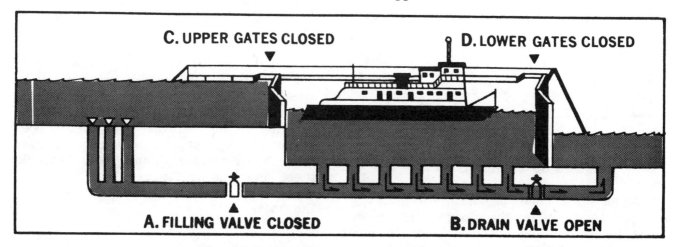

Fig. 13-9    Water Level Lowering.

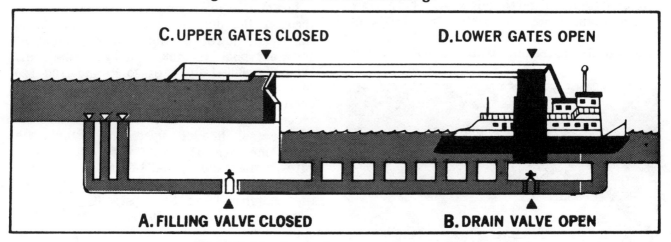

Fig. 13-10    Lock Open to Lower Pool.

A downbound vessel enters through the upstream gates, which are then closed. Valves are opened which allow the water in the lock chamber to flow into the downstream pool. When the level of water in the chamber is the same as the downstream pool, the lower gates are opened and the vessel moves out.

The building, maintenance and operation of river locks are the responsibility of the U. S. Army Corps of Engineers. Each lock is under the control of a lockmaster, who is entirely responsible for lock operations. A lockmaster will accommodate your needs if possible, but he may have other, more pressing priorities that may result in some minor inconvenience for you. Understanding all the way around will make the whole process of passing through locks much more pleasant.

Federal law establishes clear priorities for the use of locks. First priority goes to U. S. naval and military vessels, followed by mail-carrying vessels, vessels carrying passengers for hire, fishing vessels, and vessels carrying freight. Finally, at the lowest priority, is recreational boats.

This is not as bad as it may sound. As a matter of fact, naval and military vessels and mail packets are seldom seen on the waterways, and passenger-carrying vessels are not common, either. In most cases, the "competition" for lockage is commercial barge traffic.

On occasion it is possible to pass through locks in company with commercial vessels. This depends on the space available in the lock chamber, the nature of the cargo being carried, and the wishes of the towboat operator, whose first responsibility is for the safety of his vessel.

Regardless of space availability, no other vessels will be locked through with a hazardous cargo (e.g., gasoline, sulphuric acid, etc.). Such cargos are marked by the international code flag "BRAVO," a red swallow-tailed pennant, usually constructed of sheet metal so it is always visible. You should avoid such "red-flagged" barges, and give them extra consideration. While river transport of such cargos in bulk is well-proven and exceptionally safe, any accident that DOES occur has the potential of being a major disaster.

All things considered, then, you should plan on a certain amount of delay at locks. If commercial traffic is heavy and several tows are waiting at a lock, the delay may be several hours. As a practical matter, no lockmaster wants to have several dozen pleasure boats loitering in the approaches to his lock, and will make every effort to move small boat traffic through quickly.

Sometimes a barge string is too large to fit into the lock chamber. In these cases, the barge string will be broken into two or more parts and locked through in halves. It may be possible to lock pleasure boats in the opposite direction as the chamber is being filled or drained in preparation for the second half, since there is not space enough to move another tow in for that cycle. Time is of the essence, and pleasure boaters should be prepared to move quickly to take advantage of opportunities like these. Quarters will also be very tight, and you may be moving very close to the tow and/or the lock gates, so extra caution is called for.

Lockmasters may be reached by VHF-FM radiotelephone (see Chapter 12), and this can be very useful for all involved. If the lockmasters know what is headed their way they can plan their moves and make more efficient use of the facilities. If you know what is currently going on, you can adjust your speed or plans accordingly. You may be able to speed up and get into a group locking through, or you may simply plan to anchor or beach your boat for a lunch break if there is a large restricted ("red-flagged") tow being locked through.

If they are locking through a tow, or a number of recreational craft, the lockmasters may not be able to respond immediately to every radio call. If you make it a practice to listen to ongoing radio traffic you can keep track of what is happening, and may not have to make a call to the lockmaster.

Signals are provided near the entrance of the lock chamber with which the lockmaster regulates traffic. These signals typically resemble traffic lights, and indicate much the same sort of information. Horn signals are also used.

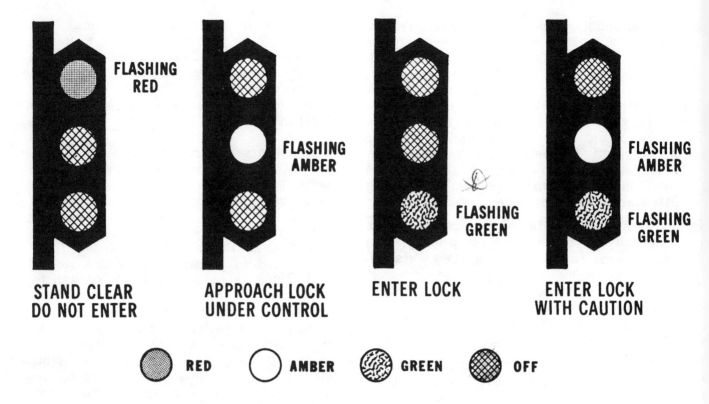

FLASHING RED

FLASHING AMBER

FLASHING GREEN

FLASHING AMBER

FLASHING GREEN

STAND CLEAR
DO NOT ENTER

APPROACH LOCK
UNDER CONTROL

ENTER LOCK

ENTER LOCK
WITH CAUTION

RED     AMBER     GREEN     OFF

Fig. 13-11   How Signals Are Also Used.

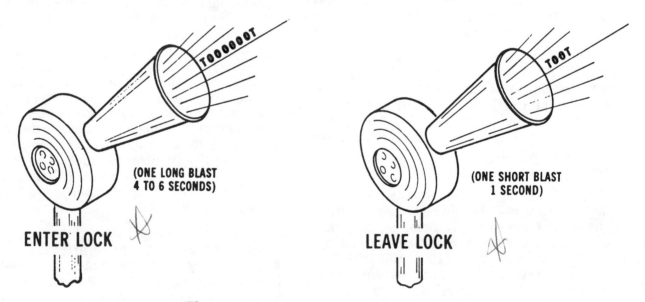

TOOOOOOT

(ONE LONG BLAST
4 TO 6 SECONDS)

ENTER LOCK

TOOT

(ONE SHORT BLAST
1 SECOND)

LEAVE LOCK

Fig. 13-12   Air Horn Signals.

A red light means "do not approach." A yellow light (often flashing) indicates that you should PREPARE to move into the lock, but do not move yet. The green light signals that the lock is ready to receive vessels. Note that the signal to enter MAY NOT APPLY TO YOU. If there are vessels waiting for lockage that have higher priority than you, the signal may apply to them.

As you approach the lock chamber, you should move at a strict no-wake speed. For most boats this means no more than a fast idle speed. There is a conflict between the urge to move into position quickly and the need to keep wakes down. Avoiding wakes should take priority. A lock chamber is a long, narrow chamber with flat concrete walls. With several boats moving in close proximity to one another, extra care is needed from everybody to avoid damaging boats or lock gate structures.

All crewmembers should wear PFD's during the entire locking operation. The lock chamber can be turbulent while the chamber is being filled, and crewmembers will be moving around tending lines, etc. It is very easy to fall overboard in these conditions, and this is nearly the worst possible conditions for a person overboard: several boats very close to one another, turbulent water, vertical walls.

A general precaution, you should also stop engines and extinguish all flames, including cigarettes. With several boats in close quarters in an enclosed chamber, a fire could be a disaster, indeed.

Locks may provide lines, or you may be expected to provide your own. You should have lines available that are AT LEAST as long as twice the depth of the lock. Small boats can be handled with one line, located midships; boats larger than 25-30' may require lines fore and aft.

Various types of locks have various means available for tying up. Small craft may use lines on bitts or bollards (large, rounded "knobs" mounted along the top of the lock wall) or on a railing. Other locks have ladders or series of recessed bollards set into the lock wall. It will be necessary to move your line from attachment point to attachment point as the boat is raised or lowered in these cases.

Perhaps the best of all arrangements is the system of floating bollards in some of the larger locks, such as those on the Tennessee River. These structures are

Fig. 13-13 Typical Lock Wall.

mounted on tracks set into the lock wall and float up and down as the water level changes. If you are fortunate enough to get one of these floating bollards, you will not have to feed out or take in line. You will, however, have to tend the lines and be prepared to take action in the unlikely event that the bollard should jam and not move up or down.

When many recreational boats are locked through, there may not be enough space available on the lock wall. You should, therefore, be prepared to raft up with other boats. The lockmaster will instruct you where to go on the wall, and may designate which boats should raft with you. You should be prepared with extra fenders and lines for this eventuality.

After the water in the lock chamber has reached its new level, do not move away from the wall until the lockmaster signals that you may. Again, move at a no-wake speed, paying close attention to other boats that will also be getting under way at the same time.

River Piloting

The charts that are used for river navigation differ somewhat from those used for coastal piloting. Since the extent of the river is essentially one-dimensional, it is not practical to publish river charts in the same form as for broader expanses of water, such as coastal waters or the Great Lakes. Instead, river charts are published as spiral-bound books. Each page of the book represents a section of a few miles of the river, which is continued on an adjacent page. Because of this arrangement, river charts can conveniently be shown in a fairly large scale, and they can still be handled conveniently even on board fairly small boats.

Anyone who is familiar with coastal piloting charts and practices should feel comfortable with river charts in short order. There are some differences, however.

It is seldom necessary on the river to plot a compass course or maintain a dead reckoning plot. It is necessary, however, to stay in a relatively confined channel, and a number of special navigation aids are provided to assist you in doing this. These include traditional buoys and daymarks, plus a liberal number of ranges and a special type of daymark, called a "crossing daymark."

The banks of the river are identified as "right bank" or "left bank," as the river flows. Thus, the west bank of the Mississippi River, which flows south, is its right bank. The right margin of the channel is marked by green buoys and daymarks, while the left margin is marked with red buoys and daymarks. (See Chapter 4, Aids to Navigation.)

The river channel is the deepest portion of the river, a sort of river within the river. When a river basin is flooded, either naturally or because of the construction of control structures (dams) downstream, the deeper channel may be lost under a broad expanse of uniform-appearing water. Since the river can be very shallow outside the channel, it is important to know where the channel lies. This is especially true since the channel can meander considerably within the limits of its banks.

Standard daymarks (red triangles and green squares) as they are used on the river imply that the channel continues as it has. They are often referred to as "passing daymarks," since they are passed without any change of course other than that necessary to follow the curvature of the river itself.

A different sort of daymark, diamond-shaped, but still marked with red or green, depending on which side of the channel it marks, indicates that the channel swings to the opposite bank. This "crossing daymark" indicates that the next marker (buoy or daymark) to be seen will be on the opposite bank.

**Fig. 13-14  Crossing Daymark.**

# Chapter 14

# Piloting

## Introduction

Navigation is the science of knowing where you are on the Earth and knowing how to get to where you want to be. Piloting is navigation in coastal waters, usually within sight of land. While some piloting makes use of electronic aids that operate at a distance, most piloting is done using visual sightings of natural or man-made landmarks.

In a basic course such as this one, we can only introduce you to some of the many facets of piloting. We can, however, give you a "leg up" on your study of this fascinating and important subject, and give you some tools and techniques that you will find useful in your recreational boating.

If you have any serious interest in advancing your skills as a pilot, and you really should if you take boating seriously, we recommend that you follow up this course with Advanced Coastal Navigation taught by the Coast Guard Auxiliary, or a similar course. See your instructor for details.

## Tools

The tools required for piloting are minimal. You can spend a great deal of money on them, however, you are advised to keep your investment small and limit yourself to only the basic tools until you have a good understanding of what is really needed.

Your basic piloting tool kit should include:

- Charts of the area of interest,

- A good-quality magnetic compass,

- Parallel rulers or course protractor,

- Dividers and drafting compass,

- Fine-lead mechanical pencil, medium-soft,

- Good-quality eraser, preferably vinyl.

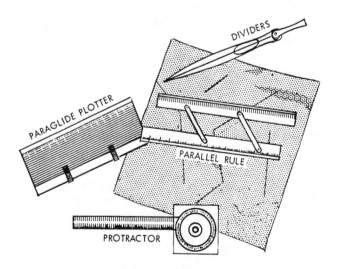

**Fig. 14-1  Basic Piloting Tools**

Additional piloting implements could include a good binocular (7x50), some means of measuring water depth (calibrated pole, lead line, or electronic depth sounder ["sonar"]), and a hand bearing compass.

As your skills increase, or as your circumstances require and permit, you may want to add electronic tools, such as a radio direction finder (RDF), satellite navigation equipment, or LORAN-C. But no matter how sophisticated your piloting equipment may become, there are times when it still comes down to chart, compass, pencil and straight edge.

## The Nautical Chart

Maps are what make serious navigation possible. A "map" is a graphical representation of a portion of the surface of the earth, generally on paper. Usually a map is drawn "to scale." That is, the sizes of objects in the drawing are proportional to the sizes of those objects on the earth.

In general, the word "map" applies to drawings of land areas. More properly, drawings of areas of water, especially those drawn specifically to aid piloting and navigation, are called "charts."

Charts are not restricted to showing water areas. Remember that piloting is navigating near the coast, using landmarks as aids. Nautical charts show areas of land near the water, and may actually include a great deal of detail about objects on the land, if those objects are useful to finding position (the shape of the coastline, landmarks visible from the sea, man-made aids to navigation) or for providing services for mariners (marinas, harbors, etc.)

Today's chart is a technological marvel. If the same information were converted into words and written down, the contents of a single nautical chart would probably require several large books. And they would be much harder to read and interpret.

This compact presentation of information is possible in part through the use of symbols. These symbols stand for various objects that cannot be represented to

scale in their true shapes. We will discuss the symbols used on a chart later in this chapter.

## Sources of Charts

Charts of U.S. waters are prepared and published by the National Ocean Service (NOS), and free catalogs are available directly from that organization. These catalogs are also provided by authorized chart sales outlets, including map stores, navigational instrument sales and service facilities, boat yards and marine service businesses.

Charts are only as good as the information on them, and because that information changes with time, you should be sure to buy and use up-to-date charts. To help you be certain of having the most recent version, charts are dated.

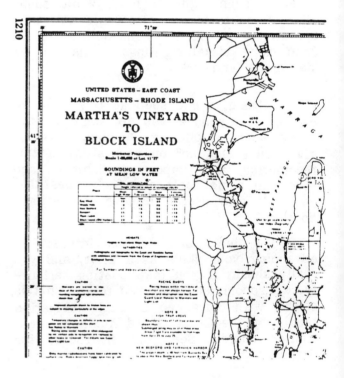

Fig. 14-2   Portion of a Nautical Chart

The "Notice to Mariners," published monthly by the local Coast Guard District, gives information on changes that are needed to charts between formal updates. Changes always occur faster than charts can be updated, printed and distributed. Even newly-purchased copies of the latest editions of charts probably require some correction.

## Projection

The surface of the earth is curved. Most maps and charts, on the other hand, are flat. It is just not possible to represent a curved surface on a flat piece of paper accurately without some distortion. If the area is small enough, the distortion may be small enough to ignore, but it will always be there.

The process of mapping a curved surface onto a flat one is called projection. It is a fairly complex mathematical process in execution, but the concept is simple.

There are several projection techniques. The one most commonly used in navigational charts is the Mercator projection. This projection works well for most purposes, but shapes and distances are increasingly distorted as you move into extreme northern and southern areas. The distortion makes these charts nearly unusable in polar and near-polar areas, but this is no serious problem for most of the areas where recreational boating occurs.

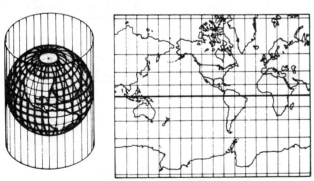

- Angles are correctly represented • Great circle appears curved
- Rhumb line appears as straight line
- Distortion in BOTH directions

### Fig. 14-3 Mercator Projection

Another common projection, used for charts of the Great Lakes, for example, is the polyconic projection. This projection gives less distortion in high northern and southern areas.

## Scale

Charts are classified according to scale. A harbor chart, for instance, may have a scale of 1:20,000. That is, the drawing of the object as it appears on the chart is 1/20,000 the size of the actual object. A harbor entrance that is 1" wide on the chart is actually 20,000" wide, or about 3/10 of a mile.

If the chart's scale were 1:40,000 the same 1" drawing would represent an object just twice that size, or about 3/5 of a mile. Conversely, the 3/10-mile wide harbor entrance would only appear 1/2" wide on the chart.

Harbor charts sometimes are drawn in scales of 1:10,000. These charts can show an enormous amount of detail, but they cannot cover a very large area. Coastal charts, on the other hand, are typically 1:80,000. They show much larger areas, with correspondingly less detail.

Even smaller scales (1:100,000; 1:1,000,000; etc.) are used for special purposes, such as planning ocean passages. Some charts show an entire ocean on one sheet of paper. In general, you should select charts to give the amount of detail you need for each portion of your cruise; small-scale, large-area charts for overall planning; large-scale, detailed charts for maneuvering within harbors; and so on.

Most nautical charts are printed on large sheets of heavy, good-quality paper. They are designed to be used with a large flat table, such as might be found on the bridge of a ship. They are difficult to work with on a small boat, however, so special folio-style charts, known as Small Craft Charts, are published for areas that have a lot of small boat traffic. These charts, generally in 1:40,000 scale, are specially designed in a format with fold-out segments to be used in the cramped quarters of a small boat. Their covers also carry other useful information, such as tidal data, descriptions of facilities available in the area, etc.

**Fig. 14-4   Small Craft Chart**

If you have an open boat, you may want to protect your chart by encasing it in a transparent plastic cover that will allow you to spread it out flat without worry of its being damaged by rain or spray.

**Datum and Sea Level**

Datum is the technical term for the base line from which a chart's vertical measurements are made - heights of land or landmarks, or depths of water. Most landsmen's maps use sea level as datum, and that is quite good enough for most purposes.

But in coastal areas with tides, depths are constantly changing. Since depth is a primary concern of the mariner, a more sophisticated datum is required.

The marine datum used for heights of objects on land is mean high water, the average (mean) level of all high tide levels (excluding unusual conditions, such as severe storms, etc.)

The figures for water depths, on the other hand, are based on a more conservative datum, mean low water (MLW). In the Pacific, there are two tides per day, generally unequal. The datum used on the West Coast is the average of the lower of the two low waters, called the mean lower low water (MLLW). On the Gulf of Mexico, the datum is the Gulf Coast Low Water Datum, and a similar low water datum is used in the Great Lakes.

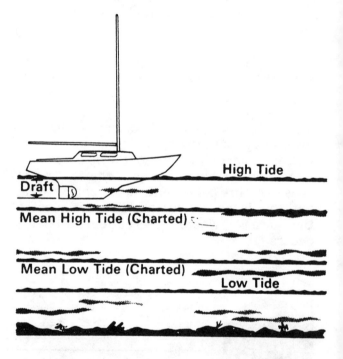

**Fig. 14-5   Datum - Depths of Water**

Note that the depth of water that appears on a chart is based on datum. The actual depth of water at any given time will depend on many factors and may differ considerably from what the chart shows.

**Units of Measurement**

Depths of water ("soundings") are usually given in feet on U.S. charts, but may also be given in fathoms (1 fathom = 6 feet) or <u>meters</u>. The units of depth measurement, <u>the scale</u>, and the datum are among the important data prominently displayed on the <u>title block</u> of the chart. (See Fig.14-2.)

## Other Charted Information

Besides heights and depths, charts also describe the type of bottom material, using special abbreviations. This information is especially useful if you are trying to select a place to set an anchor. Soft mud is not generally suitable holding ground, whereas sand or hard mud is usually excellent for anchoring. (See Chapter 5.)

| 1 |     | Ground      |
|---|-----|-------------|
| 2 | S   | Sand        |
| 3 | M   | Mud, Muddy  |
| 4 | Oz  | Ooze        |
| 5 | Ml  | Marl        |
| 6 | Cl  | Clay        |
| 7 | G   | Gravel      |
| 8 | Sn  | Shingle     |
| 9 | P   | Pebbles     |
| 10| St  | Stones      |

Fig. 14-6   Types of Bottoms

Obstructions and other hazards in the water are also charted. Symbols tell the mariner what to be ready for and what to avoid. It is worth bearing in mind that a wreck, even one that is largely exposed, soon ceases to look like the ship it once was, and may be difficult to recognize.

Shallow water is tinted light blue on a chart, while deeper water is shown in white. This gives a ready visual reference without having to look at the numbers. (As a rule of thumb, moving into the blue is generally time to switch to a larger-scale chart.)

## Shore Details

Charted details ashore include prominent structures, especially those that stand out because of their distinctive shape (churches, water towers). Land contours are frequently charted. Bridges of all types are described in detail.

The shoreline contour is one of the chart's most important features. It is usually tinted gold, or light green if it is swampy or if it covers and uncovers with changes in water level.

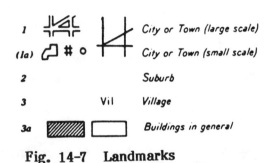

| 1   |     | City or Town (large scale) |
| (1a)|     | City or Town (small scale) |
| 2   |     | Suburb                     |
| 3   | Vil | Village                    |
| 3a  |     | Buildings in general       |

Fig. 14-7   Landmarks

(You should keep in mind that structures that were once prominent enough to warrant appearing on the chart may have been torn down, or may be screened by larger buildings that were built later. The process of keeping charts up-to-date is a continuous one, and depends on cooperation from chart users, such as you. Your instructors can tell you how you can participate in the cooperative chart updating program.)

## Aids to Navigation

Man-made structures, both fixed and floating, serve as signposts, beacons, direction signals, and warnings of danger to the mariner. These aids to navigation, placed and serviced by the U. S. Coast Guard, are described in detail in Chapter 4.

Obviously, aids to navigation -- except for major lighthouses — are far too small to appear on the chart in their true shape. Instead, symbols are used to indi-

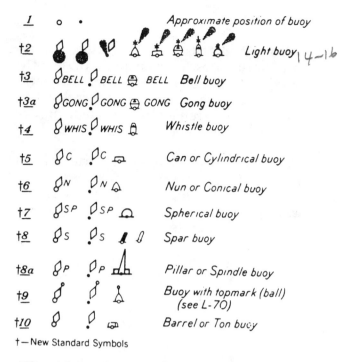

| _1_ | o · | | Approximate position of buoy |
| --- | --- | --- | --- |
| †2 | | | Light buoy |
| †3 | BELL · BELL BELL | Bell buoy |
| †3a | GONG · GONG GONG | Gong buoy |
| †4 | WHIS · WHIS | Whistle buoy |
| †5 | C · C | Can or Cylindrical buoy |
| †6 | N · N | Nun or Conical buoy |
| †7 | SP · SP | Spherical buoy |
| †8 | S · S | Spar buoy |
| †8a | P · P | Pillar or Spindle buoy |
| †9 | | | Buoy with topmark (ball) (see L-70) |
| †10 | | | Barrel or Ton buoy |

†—New Standard Symbols

**Fig. 14-8   Excerpt from Chart No. 1**

cate the position, type, number and color of the aids. These (and other) symbols used on nautical charts are shown in Chart No. 1, a sample of which is shown in Fig.14-8.

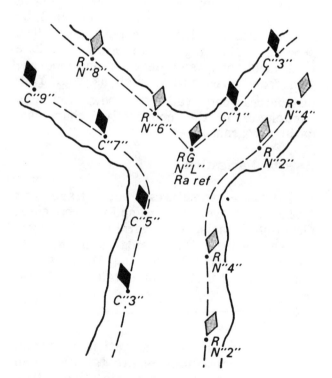

**Fig. 14-9   Channel Markers**

The actual location of a buoy is the small circle at one end of the diamond symbol. A fixed aid is marked with a small, isolated circle. Lighted buoys are distinguished by light purple (magenta) circles printed around the position circle. Lighted fixed aids have a purple (magenta) "exclamation mark" with its sharp end pointing toward the position circle.

In practical piloting, it should be remembered that buoys are anchored in place, and at low tide they may move off their charted positions. They may even end up outside the channel they mark. They may be sunk, or be displaced by ice or debris.

They may be damaged by vandals or accident. Fixed aids, on the other hand, usually stay put. Even if their lights are extinguished, they are usually recognizable.

### The Magnetic Compass

Many centuries ago, mariners oriented themselves by the sun's place or rising and setting, or by the direction of the prevailing winds. This was less than precise, especially on windless or cloudy days. The magnetic compass, perfected slowly over years of experimentation, trial and scientific endeavor, became the sailor's most common and most reliable direction-indicating aid.

In principle, the magnetic compass remains as simple as it was when it was invented in medieval times. It is a magnet, balanced so it can pivot freely in a horizontal plane. The magnet -- as any magnet will, given the opportunity — aligns itself with the earth's magnetic field. A pointer attached to the magnet will point the way toward the north magnetic pole.

The north magnetic pole is near, but not the same as, the earth's true north pole, or axis of spin. The magnetic pole wanders somewhat over many years, and is located in far northern Canada.

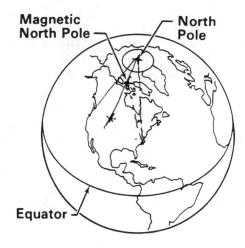

**Fig. 14-10   Relative Position of Poles**

The difference between the location of the north magnetic pole and the true north pole has important effects on the way we use the magnetic compass. This effect, and the way we handle it, are discussed below.

## Selecting a Compass

A magnetic compass should be selected carefully to suit the boat it will be used on. Power boats should be equipped with a compass designed and built to withstand the vibrations and pounding of a power boat moving at high speeds, while a sailboat compass needs to be able to operate satisfactorily when it is heeled over at an angle.

(A major achievement in the design of compasses for the Royal Navy was building one that would be accurate enough to use for navigation while not jumping off the pivot with the shock of guns being fired on board!)

In general, since large compasses tend to be more stable and more finely calibrated than small compasses, all other things being equal, the compass should be as large as practical under the situation. Most small boats have small compasses, while larger, steadier boats have larger compasses, when it should probably be the other way around. On the other hand, larger boats are used on longer passages, where greater accuracy is needed.

Whatever the size of the compass chosen, it must be installed with care. Try to locate the instrument so that it can be sighted over in all directions. But even more important, it must be easily visible to the helmsman.

Marine compasses are filled with an oily or alcohol-based liquid to help damp out vibrations and oscillations. Good quality compasses have bellows chambers to allow for expansion and contraction of this fluid with changing temperatures. All compasses should be protected from excess heat and direct sunlight, but you may find an inexpensive compass leaking fluid from a ruptured seal if it is allowed to overheat. Such a compass must be repaired or replaced, since without the fluid it is virtually useless on a boat.

Make certain that the fore-and-aft marks on the compass — the center pivot and the lubber's line — are parallel with the keel.

A good compass almost always has internal adjusters, small magnets that allow the instrument to be adjusted for local magnetic influences that contribute error. It is also useful to have a light (preferably red) installed so the compass can be read at night.

**Fig. 14-11   Small Boat Magnetic Compass**

The compass should be located at least three feet in every direction from radios, other electronic instruments, or masses of ferrous metal. This may be difficult in a small boat, but do the best you can.

When you have installed the compass in the best possible location, choose a calm day and move into an area with several charted landmarks or fixed aids to navigation. Point the boat toward each landmark in turn and check that the compass reads appropriately for each landmark.

You may wish to have your compass adjusted by a professional. The techniques for doing so are not complex, but they are tedious and not especially convenient for most recreational boaters. On the other hand, you may find, as many do, that your compass is as accurate as you can read, just as you installed it.

## Latitude and Longitude

A coordinate grid pattern gives a reference framework to describe locations and to make it possible to perform some of the operations necessary for careful navigation. This grid pattern is provided by parallels of latitude and meridians of longitude.

The parallels are numbered north (N) and south (S) from 0° at the Equator to 90°N and 90°S at the true north and south poles, respectively. Each degree is subdivided into 60 equal segments called minutes ('), and each minute can be subdivided into 60 seconds ("), or, alternatively, into tenths of minutes (00.0').

On most charts, true north is located at the top, and parallels are indicated along the side margins by divisions in the black-and-white border, as well as by lines running across the chart at intervals. (Small Craft Charts are sometimes printed to show a maximum stretch of shoreline per sheet. When this is the case, the top edge of the chart may not be north.)

It is handy to remember that one minute of LATITUDE (but not of longitude) equals one nautical mile, or 6076 feet. This is useful in measuring distances on the chart. Each chart also includes at least one printed scale, giving distances in nautical miles, statute miles, kilometers, and/or yards. (See Fig.14-13.)

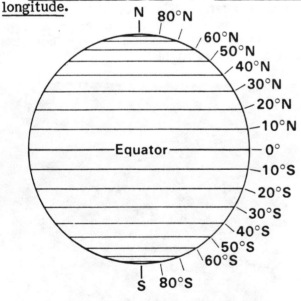

Fig. 14-12   Parallels of Latitude

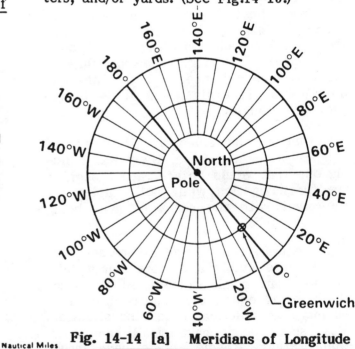

Fig. 14-14 [a]   Meridians of Longitude

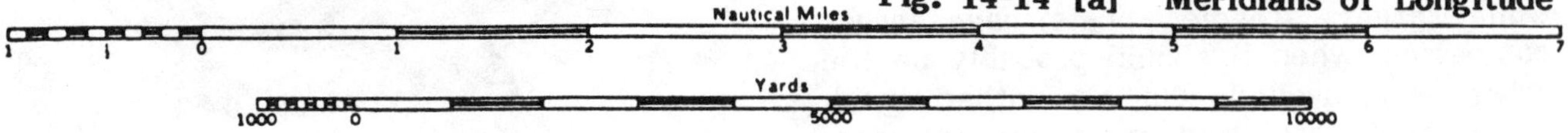

Fig. 14-13   Distance Scale

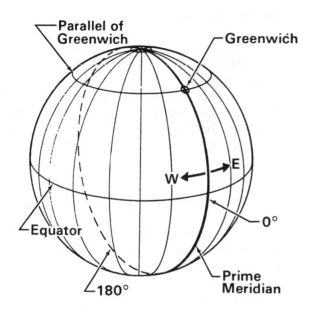

**Fig. 14-14 [b]   Meridians of Longitude**

Meridians of longitude run north (N) and south (S) between the true poles. By convention, meridians are numbered east (E) and west (W) from the Prime Meridian (000°), the one passing through the Royal Observatory in Greenwich, just outside London, England. West and east longitude meet at 180° in the Pacific Ocean. (See Fig.14-14 [a] & [b].)

Almost the entire United States is thus in west longitude -- from about 60°W on the East Coast to about 130°W in California or 150°W in Hawaii. (Several islands in the Aleutian Chain in Alaska are over the 180th meridian and in east longitude.)

Latitude and longitude always include north or south, east or west, in their designation, but they give a unique representation of position. If a boat's position is given as 45° 30.1'N, 73° 20.4'W, there is only one place on earth it can be.

**Course Plotting**

Navigational charts are constructed so that if you draw a line on the chart connecting the point representing your present location with the point representing the position you want to go to, the

angle that the (course) line makes with any meridian is the angle with true north, or direction, that you need to travel to get to your destination. Furthermore, the length of the line is a measure of the distance that you have to travel to get there.

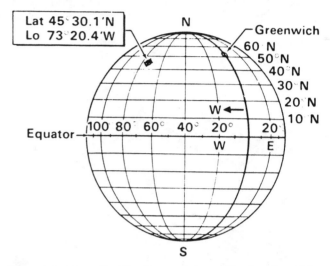

**Fig. 14-15   Latitude and Longitude Provide a Coordinate Grid System**

To "plot" or "chart" a course, the first step in piloting, first draw the course line. Extend it if necessary so that it crosses a meridian (one of the north-south lines). Use a protractor to measure the angle that the course line makes with the meridian. Always measure the number of degrees moving from the meridian around to the <u>right</u>.

Note that direction measured in degrees is a number between 0 and 360. To avoid confusion with other numbers we will be using later, <u>course directions</u> are always written as three digits. Thus 0 degrees is written 000, 25 degrees is written 025, and so on.

**Compass Rose**

The use of the course protractor is made a little bit easier on marine navigation charts, since one is provided directly on the chart, usually in more than one place. This printed protractor is called the <u>compass rose</u>. (See Fig. 14-16.)

All that is necessary to use the compass rose is to move a course line parallel to itself so that it passes through the exact center of the rose. The course angle can then be read directly where the course line cuts through the margin of the rose.

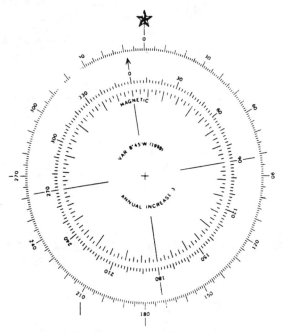

Fig. 14-16   Compass Rose

Moving the course line parallel to itself is not especially difficult, and several tools exist specifically to do that. These range from the traditional parallel rulers through a number of other patent devices, all the way up to drafting machines costing hundreds of dollars. Very simple devices, used carefully, work very well, indeed.

Fig. 14-17   Parallel Rulers

## Parallel Rulers

The parallel rulers consist of two straight pieces of wood, metal or plastic, usually 12"-15" long. The two straight edges are linked together by two movable arms so the long pieces can be brought together or moved apart several inches, but still remain parallel to one another.

To use the parallel rulers, align one edge of the collapsed rulers with the line to be measured. Then holding the other edge tight against the paper, open the ruler. You can now use the original edge to draw as many lines as you want, at whatever distance you choose from the original line, all exactly parallel to one another and to the original line, as long as the fixed straightedge does not slip.

It may be necessary to "walk" the rulers, moving one edge, then the other, avoiding slips, to get to the nearest compass rose. It may take some practice to get comfortable with the procedure, and it is always good practice to "walk" the line back again to the original course line to make sure you haven't slipped a little bit.

You should also avoid the temptation to place the lower edge along the course line and measure with the upper edge. The two edges are not guaranteed to be parallel to one another (although they should be), but only that either edge can be moved parallel to itself.

## Naming Courses

A course straight north will not cross any meridian. Another way of saying that is that it forms an angle of 0 degrees with a meridian, or the course is 000. The same line, traveled in the opposite direction (due south) forms a 180 degree line with the meridian, measured from the meridian around to the right. This is spoken of as "course 180."

Similarly, a course to the east crosses meridian (a north-south line) at right angles (course 090), while the same course line followed to the west is course 270.

It is easy to become confused and read the "reciprocal course" (same course line, opposite direction of travel), but it is equally easy to avoid the confusion. The course direction must fall between the appropriate limits. Thus a course to the northeast (045°) falls between north (000°) and east (090°). The same course line, followed in the opposite direction (towards the southwest) must fall between south (180°) and west (270°), as indeed 225° does.

## Sources of Error

As mentioned above, the magnetic north pole is located several hundred miles away from the true north pole. The magnetic compass points toward the magnetic pole, and unless you happen to live in one of those few parts of the world where the magnetic north pole just happens to lie in the same direction as the true north pole, this creates some practical problems for the navigator. The task of actually following the plotted course depends on following a compass indicator, so it is necessary to correct the compass reading or correct the course followed to get where you really want to go.

## Variation

The amount by which the magnetic compass points away from true north is called variation. The amount of variation that exists varies, depending on where you are on the globe. If you cruise off the East Coast the magnetic north pole is west of true north, and the error is called westerly variation. On the West Coast, the compass points east of true north, and the error is easterly variation. And there are some areas in the Midwest that actually are fortunate enough to have no variation at all, as the two poles are in line with one another.

The amount of variation that applies in any given area is printed on the chart as a notation in the center of the compass rose. Note that if more than one compass rose appears on the chart, you should use the variation in the rose nearest your position, since variation can differ slightly from place to place.

Also note that the compass rose has two protractor scales. The outer scale is oriented so that 000 on the protractor is pointed toward true north. The inner scale, on the other hand, is oriented to the magnetic north pole. It is possible to measure the magnetic course between two points directly from that inner scale.

Remember: Variation is the same for all vessels in a particular area.

## Correcting the Course

It is not practical to correct the magnetic compass to compensate for variation because the variation changes with the vessel's location. It is practical, on the other hand, to correct the course line. Adding westerly variation (or subtracting easterly variation) to the plotted course yields a magnetic course that compensates for the effects of variation.

For example, if the desired course is 072° (somewhat east of northeast) and the local variation is 9°W, the desired magnetic course is 072° + 9°W = 081°M.

## Deviation

Another important influence on the boat's magnetic compass is magnetic material in and on the boat itself. The engine, steering gear, radio loudspeakers, even electric currents in dashboard instruments, all cause the compass to deviate from an accurate reading. Furthermore, since this deviation is caused by the unique magnetic elements on that particular boat, the deviation pattern is different for each vessel.

Since deviation is the result of an interaction between the magnetic compass, the earth's magnetic field, and other magnetic influences on the vessel, it stands to reason that moving these elements around with respect to one another will change the effect that they have on one another. In practical terms, this means that the amount of deviation experienced by a compass depends on the direction, or heading, of the vessel.

On the other hand, since the vessel carries its magnetic environment along with it, the deviation pattern for a given small craft is, essentially not a function of its location.

It may be necessary to develop a deviation table for the vessel that shows the amount and direction of error for each heading. Generally for modern small craft, the errors are small (less than a few degrees), and a correction for deviation is unnecessary. On the other hand, if the compass deviations are large (over 3-5°), it may be necessary to make a table of these deviations (Deviation Table) and apply these corrections when converting from compass to magnetic directions and vice versa.

It may also be necessary to develop a new deviation table each time major magnetic items (radios, etc.) are added or changed. Unfortunately, construction of a deviation table is beyond the scope of this course. The subject, however, is covered thoroughly in the Advanced Coastal Navigation course.

## Positioning

It is important to be able to establish the position of the boat frequently, in order to know where you are in the event of an emergency, in case the visibility becomes restricted (i.e., fog), or simply so you can determine if you have enough fuel to get you where you want to go. A Line of Position (LOP) is a line established on a chart that can be drawn through the known position of the vessel. By itself, an LOP is insufficient to establish the position of the vessel. But, the intersection of two, or more, LOPs definitely establishes the position of the vessel.

The simplest form of LOP is the Range. Recall from Chapter 4, the discussion of Range Marks, which establish whether the vessel is on the centerline of the channel. When the two range marks align, a Range LOP is established. If that line is drawn on the chart, and the vessel is on the range, then the vessel is known to be on that line. Although this single LOP is insufficient to establish the vessel's exact position, it clearly indicates where the vessel is not.

If two LOPs observed at the same time can be drawn on the chart then the position is established. This position is established at the intersection of the two LOPs, and is termed a FIX. LOPs can be determined using the vessel's magnetic compass.

Given a reasonably accurate compass, you can use it and measurements you make with it to determine your position. Select two or more identifiable landmarks (or preferably navigational aids). The more evenly they are distributed around the horizon, the better. If you use only two marks, the angle between the lines from your vessel to each of the two objects should be as near 90° as possible. Locate the marks on the chart.

Head the vessel directly toward one mark and note the compass heading. As soon as you have recorded the compass heading, head toward the other mark and note its compass heading.

These two readings are called bearings and they will be used to draw LOPs. Since they are measured in terms of compass readings, they are called compass bearings, and they must be corrected to give true directions. Before the compass direction can be plotted on a chart as a true direction, corrections must be made for both deviation and variation.

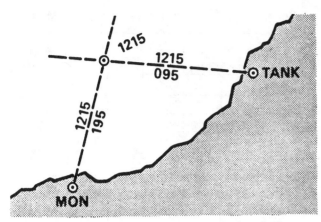

**Fig. 14-18    Positioning by Crossed Bearings on Two Landmarks**

The process of converting from compass bearings to true bearings is the reverse of the process of converting from true directions read from the chart to a compass direction to be followed. Westerly errors, either deviation or variation, must be subtracted, and easterly errors must be added when correcting, to get a true direction.

For example, suppose the first compass bearing is 095°C, and the second is 195°C ("C" for compass). Variation shown on the chart for the area is 12°E. (This would seem to imply that our example is taking place somewhere in the western part of the United States.)

For the purposes of illustration, we assume that our compass has a deviation of 3°W for a compass heading of 095°C, and a deviation of 3°E for a compass heading of 195°C. (These values for deviation would have been obtained from a deviation table constructed specifically for our compass. The table would be entered with the compass heading or the magnetic heading to obtain the respective deviation error.)

We must correct our compass bearings to true bearings in order to plot them on the chart. (Remember, the directions on the chart are true directions, relative to true north, not compass directions.) First, we correct for the deviation error. For the compass bearing of 095°C, our deviation of 3°W must be subtracted (095°C -

3°W = 092°M). Our magnetic bearing is 092°M. Now, correcting for 12°E variation, we add this easterly error to our 092°M to obtain our true bearing (092°M + 12°E = 104°). (Note that it is unnecessary to add the designator "T" to indicate true, since the chart's directions are true.) Thus, our 095°C compass bearing becomes our 104° true bearing.

Applying the same procedure to the 195°C compass bearing, we correct for the deviation on that heading of 3°E, by adding, to get 198°M, the magnetic bearing. Again, adding the 12° variation, we get a true bearing of 210°. Our two true bearings of 104° and 210° may now be plotted on the chart. These are our LOPs.

Your next task is to draw the first LOP through the first mark at a true angle of 104°, and the second LOP through the second mark at an angle of 210°. Extend the lines back (in the reciprocal direction) as needed until they pass through the area where you are likely to be. The point where these two LOPs cross is your position. A position determined in this fashion is known as a fix.

Ideally, if you conduct the same operation with three marks, the three resulting LOPs should cross at a single point. In most real situations, however, this seldom happens. The triangle that is formed by the near-intersection of three LOPs — known as a "cocked hat" — is a measure of your care in taking and recording bearings, the accuracy of your deviation table, and a multitude of other factors. The smaller the triangle, the better. With practice, and good observing conditions, you should be able routinely to get triangles so small that they can almost be disregarded and considered to be one point.

Taking visual bearings on landmarks is only one of many possible ways of obtaining LOPs. You are encouraged to continue your study of piloting and investigate the many other techniques available to you.

## Speed–Time–Distance

When you set a course, it is important to know how long it will take to reach your destination.

Unfortunately, measuring speed over the water is never very simple. Speedometers for small boats exist, but they are not especially accurate. The mechanisms used in most such instruments are not sensitive at slow speeds, but in any case, they only measure speed through the water.

Fig. 14–19    Tachometer

What is really needed is speed over the bottom. The readings you get from any speed instrument will be influenced by currents, as well as any intrinsic inaccuracy in the instrument. Part of the "art" of piloting is involved in estimating the effects of those currents and other factors and judging the true speed over the bottom.

Most inboard engines have tachometers, instruments that indicate the speed of the engine. A good indicator of a boat's speed is the reading of the tachometer, coupled with a suitable conversion table or chart relating that engine speed to speed through the water.

### Speed Trial Tabulation Over Measured Mile

| RPM | N-S | | S-N | | Average Speed | Current |
|---|---|---|---|---|---|---|
| | Time | Speed | Time | Speed | | |
| 800 | 6m 47s | 8.85 | 8m 32s | 7.03 | 7.94 | .91 |
| 1000 | 5m 46s | 10.41 | 7m 31s | 7.98 | 9.18 | 1.23 |
| 1200 | 5m 01s | 11.96 | 6m 46s | 8.87 | 10.41 | 1.55 |
| 1400 | 4m 28s | 13.43 | 6m 13s | 9.65 | 11.54 | 1.89 |
| 1600 | 4m 03s | 14.82 | 5m 47s | 10.38 | 12.6 | 2.22 |
| 1800 | 3m 42s | 16.22 | 5m 01s | 11.96 | 14.09 | 2.13 |
| 2000 | 3m 31s | 17.06 | 4m 53s | 12.29 | 14.67 | 2.39 |
| 2200 | 3m 24s | 17.64 | 4m 41s | 12.81 | 15.22 | 2.42 |

Fig. 14–20    Speed Table

It is necessary to construct a speed curve for your boat, in which you relate the engine speed (as indicated by the tachometer) to your measured speed between known points. Use a stopwatch to time the trip between buoys at various engine speeds.

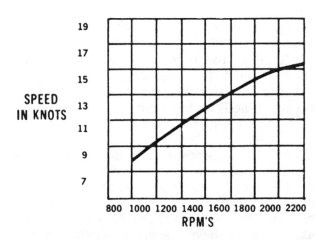

Fig. 14–21    Sample Speed Curve

Run the course in both directions to cancel out the effects of any current that may be present. Calculate the speed by the formula S(peed) = 60 x D(istance) / T(ime), in minutes. Calculate the speed for each run, then average the runs made at the same engine speed but in different directions together to get the speed table entry for that engine speed. Do not make the mistake of averaging times to compute the speed.

**Fig. 14-22 Measuring Distance.**

Distance on a Mercator chart is usually measured on the latitude scale. This is the scale that appears on the right and left edges of the chart. One nautical mile, remember, equals one minute (1') of latitude.

One important characteristic of a Mercator projection is that the size of areas is distorted. Because of this distortion, one minute of latitude will appear to get larger as you move away from the equator. On large-scale charts (1:80,000 or larger) this distortion makes very little practical difference, although it is measurable. However, with smaller-scale charts, the difference in the length of one minute of latitude from the top to the bottom of the chart is significant. For that reason, you should always choose latitude markings near the level (mid-latitude) of the line being measured as your scale of distance.

## Plotting

In almost any piloting situation, the answers to be determined concern either establishing a course line or determining position. The determination of position may be the whole problem, but most of the time position is only a point necessary to the fixing of a course line to another destination.

## Time

Time is noted on a chart using the 24-hour system, and it is always written in four digits. (Courses, remember, are always written in three digits.) The first two digits tell the hours since the previous midnight, and the last two digits tell the minutes. No punctuation marks are used.

Midnight is written 2400, 9:45 a.m. is written 0945, while 9:45 p.m. is written 2145. Mariners never use the word "hours" following a time designation.

## Plotting Symbols

There are several terms and symbols that are used in piloting. You need to be completely familiar with them.

A line of position (LOP) is a line passing through a known position along which a vessel is presumed to be located. LOP's may be obtained from bearings on a charted object (as in our example, above), from a measured distance from a charted object, from the depth of the water, two charted objects in line, or any of several other means.

An LOP is labeled with the time (in 24 hour notation) and the true bearing (in degrees). Bearings are always noted as directions from the vessel toward the object.

A true bearing at 9:30 a.m. on an object directly east of the vessel would be recorded as:

$$\frac{0930}{090}$$

If the LOP is derived from a range (two charted objects in a line), only the time is noted.

A fix is an accurate position obtained by the crossing of two or more LOP's, or by passing close aboard a charted object (such as a lighthouse or harbor entrance). It is indicated by a circle around the position dot (the <u>dot</u> marks the <u>exact</u> position on the chart) with the <u>time</u> parallel to the top or bottom margins of the chart.

A <u>DR position</u> is a position determined by applying the vessel's course and speed, and all changes in either, to the last known accurate position.

A DR position is marked with the time and a half circle around the position dot. The time is written at an angle to the charted course line.

An <u>estimated position</u> (EP) is the most probable position for a vessel, given all considerations that apply. It is often a DR position modified by additional information, such as currents and wind drift ("leeway").

An estimated position is marked with the time and a square around the position dot.

## The Dead Reckoning Plot

If a cruise is to be any appreciable length (an hour or more), it is customary practice to set up a DR plot. This is a scale drawing on the chart of the course we intend to follow, marked with hourly estimates of our position. These positions are based solely on the courses (directions) sailed and the speed, based on the speed (RPM) curve, log, or speedometer.

It is helpful if there are landmarks along the course from which good LOP's can be obtained. Again, it is accepted practice to plot fixes whenever possible and compare those known positions with the DR position for the same time. This gives valuable information about leeway that can then be applied to refine our EP as we move along the track.

Note that in nearly every case, we begin a new DR plot with every fix.

## Plotting DR Position

Outside most harbors there is a buoy or other landmark that marks the entrance to the harbor, and from which we take departure, the final fix anchoring one end of a DR plot. There will be another such marker at our destination.

If there are no obstructions between these two marks, we can simply draw a straight line between them, then sail it as best we can. More often, however, it will be necessary to travel an irregular course to avoid hazards such as intervening land, shallows, etc. If possible, select at each turning point some suitable landmark, such as another buoy, etc.

Using your plotting tools, draw in your intended course as a series of straight lines between the turning points. Measure and label the course to follow on each leg. Remember to plot only true directions. You will want to convert them to <u>magnetic</u> and <u>compass</u> courses for your own use later, and when you do so, they should be correctly labeled.

When you label your course, write the course numbers along the line, <u>above</u> the line and precede the number with the letter "C," for <u>course</u>. The fact that it is a three-digit number and <u>above</u> the line tells you immediately that it is a course, not a bearing.

Follow the numbers with "M" (for "magnetic"), or "C" (for "compass"). We don't have to label the line with a "T" for <u>true</u>, since all normal directions on a chart are <u>true</u>, and the additional label would be redundant.

Your compass course line, then, might look like this:

**C047C**

Make all measurements and calculations as carefully as possible. In piloting as in school, neatness and accuracy count.

Now use your dividers and the latitude scale to measure the lengths of the course legs. Measure carefully to the nearest 1/10 of a nautical mile.

Finally, estimate the speed that you intend to use on each leg. Write the number below the course line, preceded by a notation "S."

Calculate the amount of time that should be required to get from your departure to your first turning point at your projected speed. Use the formula $T(ime) = 60 \times D(istance) / S(peed)$, where time is measured in minutes, distance in nautical miles, and speed is measured in knots, or nautical miles per hour. (Never say "knots per hour." It is a sure sign of a person who does not know the first thing about piloting.)

(If you are operating on the Great Lakes, the rivers, or on other bodies of water where charted distances are in statute miles the speed will be noted in miles per hour. This is perfectly acceptable as long as units are not mixed.)

After you have calculated the time that should elapse between your departure and your arrival at the first turning point, add it to the departure time and note the expected time of arrival (ETA) at the turning point. This is now a DR position, so it should be marked with a dot and a half-circle and labeled with the time.

If the trip to the first turn will include the start of a new hour on the clock, calculate where you should be at that time and plot that position on your course line.

To do this, you must alter your Time-Speed-Distance calculations. You now must calculate the distance you will travel in a given time, so the formula becomes $D = S \times T/60$.

Thus, if you depart at 0930 and you do not expect to reach your first turning point until 1015, you must calculate how far down your track you should be 30 minutes after you depart. At a speed of 6 knots, traveling for 30 minutes you should cover $D = 6 \times 30/60 = 3$ nautical miles. Measure off 3 miles (3 minutes of latitude) along the track from the departure point and mark it with a dot and half-circle and the time (1000) at an angle to the course line.

In addition to the course and speed changes and the whole hours, you should compute a DR position whenever you obtain a fix or calculate an EP. In the end, you should have a plot on your chart that resembles Fig.14-23.

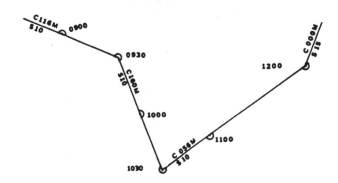

**Fig. 14-23    Typical Plot**

If the channel is narrow, or the conditions particularly hazardous, you should plan on more frequent DR positions and fixes. Large ships moving into and out of harbors take a constant series of fixes to be sure of their position. You in a small boat cannot do that, but you also have more maneuverability, so you should adjust your practice accordingly.

**Summary**

As we noted above, the navigation of the average small boat can appear to be a "seat-of-the-pants" procedure. Having mastered the basic techniques described in this chapter, however, you will be in a much better position to get where you want to go or figure out where you are, provided you practice what you have learned and hone your skills.

Even Sir Francis Chichester, arguably the greatest small boat navigator of modern times, felt the need to practice his piloting techniques if he did not actually use them for a few days at a stretch.

Another important concept is that of a "buddy system." Whenever you move into unfamiliar waters, it is always advisable to travel with a companion vessel piloted by someone who is familiar with the area. Not only will you feel more comfortable until you, too, learn the area, but you will probably have more fun in the process, and that, in the final analysis, is what it is all about.

# Glossary of Nautical Terms

## A

**ABAFT** - Toward the rear (stern) of the boat. Behind.

**ABEAM** - At right angles to the keel of the boat, but not on the boat.

**ABOARD** - On or within the boat.

**ABOVE DECK** - On the deck (not over it — see ALOFT).

**ABREAST** - Side by side; by the side of.

**ADRIFT** - Loose, not on moorings or towline.

**AFT** - Toward the stern of the boat.

**AGROUND** - Touching or fast to the bottom.

**AHEAD** - In a forward direction.

**AIDS TO NAVIGATION** - Artificial objects to supplement natural landmarks in indicating safe and unsafe waters.

**ALEE** - Away from the direction of the wind. Opposite of windward.

**ALOFT** - Above the deck of the boat.

**AMIDSHIPS** - In or toward the center of the boat.

**ANCHORAGE** - A place suitable for anchoring in relation to the wind, seas and bottom.

**ANEMOMETER** - A device which measures the velocity of the wind.

**APPARENT WIND** - The wind perceived in a moving boat which is the combination of the true wind and the wind of motion.

**ASTERN** - In back of the boat, opposite of ahead.

**ATHWARTSHIPS** - At right angles to the centerline of the boat; rowboat seats are generally athwartships.

**AWEIGH** - The position of anchor as it is raised clear of the bottom.

## B

**BACKSTAY** - Standing rigging that supports the mast from aft to keep it in an upright position. Running backstays (always in pairs) perform the same function, but may be quickly slackened to avoid interfering with the boom.

**BACKWIND** - When wind is deflected from one sail to the lee side of another sail, as when the jib is backwinding the main.

**BALLAST** - Heavy material placed in the bottom of a boat to provide stability.

**BARE POLES** - When a sailboat is underway with no sails set.

**BAROMETER** - An instrument for measuring the atmospheric pressure.

**BATTEN** - A thin semi-rigid strip inserted in the leach of the sail to provide support for the sail material.

**BATTEN DOWN** - Secure hatches and loose objects both within the hull and on deck.

**BEAM** - The greatest width of the boat.

**BEAR** - To "bear down" is to approach from windward, to "bear off" is to sail away to leeward.

**BEARING** - The direction of an object expressed either as a true bearing as shown on the chart, or as a bearing relative to the heading of the boat.

**BEAT** - To sail to windward, generally in a series of tacks. Beating is one of the three points of sailing, also referred to as sailing 'close hauled' or 'by the wind.'

**BECALMED** - Having no wind to provide movement of the boat through the water.

BECKET - A looped rope, hook and eye, strap, or grommet used for holding ropes, spars, or oars in position.

BEFORE THE WIND - Traveling in the same direction the wind is blowing toward; sailing before the wind is a point of sailing, also called running.

BELAY - To make a line fast. A command to stop.

BELOW - Beneath the deck.

BEND - To attach a sail to a spar. Also used as a term to describe a knot which fastens one line to another.

BIGHT - The part of the rope or line, between the end and the standing part, on which a knot is formed. A shallow bay.

BILGE - The interior of the hull below the floor boards.

BINNACLE - A stand holding the steering compass.

BITT - A heavy and firmly mounted piece of wood or metal used for securing lines.

BITTER END - The last part of a rope or chain. The inboard end of the anchor rode.

BLANKET - To deprive a sail of the wind by interposing another object.

BLOCK - A wooden or metal case enclosing one or more pulleys and having a hook, eye, or strap by which it may be attached.

BOAT - A fairly indefinite term. A waterborne vehicle smaller than a ship. One definition is a small craft carried aboard a ship.

BOAT HOOK - A short shaft with a fitting at one end shaped to facilitate use in putting a line over a piling, recovering an object dropped overboard, or in pushing or fending off.

BOLLARD - A heavy post set into the edge of a wharf or pier to which the lines of a ship may be made fast.

BOLT ROPE - Line attached to the foot and luff of a sail to give it strength or to substitute for sail slides.

BOOM - A spar attached to the mast for extending the foot of the sail.

BOOM CROTCH or CRUTCH - A notched board or X-shaped frame that supports the main boom and keeps it from swinging when the sail is not raised.

BOOMKIN - A short spar or structure projecting from the stern to which a sheet block is attached for an overhanging boom, and to which, on boats without running backstays, is attached the fixed backstay.

BOOM VANG - A tackle running from the boom to the deck which will flatten the curve of the sail by pulling downward on the boom.

BOOT TOP - A painted line that indicates the designed waterline.

BOW - The forward part of a boat.

BOW LINE - A docking line leading from the bow.

BOWLINE - A knot used to form a temporary loop in the end of a line.

BOWSPRIT - A spar extending forward from the bow.

BRIDGE - The location from which a vessel is steered and its speed controlled. "Control Station" is really a more appropriate term for small craft.

BRIDLE - A line or wire secured at both ends in order to distribute a strain between two points.

BRIGHTWORK - Varnished woodwork and/or polished metal.

BROACH - The turning of a boat parallel to the waves, subjecting it to possible capsizing.

BROAD ON THE BEAM - At right angles to the beam. Abeam (not aboard the vessel).

BROAD ON THE BOW - A direction midway between abeam and dead ahead.

BROAD ON THE QUARTER - A direction midway between abeam and dead astern.

BROAD REACH - Sailing with the apparent wind coming over either quarter.

BULKHEAD - A vertical partition separating compartments.

BULWARK - The side of a vessel when carried above the level of the deck.

BUOY - An anchored float used for marking a position on the water or a hazard or a shoal and for mooring.

BURDENED VESSEL - That vessel which, according to the applicable Navigation Rules, must give way to the privileged vessel. The term has been superceded by the term "give-way."

BURGEE - A small yachting flag which is either swallow tailed or pointed.

BY THE LEE - Sailing with the wind on the same side as the boom; not a recommended point of sailing as it could cause an accidental jibe.

BY THE WIND - Sailing close hauled, beating.

## C

CABIN - A compartment for passengers or crew.

CAPSIZE - To turn over.

CARVEL - Smooth planked hull construction (see LAPSTRAKE).

CAST OFF - To let go.

CATAMARAN - A twin-hulled boat, with hulls side by side.

CATBOAT - A sailboat with a single sail attached to a mast stepped well forward.

CAULK - To stop up and make watertight by filling with a waterproof compound or material.

CENTERBOARD - A plate, in a vertical fore-and-aft plane, that is pivoted at the lower forward end, and can be lowered or raised through a slot in the bottom of the boat to reduce leeway.

CENTER OF EFFORT - The center of wind pressure on a sail.

CENTER OF LATERAL RESISTANCE - The center of underwater resistance which is approximately the center of underwater profile.

CHAFING GEAR - Tubing or cloth wrapping used to protect a line from chafing on a rough surface.

CHAIN PLATE - Metal strap fastened to the side of a boat, to which a stay or shroud is attached.

CHART - A map for use by navigators.

CHART NO. 1 - A booklet prepared by the National Ocean Survey which contains symbols and abbreviations that have been approved for use on nautical charts published by the U.S.Government. Past editions of this chart were in actual chart form.

CHINE - The intersection of the bottom and sides of a flat or v-bottomed boat.

CHOCK - A fitting through which anchor or mooring lines are led. Usually U-shaped to reduce chafe.

CLEAT - A fitting to which lines are made fast. The classic cleat to which lines are belayed is approximately anvil-shaped.

CLEW - The after, lower corner of a sail to which is attached the sheets.

CLOSE ABOARD - Not on but near to a vessel.

CLOSE HAULED - Sailing as close to the wind as is possible, beating, or by the wind, one of the three points of sailing.

CLOSE REACH - Sailing with the sheets slightly eased and the apparent wind forward of the beam.

CLOVE HITCH - A knot for temporarily fastening a line to a spar or piling.

COAMING - A vertical piece around the edge of a cockpit, hatch, etc. to prevent water on deck from running below.

COCKPIT - An opening in the deck from which the boat is handled.

COIL - To lay a line down in circular turns.

COIL DOWN - To flemish down.

COLLAR - The reinforced opening in the deck or cabin roof through which the mast passes. This opening is constructed to take the strain of the mast.

COMING ABOUT - The changing of course when close hauled by swinging the bow through the eye of the wind and changing from one tack to another.

COURSE - The direction in which a boat is steered.

CRADLE - A framework, generally of wood, to support a boat when it is out of the water.

CRINGLE - A ring sewn into a sail through which a line may be passed.

CUDDY - A small shelter cabin in a boat.

CUNNINGHAM - A grommeted hole in the mainsail luff slightly above the foot through which a line or hook is pulled downward to exert stress on the luff, thereby flattening the sail.

CURRENT - The horizontal movement of water.

CUTTER - A single masted sailboat with the mast stepped further aft than that of a sloop.

## D

DAGGERBOARD - A plate, in a vertical fore-and-aft plane which can be lowered and raised vertically through a slot in the bottom of a boat to reduce leeway.

DAVITS - Mechanical arms extending over the side or stern of a vessel, or over a sea wall, to lift a smaller boat.

DEAD AHEAD - Directly ahead.

DEAD ASTERN - Directly aft.

DEAD RECKONING - A plot of courses steered and distances traveled through the water.

DECK - A permanent covering over a compartment, hull or any part thereof.

DINGHY - A small open boat. A dinghy is often used as a tender for a larger craft.

DISPLACEMENT - The weight of water displaced by a floating vessel, thus, a boat's weight.

DISPLACEMENT HULL - A type of hull that plows through the water, displacing a weight of water equal to its own weight, even when more power is added.

DOCK - A protected water area in which vessels are moored. The term is often used to denote a pier or a wharf.

DOLPHIN - A group of piles driven close together and bound with wire cables into a single structure.

DOUSE - To lower sails quickly.

DOWNHAUL - A line attached to the boom at the tack area of the sail in order to pull the luff of the sail downward.

DRAFT - The depth of water a boat draws.

DROGUE - Any device streamed astern to check a vessel's speed, or to keep its stern up to the waves in a following sea.

## E

EASE OFF - To slacken or relieve tension on a line.

EBB TIDE - A receding tide.

ENSIGN - A national or organizational flag flown aboard a vessel.

EVEN KEEL - When a boat is floating on its designed waterline it is said to be floating on an even keel.

EYE BOLT - A bolt having a looped head designed to receive a hook or towing line. This bolt is usually bolted through the deck or stem.

EYE OF THE WIND - The direction from which the wind is blowing.

EYE SPLICE - A permanent loop spliced in the end of a line.

## F

FAIRLEAD - A fitting used to change the direction of a line.

FALL OFF - To turn the bow of the boat away from the eye of the wind.

FAST - Said of an object that is secured to another.

FATHOM - Six feet.

FENDER - A cushion, placed between boats, or between a boat and a pier, to prevent damage.

FIGURE EIGHT KNOT - A knot in the form of a figure eight, placed in the end of a line to prevent the line from passing through a grommet or a block.

FIN KEEL - A thin narrow keel bolted to the bottom of the hull.

FISHERMAN'S BEND - A knot for making fast to a buoy or spar or to the ring of an anchor.

FLARE - The outward curve of a vessel's sides near the bow. A distress signal.

FLEMISH DOWN - A decorative but useless method of coiling a line flat on the deck or dock.

FLOOD TIDE - A rising tide.

FLOORBOARDS - The surface of the cockpit on which the crew stand.

FLUKE - The palm of an anchor.

FLY - A pennant at the masthead.

FLYING BRIDGE - An added set of controls above the level of the normal control station for better visibility. Usually open but may have a collapsible top for shade.

FOLLOWING SEA - An overtaking sea that comes from astern.

FOOT - The lower edge of a sail.

FORE-AND-AFT - In a line parallel to the keel.

FOREPEAK - A compartment in the bow of a small boat.

FORESAIL - The sail set abaft the foremast of a schooner.

FORWARD - Toward the bow of the boat.

FOULED - Any piece of equipment that is jammed or entangled, or dirtied.

FOUNDER - When a vessel fills with water and sinks.

FREEBOARD - The minimum vertical distance from the surface of the water to the gunwale.

FULL AND BY - Close hauled.

FURL - To roll up a sail on top of a boom or spar and secure it with small lines.

## G

GAFF - A spar to support the head of a gaff sail.

GALLEY - The kitchen area of a boat.

GANGWAY - The area of a ship's side where people board and disembark.

GANGPLANK - The temporary ramp or platform between the vessel and the wharf or pier.

GASKET - A sail stop.

GEAR - A general term for ropes, blocks, tackle and other equipment.

GIVE-WAY VESSEL - A term used to describe the vessel which must yield in meeting, crossing, or overtaking situations.

GOOSENECK - A universal joint connecting the mast and the boom, allowing movement of the boom in any direction.

GRAB RAILS - Hand-hold fittings mounted on cabin tops and sides for personal safety when moving around the boat.

GROUND TACKLE - A collective term for the anchor and its associated gear.

GUDGEON - The eye supports for the rudder mounted on the transom which receive the pintles of the rudder.

GUNWALE - The upper edge of a boat's sides.

## H

HALYARD - A line or wire used to hoist the sails or flags.

HANKS - Snap hooks which attach the luff of a headsail to the forestay.

HARD ALEE - The operation of putting the helm (tiller) to the lee side of the boat when coming about.

HARD CHINE - An abrupt intersection between the hull side and the hull bottom of a boat so constructed.

HATCH - An opening in a boat's deck fitted with a watertight cover.

HAWSER - A heavy rope or cable used for mooring or towing.

HEAD - A marine toilet. Also the upper corner of a triangular sail.

HEADER - A change in wind direction which will head or impede progress in an intended direction.

HEADING - The direction in which a vessel's bow points at any given time.

HEADSAILS - Sails forward of the foremost mast.

HEAD UP - Swing the bow closer to the eye of the wind.

HEADWAY - The forward motion of a boat. Opposite of sternway.

HEAVE TO - To bring a vessel up in a position where it will maintain little or no headway, usually with the bow into the wind or nearly so.

HEEL - To tip to one side.

HELM - The wheel or tiller controlling the rudder. (Also see LEE HELM, WEATHER HELM.)

HELMSPERSON - The person who steers the boat.

HIKING OUT - The position one assumes when positioned on the weather rail in an effort to balance the heeling forces of the wind upon the sails and or rigging.

HIKING STICK - A short stick attached to the tiller which allows the helmsperson to hike out while steering the boat.

HITCH - A knot used to secure a rope to another object or to another rope, or to form a loop or a noose in a rope.

HOLD - A compartment below deck in a large vessel, used solely for carrying cargo.

HORSE - The wire or rope bridle to which is attached the block through which the sheet(s) run through.

HULL - The main body of a vessel.

HULL SPEED - The maximum displacement speed.

## I

IN IRONS - Stalled. Said of a sailboat headed into the eye of the wind, with no wind pressure on either side of the sails.

INITIAL STABILITY - A boat's tendency to resist initial heel from the upright position.

## J

JIB - A triangular sail set forward of the mainmast (sloop, cutter, ketch, yawl) or the foremast (schooner).

JIBE - The maneuver of changing the sail (and boom) from one side of the boat to the other. Usually used as a method of changing course while keeping the wind astern.

JIB SHEET - The line, usually paired, controlling the lateral movement of the jib.

JIB STAY - A stay running from the bow to the upper part of the mast on which the jib is attached.

JUMPER - A stay on the upper forward part of the mast.

JUMPER STAYS - The wire which runs over the ends of the jumper strut to provide support for the mast against the pull of the backstay.

JUMPER STRUTS - Short horizontal spars placed above the union of the forestay and the mast designed to balance the pull of the backstay upon the mast.

## K

KEDGE - A light anchor used for moving a boat. Also the traditional yachtsman's anchor.

KEEL - The centerline of a boat running fore and aft; the backbone of a vessel.

KEEL BOAT - A boat with a fixed keel as opposed to a boat with a centerboard or daggerboard.

KETCH - A two-masted sailboat with the smaller after mast stepped ahead of the rudder post.

KNOCKDOWN - When a boat is laid over on its beam ends by wind or sea, allowing water to come in over the gunwales.

KNOT - A measure of speed equal to one nautical mile (6076 feet) per hour.

KNOT - A fastening made by interweaving rope to form a stopper, to enclose or bind an object, to form a loop or a noose, to tie a small rope to an object, or to tie the ends of two small ropes together.

## L

LAPSTRAKE - Hull construction of overlapping planks; also known as clinker-built construction (see CARVEL).

LATEEN RIG - A fore-and-aft sailing rig originating in the near east and still found there, consisting of a triangular (lateen) sail, one side of which is very short, slung from a lateen yard, a long, movable spar which crossed the relatively short mast at an angle.

LATERAL RESISTANCE - That resistance to the leeway or sideways movement of a boat caused by wind or wave forces determined by the amount of heel, keel or centerboard below the water line.

LATITUDE - The distance north or south of the equator measured and expressed in degrees.

LAY - To 'lay a mark' is to be able to reach it without tacking, close-hauled. The lay of a line is the direction in which it's strands are twisted.

LAZARETTE - A storage space in a boat's stern area.

LEE - The side sheltered from the wind.

LEEBOARD - Pivoted board attached to the side of a sailboat to reduce leeway; usually one on either side, that to leeward being lowered when in use.

LEECH - The after edge of a fore-and-aft sail.

LEE HELM - The condition, in a sailing vessel, when the helm must be kept to leeward to hold a boat on her course.

LEEWARD - The direction away from the wind. Opposite of windward.

LEEWAY - The sideways movement of the boat caused by either wind or current.

LIFT - An increase in the wind's force, causing an increase of heel of a boat close-hauled, shifting the center of effort forward, allowing the boat to sail, often advantageously, closer to the wind and faster; sometimes said of a similarly advantageous shift in wind direction; being lifted is the opposite of being headed (see HEADER; also see TOPPING LIFT).

LINE - Rope and cordage used aboard a vessel.

LOG - A record of courses or operation. Also, a device to measure speed.

LONGITUDE - The distance in degrees east or west of the meridian at Greenwich, England.

LONG SPLICE - A method of joining two ropes by splicing without increasing the diameter of the rope.

LOOSE-FOOTED - A sail secured to the boom at the tack and the clew only as opposed to a sail secured with slides.

LOWER SHROUDS - The shrouds which run from the chain plates at the sides of the boat to the mast just beneath the intersection of the spreaders.

LUBBER'S LINE - A mark or permanent line on a compass indicating the direction forward parallel to the keel when properly installed.

LUFF - The forward edge of a sail; also the action of heading up into the wind causing the sail to flutter.

### M

MAINMAST - The principal mast of a sailboat.

MAINSAIL - The principal sail that sets on the mainmast.

MAINSHEET - The sheet controlling the athwartships movement of a mainsail.

MARLINSPIKE - A tool for opening the strands of a rope while splicing.

MAST - A spar set upright to support rigging and sails.

MAST STEP - The shaped brace on which, or into which, the butt of the mast rests.

MIDSHIP - Approximately in the location equally distant from the bow and stern.

MIZZEN - The after and smaller mast of a ketch or yawl; also a sail set on that mast.

MIZZENMAST - (see MIZZEN).

MOORING - An arrangement for securing a boat to a mooring buoy or a pier.

MOORING PENNANT - A line used to secure a boat to a mooring buoy, which is permanently attached to the buoy's ring.

### N

NAUTICAL MILE - One minute of latitude; approximately 6076 feet — about 1/8 longer than the statute mile of 5280 feet.

NAVIGATION - The art and science of conducting a boat safely from one point to another.

NAVIGATION RULES - The regulations governing the movement of vessels in relation to each other, generally called steering and sailing rules.

### O

OFF THE WIND - Sailing downwind (away from the eye of the wind).

OUTBOARD - Toward or beyond the boat's sides. A detachable engine mounted on a boat's stern.

OUTHAUL - A line, or block and tackle, for stretching the foot of a sail out along the boom.

OVERBOARD - Over the side or out of the boat.

### P

PAINTER - A line attached to the bow of a boat for use in towing or making fast.

PALM - A leather fitting placed over the hand to assist in sewing heavy material with a needle and thread.

PAY OUT - To ease out a line, or let it run in a controlled manner.

PEAK - The upper outer corner of a gaff sail.

PENNANT (sometimes PENDANT) - The line by which a boat is made fast to a mooring buoy.

PIER - A loading platform extending at an angle from the shore.

PILE - A wood, metal or concrete pole driven into the bottom. Craft may be made fast to a pile; it may be used to support a pier (see PILING) or a float.

PILING - Support, protection for wharves, piers etc.; constructed of piles (see PILE).

PILOTING - Navigation by use of visible references, the depth of the water, etc.

PINCH - To sail a boat too close to the wind causing the sails to stall.

PINTLE - The pin-like fittings of the rudder which are inserted into the gudgeons mounted on the transom.

PITCHPOLING - A small boat being thrown end-over-end in very rough seas.

PLANING - A boat is said to be planing when it is essentially moving over the top of the water rather than through the water.

PLANING HULL - A type of hull shaped to glide easily across the water at high speed.

POINT - One of 32 points of the compass equal to 11 1/4 degrees.

PORT - The left side of a boat looking forward. A harbor.

PORT TACK - Sailing with the wind coming over the port side of the boat causing the main boom to be on the starboard side of the boat.

PRIVILEGED VESSEL - A vessel which, according to the applicable Navigation Rule, has right-of-way (this term has been superceded by the term "stand-on").

PUFF - A term used to describe a gust of wind.

**Q**

QUARTER - The sides of a boat aft of amidships.

QUARTERING SEA - Sea coming on a boat's quarter.

**R**

RAKE - The angle of a mast from the perpendicular, usually aft.

REACH - The point of sailing between close hauled and running, one of the points of sailing. Subdivided into close, beam and broad reach.

READY ABOUT - The preparatory command given before "hard alee" when tacking (passing the bow through the eye of the wind).

REEF - To reduce the sail area.

REEF POINTS - Short lines set into the lower portion of the sail to secure it's foot when reefed.

REEVE - To pass a line through a block or other opening.

RIG - The arrangement of a boat's sails, masts and rigging.

RIGGING - The general term for all the lines of a vessel.

ROACH - The outward curve at the leech of a sail.

RODE - The anchor line and/or chain.

ROLLER FURLING - Type of jib rigged to furl by rolling up around its own luff.

ROLLER REEFING - Reefing by rolling a mainsail around a boom.

ROPE - In general, cordage as it is purchased at the store. When it comes aboard a vessel and is put to use it becomes line.

RUDDER - a vertical plate or board for steering a boat.

RUN - To allow a line to feed freely.

RUNNING - Sailing before the wind; sailing with the wind astern.

RUNNING LIGHTS - Lights required to be shown on boats underway between sundown and sunup.

RUNNING RIGGING - Sheets, halyards, topping lifts, downhauls, vangs, etc., used for raising and adjusting sails (see STANDING RIGGING).

**S**

SAILING FREE - Sailing with the wind aft (running).

SAILS - Flexible vertical airfoils, generally made of cloth, that use wind pressure to propel a boat.

SAIL STOPS - Short length of line used to wrap around the sail when it is bundled up or furled.

SAMSON POST - A single bitt in the bow or stern of a boat, fastened to structural members.

SCOPE - The ratio of the length of an anchor line, from a vessel's bow to the anchor, to the depth of the water.

SCREW - A boat's propeller.

SCULLING - Moving the tiller or an oar back and forth to propel a boat ahead.

SEA ANCHOR - Any device used to reduce a boat's drift before the wind. Compare with DROGUE.

SEA ROOM - A safe distance from the shore or other hazards.

SEAWORTHY - A boat or a boat's gear able to meet the usual sea conditions.

SECURE - To make fast.

SEIZE - To bind two lines together with light line.

SET - Direction toward which the current is flowing.

SET FLYING - Said of a sail made fast only at it's corners, such as a spinnaker.

SHACKLE - A "U" shaped connector with a pin or bolt across the open end.

SHEAVE - The grooved wheel or roller in a block (pulley).

SHEER - The fore-and-aft curvature of the deck as shown in side elevation.

SHEET - The line used to control the forward or athwartships movement of a sail.

SHEET BEND - A knot used to join two ropes. Functionally different from a square knot in that it can be used between lines of different diameters.

SHIP - A larger vessel usually thought of as being used for ocean travel. A vessel able to carry a "boat" on board.

SHORT SPLICE - A method of permanently joining the ends of two ropes.

SHROUD - The standing rigging that supports the mast at the sides of the boat.

SLACK - Not fastened; loose. Also, to loosen.

SLIDES - The hardware which attaches either the foot or the luff of the sail to a track on the respective spar.

SLOOP - A single masted vessel with working sails (main and jib) set fore and aft.

SLUG - A fitting which is inserted into a groove on either the mast or the boom providing attachment for either the luff or the foot of the sail respectively.

SNATCH BLOCK - A block that opens at the side to allow a line to be inserted or removed without reeving the entire length of line.

SOLE - Cabin or saloon floor. Timber extensions on the bottom of the rudder. Also the molded fiberglass deck of a cockpit.

SOUNDING - A measurement of the depth of water.

SPAR - A general term for masts, yards, booms, etc.

SPINNAKER - A large, light-weather headsail used for running or reaching.

SPLICE - To permanently join two ropes by tucking their strands alternately over and under each other.

SPREADER - A horizontal strut used to increase the angle at which the shrouds approach the mast.

SPRING LINE - A pivot line used in docking, undocking, or to prevent the boat from moving forward or astern while made fast to a dock.

SQUALL - A sudden, violent wind often accompanied by rain.

SQUARE KNOT - a knot used to join two lines of similar size. Also called a reef knot.

STANDING PART - That part of a line which is made fast. The main part of a line as distinguished from the bight and the end.

STANDING RIGGING - The permanent shrouds and stays that support the mast.

STAND-ON VESSEL - That vessel which has right-of-way during a meeting, crossing, or overtaking situation.

STARBOARD - The right side of a boat when looking forward.

STARBOARD TACK - Sailing with the wind coming over the starboard side of the boat and with the boom out over the port side of the boat.

STAY - That part of the standing rigging supporting the mast from forward and aft.

STAYSAIL - A sail (usually triangular) set on one of the stays.

STEM - The foremost upright timber of a vessel to which the keel and ends of the planks are attached.

STEM - The forwardmost part of the bow.

STEP - A socket in the bottom of the boat which receives the heel of the mast.

STERN - The after part of the boat.

STERN LINE - A docking line leading from the stern.

STOCK - The cross bar of an anchor.

STORM SAILS - Small sails for heavy weather sailing.

STOW - To put an item in its proper place.

SWAMP - To fill with water, but not settle to the bottom.

SWING KEEL - a weighted extension of the keel which can be partially retracted into the hull or locked in the fully-lowered position.

## T

TABERNACLE - A hinged fitting at the base of the mast to enable the mast to be easily raised or lowered.

TABLING - An extra thickness of cloth sewn around the sail's edges and at the corners.

TACK - To come about; the lower forward corner of a sail; sailing with the wind on a given side of the boat, as starboard or port tack.

TACKING - Moving the boat's bow through the wind's eye from close hauled on one tack to close hauled on the other tack. Same as coming about.

TACKLE - A combination of blocks and line to increase mechanical advantage.

TANG - A fitting on a spar to which standing rigging is secured.

THWART - A seat or brace running laterally across a boat.

THWARTSHIPS - At right angles to the centerline of the boat.

TIDE - The periodic rise and fall of water level in the oceans.

TILLER - A bar or handle for turning a boat's rudder or an outboard motor.

TOGGLE - Small fittings which allow the turnbuckle to lie in the same straight line as the stay or shroud to which it is fitted. Also, a pin thru eye or bight of rope used as a quick release.

TOPPING LIFT - A line used to support the weight of or to adjust the horizontal set of a spar such as a boom or a spinnaker pole.

TOPSIDES - The sides of a vessel between the waterline and the deck; sometimes referring to onto or above the deck.

TRANSOM - The stern cross-section of a square sterned boat.

TRAVELER - A device that allows sheets to slide athwartships.

TRIM - Fore and aft balance of a boat.

TRUE WIND - The actual direction from which the wind is blowing.

TRUNK - The structure which houses the centerboard.

TURNBUCKLE - A threaded fitting to pull two eyes together for adjustment of standing rigging.

## U

UNDERWAY - Vessel in motion, i.e., when not moored, at anchor, or aground.

UNREEVE - To run a line completely through and out of a block.

UPPER SHROUDS - The shrouds which run from the chain plates at the sides of the boat over the spreaders to the masthead.

## V

VANG - See BOOM VANG.

V BOTTOM - A hull with the bottom section in the shape of a "V".

## W

WAKE - Moving waves, track or path that a boat leaves behind it, when moving across the waters.

WATERLINE - A line painted on a hull which shows the point to which a boat sinks when it is properly trimmed (see BOOT TOP).

WAY - Movement of a vessel through the water such as headway, sternway or leeway.

WEATHER - Windward side of a boat.

WEATHER HELM - The tendency of a boat to turn into the wind when its rudder is set amidships.

WHARF - A man-made structure bounding the edge of a dock and built along or at an angle to the shoreline, used for loading, unloading, or tying up vessels.

WHIPPING - The act of wrapping the end of a piece of rope with small line, tape or plastic to prevent it from fraying.

WHISKER POLE - A spar used to extend the jib when running.

WINCH - A device to increase hauling power when raising or trimming sails.

WIND OF MOTION - That wind which is perceived on a boat as the result of the movement of the boat itself.

WINDWARD - Toward the direction from which the wind is coming.

WING AND WING - Running with the mainsail set on one side of the boat and the jib set on the other side.

WORKING SAILS - Sails for use under normal conditions; on a sloop, the mainsail and jib.

## Y

YAW - To swing off course, as when due to the impact of a following or quartering sea.

YAWL - A two-masted sailboat with the small mizzen mast stepped abaft the rudder post.

# Hypothermia

Hypothermia is being cold. But it is being cold in a way that is far more serious than the discomfort you feel on a raw winter day. Hypothermia is life-threatening cold.

But hypothermia is not "freezing to death." It is not even frostbite. Hypothermia can kill at temperatures well above freezing, and can be a serious problem for some people even in comfortably mild temperatures.

Hypothermia is the reduction of the body's core temperature below the point where normal biological functions can occur. It represents a failure of the body's ability to generate sufficient heat to offset losses, either because heat loss is so rapid, or the resources for generating heat are not available, or the heat-generating mechanisms are impaired.

Hypothermia is a major killer of victims of aquatic mishaps, as well as people injured, ill, or unable to take shelter. It is commonly referred to in newspaper accounts as "exposure."

Hypothermia requires prompt and sophisticated medical treatment; it is not a "first aid" case. It is important to recognize the conditions that could lead to hypothermia early, take steps to avoid them, and seek prompt medical attention for people who are suffering from it. The successful management of hypothermia cases is not trivial, even for trained and well-equipped emergency medical centers.

## Recognizing Hypothermia

It is unfortunate that one of the first things affected by hypothermia is the ability to recognize and understand the implications of what is happening. A person working alone must be aware of the conditions that can lead to hypothermia and take steps to avoid or minimize them, since he probably will not recognize the degradation of his abilities as hypothermia progresses, or overestimate his own ability to "tough it out." People in groups must assume the responsibility for monitoring each other and for taking steps to counter it, even in the face of protests that everything is "all right."

The human body has a remarkably efficient mechanism for maintaining its own internal environment. The chemical and biological processes that support life can operate only within a narrow range of temperatures, and the body uses food energy to help maintain its own temperature within that range. If the body heats up, excess heat is dumped to the surroundings. If the body cools down, automatic mechanisms work to conserve heat and to generate more.

Hypothermia is a failure of the regulatory mechanism that conserves and generates body heat.

As the body's temperature falls, the temperature drop is detected by a mechanism in the brain and several things begin to happen. The blood flow within the body is altered in subtle ways so that more of the body's heat is shunted away from the skin surface and toward the vital organs (brain, heart, lungs). Stored food energy is called upon and the metabolic "furnace" starts generating more heat. These adaptations to cold are generally not visible.

What is visible is the "gooseflesh" that is one indication of the routing of blood away from the skin, and the shivering that is part of the heat-producing activity.

If these actions are not able to keep up with heat losses, they become more intense. The reduction of blood flow to the extremities (hands, arms, legs) can be so severe that functioning of the small muscle groups required for fine movement is interfered with. This can happen within a very few minutes of immersion, and may not be a direct function of the chilling of the muscles of the hands and fingers themselves. Victims thrown suddenly into 65-70 degree water have reported that they were unable to cope with the straps and buckles on a standard PFD, even though they were highly trained and motivated and had a great deal of experience with these devices.

The shivering becomes more intense as body core temperature continues to fall, involving larger and larger groups of muscles. The shivering can be so strong as to even interfere with walking.

The victim at this point may show signs of confusion and a lack of responsiveness. Speech becomes slurred, and incoherent. If he is alone, or if there is no occasion to speak to companions, this change may go undetected.

As the body's temperature continues to fall and as resources are used up, the shivering diminishes, then stops. The victim becomes increasingly lethargic and uncoordinated, eventually passing into unconsciousness and death.

**Prevention of Hypothermia**

Prevention of hypothermia is relatively easy. Most of the things you can do to combat hypothermia are "common sense" things you would normally do anyway.

Avoid situations that promote loss of body heat. Essentially, this means keeping dry and out of the wind.

Of course, if you fall overboard, or if your boat capsizes, it is difficult to avoid getting wet. On the other hand, anything you can do to get out of the water, even though you are thoroughly soaked, helps reduce the rate at which you lose heat.

There are cases on record, for example, of capsizings in which the length of survival depended on the extent to which the victims were able to get out of the water. Those who were able to get out of the water reduced the rate of loss of body heat and survived longer, while those who stayed in the water died.

After avoiding getting wet, it is important to avoid the wind. Even a wet body in wet clothing can generate enough heat to maintain it's core temperature for a time if the heat it does make is kept close. Wet clothing can, under certain circumstances, even be dried by body heat. However, if the heat trapped in the clothing is carried away by wind, it must be replaced constantly. In addition, evaporation of water from the body and wet clothes carries more heat away with it, heat that comes from the body.

Wet clothing without wind is less effective than dry clothing, but it is far better than it would be if wind were present.

The type of clothing material also makes a significant difference in rate of heat loss when it is wet. Many synthetic fibers of the sort typically found in modern outdoor clothing are effective in reducing heat loss when dry, but afford virtually no protection to heat loss when wet. Wool, on the other hand, retains a higher percentage of its insulating properties than most other fibers. Wet wool clothing is a poorer insulator than dry wool clothing, or than dry synthetic clothing. But wet wool is far more effective than wet synthetic fabric.

If you have done all you can to reduce the rate of heat loss, the next concern is to increase the resources available to produce heat. This means food.

Since you seldom can eat after an accident dunks you in the water, and you cannot predict when an accident will occur, you should make it a practice never to go into a potential hypothermia situation without having eaten a good meal. This includes not only boating activities, but anything that involves working or playing out of doors.

A typical scenario has a sportsman skipping lunch to take advantage of good fishing conditions, or to get in some extra duck hunting before bad weather gets worse. Then when an incident does occur, he has no ready food reserves to be converted into heat, and a situation that is already bad gets worse more rapidly than it would have had the victim eaten properly.

Other physical conditions can also contribute to diminished capacity to maintain body heat. The elderly, the very young, and those who have recently been ill are particularly susceptible, as are those whose metabolism has been suppressed by drugs or alcohol.

**Aftereffects of Hypothermia**

Mild hypothermia, treated by the victim, will probably have no long-term effects. In fact, it is likely that you have experienced mild hypothermia at some time in your life and were not even aware of it.

More serious cases, those in whom the signs of hypothermia are obvious, should receive medical attention. Improperly managed treatment, especially that involving body rewarming, can cause worse damage than already exists. It can even cause death.

**Summary**

In conclusion, then, hypothermia is a condition which can turn a bad situation, or even only a mildly annoying one, into a life-threatening emergency. It is important to be aware of and sensitive to the conditions that favor the development of hypothermia, and to take prompt action to minimize risk to yourself and to others with you.

If hypothermia is suspected, seek prompt and competent medical attention.

# Substance Abuse

A remarkable number of boating-related terms seem to be connected with alcohol use. Everybody knows what it means when the "sun is over the yardarm," and many even know that to "splice the mainbrace" means to take a drink.

Recreational boating is an activity that people engage in for fun: For many boaters, their entire social life revolves around boats, boating activity, and their boating friends. And some of these social activities include consumption of alcohol and other substances for the purpose of altering feelings, moods or perceptions. Some boaters have actually been heard to boast that, gallon for gallon, they consumed more beer, wine and liquor on their boat than they did fuel!

The moral and legal issues of drug and alcohol use and abuse aside, it is a simple fact that drugs and alcohol have no place on a boat underway, or in the operator or crew of a boat underway.

Operating a boat is usually a simple, relaxed affair. After all, we do it for fun and relaxation. But a single wrong choice, a single moment of inattention can turn a pleasant afternoon outing on the water into a disaster.

Over a thousand people a year die in boating accidents. Over half of those deaths involve the use of alcohol, either by the victim or by another party involved in the incident. Add to this number the thousands who each year receive serious injuries in boating accidents and you have a frightening picture of needless suffering and expense, much of which is directly attributable to unwise, and unnecessary use of alcohol and other drugs.

The fact is that boating, pleasant as it is, is a stressful activity. Studies have shown that after only a few hours on the water a normal, healthy, young boat operator's reactions, perceptions and judgment can be as impaired as if he were legally intoxicated, simply from the effects of unaccustomed exposure to fresh air, glare, ultraviolet light, motion, and noise.

If you doubt that these factors can alter behavior, spend a couple of hours at the launching ramps watching otherwise rational people trying to load their boats on trailers. Add the effects of a few drinks, and you have a truly explosive situation.

Alcohol and other drug use is not only a bad idea for the operator of a boat, but for passengers and guests, as well. It is often difficult enough to get about on the moving deck of a small boat when you are at your best. When you are unbalanced by the effects of a few beers, it is simply asking for a dunking.

If you survive the first few seconds of an automobile accident, the only additional pain you are likely to feel is in your pocketbook. In an accident on the water, on the other hand, even if you survive the initial accident, you may find your situation deteriorating rapidly. The aftermath can, in fact, be much worse than the accident itself.

If the victims of an accident have been ingesting drugs or alcohol, their chances of surviving are seriously reduced. Alcohol and depressant drugs lower the body's resistance to hypothermia (see Appendix A). An intoxicated person who falls into the water is much more likely than a sober one to become disoriented and swim downward rather than toward the surface. And finally, just when good judgment and mental sharpness is needed most, they are muddled by the intoxicants.

In summary, then, if you feel that you must serve or consume alcoholic beverages on your boat, do so after you are secured to a pier or ashore for the day. Even at that, it may be dangerous to negotiate along a pier after a few drinks.

Illegal drugs, on the other hand, are just that, illegal. If you or guests on your boat are found in possession of or using illegal drugs, the real consequences can be devastating for all involved. At the least you may stand to lose your boat and other personal assets, not to mention your freedom.

Note: Even legal drugs may impair physical ability and mental judgment (e.g., antihistamines, and other sedatives, tranquilizers, etc.).

To repeat, there is no place for alcohol or drug use, even in moderation, in boating. Don't do it, and don't tolerate it on your boat. You cannot afford the risk.

**Appendix C**

LISTING OF U. S. COAST GUARD DISTRICT OFFICES

FIRST COAST GUARD DISTRICT:

COMMANDER
U. S. Coast Guard
1st. Coast Guard District
Coast Guard Building
408 Atlantic Avenue
Boston, MA  02210-2209

SECOND COAST GUARD DISTRICT:

COMMANDER
U. S. Coast Guard
2nd. Coast Guard District
1430 Olive Street
St. Louis, MO  63101-2378

FIFTH COAST GUARD DISTRICT:

COMMANDER
U. S. Coast Guard
5th. Coast Guard District
Federal Building
431 Crawford Street
Portsmouth, VA  23704-5004

SEVENTH COAST GUARD DISTRICT:

COMMANDER
U. S. Coast Guard
7th. Coast Guard District
51 S. W. 1st Avenue
Miami, FL  33130-1608

EIGHTH COAST GUARD DISTRICT:

COMMANDER
U. S. Coast Guard
8th. Coast Guard District
Hale Boggs Federal Building
500 Camp Street
New Orleans, LA  70130-3396

NINTH COAST GUARD DISTRICT:

> COMMANDER
> U. S. Coast Guard
> 9th. Coast Guard District
> 1240 East 9th Street
> Cleveland, OH   44199-2060

ELEVENTH COAST GUARD DISTRICT:

> COMMANDER
> U. S. Coast Guard
> 11th. Coast Guard District
> Union Bank Building
> 400 Oceangate
> Long Beach, CA   90822-5399

THIRTEENTH COAST GUARD DISTRICT:

> COMMANDER
> U. S. Coast Guard
> 13th. Coast Guard District
> Jackson Federal Building
> 915 Second Avenue
> Seattle, WA   98174-1067

FOURTEENTH COAST GUARD DISTRICT:

> COMMANDER
> U. S. Coast Guard
> 14th. Coast Guard District
> Prince Kalanianaole Federal Building
> 300 Ala Moana Blvd, 9th Floor
> Honolulu, HI   96850-4892

SEVENTEENTH COAST GUARD DISTRICT:

> COMMANDER
> U. S. Coast Guard
> 17th. Coast Guard District
> P. O. Box 3-5000
> Juneau, AK   99802-1217

# Float Plan

When you go on an outing you plan as much as possible so that nothing goes wrong. You watch the weather, you carry enough fuel, and you carry spare parts for emergency repairs.

But if you were to have an accident, or be stranded with a disabled boat, or if the boat were to sink or be destroyed by fire, would anyone know where you were? Would they even know you were gone?

You can ensure that all the answers to these questions will be answered in your favor if you simply file a <u>float plan</u> with a responsible authority, family member, or friend before you leave.

A well thought-out float plan provides invaluable information that will help searchers locate you if you should be lost — information that others may simply not have, such as the sort of emergency equipment you have on board, the fuel capacity (useful in determining where you

<u>might</u> have decided to go for the day).

Most important, it will tell when you should be back, which in turn tells when you should be considered overdue, and where you intend to cruise. This helps focus search activities in areas where they will do the most good.

In this section is a sample form that you can copy or modify to suit your needs. Be sure to give it to a <u>responsible individual,</u> and be equally certain to notify them on your return or if you decide to change your plans.

You will probably never need it, but if you do become the object of a search, a good float plan will help you be found quicker, when the danger of permanent injury is less. In addition, your quick rescue will also help your fellow man, since it will free up search and rescue facilities to look for others who were not as far-sighted and well-prepared as you.

## VESSEL INFORMATION DATA SHEET

When requesting assistance from the Coast Guard, you may be asked to furnish the following details. This list should, therefore, be filled out as completely as possible and posted alongside your transmitter with the *Distress Communications Form.*

1. *Description of Vessel Requiring Assistance.*

Hull markings _____

Home port _____

Draft _____

Sails: Color _____

       Markings _____

Bowsprit ? _____

Outriggers ? _____

Flying Bridge ? _____

Other prominent features _____

2. *Survival Gear Aboard (Circle Yes or No)*

| | | |
|---|---|---|
| Personal Flotation Devices | Yes | No |
| Flares | Yes | No |
| Flashlight | Yes | No |
| Raft | Yes | No |
| Dinghy or Tender | Yes | No |
| Anchor | Yes | No |
| Spotlight | Yes | No |
| Auxiliary power | Yes | No |
| Horn | Yes | No |

3. *Electronic Equipment*

| | VHF | MF | HF |
|---|---|---|---|
| Radiotelephone(s) | | | |
| Channels/Frequencies available | 22 | Yes | No; |
| | 2670 kHz | Yes | No |
| Radar | | Yes | No |
| Depth Finder | | Yes | No |
| Loran | | Yes | No |
| Direction Finder | | Yes | No |
| EPIRB | | Yes | No |

4. *Vessel Owner/Operator*

Owner name _____

   Address _____

             _____

   Telephone number _____

Operator's name _____

   Address _____

             _____

   Telephone number _____

Is owner/operator an experienced sailor?   Yes  No

5. *Miscellaneous*

Be prepared to describe local weather conditions.

# FLOAT PLAN

Complete this plan, before going boating and leave it with a reliable person who can be depended upon to notify the Coast Guard, or other rescue organization, should you not return as scheduled. Do not file this plan with the Coast Guard.

TODAY'S DATE_____

1. NAME OF PERSON REPORTING _____

   TELEPHONE NUMBER_____

2. DESCRIPTION OF BOAT. TYPE_____COLOR_____

   TRIM_____REGISTRATION NO._____

   LENGTH_____NAME_____MAKE_____

   OTHER INFO._____

3. PERSONS ABOARD_____

          NAME           AGE       ADDRESS & TELE. NO.

   _____  _____  _____

   _____  _____  _____

   _____  _____  _____

4. ENGINE TYPE_____H.P._____

   NO. OF ENGINES_____FUEL CAPACITY_____

5. SURVIVAL EQUIPMENT: (CHECK AS APPROPRIATE)

   PFDs_____FLARES_____MIRROR_____

   SMOKE SIGNALS_____FLASHLIGHT_____FOOD_____

   PADDLES_____WATER_____OTHERS_____

   ANCHOR_____RAFT OR DINGHY_____EPIRB_____

6. RADIO  YES/NO  TYPE_____FREQS._____

7. TRIP EXPECTATIONS: LEAVE AT_____(TIME)

   FROM_____GOING TO_____

   EXPECT TO RETURN BY_____(TIME) AND IN

   NO EVENT LATER THAN_____

8. ANY OTHER PERTINENT INFO._____

9. AUTOMOBILE LICENSE_____TYPE_____

   TRAILER LICENSE_____COLOR AND MAKE OF

   AUTO_____

   WHERE PARKED_____

10. IF NOT RETURNED BY_____(TIME) CALL THE

    COAST GUARD, OR_____(LOCAL AUTHORITY)

    TELEPHONE NUMBERS_____

# Accident Reporting

If you have a boating accident that results in death or injury to a person, or in more than $200 in damage to vessels, you must file a report.

If someone dies as a result of the accident, or if a person is missing after an accident and it is reasonable to assume that that person is dead or injured, you must file the report within 48 hours of the accident. Otherwise, you must file within 10 days.

When someone dies or is missing, it is obvious that a report must be filed. Other cases may not be so obvious. If the worst injury is minor enough to need first aid only, you may not need to file a report. On the other hand, it does not take much damage to amount to $200 worth.

There are no penalties for filing a report that was not needed. There are, on the other hand, penalties for failing to report a reportable accident. You can be fined a few hundred dollars for failing to report an accident. If the case involves gross negligence and failure to file a proper report, criminal penalties up to and including a $1,000 fine and up to a year in jail may be assessed. So it is to your advantage to report all but the most trivial accidents.

If you are involved in an accident, you are expected to render whatever help you can to others who may need it. This humanitarian concern is supported by legal penalties (up to $1,000 in fines and/or two years in prison) for failure to render reasonable assistance.

Just remember that, while you are expected to help if you can, you are **NOT** expected to attempt rescues that are beyond your ability, or that are likely to result in additional injury or damage. No matter how noble the intentions, heroic efforts that result in additional victims only place an added burden on search and rescue resources. These attempts may be worse than no assistance at all.

Whom do you report to? In most cases, you should report to state conservation or department of natural resources officers. Occasionally, depending on the location and other factors, reports should go to the county sheriff, state police, or municipal police. On Federal waters, or in areas where other authorities are not available, report to the nearest Coast Guard office.

You should know who the responsible authority is in the area where you do your boating, but if you contact the wrong ones, they will direct you to the proper channels. The important thing is that you make the report.

The officers to whom you report will give you the necessary forms (Coast Guard form CG-3865 or equivalent.) These forms ensure that necessary information is provided, and that it is in a format that allows for consistent gathering of accident information. This information is compiled by the Coast

Guard, and is used to determine future directions for boating safety programs and activities.

The personal details of the report (name and address of owner, names of accident victims, etc.) are protected under Federal law. You need not worry that this information will be released to any other than appropriate law enforcement personnel.

# Bibliography

Bamford, Don, ANCHORING: ALL TECHNIQUES FOR ALL BOTTOMS, Seven Seas Press, Inc., Newport, RI., 1985.

Beyn, Edgar J., THE 12 VOLT DOCTOR'S PRACTICAL HANDBOOK, Spa Creek Instruments Co., Annapolis, MD., 1983.

Blandford, Percy W., RIGGING SAIL, Tab Books, Inc., Blue Ridge Summit, PA., 1983.

Bond, Bob, THE HANDBOOK OF SAILING, Albert A. Knopf, New York, 1980.

Bond, Bob and Sleight, Steve, SMALL BOAT SAILING, Albert A. Knopf, Inc., New York, 1983.

Bowditch, Nathaniel, AMERICAN PRACTICAL NAVIGATOR, 1977 Edition, (DMA Stock No. NVPUB9V1) Defense Mapping Agency Hydrographic Center, Washington, 1977.

Coles, Adlard, HEAVY WEATHER SAILING, John deGraff, Inc., Tuckahoe, N.Y., 1972 (revised).

Falk, Stephen, THE FUNDAMENTALS OF SAILBOAT RACING, St. Martin's Press, New York, 1973

Giannoni, Frances and John, USEFUL KNOTS AND LINE HANDLING, Golden Press, New York, 1968.

Gibbs, Tony, ADVANCED SAILING, St. Martin's Press, New York, 1975.

Henderson, Richard, BETTER SAILING, Henry Regnery Co., Chicago, 1977.

Henderson, Richard, SEA SENSE, International Marine Publishing Co., Camden ME., 1972.

Henderson, Richard, UNDERSTANDING RIGS AND RIGGING, International Marine Publishing Co., Camden, ME., 1985.

Howard-Williams, Jeremy, SAILS, John deGraff, Inc., Tuckahoe, N.Y., 1983.

Imhoff, Fred, and Pranger, Lex, BOAT TUNING FOR SPEED, Sail Books, Inc., Boston, 1975.

Institute of Advanced Sailing, THE BEST OF SAIL TRIM, Sail Books., Boston, Mass., 1975.

Kotsch, William J., WEATHER FOR THE MARINER, Naval Institute Press, Annapolis, MD., 1977 (revised).

Maloney, Elbert S., CHAPMAN, PILOTING SEAMANSHIP AND SMALL BOAT HANDLING, 57th Edition, Hearst Marine Books, New York, 1985.

Maloney, Elbert S., DUTTON'S NAVIGATION AND PILOTING, 14th Edition, Naval Institute Press, Annapolis, 1985.

McCollam, Jim, THE YACHTSMAN'S WEATHER MANUAL, Dodd, Mead & Co., New York, 1973.

Ross, Wallace, SAIL POWER, Alfred A. Knopf, New York, 1974.

Rousamaniere, John, THE ANNAPOLIS BOOK OF SEAMANSHIP, Simon and Schuster, New York, 1983.

Royce, Patrick M., ROYCE'S SAILING ILLUSTRATED, Western Marine Enterprises, Inc., Ventura, California, 1982.

SHIP'S MEDICINE CHEST AND MEDICAL AID AT SEA., U. S. Dept. of Health, Education and Welfare, 1984.

Shufeldt, H. H. and Dunlap, G.D., PILOTING AND DEAD RECKONING, Naval Institute Press, Annapolis, MD, 1985.

Thompson, Chris, THE CARE AND REPAIR OF SMALL MARINE DIESELS, 3rd Printing, International Marine Publishing Co., Camden, ME., 1984.

Watts, Alan, BASIC WINDCRAFT, USING THE WIND FOR SAILING, Dodd, Mead & Company, New York, 1976.

# Index

DEPARTMENT OF
TRANSPORTATION
U. S. COAST GUARD
CG-2730 (Rev. 6-73)

# AUXILIARY–ENROLLMENT APPLICATION

## SECTION I - PERSONAL DATA *(All Blocks Not Shaded To Be Completed By Applicant)*

| MEMBER NUMBER (1-10) | Trans Code (11-13) | LAST NAME (14-25) | FIRST NAME & INITIAL (26-37) |
|---|---|---|---|
| | Ø 1 1 | | |

Check (38-39) | (Area) HOME PHONE (40-49) | (Area) BUSINESS PHONE (50-59)

MR.
MS.

STREET OR P.O. BOX (60-79)

| MEMBER NUMBER (1-10) | Trans Code (11-13) | NAME (14-17) | CITY (18-32) | State (33-34) |
|---|---|---|---|---|
| Keypunch from above | Ø 1 2 | | | |

Zip Code (35-39) | Status (40-41) | Occ. (42-44) | Date of Birth (45-50) M M D D Y Y | Fac. (51-52, 55)

U

SOCIAL SECURITY NO. (56-64) | Date of Enrl. (65-70) M M D D Y Y | Base Enrl. Date (71-76) M M D D Y Y

OCCUPATION:

## FACILITY STATUS *(Indicate Type & Percent Owned)*

| BOAT | % | Radio Station | % | Name and Address of Facility Co-Owner *(if any)* |
|---|---|---|---|---|
| ACFT | % | Non-Facility Owner | | |

List any Yacht, Motorboat, Aeronautical, or Radio organizations to which you belong.

Describe briefly any nautical, aeronautical, or communications experience and list certificates and/or licenses held. If applying for special membership *(non-facility status)*, describe special qualifications.

| U.S. Citizen | CHECK | PRIOR AUXILIARY MEMBERSHIP DATA | | | |
|---|---|---|---|---|---|
| ➤ | YES | PRIOR MEMBER NO. | FROM *(Date)* | TO *(Date)* | HIGHEST OFFICE HELD |
| | NO | | | | |

I Pledge to support the U. S. Coast Guard Auxiliary and its purposes and abide by the governing policies established by the Commandant of the U. S. Coast Guard and the Auxiliary Manual, CG-305.

SIGNATURE OF APPLICANT | DATE SIGNED

## SECTION II - AUXILIARY RECOMMENDATIONS

| APPLICANT IS: | Reason for Non-Acceptability | BASIS FOR MEMBERSHIP |
|---|---|---|
| Acceptable | | Facility Owner |
| Not Acceptable | | Special Qualifications |

ATTACHMENTS: ☐ CG-2736 ☐ CG-2746 ☐ CG-3616 ☐ OTHER

| Date Fwd. | Signature of Flotilla Commander | Optional Endorsement | Flotilla Number |
|---|---|---|---|
| | | | |

## SECTION III - DIRAUX ENDORSEMENT

| Applicant is: | accepted | Remarks: |
|---|---|---|
| | not accepted | |
| as a: | facility owning member | |
| | specially qualified member | |
| with status as a: | flotilla member | Signature of DIRAUX / Date |
| | member-at-large | |

PREVIOUS EDITIONS ARE OBSOLETE

## SECTION IV - MEMBERSHIP RECORD

| DESIGNATION | DATE DESIGNATED & FORMS ISSUED | REMARKS |
|---|---|---|
| CONDITIONAL MEMBER | | |
| BASICALLY QUALIFIED MEMBER | | |
| AUXOP | | |
| PERMANENT MEMBER | | |
| OTHER (Specify) | | |
| INSTRUCTOR | | |
| COURTESY EXAMINER | | |
| AVIATION INSPECTOR | | |
| COMMUNICATIONS INSPECTOR | | |
| MEMBER-AT-LARGE | | |

| OFFICES HELD | | | | AWARDS AND DECORATIONS | |
|---|---|---|---|---|---|
| ELECTED | DATE | APPOINTED | DATE | TITLE | DATE |
| | | | | | |
| | | | | | |
| | | | | | |
| | | | | | |
| | | | | | |
| | | | | | |
| | | | | | |
| | | | | | |

## SECTION V - OPERATIONAL SPECIALTY RECORD

| SPECIALTY | | DATE OSC EXAM PASSED | OSC EXAM GRADE | DATE PRACTICAL FACTORS COMPLETED | CG-2836 ISSUED |
|---|---|---|---|---|---|
| PATROLS | | | | | |
| SEARCH AND RESCUE | | | | | |
| COMMUNICATIONS | | | | | |
| SEAMANSHIP | | | | | |
| PILOTING | Part A | | | | |
| | Part B | | | | |
| WEATHER | | | | | |
| ADMINISTRATION | | | | | |

## SECTION VI - TRANSFER AND DISENROLLMENT RECORD

| Transferred to (List New Member No.) | Date Transferred | Transferred to (List New Member No.) | Date Transferred |
|---|---|---|---|
| | | | |
| | | | |
| | | | |

| DISENROLLMENT | Date Disenrolled: | Reason for Disenrollment:<br>☐ INACTIVITY  ☐ DEATH<br>☐ CAUSE  ☐ OWN REQUEST<br>☐ OTHER (Specify) | CG-4949 submitted ☐ |
|---|---|---|---|
| Signature of DIRAUX | | | Date |

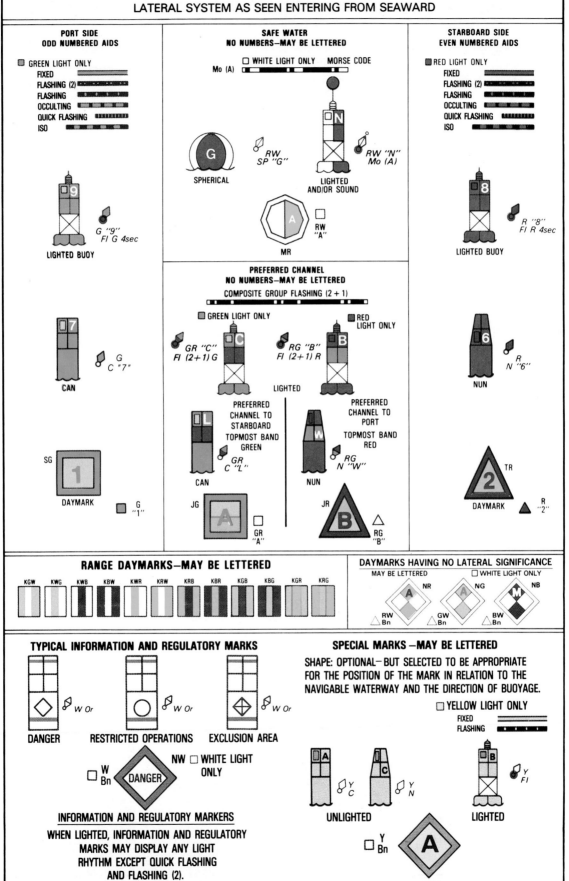

# U.S. AIDS TO NAVIGATION SYSTEM
## on navigable waters except Western Rivers and Intracoastal Waterway

### LATERAL SYSTEM AS SEEN ENTERING FROM SEAWARD

**PORT SIDE**
**ODD NUMBERED AIDS**

☐ GREEN LIGHT ONLY
FIXED
FLASHING (2)
FLASHING
OCCULTING
QUICK FLASHING
ISO

LIGHTED BUOY
9
G "9"
Fl G 4sec

CAN
7
G
C "7"

SG
DAYMARK
1
G "1"

**SAFE WATER**
**NO NUMBERS—MAY BE LETTERED**

☐ WHITE LIGHT ONLY    MORSE CODE
Mo (A)

SPHERICAL
G
RW SP "G"

LIGHTED AND/OR SOUND
N
RW "N" Mo (A)

MR
A
RW "A"

**PREFERRED CHANNEL**
**NO NUMBERS—MAY BE LETTERED**

COMPOSITE GROUP FLASHING (2 + 1)

☐ GREEN LIGHT ONLY          ☐ RED LIGHT ONLY

C
GR "C" Fl (2+1) G

B
RG "B" Fl (2+1) R

LIGHTED

PREFERRED CHANNEL TO STARBOARD
TOPMOST BAND GREEN

L
CAN
GR C "L"

PREFERRED CHANNEL TO PORT
TOPMOST BAND RED

W
NUN
RG N "W"

JG
A
GR "A"

JR
B
RG "B"

**STARBOARD SIDE**
**EVEN NUMBERED AIDS**

☐ RED LIGHT ONLY
FIXED
FLASHING (2)
FLASHING
OCCULTING
QUICK FLASHING
ISO

LIGHTED BUOY
8
R "8"
Fl R 4sec

NUN
6
R
N "6"

TR
DAYMARK
2
R "2"

### RANGE DAYMARKS—MAY BE LETTERED

KGW  KWG  KWB  KBW  KWR  KRW  KRB  KBR  KGB  KBG  KGR  KRG

### DAYMARKS HAVING NO LATERAL SIGNIFICANCE

MAY BE LETTERED          ☐ WHITE LIGHT ONLY

A    NR
RW Bn

A    NG
GW Bn

M    NB
BW Bn

### TYPICAL INFORMATION AND REGULATORY MARKS

DANGER
W Or

RESTRICTED OPERATIONS
W Or

EXCLUSION AREA
W Or

NW ☐ WHITE LIGHT ONLY
W Bn
DANGER

**INFORMATION AND REGULATORY MARKERS**

WHEN LIGHTED, INFORMATION AND REGULATORY MARKS MAY DISPLAY ANY LIGHT RHYTHM EXCEPT QUICK FLASHING AND FLASHING (2).

### SPECIAL MARKS —MAY BE LETTERED

SHAPE: OPTIONAL— BUT SELECTED TO BE APPROPRIATE FOR THE POSITION OF THE MARK IN RELATION TO THE NAVIGABLE WATERWAY AND THE DIRECTION OF BUOYAGE.

☐ YELLOW LIGHT ONLY
FIXED
FLASHING

A
Y C

C
Y N

B
Y Fl

UNLIGHTED          LIGHTED

Y Bn
A

Plate 1

# U.S. AIDS TO NAVIGATION SYSTEM
## on the Intracoastal Waterway

### AS SEEN ENTERING FROM NORTH AND EAST—PROCEEDING TO SOUTH AND WEST

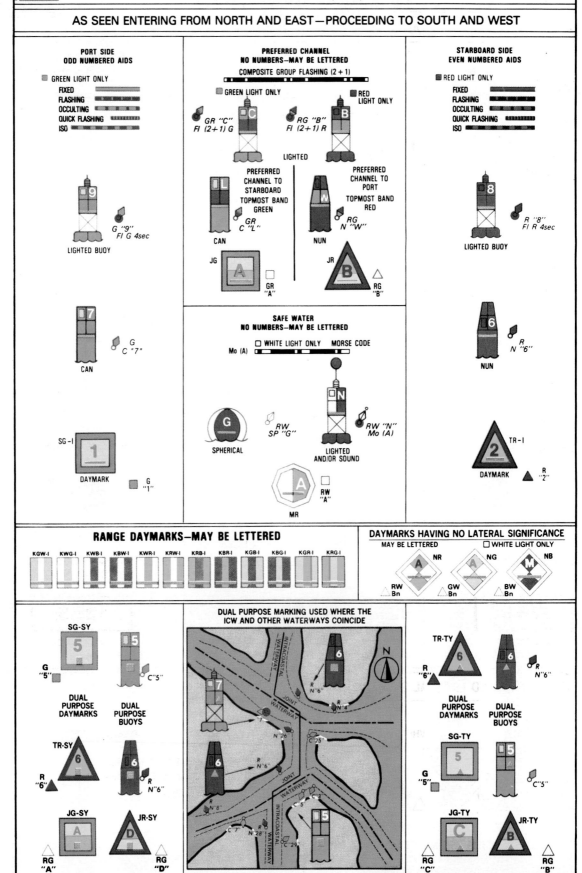

When following the ICW from New Jersey through Texas, a △ should be kept to your starboard hand and a □ should be kept to your port hand, regardless of the color of the aid on which they appear. Information and Regulatory Marks and Special Marks may be found on Intracoastal Waterway.   Refer to Plate 1.

Plate 2

# U.S. AIDS TO NAVIGATION SYSTEM
## on the Western River System

## AS SEEN ENTERING FROM SEAWARD

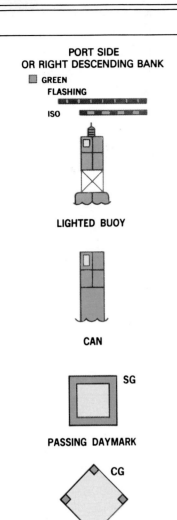

**PORT SIDE OR RIGHT DESCENDING BANK**

GREEN
FLASHING
ISO

LIGHTED BUOY

CAN

PASSING DAYMARK — SG

CROSSING DAYMARK — CG

176.9
MILE BOARD

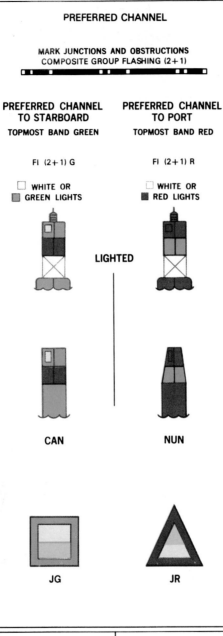

**PREFERRED CHANNEL**

MARK JUNCTIONS AND OBSTRUCTIONS
COMPOSITE GROUP FLASHING (2+1)

PREFERRED CHANNEL TO STARBOARD
TOPMOST BAND GREEN
Fl (2+1) G
☐ WHITE OR
■ GREEN LIGHTS

PREFERRED CHANNEL TO PORT
TOPMOST BAND RED
Fl (2+1) R
☐ WHITE OR
■ RED LIGHTS

LIGHTED

CAN

NUN

JG

JR

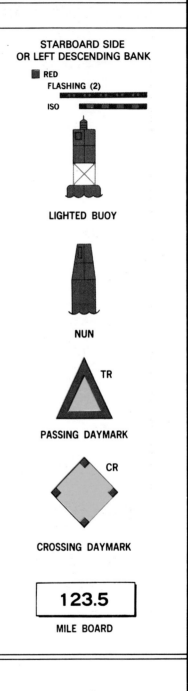

**STARBOARD SIDE OR LEFT DESCENDING BANK**

RED
FLASHING (2)
ISO

LIGHTED BUOY

NUN

PASSING DAYMARK — TR

CROSSING DAYMARK — CR

123.5
MILE BOARD

---

## DAYMARKS HAVING NO LATERAL SIGNIFICANCE

MAY BE LETTERED          ☐ WHITE LIGHT ONLY

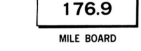
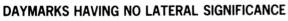
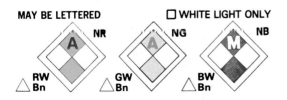

NR
RW
Bn

NG
GW
Bn

NB
BW
Bn

INFORMATION AND REGULATORY
MARKS, AND SPECIAL MARKS,
MAY BE FOUND ON THE
WESTERN RIVER SYSTEM.

Refer to Plate 1

Plate 3

# UNIFORM STATE WATERWAY MARKING SYSTEM

## STATE WATERS AND DESIGNATED STATE WATERS FOR PRIVATE AIDS TO NAVIGATION

### REGULATORY MARKERS

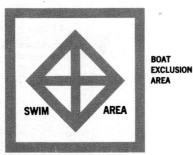

BOAT
EXCLUSION
AREA

SWIM          AREA

EXPLANATION MAY BE PLACED OUTSIDE
THE CROSSED DIAMOND SHAPE, SUCH AS
DAM, RAPIDS, SWIM AREA, ETC.

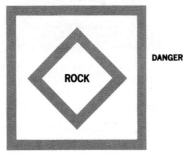

ROCK

DANGER

THE NATURE OF DANGER MAY BE IN-
DICATED INSIDE THE DIAMOND SHAPE,
SUCH AS ROCK, WRECK, SHOAL, DAM, ETC.

CONTROLLED
AREA

NO          WAKE

TYPE OF CONTROL IS INDICATED IN
THE CIRCLE, SUCH AS SLOW, NO WAKE,
ANCHORING, ETC.

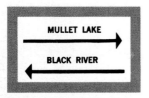

MULLET LAKE

BLACK RIVER

INFORMATION

FOR DISPLAYING INFORMATION SUCH
AS DIRECTIONS, DISTANCES, LOCATIONS, ETC.

BUOY USED TO DISPLAY
REGULATORY MARKERS

MAY SHOW WHITE LIGHT
MAY BE LETTERED

5 MPH

## AIDS TO NAVIGATION

MAY SHOW WHITE REFLECTOR OR LIGHT

**MOORING BUOY**

WHITE WITH BLUE BAND

MAY SHOW WHITE
REFLECTOR OR LIGHT

**RED-STRIPED WHITE BUOY**

MAY BE LETTERED
DO NOT PASS BETWEEN
BUOY AND NEAREST SHORE

7

**BLACK-TOPPED WHITE BUOY**

MAY BE NUMBERED

PASS TO NORTH
OR EAST OF BUOY

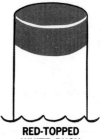

**RED-TOPPED WHITE BUOY**

PASS TO SOUTH
OR WEST OF BUOY

### CARDINAL SYSTEM

MAY SHOW GREEN REFLECTOR OR LIGHT

MAY SHOW RED REFLECTOR OR LIGHT

3

**SOLID RED AND SOLID BLACK BUOYS**

USUALLY FOUND IN PAIRS
PASS BETWEEN THESE BUOYS

4

PORT
SIDE ————— LOOKING UPSTREAM ————— STARBOARD
SIDE

### LATERAL SYSTEM

Plate 4